Other titles in the series are:

- Business Finance and Accounting for Managers
- Accounting for Value Linking business performance and value creation

Preface

This book has been written specifically with the non-financial manager in mind. Such people we know from our experience need to be financially aware and also to understand the language of Corporate Finance for their career in management, but they do not need to know everything unless they intend to specialise. We have therefore assumed that the reader of this book will have his or her sights upon general management in the true sense of the word and will seek other sources for purposes of specialisation.

The book is organised in ten chapters designed to provide a comprehensive review of the key issues, concepts and tools of Corporate Finance.

Chapter 1 provides the context for Corporate Finance and provides the foundation for subsequent chapters. This foundation draws heavily upon providing an understanding of the significance of the principles of financial economics in the form of discounted cash flow analysis from a project perspective, which is covered in Chapter 2 and, from a business perspective, which are covered in Chapters 3 and 4. Performance measurement issues and an understanding of the basis for economic returns are covered in Chapters 5 and 6.

Managers do not exist in a risk-free vacuum and risk is an essential issue to understand. This is covered in Chapters 6 and 7, the latter providing a comprehensive overview of contemporary issues and challenges.

Recent years have seen enormous Merger and Acquisition (M&A) activity and an understanding of the financial issues associated with M&A should be high on a general manager's agenda. A framework for assessing the financial implications within a practical setting is provided in Chapter 8, together with other important valuation applications and challenges, like valuations in emerging markets.

Intangible assets are frequently referred to but often given scant treatment within an accounting setting. From a Corporate Finance perspective they may play a crucial part in determining the future prospects of a business and issues associated with them are covered in Chapter 9. Last, but not least, the challenge of applying the principles of Corporate Finance internally in managing a business for value are covered in Chapter 10.

Roger W. Mills March 2007

ROGER W. MILLS

Corporate Finance - a Managerial Perspective

First Edition

LIBRARY OF CONGRESS CATALOGING IN PUBLICATION DATA

Corporate Finance – a managerial perspective

Roger W. Mills

Included bibliographies and index

ISBN 978-1-906156-02-2

Value Focus Publishing

Nieuwe Uitleg 15
2514 BP The Hague
The Netherlands

Email: info@valuefocus.co.uk

Contents

CHAPTER 1
CORPORATE FINANCE IN CONTEXT

Chapter Preview

This chapter will provide the context for Corporate Finance and enable you to:

- Define Corporate Finance.
- Appreciate shareholder value as being a key objective.
- Appreciate some of the new metrics associated with the drive towards shareholder value.
- Understand the link between shareholder value and financial management.
- Assess whether the size and composition of a company's asset structure is appropriate.
- Discuss methods to determine the size and composition of a company's future asset structure.
- Determine the volume of funds likely to be required to finance future asset structures.
- Assess the present and future capital structure.
- Understand the factors that shape a company's dividend policy.
- Review the importance of estimating the cost of capital.
- Understand the linkage between the Business Plan and the Financial Plan.

1.1 Corporate finance

Corporate Finance can be thought of as the specific area of finance dealing with the financial decisions made within corporations and focuses specifically upon the tools and analysis used to make these decisions. The discipline as a whole may be divided between long term, capital investment decisions, and short term, working capital management. The two are related in that a firm's value is enhanced when the return on capital, a function in no small part of working capital management, exceeds the cost of capital, which results from the longer term, capital decisions.

Corporate finance is closely related to managerial finance, which is slightly broader in scope, describing the financial techniques available to all forms of business enterprise, corporate or not.

1.2 Corporate finance and the drive to create shareholder value

Since the 1980s, the objective of creating 'shareholder value', by earning an economic return on capital invested in excess of the cost of that capital, has spread from the US and has been adopted increasingly by companies. A number of shareholder value approaches have emerged, which draw upon the financial theory of value, which is that value in economic terms is considered as being the present value of the firm's expected future net cash flows.

Major companies have been promoting the creation of value for their shareholders and many companies now incorporate some form of mission statement concerning the maximisation or creation of shareholder value as being a key corporate objective.

The emergence of a cash flow approach to measuring shareholder value and the adoption of the view that maximising shareholder value is epitomised in maximising the firm's current market value have occurred since the late 1980s.

The acceptance of cash flow approaches to valuation has been accompanied by a trend to place relatively less importance on traditional accounting measures, such as earnings per share, and has seen the evolution and development of a number of new methods, or metrics, for measuring company performance. These new metrics all share the same basic premise that a company only creates value if the economic return on its capital is greater than the cost of that capital. Different metrics have been developed that adopt slightly different approaches to maximising shareholder value and the following are illustrations:

1. Free cash flow

The basic free cash flow model is used to derive a view of the present value of cash available to the providers of finance, both equity and debt, over the future time period in which there is considered to be competitive advantage. Such free cash flows include investments in whatever form to support the existing and future business, but exclude any financing costs. Any financing costs are included when measuring the cost of capital, which is used as the rate at which to discount the free cash flows to a present value. This present value represents the value of the business as a whole and needs to be adjusted for the impact of any external investments and debt to convert it to the value of the equity. When divided by the number of ordinary shares, this gives an estimate of the value per share which, for a publicly traded company, can be compared with its share price.

In some cases, like banks and financial institutions, such an approach may be inappropriate for a number of reasons. For example, the cash inflow of a bank arises from interest and banks do not have debt in the traditional sense of a non regulated business. For this reason, instead of using pre financing cash flows, the cash flows from all activities are used. These are the cash flows that will be available to equity holders and, since only cash flows to equity holders are considered, they need to be discounted by the cost of equity, rather than the cost of capital to the business (known as the weighted average cost of capital).

The free cash flow approach to valuation is depicted in Figure 1.1 where the value of a business is the present value of the expected future free cash flows discounted at the appropriate cost of capital. To simplify the task of forecasting cash flows into perpetuity, typically cash flows are forecast over a finite time period, the planning period and any value beyond is captured in a terminal value.

Figure 1. 1: Free cash flow valuation

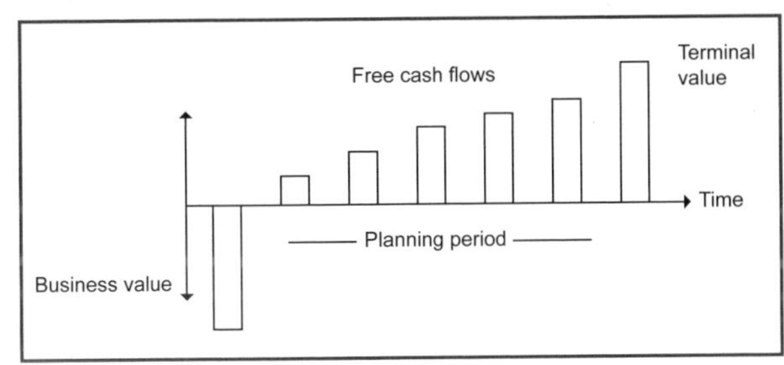

2. Economic profit (EP)

Measures of economic profit focus upon the difference between the economic return on capital and the cost of capital invested in the company over a given time period. For example, if a company earns a 15% annual economic return on capital invested, its cost of capital is 10% and the capital invested is £1 million, then the economic profit generated is £50,000 ([15% - 10%] x £1m).

Economic profit measures have been popularised through EVA®, an approach trademarked by Stern Stewart & Company, and are considered by some to have an advantage over free cash flow approaches for purposes of measuring performance period by period.

Figure 1.2 depicts graphically a typical EP profile for a business which is able to generate positive EPs for its competitive advantage period. Typically, it is assumed that during the competitive advantage period competitors enter the market driving returns down to the cost of capital where no EP will be generated.

Figure 1.2: Economic Profit profile

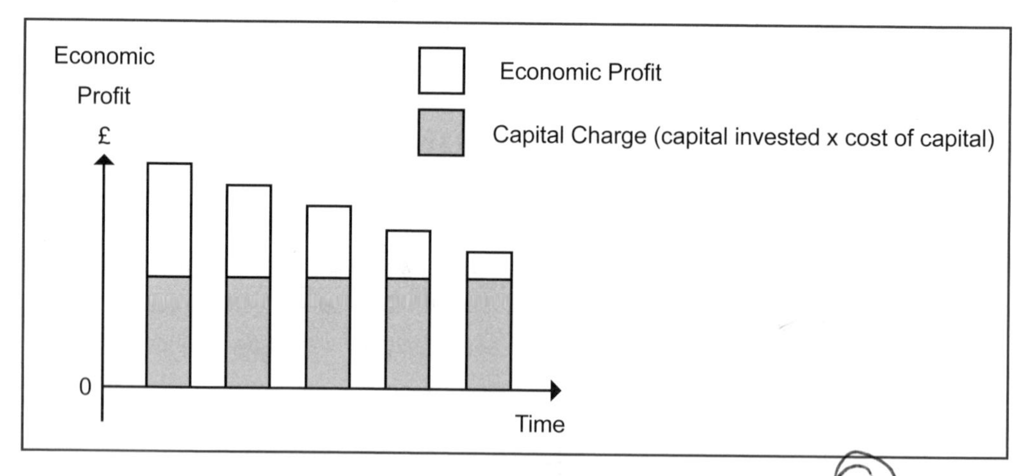

While economic profit focuses upon a given time period, Market Value Added (MVA) is used to show long term total value creation or destruction. MVA represents invested capital plus the present value of projected economic profit figures. The one crucial difference between the two is that MVA embodies the market's expectations and it takes a forward looking perspective. In fact, the results of applying free cash flow analysis and economic profit measures can be shown to be the same in principle when using the same assumptions. Furthermore, MVA is mathematically the same as the Net Present Value of the business, a technique widely used in capital investment appraisal and which is covered in Chapter 3.

Figure 1.3 Depicts the basis of the calculation of MVA at a point in time for a business.

Figure 1.3: Calculation of MVA

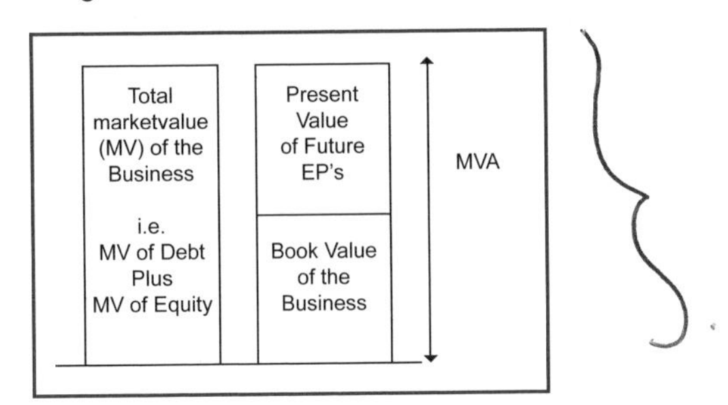

There are a number of variants of this economic profit approach, one being where equity cash flows are compared with the cost of equity to calculate an equity economic profit. For the reasons discussed earlier with reference to the free cash flow approach, this variant would be that most likely to be adopted by a bank.

1.3 Linking shareholder value and financial management

The implications of the drive to create shareholder value are profound. Companies that implement shareholder value typically adopt what has come to be known as Value Based Management (VBM) in some form that seeks to achieve the changes in behaviour and attitude consistent with creating value. VBM typically has important implications for all parts and functions of the business, not least of which is the finance function and financial management and is covered extensively in Chapter 10, once the basic tools of Corporate Finance have been reviewed.

Good financial management is vital to the success of the business. Whereas production management is concerned with handling physical resources to increase corporate profitability and value, financial management is concerned with improving the use of financial resources for the same objective. Financial resources represent the funds available to the business for which financial management is required to plan and control both their supply and use within the business.

A key issue in this book is the development of the link in principle between creating shareholder value and financial management. Against this, a number of key questions can be seen as follows:

- Are the size and the composition of the present asset structure appropriate to the returns being achieved?
- What should be the size and composition of the future asset structure in relation to projected returns?
- What volume of funds is likely to be required to finance the future asset structure?
- What should be the composition of the capital structure both now and in the future?

1.4 Present Asset Structure

Concern with the present asset structure focuses upon one key question,
'Is the volume and the composition of the assets currently employed justified by the value of sales activity being achieved?'
One approach that can be used to answer this question is reliant upon extracting financial data to calculate a ratio that is known as the sales generation ratio which is calculated as follows:

$$\text{Sales Generation Ratio} = \frac{\text{Sales Revenue}}{\text{Total Assets}}$$

This ratio, which shows how many £ of sales are generated per £ of total assets, can be subdivided into a number of interrelated component ratios to identify the success or otherwise of particular areas of the business such as:

- Inventory control, to ensure that inventory and work in progress are no higher than is necessary to service the volume of activity achieved.
- Credit control, to ensure that sales effort is channelled into areas of low credit risk and that outstanding receivables (accounts receivable) are collected and banked with the minimum of delay.
- The control of cash and near cash funds to prevent them from lying idle and therefore not generating any return.
- The existing fixed asset base. Would it be worthwhile realising the value from certain assets and subcontracting outside?

In considering the present asset structure we need to look at the assets used within the business and a core issue relates to the short-term assets and liabilities in the form of inventories, trade receivables and trade payables. These are often grouped together in financial management and known under the 'umbrella' of working capital. We now turn our attention to the measurement and management of working capital.

1. Working Capital Measurement and Management

Working capital is the lifeblood of all businesses and has to be managed carefully to ensure that money and inventory are available when required. Poor working capital management is a sure way of threatening profitability and survival.

The main components of working capital for a manufacturing or trading organisation are inventory (from suppliers), receivables (money due from customers), cash and payables (money owed to suppliers). These are all linked by the cycle of events shown in Figure 1.4. Inventory is acquired, very often on credit from payables, and then sold as goods to receivables, to customers who eventually pay cash used to pay payables and so on. For a service business there may be no inventory, in which case a service is provided to a client (now a receivable) who pays cash eventually which in turn is used to pay payables for goods and/or services and so the cycle goes on.

Figure 1.4 Cash Conversion Cycle

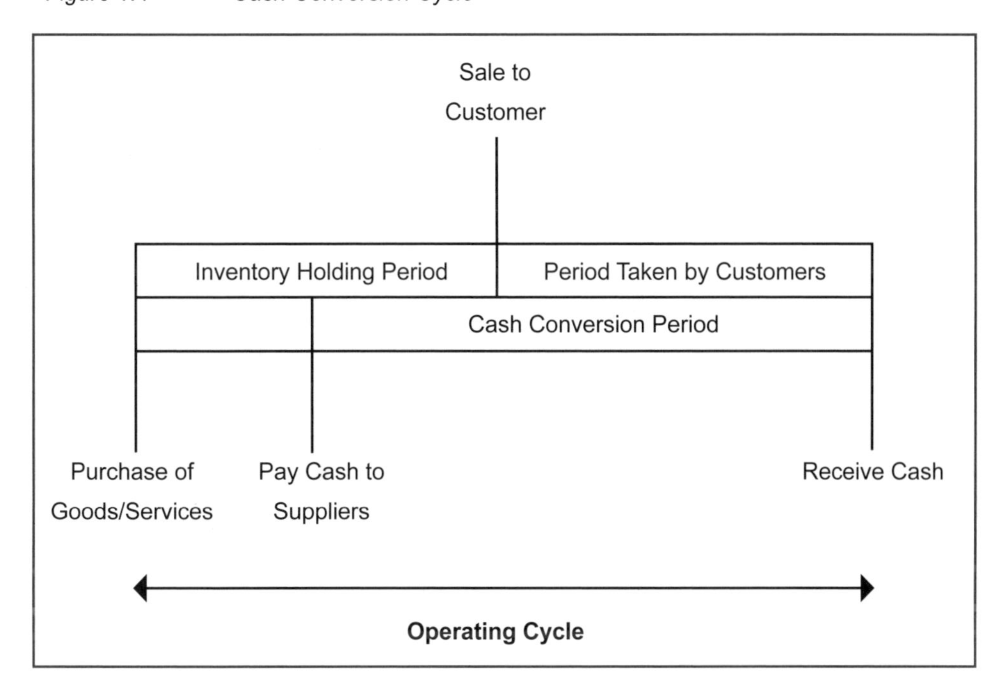

In Figure 1.4 there are two key time periods. The first is the **operating cycle**, which is the period of time between receiving/buying the goods from suppliers and receiving the cash from customers. This operating cycle reflects the normal day-to-day activities of a business.

The second is the cash **conversion period**, which is the time period between paying suppliers and receiving cash from customers. In other words the cash conversion period is the period of time that cash is tied up in the business.

It is important to control working capital. Too little or too much can be a severe disadvantage, so how can control be achieved? We will now consider the main issues involved in controlling three of the parts of a business' working capital – inventory, receivables and cash. The management of payables is largely a mirror image of receivables management.

a. Inventory Control

The financial objective of inventory control is to minimise the overall costs of holding inventory while taking into account the various objectives of other functions within a company. For example, marketing might want to maintain a full range of merchandise, purchasing might want to concentrate on a reduced range but in greater volumes because they can obtain better prices and finance might want to minimise the amount of working capital tied up in inventory. An effective system of inventory control seeks to optimise the needs of these various users. Inventory control is achieved through implementing the following system that involves:

- Setting inventory levels
- Monitoring movements against inventory levels
- Taking corrective action.

Calculating inventory levels

A company should set maximum, minimum and reorder levels. Inventory levels should take account of historic and forecast volumes, lead times and cost of holding and reorder size.

Monitor movements against inventory levels and corrective action

Once levels have been calculated for all inventory items it is important to monitor movements and take the necessary corrective action. For example, if following a receipt of goods the inventory goes above the maximum level, any outstanding purchase orders should be cancelled. If it is forecast that the usage will reduce, then the company might consider a special offer or sale.

Similarly, following an issue of goods, if inventory reaches the reorder level, this should automatically trigger the preparation of a purchase order, where it would be anticipated that the goods would be received before inventory reaches the minimum level. Should an issue of goods cause the inventory level to fall below minimum then outstanding purchase orders should be referred to the supplier to obtain a delivery date.

b. Credit Control

The main objective of credit control is to minimise bad debts. This requires that a balance is achieved between the risk of granting credit to a customer and the loss of profits through not trading with that customer.

It is not uncommon when discussing credit control with a group of managers for the first thoughts to be 'how quickly can we collect monies owed from customers'? What needs to be borne in mind is that this is a control system and will require the following:

- The establishment of a credit control policy
- The vetting of new customers
- The monitoring of the ageing of debts
- The taking of corrective action.

Establishing a credit control policy

A credit control policy sets the general terms by which a company will offer credit. This will include the period of credit, for example 'net 30 days', and the timings and actions that will take place should the credit period be extended by the customer. A good example of the actions taken is provided by the (UK) electricity, telephone and gas companies: first there is a reminder, then usually two weeks later a final reminder, followed by a polite letter advising that your supply will be 'cut-off' if payment is not made within, say, seven days. This is often followed up by a further letter advising that supply will be 'cut-off' from a specified date unless payment is received.

When a company establishes its credit period it is important to take into account the competitive environment. For example, if other companies in the same industry are granting 60 days credit, a company offering 30 days would tend to lose customers to its competitors.

Vetting new customers

All new customers should be vetted to determine their creditworthiness and establish credit limits. This process takes many different forms but attempts to determine customers':

- *Ability to pay.* This should be relatively simple, requiring a review of a customer's financial position. This could be achieved through bank references, analysing the annual accounts or by using a credit bureau.
- *Willingness to pay.* Assessing a company's willingness to pay by assessing their track record. For example, if individuals pay their household bills within the accepted time limits they would be deemed as showing a willingness to pay.

Establishing credit limits can take the form of making an allowance for an initial sum with regular reviews to increase the credit limit if required. Other systems involve complex models that take into account a number of variables or the use of a credit bureau.

Monitoring the ageing of debts

On the receipt of an order from an existing customer the credit department should check that:

- the new order would not make their balance outstanding exceed their credit limit
- there are no outstanding debts on the account.

When the order has been fulfilled and an invoice sent to the customer there should be a continuous monitoring of the account. Regular reports should be produced to show the age of all outstanding amounts – for example, between one month to two months, two months to three months and over three months. An ageing report can take the following format:

Table 1.1 Age Classification of Receivables

Invoice	Amount £	1 to 2 Months	2 to 3 Months	Over 3 Months	Remarks
MR 201	30,000			30,000	Court action
MR 209	15,000			15,000	Receiver
MR 245	60,000		60,000		Letter sent
MR 246	25,000		25,000		Cheque promised
MR 247	100,000	100,000			
MR 260	40,000	40,000			
	270,000	140,000	85,000	45,000	

Corrective action

It is important that corrective action is taken in accordance with the credit control policies of the company. If customers know that they can extend their credit periods without losing their rating then the marginally good 'payer' may move to being a marginally bad 'payer'. The forms of corrective action should include:

- A review of the credit limit of a customer
- Reject orders due to poor creditworthiness - for example, when a customer attempts to extend the credit limit or a potential customer fails the creditworthiness checks
- Send out regular statements, a final reminder and, if necessary, final offer
- Start court proceedings. This will often mean a lengthy procedure of claim and counter claim taking at least six months. If successful with a court action, there is no guarantee that the debt will be paid and a small company may have to rely on the courts to recover the debt.

How to improve collection

One of the simplest methods of reducing the overall credit is to ensure that customers are invoiced promptly. In many cases this can reduce the payment period by anything up to two weeks.

Offering cash discounts for earlier payment can result in a significant improvement of cash flow. For example, if a company's credit terms were net 30 days, it might offer a cash discount of two percent for payment within 10 days.

Many small companies charge interest of up to 10% on overdue accounts in an effort to encourage prompt payment despite the competitive risk involved.

An area that has grown in significance over the past few years has been that of factoring of debts, which is a means of accelerating cash inflow by selling debts to a third party. Some of the major banks offer these services, which of course have a cost. The usual process means that when an invoice is raised by a company all proceeds from that invoice are paid to the company by the factor. The factor pays (usually) around 80 per cent of the invoice value to the company immediately and the balance less interest and charges when the account is finally settled by the customer. It is possible to arrange that the factor also manages the customer account and chases payment, as well as taking the burden of unpaid debt. The advantage for the company is improved cash flow and, if the additional services are bought, savings in credit management, but it is important to remember that factors are careful about the type of debts they buy – usually only accepting 'clean and unencumbered' debts.

c. Trade credit

In most industries trade credit is the 'norm' and is an important source of finance for many businesses. As a business grows and purchases more on credit so the amount of this essentially interest-free finance grows. Just as with credit control a business needs to ensure that it has good processes and procedures in place, to enable it to take advantage of this source of finance without abusing those businesses granting the credit.

d. Cash control

The main objective of a system of cash control is to plan the expected operations of a company over a future period of time. Such a plan requires forecasts of future sales and cash expenditure covering purchases of materials, wages, equipment and so on. Assumptions will also have to be made concerning the time delays from sales to receipts and from purchases to payments. The following example, set out in Table 1.2, shows the three main components of a cash budget:

1. Forecast of sales and cash receipts
2. Forecast of cash expenditure
3. Monthly net cash flow and cash balance

Sales forecast for the six month period July to December, together with a forecast of 75% being credit sales.

Credit periods are expected to be 80% collected after one month and the remaining 20% after two months.

Table 1.2 Components of a Cash Budget

1. Forecast Sales and Cash Receipts

	May	Jun	Jul	Aug	Sept	Oct	Nov	Dec
	£m	**£m**	**£m**	**£m**	**£m**	**£m**	**£m**	**£m**
Forecast Sales	40.0	44.0	68.0	80.0	64.0	32.0	24.0	44.0
Credit sales	**30.0**	**33.0**	**51.0**	**60.0**	**48.0**	**24.0**	**18.0**	**33.0**
Credit receipts								
1 month (80%)		**24.0**	**26.4**	**40.8**	**48.0**	**38.4**	**19.2**	**14.4**
2 months (20%)			**6.0**	**6.6**	**10.2**	**12.0**	**9.6**	**4.8**
Total credit receipts		**24.0**	**32.4**	**47.4**	**58.2**	**50.4**	**28.8**	**19.2**
Cash Sales	10.0	11.0	17.0	20.0	16.0	8.0	6.0	11.0
Total Cash Receipts	10.0	35.0	49.4	67.4	74.2	58.4	34.8	30.2

Note: The above calculations show the variation in forecast sales and the expected total cash receipts. For example, in October the forecast sales are £32 million with expected total cash receipts of £58.4 million. In practice, a company would not prepare a forecast without making adjustments for bad debts.

Forecast of Cash Expenditure

	Jun	Jul	Aug	Sept	Oct	Nov	Dec
	£m	**£m**	**£m**	**£m**	**£m**	**£m**	**£m**
Forecast Purchases	26.4	40.8	48.0	38.4	19.2	14.4	26.4
Cash Payments for Purchases		26.4	40.8	48.0	38.4	19.2	14.4
Wages paid		5.6	5.6	5.6	5.6	5.6	5.6
Overheads and Expenses Paid		9.0	9.0	9.0	9.0	9.0	9.0
Capital Expenditure		15.0	15.0	0	0	15.0	0
Total Cash Expenditure		56.0	70.4	62.6	53.0	48.8	29.0

Monthly Net Cash Flow and Cash Balance

	Jul	Aug	Sept	Oct	Nov	Dec
	£m	**£m**	**£m**	**£m**	**£m**	**£m**
Total Cash Receipts	49.4	67.4	74.2	58.4	34.8	30.2
Total Cash Expenditure	56.0	70.4	62.6	53.0	48.8	29.0
Net Cash Flow	–6.6	–3.0	11.6	5.4	–14.0	1.2
Opening Cash Balance	3.0	–3.6	–6.6	5.0	10.4	–3.6
Closing Cash Balance	–3.6	–6.6	5.0	10.4	–3.6	–2.4

2. Investment in Working Capital

We obtain an estimate of the cash conversion period as follows:

Inventory holding period	X
plus: Receivable days	X
less: Payable days	-X
Cash Conversion period	X

The example below shows how this principle can be applied to calculate the investment required in working capital:

2006 Figures

Inventory days	=	60 days
Trade receivables days	=	30 days
Payables days	=	30 days

2007 Forecasts

Revenue	=	£100m
Costs of sales	=	£60m

Calculations of Working Capital for 2007

Inventory	=	£60m x 60 / 365	=	£9.9m
Receivables	=	£100m x 30 / 365	=	£8.2m
Payables	=	£60m x 30 / 365	=	£4.9m

The amount of capital tied up in working capital is:

Inventory	£9.9m
plus Receivables	£8.2m
less Payables	- £4.9m
Total Working Capital	£13.2m

What this means is that an investment in working capital of £13.2m is required in terms of cash, hence there will have to be a cash outflow from the business in the sum of £13.2m.

In terms of the operating cycle from purchase to production to selling, the level of investment increases over the period of the cycle. See Figure 1.5.

Figure 1.5 Investments in Working Capital

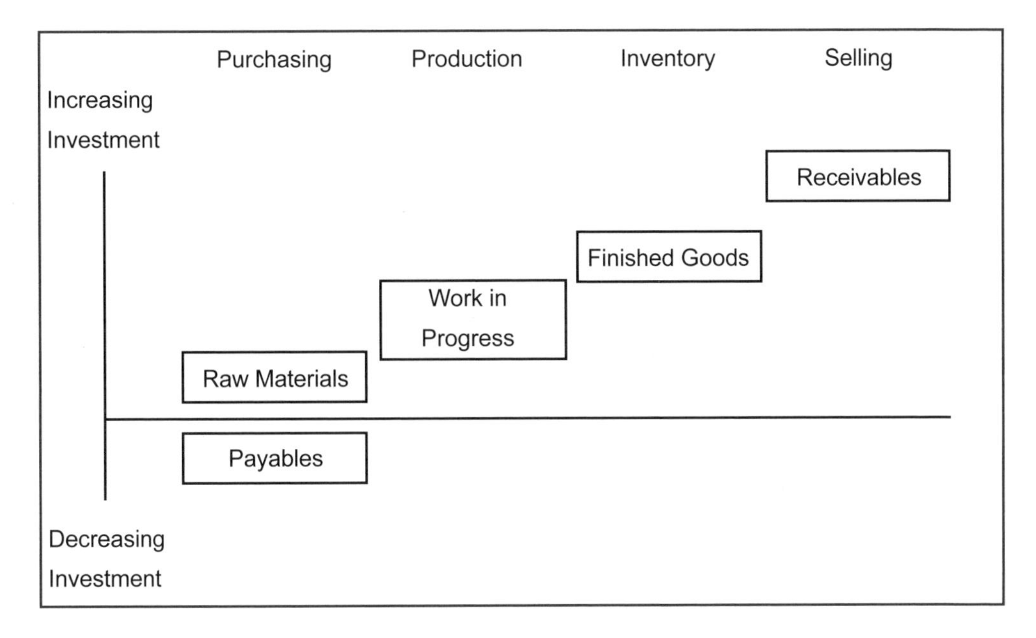

When carrying out these working capital ratio calculations the implicit assumption is that the relationships remain constant over time, that is, inventory turnover period, receivables days and payables days remain constant. As a check it is recommended that one considers whether the future will resemble the past.

Factors affecting investment in working capital

There are a number of factors that affect these ratios and the underlying relationships:

- **Industry:** In terms of the external environment every industry has its own particular structure in terms of customers, suppliers, competitors, regulation and technology. Similarly each industry may be at a different stage of the life cycle and have correspondingly varying strategic intents. Thus working capital can vary enormously across industries.
- **Attitude to risk.** At the level of the economy one of the key influences on working capital is the health of the economy and hence the stage of the business cycle the economy is in. At the company level, the strategy of the business and the management team's aversion to risk plays an important role on working capital levels. In essence what we have here is a trade-off between risk and return, that is, the risk avoided by having working capital versus the costs associated with investment in working capital.

We should also not ignore that different working capital practices may exist between countries. This in part results from cultural and social factors and partly from the efficiency and effectiveness of the distribution infrastructure within the country.

Table 1.3 highlights the trade-offs that exist in managing working capital.

Table 1.3 Working Capital Trade-Offs

	Risk avoided	Costs incurred
Inventory	Lack of inventory and loss of customer who cannot wait	Cash tied up in inventory and cost of physically holding inventory
Receivables	Loss of customers who find attractive opportunities elsewhere	Cash tied up in receivables and more possible bad debts
Payables	Reliance on alternative forms of financing, for example, higher prices	Damage to market reputation and being charged bank overdraft

1.5 Future Asset Structure

Future assets required by a business are usually the result of business plans which project business activities into the future, taking account of product/market strategies and their impact on growth and diversification. Sound financial management requires that those future assets acquired as part of the plan are indeed worthwhile to the business. As will be illustrated in the next two chapters analytical techniques can be used to appraise projects, but there is the overriding requirement that particular attention should be paid to the quality of the input data. In our opinion too much attention can be and has been given to the techniques which can only be as good as the user's judgments in selecting appropriate input data.
There are two key issues concerning input data:

- How are initial estimates to be generated as accurately as possible?
- How can the importance of the various components within the estimates be judged?

With regard to the first of these, forecasting methods can be used reliant upon one or more of the following: subjective managerial judgment, sensitivity analysis, consensus of expert opinion and computer simulations. The evidence available suggests that most large companies use two or more of these and, where larger capital expenditures are involved, more quantitatively orientated methods reliant upon probability theory may well be used.

Further, and related to the second issue, the initial estimates should be broken down as far as possible. For example, in discussing the basic principles, we used information about only annual cash flows from a project, which alone would be unsatisfactory for larger and therefore riskier projects. In their case, such information should be broken down into key factors and such a breakdown can be powerful when using a computer spreadsheet package to investigate the importance of each factor to the end result.

Just exactly what are the factors that should be used in cash flow estimation? It is difficult to be entirely prescriptive because some factors will vary from project to project, but a useful way of considering them is within the following three groupings:

1. Financial Factors

- Inflation
- Risk
- Working Capital Requirements
- Taxation
- Residual Value

2. Marketing factors

- Sales Forecast
- Product Life
- Discount Policy
- Promotional Costs
- Selling Costs
- Market Test Costs
- Competitive Advantages and Disadvantages
- Transportation Costs

3. Operating factors

- Operating Costs
- Material and Supply Costs
- Start up costs
- Shutdown Costs
- Maintenance Costs
- Repair Costs
- Capacity Utilisation

The effects of the business life-cycle

It has been widely observed that businesses, and the industries that they form a part of, typically go through a life cycle comprising four stages; start-up, growth, maturity and decline. Table 1.4 shows how various characteristics of a business, grouped under three categories, typically evolve over the life-cycle and will impact the future asset structure of the business.

Table 1.4 Business Life–Cycle

	Start–up	Growth	Maturity	Decline
Operational and Strategic Aspects				
Growth Prospects	Very High	High	Medium	Lower
Business Risks	Very High	High	Medium	Lower
Revenue	Often None or Small	Some and Growing rapidly	Significant and steady	Significant and declining
Profits	Often none or negative	None or small	Significant	Significant
Investment Needs	High	High	Replacement only	Minimal
Cash Flow	Negative	Neutral to slightly positive	Significantly positive	Positive to neutral
Financing Aspects				
Financing Type	Entirely equity	Largely equity	Debt and equity	Largely debt

	Start–up	Growth	Maturity	Decline
Financial Risk	Lower	Low	Medium	High
Dividend payout				
Dividend Payout	Nil	Minimal	High	Medium

During the start-up phase, a business is typically making heavy investment expenditures to grow its product/service and its market. As a result the business may have little revenue, small or no profits and hence negative cash flow. Such a business is often funded by capital providers who are willing to take high risks for a period of time, taking a deferred return in the form of a capital gain at the end of their investment period. Given the fact that the start-up phase is cash negative it makes no sense to pay dividends or borrow debt which cannot be serviced as all cash is needed to grow the business.

Moving into the growth phase, sales are growing rapidly and the business is still making significant market building expenditures and capital investments to grow the market. As a result, cash flow is likely to be at best small or neutral and the most appropriate source of funding is still equity. As the market is growing rapidly, investors will want the business to invest to take advantage of the growth opportunities that exist rather than return cash in the form of dividends. During this phase the venture capitalists will want to realise their capital gain, at the same time new investors need to be attracted to the business with an offering of a small dividend. However most of the return to new investors will be in the form of a capital gain in the value of their shares.

As market growth slows and expenditures and investments are curtailed, both profits and cash flow become significantly positive. At this stage business risks are receding and its makes sense to change the funding policy of the business by introducing debt capital which can now be serviced more easily – this change in capital structure introduces financial risk into the business. In addition, a change to the dividend policy is appropriate in that as growth slows there are unlikely to be the same level of growth opportunities for the business to invest in and hence surplus cash should be returned to the shareholders. The growth investors who want their return in the form of capital gain will have started to exit and be replaced by investors wanting steady returns in the form of annual dividends.

As one would expect the strong profit levels and positive cash flow will fade as the business moves into the decline phase. As the growth prospects for the business are minimal it makes sense to curtail significantly all investment and expenditure to that required to sustain the business for as long as is possible to squeeze out returns. The resultant cash flow freed up is best returned to shareholders in a high dividend payout. Given business risks are lower it makes sense to replace expensive equity funding with cheaper debt, which has the benefit of disciplining the business to focus on cash flow generation to service it.

In summary, what is important to notice is the changing picture of investment needs, capital structure and dividend policy over the life cycle as the profile of business and financial risks change over time. What also changes is the profile of investor, both equity and debt, and the nature of their risks and returns.

1.6 Future Requirement for Funds

One of the most frequent causes of bankruptcy is the inability to forecast future requirements for funds. The form that a forecast of future requirements for funds might take depends largely on the purpose for which it is needed. If concern is with a general indication of average future requirements, then a forecast funds flow statement will be sufficient. However, the problem with this is that the forecast will only illustrate the final financial position. In Table 1.5 we illustrate the cash flow forecast for a company where an equilibrium cash position is achieved at the end of the 6 month forecast but significant cash deficits were incurred at the end of some individual months. This provides an example which highlights the importance of forecasting at frequent time intervals.

Table 1.5 *Cash Flow Forecast*

Part A							
Receipts £'000	**July**	**Aug**	**Sept**	**Oct**	**Nov**	**Dec**	**Total**
Sales	430	600	600	800	1,300	1,600	5,330
5 year Loan	250						250
Share Capital		150					150
Sub–Total A	830	600	600	800	1,300	1,600	5,730
Part B							
Payments £'000 (unchanged)							
Sub–Total B	1,430	1,180	780	780	780	780	5,730
Part C	**July**	**Aug**	**Sept**	**Oct**	**Nov**	**Dec**	**Total**
Balance A – B	–600	–580	–180	20	520	820	
Part D							
Balance c/f,							
Cumulative							
Cash Position	–600	–1,180	–1,360	–1,340	–820	0	

Many large organisations forecast their cash flows daily, the benefits of which may be summarised as the following:

- Future requirements for funds can be planned both with respect to volume and timing. The advantages will be that time will be available to negotiate acceptable terms in advance with any prospective lender and such a demonstration of effective management planning will assist by building confidence in the business
- Future surpluses will be evident and early steps can be taken to ensure that any available are utilised adequately
- The future shape of any funds required will be revealed. Such an early warning system will prevent following a course of action which is ultimately destined for disaster. Of course, even with the best possible forecasting there will always be a chance that unexpected funds will be required not only because of poor conditions but maybe because of good opportunities. Contingency planning is an important part of financial management and can be assisted by:
- Attempting to develop an awareness of the nature of the likely future contingencies and quantifying them with respect to the sensitivity of their impact upon financial resources
- Developing an inventory of resources that can be called upon in case of need, indicating in each case the speed by which they can be realised in cash

- Formulating a strategy which can be implemented immediately to deal with emergencies that might arise.

Understanding cash flow

When we refer to cash flow it is imperative to be clear as to what cash flows are being referred to. There are several possible definitions depending upon the purpose for which the cash flow is being calculated. For example, in Table 1.5 we looked at the cash flows in a cash flow forecast but there are other definitions. These are best understood if we consider selected data in Table 1.6 - for the 2006 Income Statement and Balance Sheet for our example company, RWM plc, from which we will derive the various cash flows used in financial management. (For full details refer to the Appendix to this chapter)

Table 1.6 RWM plc – Selected Data for 2006

Income statement Account		**Balance Sheet**		
All figures in £m	2006		2005	2006
Gross Margin	108.8	Fixed Assets	76.2	86.7
less Operating Expenses*	96.7	Current Assets	86.4	105.6
Operating profit (PBIT)	12.1	Current Liabilities	69.6	96.3
less Interest	3.4	Payables: after one year	27.0	20.1
Profit Before Tax (PBT)	8.7	**Increase/Decrease**		**2006 less 2005**
less Taxation	2.4	Fixed Assets	(86.7 – 76.2)	10.5
Profit After Tax (PAT)	6.3	Current Assets	(105.6 – 86.4)	19.2
Dividends	5.5	Current Liabilities	(96.3 – 69.6)	26.7
		Payables: after one year	(20.1 – 27.0)	(6.9)
* Includes depreciation of £5.9m				

Operating Cash Flow (OCF)

This refers to the cash flow generated by the underlying operations of the business, whether they be manufacturing a product and/or supplying a service. Such cash flows ignore any cash flows associated with the financing of the business in the form of interest payments made on debt capital and dividends payments made on the equity capital of the business.

Operating cash flow can be calculated on either a pre or post tax basis by taking the difference between receipts from customers and payments made to suppliers, employees and others providing services to the business, for example rent on premises, lease cost of cars and so on. An expedient short cut is to take operating profit and add back the depreciation figure that was deducted in arriving at the operating figure. Note that interest is always excluded as we are looking at the operating performance of the business and do not want financing effects distorting the picture.

Operating cash flow = Operating profit (pre or post tax) plus Depreciation

For RWM plc the pre tax operating cash flow is:

= £12.1m + £5.9m = £18.0m

On a post tax basis operating cash flow is:

= £12.1m – (£2.4+ £1.1m)[1] + £5.9m = £14.5

Depreciation is not a cash flow item as it is an accounting adjustment designed to try and reflect the consumption of an asset with use in the business or the fall in its value over time.

Free Cash Flow to the Firm (FCFF)

Free cash flow to the firm represents the cash flow that is freely available to the providers of capital to a business, both the debt-holders and equity-holders. The cash flows that debt-holders receive are in the form of interest and debt repaid/raised whilst the cash flows to equity-holders are in the form of dividends and equity brought back/raised. Typically it is calculated on an after tax basis. The calculation of free cash flow to RWM is shown in Table 1.7.

[1] For ease of calculation taxation payable is taken as a proxy for the cash tax paid such that timing differences and the deductibility of interest on debt are ignored. The addition of £1.1m is to reflect the cash tax situation. A company's taxes are influenced by how much debt a company has, as interest payments on that debt shield pre-tax profit from taxation. When calculating cash taxes, we remove this distortion by calculating a company's tax burden assuming a company was 100% equity financed with no debt.

Table 1.7 RWM plc – Calculation of Free Cash Flows for 2006

	£m
Operating Cash Flow (OCF) after tax	14.5
(less): Investment in Fixed Assets [1]	–16.4
(less)/add: (Investment)/Divestment in Working Capital [2]	7.5
Free Cash flow to Firm (FCFF)	5.6

1 Calculated as change in net book value of fixed assets plus depreciation (see Table 11.6), i.e. £86.7 – £76.2m + £5.9m = £16.4m. The figure of £16.4m represents an increase in fixed assets therefore a reduction in cash flow.
2 For ease of calculation calculated as current assets less current liabilities (see Table 11.6), i.e. (£105.6 – £86.4m) – (£96.3m – £69.6m) = £7.5m. The figure of £7.5m comprises of an increase of £19.2m in current assets and an increase of £26.7m in current liabilities. This represents an overall increase in cash flow to the firm i.e. an additional £7.5m from current liabilities.

If FCFF shows a surplus, the question arises as to what to do with the surplus? Invest in the future of the business or repay the capital providers of the firm. In the case of a deficit of FCFF the question arises as to how to finance the deficit: from debt or equity holders? This topic is considered in a little more detail in Section 1.7 on Capital Structure.

Free Cash Flow to Equity holders (FCFE)

Free cash flow to equity holders represents the cash flow that is attributable to equity holders which may take the form of dividend payments, equity bought back or equity raised. FCFE is for the most part calculated on a post tax basis by taking the FCFF and removing all the cash flows associated with the debt holders – that is, after tax interest costs and any debt repaid or raised. The calculation of free cash flow to equity is shown in Table 1.8.

Table 1.8 RWM plc – Calculation of Free Cash Flow to Equity for 2006

	£m
Free Cash Flow to Firm (after tax basis)	5.6
less: After Tax Interest Costs at 33% [a]	
Marginal Tax Rate i.e. £3.4m x 67%	–2.3
less: Debt Repaid/(Debt Raised) [b]	–6.9
Free Cash Flow to Equity	–3.6

a Interest payable is £3.4m (see Table 1.6). Assume taxation at 33%. Therefore the after tax interest costs = £3.4m x 67% = £2.3m.
b For ease of calculation, calculated from payables: amounts falling due after one year which are assumed to consist entirely of debt.

If the FCFE is positive the surplus may be used in one of two ways, first, to pay cash to equity holders either in the form of dividends or by buying back their shares or, second, retaining the surplus within the business for future reinvestment. This topic is considered in a little more detail in Section 1.8 on Dividend policy. If FCFE is negative the question arises as to whether the dividend is cut to finance such a deficit.

The importance of time horizons

The focus on Planning, Cash flow and Working Capital really arises from the requirement to look at an extended time horizon when undertaking any sort of cash flow planning.

When examining an extended time horizon it may usefully be divided into a number of parts as shown in Figure 1.6 below.

Figure 1.6 Extended Time Horizon

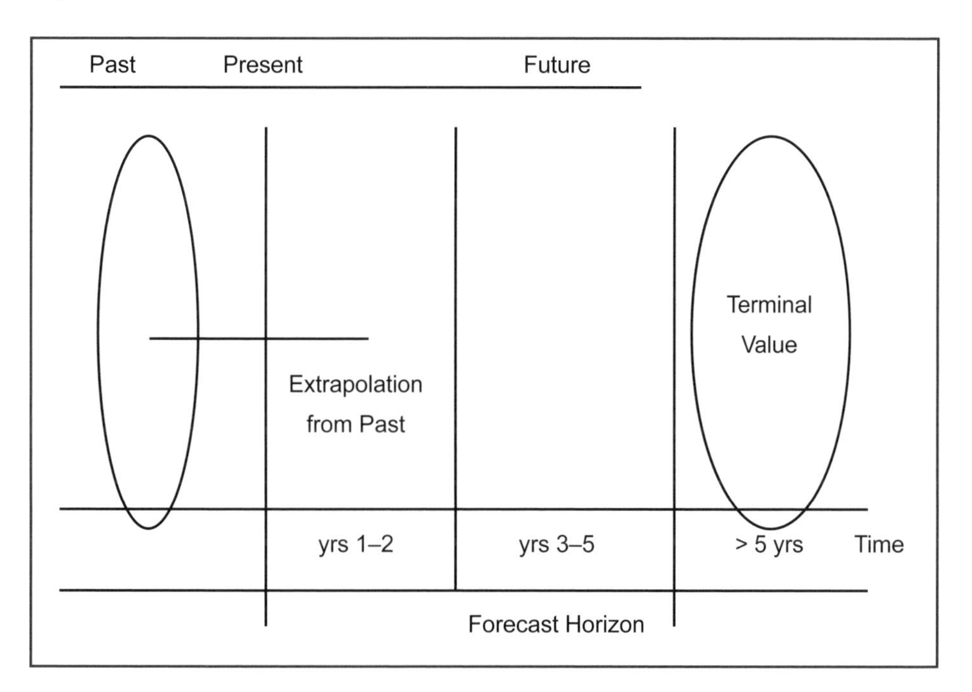

1. Years 1–2

Past historical information is often used as a guide to forecasting for years 1 and 2 provided one assumes that the past is a good guide to the future. In general most managers are comfortable with this type of forecasting for the first two years. If things are expected to change from the past they are typically able to make the appropriate allowances relatively easily.

2. Years 3–5
This period of time often does not get the attention it deserves. Typically the formulas in the spreadsheet for years 1 and 2 are copied across without any real interrogation of whether it is appropriate to do so. One needs to investigate whether the business environment and hence the firms strategy are likely to remain unchanged. In addition one of the things that may be overlooked when examining this time period is Working Capital.

The importance of focusing on this time period derives from the fact that what a business does during these years is often what gives it its competitive advantage. The sustainability of this competitive advantage enables the business to continue creating value into the period beyond five years.

3. Beyond 5 years
As mentioned above the sustainability of the businesses capital advantage is what underpins whether value is captured by a business beyond five years. The value captured is reflected in a terminal value which is the subject of a later chapter.

1.7 Capital Structure and Gearing (Leverage)

The key point about capital structure is that by raising a larger proportion of funds from debt than equity, it is quite possible to improve the return on capital employed. If debt capital can be raised and employed in the business to earn a rate which exceeds that rate being paid in fixed interest, then it must follow that a surplus will remain after payment of the interest. This surplus will clearly add to the profits available to the equity shareholder, which the following simple example demonstrates:

Example
Assume a company which presently has an all equity capital structure is to undertake an investment of £50 million which will earn incremental profit before interest and tax of £7 million. It may finance this investment either by additional equity or by a long term loan carrying an interest of 10%. Table 1.9 demonstrates that the use of further equity dilutes the return on equity, whereas the use of debt enhances it.

Table 1.9 Return on Equity (ROE)% – Effect of Equity v Debt Financing

		Before	After	
			All Equity	Debt and Equity
		£'m	£'m	£'m
Equity Capital	(A)	100.0	150.0	100.0
Debt		0.0	0.0	50.0
Profit Before Interest and Tax		20.0	27.0	27.0
less Interest Payable		0.0	0.0	5.0
Profit Before Tax		20.0	27.0	22.0
less Taxation (35%)		7.0	9.5	7.7
Profit After Tax	(B)	13.0	17.5	14.3
ROE %	**(B / A x 100)**	**13.0%**	**11.7%**	**14.3%**

This example suggests a tremendous advantage in the use of significant amounts of debt. However, in practice, the following factors would be taken into consideration in determining the amount of debt to be used:

- The articles of association of a limited company normally restrict the volume of debt
- The nature of the security which could be offered may detract from the acceptability of further debt
- The anticipated level of future profits may provide an insufficient safety margin for future interest payments
- The equity holders may not wish to accept any greater risk to dividends or share value caused by the creation of additional prior debt charge
- The anticipated level of cash flow may be inadequate to service interest, debt repayment and equity dividend, thus the risk of insolvency presents itself.

Careful assessment of all of these factors enables a safe amount of debt that does not jeopardise the value of equity shareholders' investment to be determined. The determination of the debt capacity of an organisation is an essential part of financial management and organisations do monitor their debt position very carefully.

What is Gearing (Leverage)?

There are a number of methods used to determine the gearing or leverage of a company. For the purpose of this example we are using the components of the Borrowing Ratio, that is, total borrowings divided by equity.

An Example

Imagine two identical companies, run by twins; where one twin owns Company A while the other twin owns Company B. They have similar premises in the same street and each manufactures the same products, to the same specification and using the same machinery. The costs and volumes of both companies are the same and they employ similar staff, that is, the twins, each employing one twin. The only difference between the two companies is the way in which they are financed. Twin A financed Company A mainly from equity capital, while Twin B financed Company B mainly from borrowings. The relative proportions of debt to equity and the gearing ratio for the two companies would be as follows:

	A	B
Borrowings	20	80
Equity	80	20
GEARING	LOW	HIGH

It can be seen that the gearing for Company A is 20 / 80 which equals 0.25 to 1, while the gearing for Company B is 80 / 20 and equals 4.00 to 1.

In Table 1.10 we show both companies have achieved an operating profit of £1,000. We have also assumed that interest payable is in proportion to the company's borrowing, therefore, Company A has £200 of interest payable while Company B has £800.

Table 1.10 Income Statements for Company A and B

	A	B
Operating Profit	1,000	1,000
less Interest Payable	200	800
Profit Before Taxation	800	200
less Taxation at 25%	200	50
Profit After Taxation	600	150

Why do Companies Move Towards Higher Gearing?

Quite simply, in good times it pays to finance a business by debt provided that the return is in excess of the cost of the debt.

	A	B
Borrowings	20	80
Equity	80	20
GEARING	LOW	HIGH
RETURN	LOW	HIGH

Companies that move towards higher gearing will provide a higher return to each individual share when the economic climate is good. If we take the previous example and add an extra £500 to the Operating Profit for both companies, the result is shown in Table 1.11.

Table 1.11 Income Statements – Increase in Operating Profit

	A	B
	£	£
Operating Profit	1,500	1,500
less Interest Payable	200	800
Profit Before Taxation	1,300	700
less Taxation at 25%	325	50
Profit After Taxation	975	650
less Dividend	300	75
Profit After Taxation and Dividend	675	575
No. of Shares	80	20
Profit After Taxation and Dividend Per Share	8.44	28.75

We can see from Table 1.11 that an incremental Operating Profit of £500 means that the Profit before Taxation is increased by £500 since the Interest Payable is covered from the initial £1,000 profit. Given that both companies pay the same rate of tax and pay the same amount of dividend, it means that the Profit After Taxation and Dividend is £675 for Company A and £575 for Company B. Extending the calculation we obtain Profit After Taxation and Dividend Per Share of £8.44 for Company A and £28.75 for Company B. We can now see that Company B achieves a higher return (per share) given an increase in the profits earned by the company. Therefore, higher gearing or leverage produces a higher potential return to shareholders.

What can happen to highly geared companies when there is an economic downturn?

Companies that move towards higher gearing should always keep a look out for the possibility of an economic downturn. Many companies fail to consider their financial structure and find that they are highly geared at the start of a recession. A substantial number of these companies will fail or will have to be restructured. The results of high gearing that produce a high return (per share) will place companies in a high risk category. Therefore:

	A	B
Borrowings	20	80
Equity	80	20
GEARING	LOW	HIGH
RETURN	LOW	HIGH
RISK	LOW	HIGH

As indicated, companies that move towards higher gearing will provide a higher return to each individual share when the economic climate is good. If we take the previous example and deduct £500 from the Operating Profit for both companies, the result is shown in Table 1.12.

Table 1.12 Income Statements – Decrease in Operating Profit

	A	B
Operating Profit	500	500
less Interest Payable	200	800
Profit/Loss Before Taxation	300	–300

Here we can see the risk involved. At times of recession, sales often decline. This will inevitably cause a decline in profits which in turn will cause a decline in the amount of funds coming into the business. The only thing which does not decline is the borrowings and the interest payments. In many cases interest rates will increase, therefore causing an even larger outflow of funds and an eventual, long-lasting cash crisis.

What is an acceptable level of gearing?

The potential tax related benefits of debt capital and 'gearing up' on the one hand and the disadvantages of increased risk on the other has given rise to the view of there being an optimal, or ideal, capital structure. That is, there is some mix of debt relative to equity at which the tax advantage can be maximised before the perception by debt and equity providers that the risk needs to be compensated for by a higher return.

The answer to the question is that it all depends upon the economic climate and the business itself. As for the economy, we know that perceptions and the reality of borrowing can change given different economic conditions. For instance, in times of recession a massive change typically occurs in views about what constitutes an acceptable level of borrowing. Individuals and corporations often see the upside of borrowing from boom-time turn into a very real downside as interest rates rise at a time when effective demand and confidence are falling. In addition to what is regarded as an acceptable level of gearing from a broad economic perspective, there is a need to consider specific business/industry characteristics since different types of business have different types of asset and repayment structures. Those with more to offer as security, or with more robust cash flows, should be able to gain most benefit from debt financing. The same is also the case for businesses with a good track record, even though their tangible sources of collateral may be limited.

Many believe that it is difficult to determine a single truly optimal capital structure in practice, but that it is more valuable to see it as corresponding with a limited range of possible debt and equity mixes.

Irrespective of the exact characteristics of the capital structure, the real challenge is to locate where it potentially lies when taking a forward-looking view. This is because, in terms of undertaking a valuation, the real concern is typically to find the required rate of return or cost of capital to apply in valuing a potential opportunity from a series of estimated future cash flows. This means that the cost of capital should relate to the future, which is achieved by attempting to identify the most beneficial blend of debt and equity over the future planning period. Attention will have to be paid to the most appropriate debt structure, which will have to take into consideration conditions relating to both the economy and the business.

1.8 Dividend Policy

A substantial amount of research has been undertaken about the decision to retain profit or whether to distribute it by way of dividend. The conclusion in practice suggests that dividend policy is a vital factor in enhancing the value of shareholders' equity. However, there is still inadequate empirical evidence to confirm exactly the importance of dividends in market value and one source of difficulty is that different shareholders have different expectations from their individual investments. Whereas some investors look for dividends, others look for capital growth. Except for very closely controlled companies, it is very difficult to establish the attitude of shareholders with any precision. Nevertheless, in determining a dividend policy, the following factors do appear to be of significance:

- A stable dividend rather than a fluctuating one is generally regarded as a sign of strength and should have a favourable impact upon market value
- Steady growth in dividend is generally desirable, even though such growth may lag slightly behind earnings growth. Such a conservative approach is preferable to a hasty response which may subsequently require a cut in dividend
- Dividend cover, although questioned by some, does provide a crude indication of the amount of retained profit which should, in principle, result in a growth in market value in the future. However, this does assume that any such retained profit will be employed successfully within the business.

In determining dividend policy, the balance between how much to distribute and how much to retain is vital and there is a crucial link between the capital investment decision and the financing decision.

Theoretically, the shareholders are no worse off (they may even be better off!) whether or not a dividend is paid. The proviso is that the cash flows from profits retained (rather than paid out as a dividend) are invested in projects which earn at least the corporate cost of capital.

In practice, dividends do matter. The theoretical arguments outlined above are not supported by experience in the real world. For the most part in finance, it can be assumed that investors are rational and that they would therefore accept the argument about dividend policy outlined above. But in this one case, investors do not appear to be rational. They prefer dividends now rather than in the future – even if the future dividends will be high enough to compensate. Thus, a company may miss profitable investment opportunities because the cash is not immediately available – because it has to be paid out as a dividend, to maintain the company's earlier dividend policy.

If a company has set a level of dividends in the past, they will be expected in the future. If the dividends have been so much per share, perhaps growing at the rate of inflation, then that dividend payment has set a precedent for the future. Company directors will deviate from that at their peril. If dividends are reduced, the share price will typically be most adversely affected. Conversely, directors will be reluctant to increase dividends much, because, once the dividend has been increased to a higher level, it will be expected that the new level will be maintained. So, corporate boards of directors tend to maintain a policy of steadily increasing dividends.

Why should investors be irrational on this one point of policy? Over the years, analysts have come up with arguments and suggestions to provide logical reasons for investors' attitude towards dividends and these, in summary, are as follows:

- Dividends have information content. This means that investors can be sure that the company really has made some money in the year. The cash is available to pay the dividend
- Uncertainty about the future prospects of the company means that investors prefer current dividends to distant dividends
- Shareholders do rely on cash income (from the dividends on their investments)
- Maintenance of a steady dividend policy will mean that the share price is maintained and that it is not trading at a discount.

1.9 Cost of Capital

The one remaining area for consideration is the cost of capital which is a very contentious topic. This subject is supported by a substantial body of research and literature and the following discussion represents only a very brief review.

How can a business evaluate whether a potential investment is really worthwhile? In every day life it is common practice to answer this question with reference to the rate of return that will be earned on funds invested. If money needs to be borrowed to undertake such a potential investment then there will be a cost associated with it, typically expressed as the percentage return required by the lender. Common sense would dictate that the return required from an investment should at the very least cover the cost of funds needing to be raised to finance it. What applies in everyday life also applies in corporate life. Organisations have to ensure that the opportunities in which it invests are those that will at minimum satisfy the returns required by the providers of funds. In other words, the cost of capital should equate with the opportunity cost of the funds tied up; that is, the return which would be achieved from their next best use.

The importance of understanding the role of the cost of capital in value creation may be simple, but in practice its estimation is far more problematic, as will be discussed further in Chapter 6. One source of complication is that the providers of funds to a company are not typically a homogeneous group with identical requirements and expectations from their investment. At one extreme they may comprise long-term debt-holders seeking a secure and fixed rate of interest, while at the other they may be ordinary shareholders who accept that the return received is most likely to be contingent on the company's performance. Somehow the requirements of all providers have to be captured. One commonly accepted way is via the Weighted Average Cost of Capital (WACC) in which the requirements of all providers of funds are expressed in one percentage rate of return.

Weighted Average Cost of Capital (WACC)

Opinions may often differ about the size of the cost of capital and to understand the source of such differences we will review the subject in Chapter 6 with reference to the Weighted Average Cost of Capital, looking at three steps involving estimation of the:

1. Cost of Equity
2. Cost of Debt
3. Capital Structure

These three steps and the building blocks associated with them are illustrated in Figure 1.7.

Figure 1.7 Three Steps for Estimating WACC

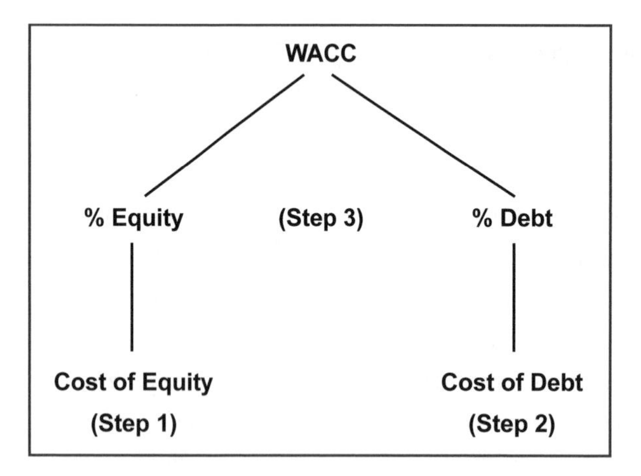

1.10 Linking the Business Plan and the Financial Plan

This section aims to provide a framework that brings together the two aspects of any firm; the business aspects or Business Plan and the financial aspects or the Financial Plan. The glue that ties these two parts together is cash flow as will be illustrated below.

The business plan

In essence, the business plan is all about the strategy of the firm and how it intends to create value, the investments it makes in deployment of that value creating strategy and its operations in execution of this strategy. The Business Plan both needs cash to execute the strategy in terms of its expenditures and investments and produces cash when the strategies are being realised. The cash flows that are important to the Business Plan are OCF and FCFF, the relationship between the two is shown in Table 1.13 for our example company RWM plc. In terms of cash flow, the Business Plan answers two questions; how much cash is required to fund the business' strategy and how much cash will the business' strategy eventually produce?

Table 1.13 Operating Cash Flow (OCF) to Free Cash Flow to Firm (FCFF)[2]

	£m
Operating Cash Flow (OCF)	14.5
less: Investment in Fixed Capital (both replacement and incremental)	-16.4
less: Investment in Working Capital	7.5
Free Cash flow to Firm (FCFF)	**5.6**

The Financing Plan

In order to be able to undertake its strategy a business needs capital to do so. This is the raison d'être of the financing plan. It provides answers to the two questions; how will the business strategy be financed and what should be done with any surplus cash?

The following table helps us to answer these questions. Taking the FCFF as our starting point, if it is positive the cash flow may be used to service debt in the form of interest or repay principal leaving FCFE which may be returned to shareholders or retained within the firm for future reinvestment. Conversely, if FCFF is negative it may be funded through borrowing, raising equity, curtailing dividends or by using internally generated funds.

Table 1.14 Free Cash Flow to Firm (FCFF) to Net Cash Movement

	£m
Free Cash flow to Firm (FCFF) (after tax basis)	5.6
less: After Tax Interest Costs	–2.3
less: Debt Repaid/(Debt Raised)	–6.9
Free Cash Flow to Equity (FCFE) [3]	–3.6
less: Dividends	–5.5
less: Equity Raised/(Bought Back) [4]	9.1
Net Cash Movement	**0**

[2] Reproduced from Table 1.7

[3] This part of the table is reproduced from Table 1.8.

[4] Calculated by taking the difference between the 2006 less 2005 figures for issued share capital plus share premium account. The basic data is taken from the balance sheets on page 39, that is, (£13.9m + £38.7m) – (£13.2m + £30.3m) = £9.1m.

1.11 Framework for Business Decisions

When we look at Tables 1.15 and 1.16 the common element is FCFF. For any one firm the FCFF in the Business Plan and the Financing Plan must be the same and we can write the following statement:

Business Plan = Financing plan

If we now expand on what is encompassed under each plan we can write the following expression Figure 1.8, which highlights the high level business decisions that any management team has to consider:

Figure 1.8 High Level Business Decisions

Component	**Strategy and Operations**	**Capital Structure Policy**	**Dividend Policy**	**Net Surplus/ Deficit Cash**
Key Management Decisions	What business are we in, how should we allocate our resources and what are the key investment decisions?	What is the appropriate mix of debt:equity to finance the business?	How much to return to shareholders vs retain to finance the future of business?	What is the appropriate level?

In summary, there are three key interrelated management decisions as shown in Figure 1.9.

Figure 1.9 Three Key Interrelated Management Decisions

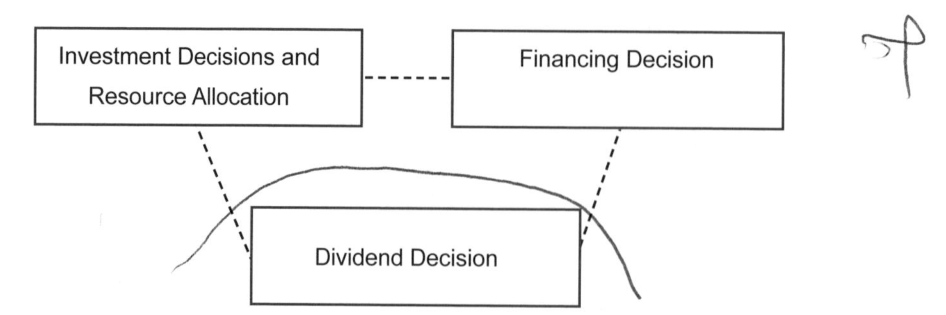

Some observers say that the Dividend decision should be a residual decision after the other two decisions. The rationale for this is that if there are investment opportunities to grow the business which create value then these should be undertaken and financed accordingly because this will generate returns to shareholders over the longer term. If there are no value creating investments in the medium term then it makes sense to return surplus capital to shareholders either in the form of dividends or in the form of share buy backs (legislation permitting). What this rationale ignores is that a company may already have an existing commitment to pay a certain level of dividends to its shareholders.

Although this commitment is not binding, shareholders may sell the shares if the dividend is cut which may depress the share price opening the company to a possible take-over.

RWM plc

Consolidated Income Statement for the years ended 31st December

	Notes	2004	2005	2006
		£m	£m	£m
Revenue		187.4	199.6	210.6
Cost of Sales		80.6	94.1	101.8
Gross Profit		106.8	105.5	108.8
Operating Expenses		86.6	90.8	96.7
Operating Profit		20.2	14.7	12.1
Interest Payable	(1)	3.9	5.3	3.4
Profit Before Tax		16.3	9.4	8.7
Taxation		5.0	2.7	2.4
Profit Attributable to Shareholders		11.3	6.7	6.3

RWM plc

Consolidated Balance Sheet as at 31st December

	Notes	2004	2005	2006
		£m	**£m**	**£m**
Non Current Assets				
Tangible Fixed Assets		66.9	76.2	86.7
Current Assets				
Inventory		50.1	54.9	70.2
Receivables	(2)	28.6	31.2	35.1
Cash		0.2	0.3	0.3
		78.9	86.4	105.6
Creditors: amounts falling due within one year	(3)	58.4	69.6	96.3
Net Current Assets		20.5	16.8	9.3
Total Assets less Current Liabilities		87.4	93.0	96.0
Creditors: amounts falling due after one year	(3)	25.1	27.0	20.1
		62.3	66.0	75.9
Capital and Reserves				
Called up Share Capital (10p shares)	(4)	13.0	13.2	13.9
Share Premium Account		28.3	30.3	38.7
Revaluation Reserve		2.1	2.1	2.1
Income statement Account		18.9	20.4	21.2
Equity		62.3	66.0	75.9

RWM plc

Notes to the accounts

	2004	2005	2006
	£m	£m	£m
1. Dividends Payable	4.9	5.2	5.5
2. Interest Payable:			
Bank Borrowings and other loans			
repayable within 5 years	3.3	4.2	2.6
Finance Leases	0.3	0.5	0.6
Hire Purchase and Sundry Loans	0.3	0.6	0.2
	3.9	3.3	3.4
3. Debtors: amounts falling due within one year:			
Trade Receivables	24.3	25.9	26.7
Other Receivables, Prepayments			
and Accrued Income	4.3	5.3	8.4
	28.6	31.2	35.1
4. Creditors: amounts falling due within one year:			
Bank Borrowings	28.0	16.0	24.4
Loan Notes	0.0	0.0	12.0
Trade Payables	16.4	24.3	26.7
Bills of Exchange	0.9	0.2	3.2
Taxation and Social Security	3.1	7.2	5.4
Finance Leases	1.3	2.5	1.6
Hire Purchase Payables	1.8	3.6	4.2
Other Payables	0.8	2.4	7.5
Accruals and Deferred Income	3.1	10.1	7.8
Proposed Dividend	3.0	3.3	3.5
	58.4	69.6	96.3

RWM plc

Notes to the accounts

	2004	2005	2006
	£m	**£m**	**£m**
5. Creditors: amounts falling due after one year:			
Loan Notes	12.0	12.0	0.0
Bank and Other Loans	3.6	2.2	5.6
Finance Leases	1.2	1.5	1.8
Hire Purchase Payables	4.2	6.8	7.6
Other Payables	4.0	4.3	4.9
Accruals Deferred Income	0.1	0.2	0.2
	25.1	27.0	20.1
Proposed Dividend	3.0	3.3	3.5

6. Called up Share Capital

Ordinary Shares 10p each. 2006, 139 million *(2005, 132 million)*

CHAPTER 2
THE FUTURE ASSET STRUCTURE AND CAPITAL PROJECT APPRAISAL

Chapter Preview

This chapter will enable you to:

- **Describe the need for organisations to identify, evaluate and invest in high quality capital projects.**

- **Prepare a list of the main financial variables required for project appraisal.**

- **Identify the main points to consider when assessing the quality of input data for use in project appraisal.**

- **Calculate the cash flows for use in a project appraisal.**

- **Appreciate the importance of:**
  - **Project monitoring**
  - **Project control**
  - **Post completion audit.**

- **Evaluate capital projects using a range of appraisal methods, including:**
  - **Payback period**
  - **Accounting rate of return**
  - **Net present value**
  - **Profitability index**
  - **Internal rate of return.**

- **Describe and illustrate the differences that can arise in evaluating projects using Net Present Value (NPV) and the Internal Rate of Return (IRR).**

- **Describe the reasons for making inflation and taxation adjustments to project appraisals and apply such adjustments.**

2.1 Introduction

Growing a business by internal development, as opposed to external investment in other organisations, requires sound commercial judgement. Such growth only occurs when the future returns from internal investment exceed the financing costs; this means that managers must test their judgement against the difficulties presented by a highly unpredictable and uncertain future.

In considering this problem we ask:

- Are there any tools or techniques available from the realms of accounting and finance to help assess the desirability of particular investments?
- What are the differences between these tools and techniques?

We will consider these questions and other important issues in this chapter in relation to the evaluation of investments within the business. Such evaluations are similar to those made by private individuals when, say, buying a car. The decision needs first to be weighed against other spending priorities. Various models would then be considered evaluating the costs and benefits of each before the actual choice is made. After the purchase a conscious or perhaps sub-conscious evaluation would be undertaken on the quality of the decision.

The process is roughly the same for commercial decisions except that the financing of capital expenditure projects is treated separately.

2.2 Organising Investment Decisions

A major stimulus for much investment is often the concern about the future performance of the business if investment does not take place. However, in practice many businesses actually consider investment requirements according to the particular needs to be addressed. Let us consider such needs with reference to the following four categories of investment:

1. Asset replacement
2. Cost saving
3. Expansion
4. Reactive.

Asset Replacement

If a company fails to replace those assets which currently generate its cash flow and profit, then in the absence of any other investment, its performance will decline, whether quickly or slowly. If the current profile of activities are appropriate to future long-term plans then, in order to continue to generate adequate cash flows and profit, the business must replace assets as they become worn out or obsolete.

Cost Saving

Cost saving projects are critical to companies which have products or services where sales revenues have reached the maximum level that can be sustained by the market. Irrespective of whether this maximum is temporary because of depressed economic conditions or more permanent because the maximum achievable share of a mature market has been reached, a reduction in the firm's costs is possible by improving the efficiency of existing asset use. Sales generation ratios (discussed in the previous chapter) can be used to identify possible areas for improvement, such as the automation of a previously labour intensive production system. This usually involves the substitution of an avoidable variable cost with an unavoidable fixed cost in order to secure forecast savings.

Finally, cost saving projects may be important to the not–for–profit organisation in which there may be no revenues associated with a project. The analysis of cost savings enables comparisons to be made with existing practice and between alternatives.

Expansion

Business growth can result from internal or organic expansion or by focusing upon external targets via an acquisitive strategy. Much investment activity can be related to the desire to achieve growth which many organisations (particularly smaller ones) will attempt to achieve internally. Successful internal growth will eventually permit an organisation to contemplate external expansion, particularly where its shares may be traded publicly. However, even companies with a successful track record of acquisitions will undertake internal investment resulting in business expansion to achieve growth.

Reactive Investment

Reactive investment covers two particular types of capital expenditure. The first is that which is required as a defensive response to threatening changes in the commercial environment. For example, some of the changes which can be observed in the major UK clearing banks services are the result of substantial investment caused by threats from previously dormant players in the financial services sector, such as Building Societies, in recent years. The second embraces that imposed upon the business because of legislative or other reasons where the benefits of the expenditure are not always readily measurable. It is perhaps, best illustrated by the following examples:

- As a result of legislation, the UK furniture industry was required to undertake substantial investment in fire resistant foam filling
- Following a major oil disaster in the North Sea, oil companies were required to undertake safety modifications to offshore installations estimated to cost hundreds of millions of pounds.

Managerial Responsibility for Investment

In larger organisations, managerial responsibility for investment is usually delegated from top management to lower levels of management. This delegation will usually exclude the raising of finance other than from short-term sources. Decisions about sources of finance with long-term implications are usually taken by top management who will try to balance proportions of debt and equity so as to minimise the cost of capital to the business.

The delegation of managerial responsibility for the evaluation of capital expenditure can be achieved by specifying cut-off levels, the amount of which corresponds with given levels of seniority. For example, senior divisional management may be responsible for capital expenditure up to an agreed cut-off sum and approval would have to be obtained from top management for capital expenditure above the agreed cut-off. In addition, such senior divisional management may also be required to approve submissions for capital expenditure from its divisional management, where the capital expenditure required exceeds the level of delegated responsibility.

2.3 Appraising Investment Opportunities

In this section we provide a background to the financial appraisal of potential investment opportunities. In common with many areas of accounting and finance, numerous terms are used to describe the financial appraisal process of which investment appraisal, project appraisal and capital budgeting are common. To avoid confusion and to reinforce the point that our concern is not with investing in securities of other organisations, we will adopt the term project appraisal to refer to the evaluation of capital expenditure.

You may find it easy to become lost in the detail of the financial issues associated with project appraisal, so let us take stock of the key financial requirements to be met:

- Only those projects which meet the objectives of the business should be selected, that is, those which provide what the business regards as a satisfactory return for the risks involved
- The return to be expected from a project must exceed the financing cost that the capital expenditure will necessitate
- The most financially desirable project must be selected from the range of opportunities available (assuming, as is normally the case, that resources are limited and that not all projects can be undertaken).

In addition to these financial requirements it is important to stress that for many investments non-financial factors may be very important. Therefore account must also be taken of these so that both financial and non-financial considerations are given appropriate weight.

With these points in mind and before we consider individual techniques for gauging the financial benefit, let us consider the main financial variables of a project appraisal. A definitive list is impossible, but the following items will usually occur in one form or another:

- The initial capital outlay including the cost of fixed assets, working capital and, if appropriate, deliberate start-up losses
- The expected useful economic life of the project
- An estimate of the residual value of assets remaining at the end of the project's useful economic life
- The amounts and timing of all cost and revenue components associated with the project
- Expected price level changes for each cost and revenue component
- Taxation assumptions and any regional grants likely to affect the corporate position
- The relevant cost of financing the project (cost of capital)
- Likely estimates of variation for each of the above variables.

Many of these financial variables will be discussed in the review of major project appraisal techniques but before considering these techniques, let us consider certain key points concerning the requirements of data for purposes of decision making. It is all too easy to focus upon the mechanics of the techniques themselves whilst losing sight of their limitations in the absence of good quality input data. It cannot be over–stressed that the benefit to be derived from any technique used for appraising a project can be no better than the quality of the input data employed.

2.4 Assessing the Quality of Input Data

The main points to consider in assessing the quality of input data are:

Future Orientation

The only capital outlay, operating costs and revenues relevant to a proposed capital project are those that concern the future. Sunk, past costs are irrelevant even though there may be a temptation to treat them otherwise, as are costs to be found in a company's cost or management accounting system. This is the case whether they are past or present and they are useful only as a guide in forecasting future cost levels.

It is not only that some of the costs themselves are irrelevant, but also the patterns of cost behaviour may be different. Such patterns may be appropriate to the routine accounting functions of budgeting and variance analysis, but may not be suitable for decisions where the relevant time span is longer than that required for effective control. Assumptions which ordinarily permit different costs to be described as fixed, variable or semi–variable in their behaviour may need to be adapted when five or ten year time scales are involved, since at the time a capital project decision is being made all costs relevant to the decision are variable. It is only when the project is accepted and implemented that project associated costs become fixed.

Attributable Costs and Revenues

The costs and revenues relevant to a capital project are only those which can be legitimately attributed to it rather than any other source. Whilst this notion is simple and manageable in principle at the level of the individual project, difficulties can be encountered in practice when the cumulative effects of several proposed capital projects need to be anticipated.

Differential Costs and Revenues

Where decisions require more than one course of action to be examined, the only costs and revenues to be considered are those that will differ under the alternative courses of action. Common costs and revenues may be ignored, provided they are expected to behave identically in each of the alternatives under consideration.

Opportunity Costs and Benefits

These costs and benefits are usually the most difficult of all to deal with. Nevertheless, opportunity costs and benefits must be included in any project decision. For example, if a consequence of introducing a new model of a product currently sold at a profit is that sales of the existing product will be lost, then the lost contribution on the existing product is an opportunity cost of the new model which must be included in the appraisal.

Financing Costs

It is often tempting, but incorrect, during a project appraisal to include the financing costs associated with a proposal within the estimated operating costs. As we will show in the next section, how the financing costs are compared with the financial benefits does vary according to the appraisal techniques used, but they should not be included with the estimated operating costs.

Uncertainty and Inflation

It is important that the risk and uncertainty associated with projects is incorporated within any appraisal, together with expectations about changes in costs and prices. Any failure to make appropriate allowances for risk, uncertainty and inflation can result in an appraisal of questionable value.

Qualitative Issues

A serious limitation of conventional project appraisal is the omission of non-financial issues, such as improvements in product quality for corporate image or a lower susceptibility to adverse social pressures. Whilst such benefits are often extremely difficult to assess, they should not be ignored.

2.5 Determining the Cash Flows

Very often, for convenience, the input data for an investment appraisal is assumed to be available. In practice, the determination of the cash flows is a very demanding task. Here we will consider how a cash flow profile may be built up by drawing upon information from a wide range of sources.

Example Using Capital Outlay and Savings

The cost of the equipment is relatively easy to obtain via quotes from a number of suppliers. Other items of cost may also be important, for example in certain projects the cost of services could be quite large if it meant laying a mains cable or an access road.

The following example provides an indication of the amount of detail that is needed in order to estimate future cash flows. The figures are taken from a project undertaken by a printer to set up a new press dedicated to printing training manuals.

Table 2.1 Determining the Capital Outlay

	£'000
Equipment	£1,700
Services	£50
Contingency	£35
Expenses	£15
	£1,800

From the following list it can be seen that the basic data required to determine savings must be obtained from a number of sources. The sales forecast, expected selling price and average page count of the manuals could be obtained from the marketing department, while the technical data concerning pages per impression and run speed would be obtained from the equipment manual and the average run length and set up could be obtained from past experience.

Table 2.2 Basic Data for Calculation of Annual Cash Flows

Sales Forecast per annum	£6,000,000
Average Selling Price per Book	£30.00
Average Page Count	200 pages
Pages Per Impression	16 pages
Run Speed	10,000 impressions per hour
Average Run Length per job	2,000 books
Set-up	30 minutes

Table 2.3 Calculation of Forecast Annual Volumes

Total Books	(£60,000,000 ÷ £30.00)	200,000 books
Total Impressions	(200,000 x 200 ÷ 16)	2,500,000 impressions
Total Print Jobs	(200,000 ÷ 2,000)	100 jobs

We now require data concerning the time taken to prepare, print, bind and warehouse. This will be obtained from work study records and hourly rates to produce the following:

Table 2.4 Additional Data to Establish Annual Costs

Preparation	30 hours (per average run length job)	£250 per hour
Paper and materials	£16,800 per job	
Printing:		
Setup	£200 per hour	
Text	£200 per hour	
Covers	7 hours, rate £140 per hour (per average run length job)	
Binding	150 minutes per 1,000, rate £140 per hour	
Warehousing	£200,000	

Table 2.5 Calculation of the Annual Costs

			£
Materials		(£16,800 x 100)	1,680,000
Preparation		(100 x 30 hours x £250)	750,000
Printing	Setup	(2.5 m x 30 ÷ 60 ÷ 2,000 x £200)	125,000
	Text	(2.5 m ÷ 10,000 x £200)	50,000
	Covers	(100 x 7 hours x £140)	98,000
Binding		(200,000 x 150 ÷ 60 ÷ 1,000 x £140)	70,000
Warehousing			200,000
			2,973,000

The annual cash flows can now be established using the sales forecast as the income then deducting materials and the costs of printing, binding and warehousing. The results are shown in Table 2.6.

Table 2.6 Annual cash flows

		£
Income	(Sales Forecast)	6,000,000
less:	Annual Costs	2,973,000
Annual Cash Flow		3,027,000

Example – Forecasting Cash Flows Using 'Drivers'

As we indicated at the beginning of this chapter, there are cases where the purpose of the investment is to expand – as was the case for the printer above. In such circumstances, an alternative approach to deriving the cash flows is by the use of a number of cash flow 'drivers'. Using this approach, the implications of an expansion can be mapped out by their impact upon the business which we illustrate with a simple example.

Imagine a business which has achieved sales revenue of £10 million from, for the sake of simplicity, a single product. With the usual forecasting difficulty it estimates 'an expansion' potential of 10% in the market in which it operates. What does the firm need to consider?

Assuming it has the production capacity; it will receive cash revenues from the increased sales after deducting operating expenses (excluding depreciation) and taxation. To take advantage of such a market it may also incur cash expenses from increases in working capital: increased debtors as a result of more aggressive marketing and more stock to provide a better service to customers. If the firm does not have the capacity it must provide for increased production by incurring capital expenditure; another drain on its cash.

To see how the cash flow driver approach works our example will now assume the following:

- Depreciation of £40,000
- Sales growth rate of 10%
- Operating profit margin of 20%
- Tax rate of 25%
- Additional fixed capital requirement of 5%
- Additional working capital requirement of 10%

Table 2.7 First Year Cash Flow

	£M
Sales Revenue (£10m increased by 10% sales growth rate)	11.00
Operating Profit Margin Before Tax (£11m x 20%)	2.20
less Tax at 25%	0.55
Operating Profit Margin	1.65
plus Depreciation	0.04
Operating Cash Flow	1.69
Replacement Capital Expenditure	–0.04
Additional Fixed Capital Expenditure (£1m x 5%)	–0.05
Additional Working Capital (£1m x 10%)	–0.10
Free Cash Flow	**1.50**

Using this approach cash flow can be readily estimated. Different assumptions about the growth rate potential, the operating profit margin, the tax rate and the fixed and working capital needs can be readily built in so as to build up a profile of cash flows for a given time period. As with any matter concerning cash, depreciation has to be taken into consideration and added back to the profit margin. In this example, the simplified assumption has been made that depreciation is a reasonable proxy for what would be required to maintain the quality of existing assets in terms of their replacement as they wear out. This is what we have referred to as 'Replacement Capital Expenditure'.

The most difficult part of this exercise is actually determining the percentages and there is no easy solution to this. Historical records and competitor analysis will be required in order to produce an accurate picture. For example, the ability to achieve sales growth will be dependent upon internal resourcing and any limiting factors, as well as the action of competitors. A major advantage of the approach is that is does force trade-offs to be considered; to achieve future cash inflows by expansion, additional fixed and working capital expenditure will be necessary.

2.6 Project Monitoring, Control and Post Audit

Considerable emphasis is often given to the appraisal process and, although this is important, it is not the 'be all and end all' in making sound investment decisions. Appropriate monitoring and control procedures ensure that funds committed to a particular project are used effectively.

These may involve ongoing procedures to monitor expenditure regularly and/or the use of what is known as the 'post audit'. Typically, this is focused upon apportioning blame, although this need not necessarily be so. An increasing number of companies (usually very large companies) have developed procedures at varying stages of a projects development, with a terminal evaluation sometime after project completion. Companies with such procedures have used them as part of a learning process.

It would be rare for all projects to be post audited. More often, on a regular basis, a sample of completed capital projects is submitted for post audit. For those selected there is a thorough investigation of all aspects of each project from the original idea through to eventual implementation. The main purpose of post audit being to provide a feedback mechanism to benefit future projects. It should cover:

- How does each project fit into the present and future resource requirements?
- What improvements might be made in the collection of better data for each project?
- To what extent have savings been overestimated and capital requirements underestimated?
- Were projects properly evaluated, including sensitivity and risk?
- Did all projects produce the forecast savings? Have the necessary standards been amended?
- What are the main recommendations for improvement to future capital projects?
- Should the procedures for capital projects be amended?

2.7 *Project Appraisal Techniques*

We have now set the scene for project appraisal in our discussions of the financial variables required and important issues associated with the quality of cost and revenue inputs. The important issue for consideration now is how such data is organised for purposes of appraising a project. This we will illustrate with reference to the four major project appraisal techniques.

1. Payback period
2. Accounting rate of return
3. Net Present Value (NPV) and profitability index
4. Internal Rate of Return (IRR)

The distinguishing characteristics of these four project appraisal techniques and their respective advantages and disadvantages are best illustrated with financial data. Accordingly we will use data for an imaginary organisation contemplating the following four alternative projects which are summarised in Table 2.8 below.

Table 2.8 Basic Data for Four Projects

	Project A	**Project B**	**Project C**	**Project D**
	£'000	**£'000**	**£'000**	**£'000**
Capital Outlay	–15,000	–18,000	–10,000	–18,000
Net Cash Inflows:				
Year 1	7,000	6,000	5,000	4,000
Year 2	4,000	6,000	5,000	5,000
Year 3	3,000	6,000		6,000
Year 4	2,000	6,000		7,000
Year 5	1,000	6,000		8,000

Payback Period

The payback period is calculated with reference to cash flow data. It is expressed in terms of a number of years (or years and months) and summarises the time required for a project to recover its capital outlay from cash inflows. For example, for Project B which has a capital outlay of £18 million and cash inflows of £6 million for each year of its five year expected economic life, the payback is exactly three years:

$$\frac{\text{Capital Outlay}}{\text{Net Cash Inflow}} = \frac{\text{£18 million}}{\text{£ 6 million}} = \text{3 years}$$

Project B is straightforward because the payback period occurs exactly at the end of year three, but this is not usually the case. For example, if you try to calculate the payback period for projects A and D you will find that it does not occur at the end of a single year. Let us see how this can be dealt with using the data for Project A. The first step is to accumulate the cash flows as follows:

Table 2.9 Calculation of Payback Period – Project A

	£'000		
Capital Outlay	–15,000		
Net Cash Inflows:	**(i)**	**(ii)**	**(iii)**
	Annual	**Annual to Payback**	**Cumulative to Payback**
	£'000	**£'000**	**£'000**
Year 1	7,000	7,000	7,000
Year 2	4,000	4,000	11,000
Year 3	3,000	3,000	14,000
Year 4	2,000	1,000	15,000

The figures in column (iii) show that in each of the first three years the whole of the net cash inflows are used to accumulate to £14 million. In the fourth year, only £1 million of the net cash flows is required to make the accumulated net cash flows equal to the capital outlay. Therefore, the payback period takes place in three and one half years that is, three years, plus £1 million out of £2 million of Year 4.

The results for all four projects may be summarised as:

	Project A	**Project B**	**Project C**	**Project D**
Payback Period (years)	3.5	3.0	2.0	3.4

The main aim in using any project appraisal technique is to find out which project should be selected from a number of competing projects. A simple ranking, in this case based on the project offering the shortest payback period, would reveal that Project C is the best project. However, some companies will evaluate the payback period in relation to the project's useful economic life. This means that Project B which pays back after three years of its estimated five year life may be viewed far more favourably than Project C, which pays back at the end of its useful economic life. The relationship between the payback period and the useful economic life for each of the projects may be summarised as:

	Project A	**Project B**	**Project C**	**Project D**
Payback Period (years)	3.5	3.0	2.0	3.4
Useful Economic Life (years)	5	5	2	5
Payback ÷ Economic Life	0.70	0.60	1.00	0.68

Payback period has a major advantage over other methods because it is simple to calculate, understand and implement. Against this, the payback period focuses upon time taken to recover the capital outlay but cash flows generated after the payback period may not be taken into consideration. One other major shortcoming, the substance and importance of which will become evident shortly in our discussion of the discounting principle, is that unless the cash flows are specifically adjusted, the time value of money is ignored.

Accounting Rate of Return

The accounting rate of return differs from the payback period since its calculation draws on data relating to the whole life of a project. You must be aware, however, that it is calculated using a project's profit, rather than cash flows and thus suffers from the ambiguity of the definition of profit. Once profit is defined the accounting rate of return is relatively straightforward to calculate. Take note that different users may arrive at different accounting rates of return using the same input data and what is even more confusing is that none of the resulting calculations are necessarily incorrect!

The first step in calculating the rate of return is to add the estimated annual profit flows to establish the total profit of the proposed project. If only cash flow information is available then the annual cash flows must be added together to find the total cash flows, which in our example are £17 million, £30 million, £10 million and £30 million for Projects A, B, C and D, respectively. From this total the capital outlay (the total depreciation) is deducted to give the total profit. The average annual profit required for the calculation is found by dividing the total profit by the life of the project. This is illustrated for our four example projects in Table 2.10.

Table 2.10 Calculation of Accounting Rate of Return

		Project A	Project B	Project C	Project D
		£'000	**£'000**	**£'000**	**£'000**
Total Net Cash Inflow	(A)	17,000	30,000	10,000	30,000
Capital Outlay	(B)	–15,000	–18,000	–10,000	–18,000
Total Profit	(C)=(A)–(B)	£2,000	£12,000	0	£12,000
Life (years)	(D)	5	5	2	5
Average Annual Profit	(C)÷(D)	£400	£2,400	0	£2,400

The accounting rate of return is then calculated by dividing the average annual profit by the capital outlay. For Project A, the calculation is:

$$\text{Accounting Rate of Return (\%)} = \frac{\text{Average Annual Profit}}{\text{Capital Outlay}} \times 100$$

$$= \frac{\text{£0.4 million}}{\text{£15 million}} \times 100$$

$$= 2.7\%$$

Similar calculations for Projects B, C and D produce accounting rates of return of 13.3%, 0% and 13.3% respectively. A simple ranking from highest to lowest rate of return shows that Projects B and D are ranked equal.

	Project A	**Project B**	**Project C**	**Project D**
Accounting Rate of Return %	2.7	13.3	0	13.3
Ranking	3	1 =	4	1 =

It was indicated earlier that using the same input data, different accounting rates of return can be produced. How can this happen? It is conceivable that one might use some notion of average capital outlay rather than the total capital outlay adopted in our example and, indeed, some organisations do just this. As you will appreciate, anything which has the effect of reducing the capital outlay in the calculation will increase the accounting rate of return. Consider for example the effect on Project B if the average capital outlay was calculated as being £9 million. The rate of return percentage would double!

The potential ambiguity in accounting rate of return results is sometimes presented as being a shortcoming. Nevertheless, the technique is used and with some success particularly where manuals of capital expenditure procedure within companies provide a specific definition of the items to be used in accounting rate of return calculations.

The Principle of Discounting

The two remaining techniques for discussion, the net present value (NPV) and the internal rate of return (IRR) are both reliant upon a principle which involves discounting, or scaling–down, future cash flows. In order to appreciate the principle involved we will compare discounting with the more familiar but related technique of compounding.

Compounding is applied to a sum of money so that its value in future may be calculated given a required rate of interest. Discounting is the reverse. Future cash inflows are discounted at a given rate of interest so that they may be directly compared to the present outlay of cash.

Figure 2.1 *Compounding and Discounting Cash Flows* 

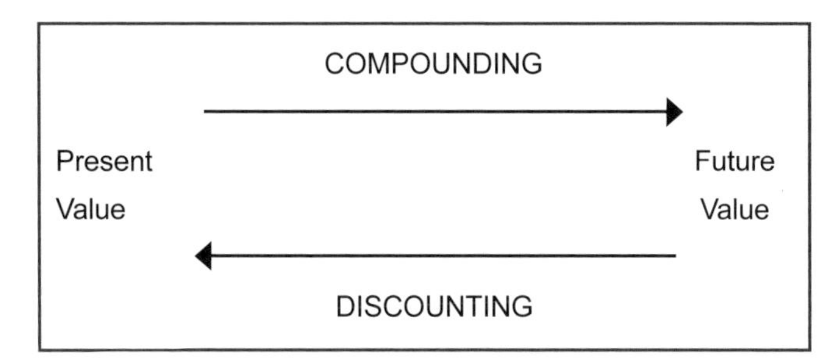

How is this discounting achieved? Cash flows can be discounted using factors which are readily available in statistical tables. The basis for their calculation is similar to the principles used in calculating compound interest. We will use the information in Table 2.11 to show the relationship between compounding and discounting. There we make specific reference to the factors used to compound and discount cash at a 10% rate.

Table 2.11 Compound Interest and Discounted Cash Flow Factors

	Compound interest factors 10%	**Discounted Cash Flow (DCF) factors 10%**
Year 0	1.000	1.000
Year 1	1.100	0.909
Year 2	1.210	0.826
Year 3	1.331	0.751
Year 4	1.464	0.683
Year 5	1.611	0.621

Using the factors in Table 2.11, £1,000 invested today at 10% compound interest would yield £1,210 at the end of year two - that is, £1,000 x 1.21. The reverse can be seen if we assume a forecast cash flow of £1,210 at the end of year two, discounted at 10% back to a present value would produce £1,000 - that is, £1,210 x 0.826. The principle of discounting thus operates by scaling down future cash flows to produce a present value. In this way future cash flows can be readily compared with the present value of capital outlays. The reduction in the value of future cash flows using the discounting process is dependent upon the rate of interest. The higher the rate of interest, the more severely the cash flows will be scaled down. The technique of adjusting cash flows might seem tedious but the discount factor tables are readily available in Appendix A at the end of the book. In that table the present value of £1 has been calculated for a wide range of interest rates.

Determining the Relevant Discount Rate

In order to calculate the net present value technique (and other discounting techniques such as the profitability index or the discounted payback period that we will discuss), the relevant discount factor must be known. This discount factor should be the company's required rate of return (sometimes known as the hurdle rate from the sporting analogy where hurdles have to be jumped to even stand a chance of being successful). This rate as represented by the company's cost of capital is a project's break–even point. Projects undertaken yielding a return above this hurdle rate will increase the value of the business whilst those below will decrease value.

The components involved in the determination of a company's cost of capital have been the subject of much academic research and debate. However, there does seem to be some agreement that the appropriate rate should comprise the weighted average of the after tax cost of debt capital and the equity cost of capital. In the case of debt capital the after tax cost is used because interest is deductible before tax thus providing a reduced real cost. This is unlike dividend payments which have to be met from after tax profits. How this cost of capital is arrived at is best understood from the following example: A company has an after tax cost of debt of 6 per cent, an estimated cost of equity of 16 per cent and future gearing comprising 20 per cent debt and 80 per cent equity. In this simple case, the company's weighted average cost of capital is 14%. The basis for the calculation is illustrated in Table 2.12.

Table 2.12 Weighted average cost of capital (WACC)

	Weight	**Cost**	**Weighted cost**
	A	**B**	**A x B %**
	(%)	**(%)**	**(%)**
Debt	20	6	1.2
Equity	80	16	12.8
			9.0

This cost of capital includes the returns demanded by both debt–holders and shareholders because pre–interest cash flows are those to be discounted. Given that both debt–holders and shareholders have claims against these, the appropriate cost of capital will be one that incorporates the relative capital contribution of each group. Thus, total pre–interest cash flows which are attributable to both lenders and shareholders are discounted by a weighted cost of capital to yield a value to the business.

It is important to realise that the relative weights attached to debt and equity within the calculation should be based on the relative proportions of each estimated for the future. This is because the concern of a capital project appraisal is with the future and not with the past. Thus, the present or previous debt to equity proportions is irrelevant, unless they apply to the future. There is also a useful analogy with the matching principle in accounting where the objective is to compare like with like, hence the use of a future orientated gearing ratio for establishing the cost of capital at which to discount future cash flows.

The determination of the relevant discount factor is important not only to project appraisal. In recognition of its importance it is discussed more fully in Chapter 6.

Net Present Value (NPV)

We will now illustrate the application of the net present value (NPV) technique, where, for a given rate of interest, future cash flows are discounted using the principle discussed in the previous section. The sum total of these discounted future cash flows is compared with the capital outlay and where it is greater than that outlay, the NPV is said to be positive and the project is acceptable on economic grounds. Conversely, if a negative NPV results (capital outlay is greater than the sum of discounted future cash flows) the project is not acceptable on economic grounds.

Using basic data for the four proposed projects illustrated earlier, and assuming a 10% cost of capital, the following NPV analysis can be carried out for Project B.

Table 2.13 Calculation of Net Present Value – Project B

	Column 1	**Column 2**	**Column 3**
			(Col. 1 x Col. 2)
	Discount Factor	**Cash Flows**	**Present Value**
	Year	**10%**	**£000**
1	0.909	6,000	5,454
2	0.826	6,000	4,956
3	0.751	6,000	4,506
4	0.683	6,000	4,098
5	0.621	6,000	3,726
Present Value of Cash Inflows			22,740
less Capital Outlay			18,000
Net Present Value			**£4,740**

The annual net cash flows shown in column 2 are multiplied by the 10% discount factors in column 1 to produce the annual present value of the cash flows in column 3. These annual present values are then added together to give the total present value of the cash inflows of £22.740 million. The net present value is calculated by deducting the capital outlay from the total present values of the cash inflows (that is, £22.740 million – £18.000 million) giving £4.740 million. The effect of discounting the cash flows is also illustrated in Figure 2.2.

Figure 2.2 Comparison of Cash Flows – Project B

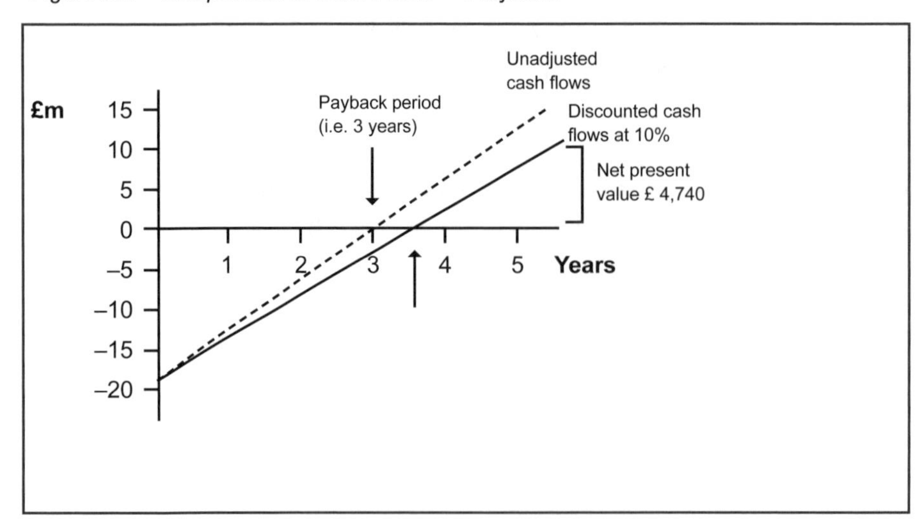

The capital outlay of £18 million is the starting point of the upper diagonal which is constructed from accumulating the annual net cash inflows of £6 million. The result is a cumulative cash inflow of £30 million at the end of year five. When these annual cash inflows of £6 million are discounted at 10% and plotted in the diagram, the lower diagonal results. The application of the 10% discount factor can be seen to cause a scaling-down which results in a net present value of £4.740 million. Raising the discount factor would scale-down the cash flows even further, thereby resulting in a lower net present value. One other observation from the diagram is the effect upon the payback period when discounted rather than undiscounted annual net cash inflows are used. You will see from the diagram that the discounted payback period is 3.75 years (rather than the original three years) when the net cash inflows are discounted at 10%. Furthermore, should the discount factor be increased resulting in a greater scaling down of cash flows, the discounted payback period becomes even longer.

We will consider the discounted payback and profitability index once we have reviewed the net present value calculations for all four projects.

Table 2.14 Comparison of Net Present Values

	Project A	Project B	Project C	Project D
	£000	**£000**	**£000**	**£000**
Present Value of Cash Inflows	13,907	22,740	8,675	22,021
Capital Outlay	15,000	18,000	10,000	18,000
Net Present Value	£–1,093	£4,740	£–1,325	£4,021

The results show that only Projects B and D produce a positive net present value and on economic grounds would be acceptable because they:

- Exceed the required rate of return (cost of capital) of 10%
- Cover the capital outlay
- Produce a sum in excess of the capital outlay which is referred to as the net present value.

Discounted Payback

The discounted payback period is similar in principle to the simple payback period, the only difference being that we use the discounted annual flows and accumulate them until their sum equals the capital outlay.

In Figure 2.2 we illustrated the discounted payback period for Project B of 3.75 years, but how is this calculated? Using the discounted annual cash flows for Project B, the discounted payback period can be calculated in a similar manner to simple payback:

Table 2.15 Calculation of Discounted Payback – Project B

	£'000		
Capital Outlay	–18,000		
Discounted Cash Flows:	**(i)**	**(ii)**	**(iii)**
	Annual	**Annual to Payback**	**Cumulative to Payback**
	£'000	**£'000**	**£'000**
Year 1	5,454	5,454	5,454
Year 2	4,956	4,956	10,410
Year 3	4,506	4,506	14,916
Year 4	4,098	3,084	18,000

Note. The adjusted cash flows shown in column (i) have been extracted from Table 2.13

The discounted cash flows to achieve the £18 million capital outlay can be monitored from column (iii). At the end of Year 3 £14.916 million will be recovered, leaving £3.084 million to be recovered in Year 4. Given that £4.098 million will be recovered from Year 4, the proportion of a year represented by £3.084 million can be readily calculated. Thus, discounted payback is achieved in three years plus £3.084 million divided by £4.098 million, which equals approximately 3.75 years.

Similar calculations for the discounted payback can be performed for Projects A, C and D to produce the following results:

Table 2.16 Comparison of Discounted Payback

	Project A	**Project B**	**Project C**	**Project D**
Discounted Payback (years)	n/a	3.75	n/a	4.19*

* A & C have negative NPVs and therefore there is no discounted payback because the outlay is never repaid in present value terms.

Profitability Index

Where the capital outlay differs from project to project the profitability index is calculated and provides useful information to assist in the decision making process. The profitability index is a ratio which relates the present value of the cash inflows from a project to its capital outlay. For Project A this would be £13.907 million divided by £15 million which gives 0.93. For Projects B, C and D the index is 1.26, 0.87 and 1.22, respectively. It is now possible to rank all projects competing for limited funds using the profitability index – all other things being equal, the higher the profitability index the better.

Table 2.17 Calculation of Profitability Index

		Project A £000	Project B £000	Project C £000	Project D £000
Present value of Cash net Inflows	(A)	13,907	22,740	8,675	22,021
Capital Outlay	(B)	15,000	18,000	10,000	18,000
Profitability Index	(A) ÷ (B)	0.93	1.26	0.87	1.22

The index of 1.26 for Project B means that the capital outlay is covered once plus an additional 26%. That project, where capital is restricted, should be preferred to the other alternatives on economic grounds. Where the profitability index is less than 1, for example, for Project A, this means that the project does not cover its capital outlay, therefore, does not provide the minimum return, that is, the company's cost of capital. However, before drawing any further conclusions let us consider the internal rate of return.

Internal Rate of Return (IRR)

The net present value, the profitability index and the discounted payback calculations require knowledge of the company's cost of capital as necessary data input for their calculation, but internal rate of return (IRR) does not.

The IRR is a discounted cash flow method which seeks to find the discount rate at which the present value of net cash inflows from a capital project exactly equal the capital outlay - in other words, at the IRR the net present value is zero.

The IRR can best be understood with reference to Figure 2.3 in which you can see that the lowest line corresponds with a NPV of £0. This is achieved by scaling–down the net cash inflows by applying a discount factor corresponding with the IRR percentage. Thus the percentage, which when converted to a discount factor and multiplied by the net cash inflows gives a present value equal to the capital outlay, is the internal rate of return.

Figure 2.3 Graphs Showing Internal Rate of Return (IRR)

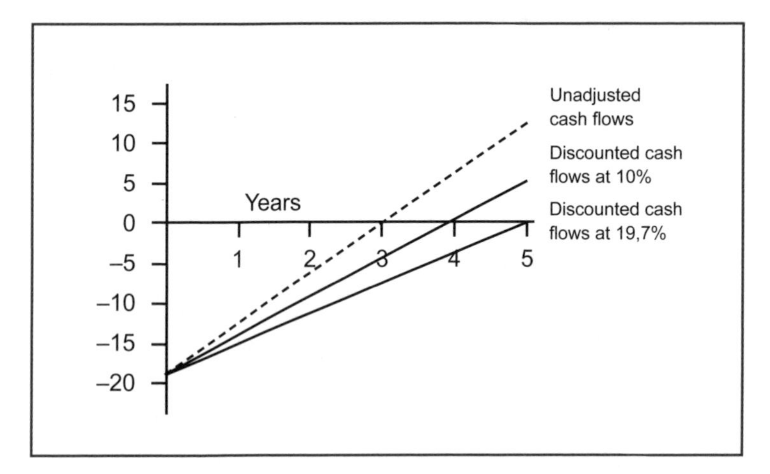

Once determined the IRR percentage should then be compared with the company's cost of capital in order to establish the economic acceptability of a project. The principle is that if the IRR exceeds the cost of capital then a project is acceptable on economic grounds. On the other hand, if the IRR from a project is lower than the cost of capital the project is not acceptable on economic grounds.

The calculation of the IRR is based on trial and error to find the discount rate corresponding to a zero net present value. As such, several calculations may need to be made and are best facilitated with the aid of a computer. The calculations necessary to find the IRR for Project B are based upon data summarised in Table 2.18.

Table 2.18 Trial and Error Calculation of Internal Rate of Return (IRR) – Project B

Year	Cash Inflows £'000	DCF factor 18%	Present value £'000	DCF factor 21%	Present value £'000
1	6,000	0.847	5,082	0.826	4,956
2	6,000	0.718	4,308	0.683	4,098
3	6,000	0.609	3,654	0.564	3,384
4	6,000	0.516	3,096	0.467	2,802
5	6,000	0.437	2,622	0.386	2,316
Present Value of Net Cash Inflows		18,762		17,556	
less Capital Outlay			18,000		18,000
Net Present Value			£762		£–444

Table 2.18 shows that cash flows for Project B when discounted at 18% provide a net present value of £0.762 million. To find the IRR (where the net present value is zero), in this case a higher discount is required. The result of increasing the rate to 21% shows that the net present value is negative at £–0.444 million. The internal rate of return must therefore fall between 18% and 21% and can be found approximately by linear interpolation.

$$\text{IRR} = d_1 + [n_1 / (n_1 + n_2) \times s]$$

Where: d_1 = lower dcf; d_2 = higher dcf; n_1 = NPV at lower dcf;
n_2 = NPV at higher dcf; $s = d_2 - d_1$

Therefore the IRR for Project B is calculated as follows:

$$\begin{aligned} \text{IRR} &= 18 + (762 / 1{,}206 \times 3) \\ &= 18 + 1.9 \\ &= 19.9\% \end{aligned}$$

Similar calculations carried out for Projects A, C and D produce the following results shown alongside that for Project B:

	Project A	Project B	Project C	Project D
Internal Rate of Return %	6.1	19.9	0	17.5

The approximations of the IRR percentages in this case are fairly accurate and in fact those obtained from using both a computer and a programmable calculator were 6%, 13.9%, 0% and 17.4% for Projects A, B, C and D respectively.

The results achieved from using manual calculations for the IRR produce satisfactory results provided that the difference between the two discount rates is not too large (for example, greater than 5%). However, it is preferable to use a computer or programmable calculator which allows the user to change any of the figures with relative ease.

One major problem with the IRR is that it may be impossible to provide a clear cut solution to projects that have irregular cash flows, that is, those that are positive in some years and negative in others. In such a situation there may not be an internal rate of return, or if there is, it may not be unique.

2.8 Using Annuity Tables

In addition to the arithmetical tables which provide a stream of discount factors it is also possible to obtain arithmetical tables which give cumulative discount factors over a specific period of time. These tables which are included in Appendix B at the end of the book convert a lump sum into a stream of equal annual payments called an annuity. To find out the total present value of £100 over 10 years we could undertake 10 individual calculations in a similar manner to that illustrated in the Table 2.13. Alternatively, we can achieve the same result from a single calculation by multiplying £100 by the cumulative discount factor found from the annuity tables.

Before we go any further it might help to consider the benefit of using cumulative discount factors in appraising potential investment opportunities. From Table 2.19 we can identify the cumulative discount factors for any period between one and five years. If we return to Project B we can calculate the present value of the net cash inflows at 10% in one operation:

£6 million x 3.790 = £22.740 million

This is a quicker method than that used before; see Table 2.13, where five multiplications were required! However, this method can only be used where the annual cash flows are equal.

Table 2.19 Discount Factors at 10%

Period	Discount Factors at 10%	Cumulative Discount Factors at 10%
1	0.909	0.909
2	0.826	1.735
3	0.751	2.486
4	0.683	3.169
5	0.621	3.790

There is one final point regarding the cumulative discount factors. If you compare the figures we have just used in Table 2.19 above with the corresponding figures in Appendix B, the slight difference is due to rounding. For the calculation of further examples we will use the figures from the Appendix B.

Example – Using Annuity Tables

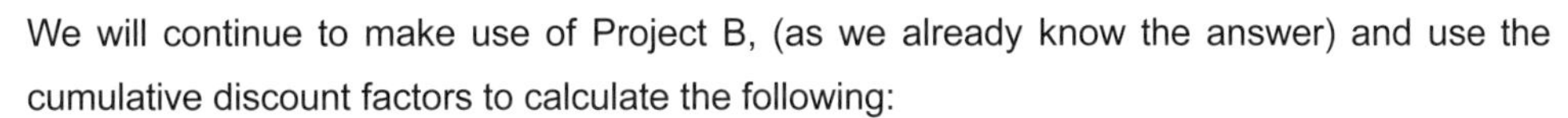

We will continue to make use of Project B, (as we already know the answer) and use the cumulative discount factors to calculate the following:

1. The internal rate of return given a capital outlay of £18 million, average annual savings of £6 million and a five year life
2. The minimum annual savings for the project to be acceptable on economic grounds, given a cost of capital (discount rate) of 20%, a capital outlay of £18 million and a five year life
3. The maximum capital outlay worth expending on such a project, given only that the cost of capital is 20%, average annual savings are £6 million and the expected life is five years.

1. Calculate the Internal Rate of Return

First, we calculate the cumulative discount factor as follows:

Capital Outlay / Average Annual Savings

£18 million / £6 million = 3.000

Second, we use the table in Appendix B and check the cumulative discount factors on the line for a five year life until we obtain a value which is close to the 3.000. In this case we will see

that a figure of 2.991 is the closest and this represents the cumulative discount factors at 20%. With the use of interpolation, say between 19% and 20% it is possible to arrive at rates correct to one decimal place.

2. Calculate the Minimum Annual Savings

We are given a cost of capital and the life of the project therefore we refer to Appendix B and extract the cumulative discount factors at 20% for a period of five years which give 2.991. The minimum annual savings is found from:

Capital Outlay / Cum Discount Factors

£18 million / 2.991 = £6.018 million

In this case, we conclude that if the capital outlay is expected to be £18 million and the company's cost of capital is 20% then the project will need to provide a minimum average annual savings of £6.018 million for five years.

3. Calculate the Maximum Capital Outlay

We follow the same procedure as in 2. above and obtain a cumulative discount factor of 2.991. The maximum capital outlay is found from:

Average annual savings x the cumulative discount factor

£6 million x 2.991 = £17.946 million

Here we conclude that if the average annual savings for five years are expected to be £6 million and the company's cost of capital is 20% then a maximum capital outlay of £17.946 million can be spent.

2.9 Project Appraisal in Practice

Many studies of project appraisal practice have been undertaken. Most have been orientated towards the practices of large organisations to which the following general observations apply:

1. The most frequently used technique is the payback period. This is often in conjunction with other techniques, but it may be used on its own for smaller projects
2. When a discounted cash flow technique is used it is more likely to be the internal rate of return method rather than the net present value method
3. Qualitative judgement is regarded as important.
4. The accounting rate of return is used despite potential ambiguities in definition
5. The use of techniques is guided by standard procedures, usually in the form of a capital budgeting manual of practice.

In addition to these five observations relating to the techniques, three others are noteworthy. Observations 6 and 7 will be dealt with in Sections 2.11 and 2.12 below. Observation 8 is considered in detail in Chapter 7.

6. Inflation adjustments are made in appraising projects using rates applicable to specific inputs, although the use of a single general rate is also practised
7. Adjustments for taxation are made to take account of the tax benefits - that is, allowances on capital projects - and the tax liabilities - that is, payments due on any savings (profits)
8. A formal analysis of risk is a standard pre-decision control procedure in many organisations, most often in the form of testing the sensitivity of key inputs and underlying economic assumptions.

2.10 Differences between NPV and IRR

One important question which emerges from the observations from the studies of practice is – 'Why the IRR is far more popular than the theoretically preferred NPV technique'? This has been attributed to a number of reasons, such as the appeal of a percentage to managers who, apparently, would be far less comfortable with interpreting a NPV calculation.

Using IRR calculations, a ranking of projects can be obtained without the need for knowledge of the company's required rate of return although, as indicated Section 2.7, this ranking may be inferior to that provided by NPV calculations. Associated with there being no need for a predetermined cut-off rate is the political appeal of the IRR. One recognised feature of the appraisal process is the potential for playing the system by ensuring that projects which have acquired the personal commitment of management always meet or exceed the prescribed hurdle rate. If the hurdle is not formally communicated then perhaps this problem can be removed. Certainly our observations of practice have found some confirmation of this view in some organisations. In such cases, the IRR usually in conjunction with other techniques is prescribed for use below corporate level. At corporate level, however, where the desired hurdle is known, the NPV technique may play a more significant role.

NPV and IRR will provide the same accept/reject for the majority of capital projects. However there are a number of situations where this is not the case and it will be seen that the use of IRR will produce an incorrect decision. These are because:

1. The output from an IRR calculation is a percentage return rather than the physical size of the earnings
2. There are differences in the reinvestment assumptions
3. The IRR can give more than one rate of return
4. The IRR can incorrectly rank mutually exclusive projects.

The output from an IRR calculation is a percentage

This difficulty is best understood with reference to the following example:

	Project X	Project Y
Capital Outlay	£18,000	£60,000
Annual Savings (5 years)	£ 8,000	£20,000
IRR	34.2%	19.9%
NPV (at 10% Cost of Capital)	£12,328	£15,820

Project X has an IRR of 34.2% compared to only 14.9% for Project Y but this does not take into account the difference in the absolute size of the earnings. Project Y is clearly preferable in terms of the NPV it generates despite its lower IRR.

Differences in the reinvestment assumptions

In using the NPV and IRR approaches there is an assumption that future cash flows from projects are available for reinvestment. However there are major differences in the way in which these reinvestment assumptions are made.

NPV assumes that annual cash flows are reinvested at the company's cost of capital. On the other hand, IRR assumes that annual cash flows are reinvested at the percentage IRR obtained from each project.

For Project X, NPV assumes that the £8,000 annual cash flow is reinvested at the cost of capital of 10%. IRR assumes that it is reinvested at 34.2%.

The reality is that the company has determined that the return it expects from reinvestment is its stated cost of capital. IRR requires that the reinvestment is often much higher and as such is not theoretically correct.

To overcome the concerns with the reinvestment assumption a 'modified' version of IRR has been developed – the MIRR – Modified Internal Rate of Return. It is founded on NPV analysis, which is then converted to a rate of return. Instead of discounting cash flows to present value, the cash flows are compounded forward to a terminal value and on the basis of the project's outlay and the terminal value of its net cash inflows an IRR - the MIRR – is calculated. Table 2.20 shows this calculation using the data from Project B in Section 2.7.

From Table 2.13 the NPV for Project B is shown as £4,740 and from Table 2.18 the IRR for Project B is shown as 19.9% (for the purposes of the MIRR calculation we will assume 20%)

Table 2.20 MIRR Calculation

Calculation of terminal value of project:						
Year	**1**	**2**	**3**	**4**	**5**	**£**
Cash flows £k:	6,000	6,000	6,000	6,000	6,000	
	@ 10% for 4 years					8,785
		@ 10% for 3 years				7,985
			@ 10% for 2 years			7,260
				@ 10% for 1 year		6,600
					@10% 0 years	6,000
Terminal Value =						36,627

(M)IRR calculation (linear interpolation)					
		10%		**20% (proxy for 19.9%)**	
Year 0 - Investment	18,000	1.00	18,000	1.00	18,000
Year 5 – Terminal Value	36,627	0.621	22,745	0.402	14,724
NPV			4,745		(3276)

MIRR = 10% + [(4745/8021) x 10%] = 15.9%

In this case the MIRR is 15.9 % compared to the IRR of 19.9%. It is felt that by not assuming that the cash flows generated by the investment can be reinvested at the IRR percentage a truer view of the project's return is estimated.

IRR can produce more than one rate of return

In capital projects where the cash flows are irregular, that is, not consistently positive, it is possible to find that the IRR method produces more than one rate of return.

		Project Z	
Capital Outlay			£5,387
Cash Inflows	Year 1	£7,575	
	Year 2	£5,353	
	Year 3	–£8,000	

Figure 10.2 Calculation of NPV's from 14% to 28%

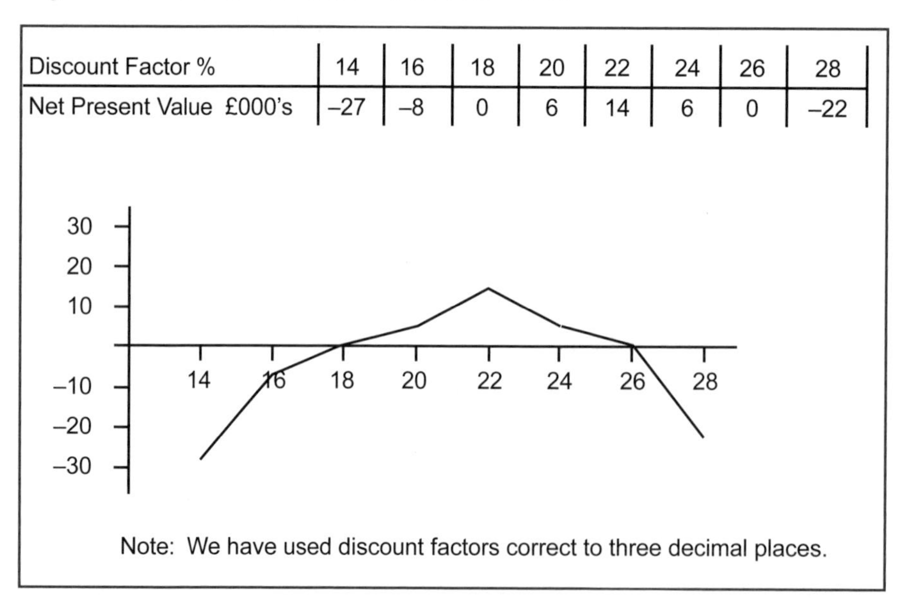

Discount Factor %	14	16	18	20	22	24	26	28
Net Present Value £000's	–27	–8	0	6	14	6	0	–22

Note: We have used discount factors correct to three decimal places.

IRR can incorrectly rank mutually exclusive projects

Mutually exclusive projects exist where there are two or more projects, any of which is acceptable in technical terms, but only one is required to perform the task demanded. In this case the decision rule is that the most acceptable in economic terms should be selected first. The question is what decision rule do we use? Should we use internal rate of return (IRR), or net present value (NPV)? Do the IRR and NPV methods always produce the same results? To answer these questions we will use the following example.

A company is considering which of two mutually exclusive projects it should undertake. The company anticipates a cost of capital of 10% and the net cash inflows for the projects are as follows:

	Project X **£**	**Project Y** **£**
Capital Outlay	120,000	120,000
Net Cash Inflows:		
Year 1	21,000	130,000
Year 2	48,000	6,000
Year 3	54,000	6,000
Year 4	45,000	2,000
Year 5	12,000	2,000
NPV at 10%	**+17,478**	**+10,240**

We will:

1. Draw a graph to show the relationship between the net present value and the discount rate for the two projects using discount rates at 10, 14, 18 and 22%.
2. Use the graph to estimate the internal rate of return for each project.
   First we will calculate the net present value for each project. These are shown in Table 2.21.

Table 2.21 Net Present Value for Project R and S

	Discount Rate %	**Project X NPV £**	**Project Y NPV £**	**Incremental NPV £ (X–Y)**
(a)	10	+17,478	+10,240	+7,238
(b)	14	+4,647	+4,896	–249
(c)	18	–6,399	–22	–6,377
(d)	22	–16,035	–4,420	–11,615

In Table 2.21 an analysis of NPVs for Projects R and S is shown for discount rates of 10%, 14%, 18% and 22% and in the final column of Table 2.21 the incremental net present values are shown which are simply the net present value for Project R less the net present value for Project S.

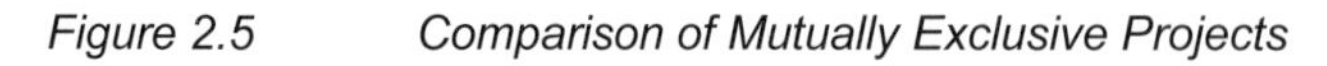

Figure 2.5 Comparison of Mutually Exclusive Projects

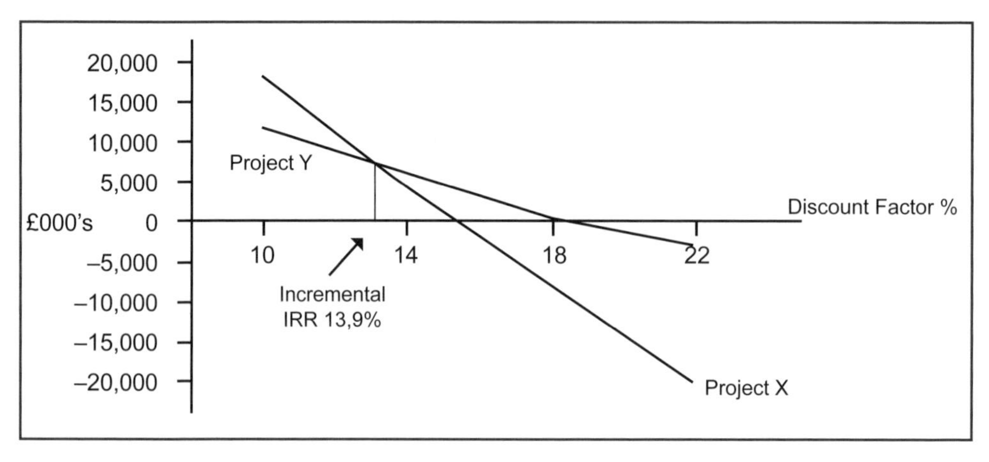

In Figure 2.5 the relationship between the NPVs from Table 2.21 and the discount rates are shown and the line for Project R cuts the horizontal axis at 15.5% (approximately) while for Project S the IRR is 18% (approximately). The incremental IRR - the point where there is no preference for Project R or Project S - is illustrated as well.

The decision rule is that we should choose the project with the highest net present value provided that the company's cost of capital is less than the incremental IRR. In this case, if the cost of capital is less than the incremental IRR, that is, between 0 to 13.9% then we would choose Project R. If the cost of capital was greater than 13.9% but less than 18% we would choose Project S provided that it produced a positive net present value.

A summary of the results produces the following:

	Project X	**Project Y**	**Incremental**
NPV at 10%	+17,478	+10,240	
IRR	15.5%	18.0%	13.9%

2.11 Effect of Inflation

In our discussion of discounting, we assumed that the discounting process simply reflects the opportunity cost of money. Perhaps the easiest way to understand this opportunity cost is that in a world with no change in prices, individuals would still have preference for cash now versus cash later. This is understood by considering whether if you sought to borrow money from a bank in a world with zero inflation it would still require you to pay interest. The answer is undoubtedly, yes! What happens in an inflationary environment is that the rate of interest is increased to compensate for the loss of the purchasing power of money.

If the rate at which a project is discounted incorporates expectations about inflation, then similar expectations need to be incorporated in the cash flows. If we refer back to examples in previous sections, you will see that we have made no allowance for inflation in the cash flows. This is a problem if inflation is seen to be present in the cost of capital. If not, then there is no problem because the rule in dealing with inflation is:

1. If cash flows and the cost of capital are in real terms, such that no inflation expectations have been built into either, then the real cash flows can be discounted to reflect the real cost of capital
2. If inflation expectations are present in either the cash flows or the cost of capital, then an adjustment must be made to ensure that the two are matched. In other words, inflated cash flows should be discounted by a cost of capital that includes inflationary expectations.

An adjustment can be made for inflation in the discount rate by rearranging the formula as in the following example:

$(1 + m) = (1 + i) \times (1 + r)$

Where

m = the money or nominal rate

i = the expected rate of inflation, and

r = the real rate

Using this formula, we can adjust the cost of capital expressed in real terms to one that incorporates inflation and vice versa. For example, if the cost of capital in real terms (r) is 10% and the expected rate of inflation is 10%, then the money rate is 21%, that is:

$(1 + m) = (1.10)(1.10) = 1.21$, and
$m = 1.21 - 1 = 0.21$, or 21%

Or, if we know the money rate, quoted by a financial institution like a bank, is 21%, and the expected rate of inflation is 10%, then we can find the real rate of 10% by rearranging the formula, that is, $(1 + r) = (1 + m) \div (1 + i)$. This type of adjustment we will demonstrate shortly.

Alternatively, as we will illustrate, if the cost of capital available incorporates the expected rate of inflation then this can be left and adjustments can be made to the cash flows. The advantage of this approach is that inflation does not necessarily impact on all sectors of the economy evenly and it may, therefore, be necessary to take into account the differential effects of inflation. For example we know that on occasion retail prices and wage rates have moved at differential rates.

An Example

Consider the following example where there is a capital outlay of £90,000, which will result in annual savings of £30,000 for five years and a cost of capital of 10%.

We will now show the effect of inflation on a capital project on which no adjustments have been made for inflation (see Table 2.22). In what follows we will illustrate:

- Adjustments are made to the cash flows and discount rate to allow for inflation at 6%
- Different inflation factors are applied to revenues, costs and the discount rate.

Table 2.22 Net Present Value of Capital Project with no Inflation

	£
Present Value of Cash Inflows (£30,000 x 3.791)	113,730
less Capital Outlay	90,000
Net Present Value (NPV)	**£23,730**

Adjustments to cash flows and discount rate

First, we must adjust the cash flows to increase them by 6% per annum compound.

Table 2.23 Adjustment of Cash Flow/Savings

Year		Factor	Adjusted Cash Flows
	£		£
1	30,000	1.06	31,800
2	31,800	1.06	33,708
3	33,708	1.06	35,730
4	35,730	1.06	37,874
5	37,874	1.06	40,146

Next we adjust the discount rate to include 6% inflation, as follows:

(1 + rate) x (1 + inflation)

1.10 x 1.06 = 1.166

Therefore the new discount rate is 16.6%. To obtain discount factors at 16.6% with the aid of a calculator or a spreadsheet divide 1 by 1.166 which will give 0.858 for year 1. Successive divisions of the resulting number by 1.166 can be undertaken until the required number of factors is found as illustrated in Table 2.24:

Table 2.24 Calculation of Discount Factors at 16.6%

1	1 / 1.166	=	0.85763	0.858
2.	0.85763 / 1.166	=	0.73553	0.736
3.	0.73553 / 1.166	=	0.63081	0.631
4.	0.63081 / 1.166	=	0.54100	0.541
5.	0.54100 / 1.166	=	0.46400	0.464

Table 2.25 Net Present Value – With Inflation

Year	A Cash Flow	B DCF Factor 16.6%	C Present Value
	£		£
1	31,800	0.858	27,284
2	33,708	0.736	24,809
3	35,730	0.631	22,546
4	37,874	0.541	20,490
5	40,146	0.464	18,628
Present Value of Net Cash Inflows			113,757
less Capital Outlay			90,000
Net Present Value (NPV)			**£23,757**

You will notice that the net present value is the same in Table 2.25 as it was in Table 2.22. (The slight difference is due to rounding). This result shows that if inflation is ignored completely, or that if inflation is applied equally to the cash flows and the discount factors, the result is the same. In this case, for Table 2.25 we have increased the cash flows by 6% and increased the discount factors by 6% – therefore, we are discounting higher cash flows at higher discount rates.

Differential inflation

Differential inflation adjustments need to be made where the cash inflows and cash outflows inflate at different rates. Different inflation assumptions need to be incorporated in each of the components which make up the total cash flow and within the discount rate.

In this example we will assume that the discount rate includes expected inflation of 6% per annum, while the components making up the annual cash flows are affected as follows:

Cash Inflows	£130,000	+ 5% per annum
Cash Outflows	£100,000	+ 7% per annum.

Table 2.26 Adjusting Revenues and Costs for Inflation

Year	Cash Inflows 1.05	Cash Outflows 1.07	Net Cash Inflows
	£	£	£
0	130,000	100,000	n/a
1	136,500	107,000	29,500
2	143,325	114,490	28,835
3	150,491	122,504	27,987
4	158,016	131,079	26,937
5	165,917	140,255	25,662

In Table 2.26, we have adjusted the revenues by 5% per annum and the costs by 7% per annum. The third column shows the net cash flows which now show a decline over the lifetime of the project.

Table 2.27 Net Present Value – With Differential Inflation

Year	A Cash Flow	B DCF Factor 16.6%	C Present Value
	£		£
1	29,500	0.858	25,311
2	28,835	0.736	21,223
3	27,987	0.631	17,660
4	26,937	0.541	14,573
5	25,662	0.464	11,907
Present Value of Net Cash Inflows		90,674	
less Capital Outlay			90,000
Net Present Value (NPV)			**£674**

In Table 2.25, with a single inflation rate applied to the individual cash flows and the discount rate, the net present value was +£23,757. This meant that the project was viable and could be considered for selection.

However, in Table 2.27, with differential inflation, the net present value is now only +£674. This shows the effect of a small change in the inflation assumptions; in this case, we reduced the revenue inflation from 6% to 5% while we increased the cost inflation from 6% to 7%.

It is possible to show that the arithmetic effect of applying the same inflation rate to the individual cash flows and to the discount rate produces the same net present value – as demonstrated in the example in Tables 2.22 and 2.25. It is tempting to conclude that it is possible to ignore inflation in the cash flows and the discount rate. The application of different inflation assumptions to individual components of the cash flows and to the discount rate, however, can have a significant effect on the accept/reject of a project. You will also find that the issue becomes even more complex when both taxation and inflation have to be taken into consideration.

2.12 The Treatment of Taxation

Taxation will have an impact on both cash and profit streams used in project appraisal. Although taxation is beyond the scope of this book the general principle to follow in project appraisal is similar to that of inflation discussed earlier in this chapter. This means that in addition to cash flows being discounted using an interest rate allowing for inflation, the discount rate must also allow for taxation.

In reality the detail of taxation as applied to project appraisal is beyond the concern of most non-financial managers. Provided you have understood the principle of comparing 'like' cash flows with a 'like' discount rate discussed with regard to inflation that is sufficient. It is then time to involve a taxation specialist!

The Effect of Taxation on Cash Flows

In this section it is assumed that the capital projects that are being appraised relate to companies which operate in a profit making environment and that these companies purchase capital assets which qualify for capital allowances and are subject to the payment of corporation tax.

There are three areas for consideration when applying tax adjustments to capital project cash flows. These are:

- The timing of tax receipts/payments[5]
- Tax payable on project savings
- Capital allowance.

[5] Please note, the timing of tax receipts and payments will reflect the tax laws of a specific country.

The timing of tax receipts/payments

When appraising capital projects, companies assume that:

- Tax will be paid in the year following the one in which taxable profits (that is, project savings/revenues) are made
- Tax will be recovered in the year following the one in which tax allowance are available.

Tax payable on project savings

It is often not appreciated that any financial benefits (that is savings) resulting from a capital project will have tax consequences. Other things equal, greater savings will produce higher profits, not all of which will be of benefit to the project initiator – the tax authorities will demand their share less, of course, any capital allowances (discussed in the next section).

Capital allowances

In certain circumstances the expenditure incurred on the capital outlay for a project can be deducted from the profit generated by a company in the form of a capital allowance.

These capital allowances reduce future tax payments according to the amount of allowance available, the tax rate in operation and the economic life of each project.

Capital allowances can be likened to a personal tax allowance in so far as they reduce the amount of earnings subject to assessment for tax. A company can normally reduce its taxable profits by the amount of capital allowances available.

An Example

If we take the same example we used for inflation where there is a capital outlay of £90,000 which will result in annual savings of £30,000 for five years. We will now assume:

1. A cost of capital of 10%
2. Capital allowances, calculated on a 25% reducing balance, apply
3. Corporation tax at the rate of 35%
4. A one year delay in the effect of taxation on receipts and payments
5. Sufficient profits available to offset capital allowances

The £90,000 shown in year 1 of Table 2.28 is the original capital outlay. The availability of the 25% capital allowance means that we are allowed 25% of this amount that can be offset against taxable profits, hence the £22,500 in column B. However, the net tax effect is 35%

of the £22,500 which equals £7,875. In year 2, the reduced balance (that is, from £90,000) is £67,500 (£90,000 – £22,500) and the process continues. In year 6, the reduced balance is £21,358. We have assumed that the project ends in year 5; therefore the whole of the remaining balance is taken and offset against our taxable profits.

Table 2.28 Calculation of After Tax Capital Allowances

Year	A Reducing Balance	B Capital Allowance (at 25%)	C Tax Saved Using Capital Allowance
	£	£	£
1	90,000	22,500	7,875
2	67,500	16,875	5,906
3	50,625	12,656	4,430
4	37,969	9,492	3,322
5	28,477	7,119	2,492
6	21,358	21,358	7,475

The tax payable on the annual savings is simply 35% of £30,000 which equals £10,500. For project appraisal we assume that tax will be payable one year later, that is, from year 2 through to year 6.

A full appraisal incorporating tax is given in Table 2.29.

Table 2.29 Project Appraisal Incorporating Taxation

Year	A Tax Saved Using Capital Allowances	B Savings	C Tax on Savings at 35%	D Cash Flow (A+B+C)	E DCF 10 % Factor	F Net Present Value
	£	£	£	£		£
1	7,875	30,000		37,875	0.909	34,428
2	5,906	30,000	–10,500	25,406	0.826	20,985
3	4,430	30,000	–10,500	23,930	0.751	17,971
4	3,322	30,000	–10,500	22,822	0.683	15,587
5	2,492	30,000	–10,500	21,992	0.621	13,657
6	7,475		–10,500	–3,025	0.564	-1,706
Present Value of Net Cash Inflows						100,922
less Capital Outlay						90,000
Net Present Value (NPV)						**£10,922**

The tax saved by claiming capital allowances, column A, is shown above in Table 2.29. The savings for the project are shown in years 1 through to 5, whilst the tax due on the savings is shown in column C. This is delayed one year with the final tax being due in year 6. The cash flow in column D is the sum of columns A plus B plus C.

The individual cash flows can then be adjusted by the company's cost of capital to find their present value. Finally, these are aggregated and the capital outlay is deducted to give the net present value of £10,922. Compare this with the result of the project without any adjustment for taxation, Table 2.25 shows a net present value of £23,757.

2.13 Putting Together a Business Case for a Project

In seeking the approval of a project most organisations require a business case to be put together that should at least include the following:

- What is this project about?
- Why do it? What is the rationale?
- When is it to be done? What is the timing?
- How will it be done? What is the implementation plan?
- Where in the organisation will it be done?
- Who will do it? Who is responsible and accountable?

It is very important to structure projects correctly to include the most important issues, such as those included in the foregoing questions. An example of a typical structure for a project is illustrated in Table 2.30.

Table 2.30 Typical Structure for a Business Project

Summary

- Statement of the objectives that the project aims to achieve
- The rationale for why undertake the project and why now
- How it fits with the company's vision and mission
- A resume of the key risks & uncertainties impacting the project

Definition and Scope of project
Description of the project from the perspective of:

- Strategy: How it fits with the company's strategy, what the strategic rationale is in terms of the scope of the company's business activities.
- Finance: Key headlines from the financial evaluation
- Operations: Key resources required to enable this project to be undertaken including people and their skills, critical business processes and so on

Alternative options
Discussion of the options open to management in terms of the timing of the investment, scaling it up or down, the flexibility that is built into the project to enable management to respond to changing circumstances

Underpinning assumptions
List of critical internal and external assumptions that underpin the project, together with the interdependencies between them plus identification of the key risks and uncertainties and their potential financial impact

Implementation plans
A high level implementation plan showing key milestone dates for:

- commitment of resource
- critical decision points
- impact on other projects and the rest of the business
- possible contingency options

Evaluation
Details of the financial evaluation techniques used plus their appropriateness together with a list of the relevant qualitative/ non-financial factors used to reach a decision.

2.14 Key Issues in Capital Project Appraisal

The successful introduction of a new product will attract competing products. This competition may force a reduction in price to a level that renders further investment non-economic. Although first entrants to a market may establish competitive advantage through the experience curve or product protection by trademarks or patents, cash flow projections should recognise market developments and competitor reactions.

To make an assessment of competitor reactions existing managerial knowledge and judgement needs to be used in conjunction with expert systems specially designed to model cash flows in a dynamic environment. This will avoid an over–reliance on projections of sales and cost of sales which, although internally consistent, do not reflect the real world.

In summary, sound financial management of capital projects should ensure that:

- Individual requests are in harmony with the plan for corporate growth and development and the risks of accepting 'no hope' capital projects should be minimised
- An appropriate hierarchical structure exists for authorising capital expenditure, which should encourage all good projects, even those proposed at low levels of authority
- The numbers used in appraisal calculations are complete and valid in light of the circumstances surrounding a project request
- Any method used to provide a measure of the relative desirability of projects is valid
- Actual expenditures are compared to planned capital outlays and that there is an appropriate control system to prevent a waste of resources
- A post completion audit of selected major projects should be conducted to identify both good practice and mistakes to feed forward into new projects

- A balance is maintained between those projects acquired on economic grounds and those that are a matter of necessity
- A balance is maintained between high risk/high return projects and low risk/low return projects in order to prevent suffering the consequences of being at either end of the scale.

With the developments in personal computers and pre-programmable calculators, no technical barrier should exist to the widespread use of discounting procedures for evaluating proposed capital projects. However, in spite of the extensive experience of many companies with the techniques, problems still arise with the use and interpretation of project appraisal techniques. These problems arise when:

1. Payback is required over time periods far too short for certain types of capital projects
2. Inappropriately high discount rates are used
3. New capital projects are compared with unrealistic alternatives
4. Capital projects selected are biased towards incremental opportunities
5. Evaluations ignore important capital project costs and benefits.

Payback is required over time periods far too short for certain types of capital projects
Considerable judgement is required in appraising certain types of capital project, particularly those in new untested process technologies. Many companies have been known to impose very short payback periods, such as two or three years, on all types of capital projects.

Some types of capital project, particularly those involving process technologies like Flexible Manufacturing Systems (FMS) or Computer-Integrated-Manufacturing (CIM) are difficult to justify when subjected to such payback criteria in the face of more traditional alternative projects. Given that the benefits from such projects will arise several years in the future, when major renovation or replacement of traditional automated machines would be required, discounted cash flow analysis is far more appropriate. However, there are problems associated with quantifying the costs and benefits of such projects that make the practical use of discounted cash flow techniques very difficult.

Inappropriately high discount rates are used
It is not uncommon to find companies using excessive discount rates for appraising capital projects. The use of an excessively high discount rate in appraising a long-lived capital project has as many drawbacks as using an arbitrarily short appraisal time. This is because discount rates compound geometrically every time period penalising cash flows received five or more years in the future.

New capital projects are compared with unrealistic alternatives

Making a decision typically requires a comparison to be made against an alternative, the consequence of which may involve doing nothing. However, where an evaluation is made with the status quo, it is quite incorrect to assume that present cash flows can necessarily be maintained. When a new technology becomes available and requires a substantial investment of funds, it will probably also be available to others. This means that a likely alternative to adopting the technology will be vulnerable market share and gross margins, with the possible consequence of declining cash flows in the future.

Capital projects selected are biased towards incremental opportunities

The project approval process for many companies specifies different levels of authorisation for different levels of management. Such a procedure can create an incentive for managers to propose a sequence of small projects that fall just below the cut-off point for higher-level approval.

A consequence of this approach is that the company can become less efficient because a division never receives the full benefit from a completely redesigned and re-equipped plant that can exploit the latest technology.

Evaluations ignore important capital project costs and benefits

It is not uncommon for capital project proposals to underestimate costs quite significantly. This is particularly the case for projects that embody revolutionary new technological features. Computer software and the training of staff may be significant costs associated with the project that can be easily overlooked.

While some costs are readily identified, but overlooked, others are more difficult to measure. Innovative technologies provide benefits in reduced stocks, improved quality and reduced floor space which can be estimated. But other returns such as improved flexibility, faster response times to changing market conditions, reductions in lead times and opportunities to learn, innovate and grow from new technology use will be much more difficult to quantify.

The inadequacy of the information provided by costing systems in relation to the complex characteristics of new processes is a major source of the problem. Very simply, procedures used within companies may not be updated to respond to such complexities in the required time frame.

Shorter product life cycles and more flexible technologies mean that plant is now being installed which may last for several product life cycles, and may also be used to produce several products simultaneously. The result is that the relationship between plant life and product life has changed, with the consequence that the basis for investment must also be changed, as must the costing systems to permit an allocation of capital and running costs over a range of products.

Thus, the key problem with the conventional application of project appraisal techniques is that they are unable to quantify the technological benefits of a new investment, many of which are seen as being unquantifiable and intangible. Such intangible benefits (apparently) almost invariably appear in a different department from that where the investment is made. Furthermore, because they were not forecast or quantified, when they do appear they are recorded as an unplanned variance that is not attributed to the project.

There are no simple solutions to these problems. Current experience with such new technologies is limited such that the benefits of flexibility, reduced throughput time and lead-time, organisational learning and technology options are difficult to estimate. This does not mean however that they need necessarily be assigned a zero value when conducting a financial appraisal. As with all projects, there will be those factors difficult to quantify but which must be taken into consideration if a real view is to be formed. These are no exception.

CHAPTER 3
SHAREHOLDER VALUE AND FINANCIAL STRATEGY

Chapter Preview

This chapter will enable you to:

- **Describe the shortcomings of accounting based measures like earnings per share for evaluating financial strategy.**
- **Describe the relevance of the tools of financial economics and in particular discounted cash flow analysis to financial strategy.**
- **Describe the principles underpinning Shareholder Value Analysis (SVA).**
- **Describe and estimate the key value drivers that can be used to perform a Shareholder Value Analysis calculation.**
- **Estimate free cash flows for use in a Shareholder Value Analysis calculation.**
- **Perform a basic SVA calculation, including estimating residual value, business value, corporate value and shareholder value.**

3.1 Introduction

The price placed by the market upon a public limited company's shares is taken to be an indicator of its perceived success. The competition for shareholders as well as customers and the potential for hostile corporate raids that now span national barriers require that a company's share price performs well relative to the rest of the market and, in particular, within its own market sector.

So far, little reference has been made to share price but in this chapter we will illustrate how the kinds of tools and techniques reviewed in previous chapters can be linked to it from a strategic perspective. The focus is upon strategic financial management and the use of the principles of financial economics in assessing and driving performance. The use of such principles is essential because as we will illustrate there are some important shortcomings in using accounting measures for financial strategy. In fact, we have considered some of the limitations of accounting measures in relation to short and long term decision making. For example, the theoretical benefits of discounted cash flows measures, particularly net present value, were illustrated in the previous chapter and compared with accounting based measures such as the rate of return. The relevance of accounting measures can also be questioned for purposes of making decisions associated with financial strategy as we will illustrate in the next section.

3.2 Shortcomings of Accounting Measures for Financial Strategy.

Why are accounting measures like profit and earnings per share inappropriate to financial strategy? The simple answer is that they have the following important shortcomings:

- Earnings can be calculated using alternative and equally acceptable accounting methods
- Business and financial risk are excluded. A business evaluating two alternative strategies with a mean earnings growth rate of 10% might at first sight find them equally acceptable, even though the variability in their return because of financial or business risk was significantly different.

With regard to financial risk the effect of changes in the level of gearing is the important consideration. A company can improve earnings per share by using debt rather than equity financing, because of the tax shield associated with debt. Does this improvement in earnings per share necessarily improve economic value? The simple answer is no. Increases in the level of debt may increase financial risk because of the danger of insolvency. Shareholders may therefore demand higher rates of return as a consequence. The simplest way to view this is to remember that one measure of value is:

$$\text{Value} = \frac{\text{Earnings}}{\text{Required Rate of Return}}$$

Unless any added earnings are sufficiently large to offset the rise in the required rate of return, value may decline.

With accounting measures it is important to realise that:

- The timing of the impact of investment is ignored. Investments in working capital and fixed capital needed to sustain and make a company grow are excluded from the earnings calculations. It is therefore possible for a company to achieve high earnings even though the associated cash flow figure is much lower. For example, a company might report a net profit of £1 million but only generate £50,000 cash, the difference between the two figures being because of significant cash outflows for working capital and replacement capital expendi¬tures, with only a small proportion being reflected in the profit re¬ported via the depreciation charge. Thus, the net profit figure conceals the real position of a company in such a replacement programme. A relatively good net profit may not always be associated with increases in economic value which might at first sight be expected
- The time value of money is ignored. Consider our earlier company evaluating two alternative strategies with a mean earnings growth rate of 10%. Both strategies might appear to be equally acceptable using an earnings criterion even though the annual cash flows associated with each may be very different. From our discussions in the last chapter we know that on economic grounds the preferred strategy would, other things equal, be that yielding cash flows earlier rather than later.

Our review of the shortcomings of accounting measures has focused upon earnings and earnings per share, but caution is also necessary in using the other alternatives that are available. Accounting measures, like return on capital employed (total assets) are sometimes compared to the company's cost of capital. The difference between the return on capital employed and the company's cost of capital is referred to by some authors as the 'spread'. Successful corporate performance is usually considered to correspond with a positive spread that is where:

Return on Capital Employed is GREATER THAN Cost of Capital

For example, if the company's return on capital employed and the cost of capital have been calculated as 15% and 10%, respectively, then the spread is 5% and should, in principle, add to the value of the business. The problem with such 'spread' approaches is their reliance upon accounting numbers and, according to evidence available, the best of them leaves more than 60% of the variation in share prices unexplained. Why is this so? In effect, the return on capital employed is really adopted as a substitute for the internal rate return, but, unfortunately, it is not an accurate or reliable estimate. Furthermore, there is no systematic pattern enabling a specific correction to be made to adjust a return on capital employed percentage to a percentage internal rate of return. With a given set of cash flows and therefore a known internal rate of return, a book value return on capital employed calculation will either over or understate the real rate because of such factors as the:

- Length of project life
- Capitalisation of investments in a company's books
- The depreciation policy
- The lag between investment outlays and their recovery in the form of cash inflows.

These problems are exacerbated when total return on capital employed is measured rather than just the increment arising from a particular strategy. This is because the measure will incorporate not only prospective investment and cash flow, but also that from earlier periods. The implications of this are that two divisions or business units with identical strategies, but with different initial values of capital employed, would face different accounting returns during the forecast/planning period in spite of identical internal rates of return!

It should also not be ignored that accounting–based measures of return typically only measure the benefits to be gained during the forecast period of the strategy and by themselves ignore key information about the value of the business after the forecast period has elapsed. In many cases, the real benefit of a strategy can only be properly evaluated with reference to the total economic return that results. This total economic return comprises not only that return provided during the forecast period of the strategy, but also the estimated value of the business at the end of the period. We will provide a numerical example which will cover this aspect in more detail later in this chapter.

Some strategies require substantial investment during the forecast period in order to grow the business and to achieve benefits beyond the forecast period. The logic of measuring the total return comprising the return associated with the plan and increases in value in the post planning period can be likened to the increase in economic value sought by shareholders in the form of both dividends and capital gains. In fact, as we will illustrate, increases in return from a planning period may be associated with different residual values for different types of strategy, thereby making reference to a measure related to the planning period alone wholly inadequate.

However, while accounting based numbers such as earnings per share and return on capital employed are not reliable indicators of long term strategy and shareholder value, accounting should not be viewed as having no purpose. It may be inappropriate for evaluating financial strategy, but it is essential for assessing past performance. Performance for the most recent year cannot be properly evaluated without recognising that investments made during this and previous years may not be recouped until later years.

Accounting based numbers do deal with this time lag and the uncertainty surrounding the amounts and timing of prospective cash flow by assigning costs systematically to a set of future time periods.

The conclusion to be drawn from this review of accounting measures is that shareholders may not be satisfied with only excellent financial performance as conveyed by accounting numbers, particularly when such numbers can be influenced significantly within the principles of accounting and by individual company policy. At the end of the day the concern of shareholders is most likely to be with the total return they receive on their shareholding from dividends plus share appreciation.

In this chapter we consider financial strategy within the context of the economic orientated discounted cash flow approach discussed in the preceding chapters. Before we consider the applications and implications of discounted cash flow analysis within strategy, we offer the same word of caution mentioned earlier with reference to project appraisal. It is all too easy to become immersed in the apparent precision of numbers relating to uncertain future financial data and lose sight of less tangible but equally important issues.

3.3 Discounted Cash Flow Analysis and Financial Strategy

The use of discounted cash flow analysis in financial strategy has been popularised as Shareholder Value Analysis (SVA). In using SVA, the quest for management is to maximise the value generated from the business (or part of the business) in terms of the projected cash flows that are discounted at the cost of capital. By adopting this approach top management and the board of directors should be better equipped to answer the following basic questions:

- Will the current strategy as conveyed within the corporate plan create value for its shareholders and, if so, how much?
- Which business units below the corporate level are creating value and which are not?
- How would alternative strategic plans affect shareholder value?

In principle, the approach can be applied throughout a company and be translated into a language for all levels of management and managerial functions. This means that alternative future courses of action may be compared and their desirability can be assessed by the process of discounting cash flows at the relevant cost of capital. The returns obtained from these alternatives can be converted into conventional accounting performance indicators, making the approach relevant and usable by all managerial levels. Of course, as we will demonstrate, the principles involved are not without their difficulties in terms of their application.

We will illustrate that one major advantage of adopting a discounted cash flow rather than an accounting approach is that life after the end of the current financial year is taken into consideration. In contrast to the accounting approach, where a loss in a particular activity this year may be regarded as unacceptable, that reliant upon discounted cash flow analysis takes a longer term perspective and recognises that it may well be desirable to accept such a loss in a year, if there will be a substantial profit in future years.

3.4 The Principles Underpinning Shareholder Value Analysis (SVA)

In what follows we will direct our discussion of discounted cash flow analysis for financial strategy towards SVA and the measurement of shareholder value. In common with our discussion in Chapter 3 on project appraisal we require the measurement of forecast cash flows and the cost of capital in order to compute the net present value of the business according to alternative strategies. Those strategies that create positive net present values should, depending upon the quality of the assumptions made, increase shareholder value, whereas those with negative net present values are likely to reduce such value. The logic of the approach is straightforward but, as we will identify, there are some practical difficulties.

In order to apply the net present value approach to business strategy a number of stages need to be followed:

- A projection is required of annual operating cash flows for the planning period in question for each business defined as being in the corporate portfolio. The difficulty of their estimation discussed with reference to project appraisal is equally applicable within the context of a financial strategy model
- The cash flows, once estimated, must be discounted at the cost of capital relevant to the company during the planning period and summed to give the present value of projected cash flows
- The final stage, and often the most difficult in practice, is the estimation of the residual or terminal value of the individual businesses at the end of the planning period, discounted to its present value
- The total present value for any particular strategy is the sum of the present values of annual operating cash flows and the residual value. As indicated earlier, there are parallels between the net present value approach and the measurement of value derived from holding a share. Just as a shareholder will usually be concerned with both dividend and capital growth potential, a company will be concerned with annual operating cash flows and the residual value.

Terminal value

As indicated, however, one significant problem in practice is the calculation of the residual or terminal value for the business at the end of the planning period. Whereas for capital projects terminal values are not usually a significant influence and can usually be estimated with reference to realisable value sources, it is far more difficult for businesses which will still be going concerns at the end of the planning period.

Various approaches have been proposed for establishing residual values. Realisable values from disposal may be appealing but are not relevant if the business is to be viewed as a going concern. Two alternative traditional methods are to use the price earning (PE) multiple method and the market to book (MB) ratio method. Using the PE ratio method, residual value is the product of some measure of after tax earnings at the end of the forecast period and the projected PE at the end of the forecast period. A claimed advantage of this approach is that the PE is widely used and readily available from, for example, the Financial Times. Against this must be weighed the assumption implied by its use that price is driven by earnings and the difficulty of predicting future PE multiples.

The problem of earnings and other accounting based measures have been discussed at length! To the concerns we have expressed about the use of earnings we need to recognise that PE ratios move over the course of time and no reliable models exist for forecasting their future value accurately. With the MB ratio method, the residual value is the product of the book value of equity and the projected MB ratio at the end of the forecast period. Similar to the PE ratio, the MB is relatively easy to calculate but it has all of its shortcomings.

An alternative to both of these is to capitalise cash flow in the last planning period. This approach treats the cash flow in the last planning period as a perpetuity in the same way as a fixed income security. For example, consider a £1,000 security offering a £100 per annum. The interest rate for one year is calculated by:

£100 / £1,000 x £100 = 10%

Alternatively, if we know the fixed income from the security and the interest rate, the capital value of the security can be calculated by rearranging the formula:

£100 / 10% = £1,000

Using such an approach the value of a fixed income security can be readily calculated in the event of a change in the interest rate. Thus, at a rate of 5.5 percent the value of the security would be:

£100 / 5.5% = £1,800

For the calculation of the residual value from a strategy, a perpetuity cash flow is taken to represent the fixed income, which is then divided by the company's cost of capital, that is:

$$\text{Residual Value} = \frac{\text{Perpetuity Cash Flow}}{\text{Cost of Capital}}$$

The support for the perpetuity method for estimating residual value is that it is argued as corresponding broadly with the realities of business. Value creating strategies are those that yield positive net present values as a result of producing returns over the cost of capital demanded by the market. By the end of the planning period corresponding with a value creating strategy, there are likely to have been additional entrants to the market who will have identified opportunities for themselves, such that any company is not expected on average to be able to produce positive net present values.

3.5 Calculating Shareholder Value

As will be illustrated, strategic value can represented by two related parts, that from the period over which forecast plans are made, known as planning period, and the period beyond, known as the continuing period. Associated with each of these will be a value, the size of which will depend upon a number of factors, including the type of business to be analysed.

The starting point on the journey to estimate strategic value is the estimation of the free cash flows using five value drivers, that is:

1. Sales growth rate
2. EBITDA (Earnings Before Interest Tax Depreciation and Amortisation) margin
3. Cash tax rate
4. Fixed capital investment
5. Working capital investment.

Once these five have been reviewed, two more will be introduced in the form of:

6. The cost of capital.
7. The planning period.

Using these seven value drivers an illustration of how a picture of value can be estimated will be provided.

Estimating free cash flow

Given the focus of attention upon VBM discussed in Chapter 1 and the quest to understand how to create value from better management, let us assume a business that has a five year strategic plan, which it wishes to evaluate. As will be illustrated, this five year plan can be valued from these five cash flow value drivers. The all important question is: how can values for the free cash flow drivers be estimated? The answer is that they are typically estimated by looking at a mix of past experience, management judgement about what is likely to happen in the future and observations about the marketplace.

The importance of cash flow data should not be underestimated in measuring strategic value. The expression Garbage In, Garbage Out (GIGO) is very appropriate for issues relating to business valuation, where the quality of any business valuation can only be as good as the input data upon which it is based. With this in mind let us review the issues associated with estimating the cash flow drivers.

Sales growth forecasts

Estimated future sales can be projected from market information to produce forecasts about the market for goods or services. Such market forecasts should be based upon an analysis of market opportunities. A pricing policy will also have to be established in each sector in order to put a monetary value on the forecast sales quantities. Prices (in most markets) affect the quantity sold, so there will be an iterative process to estimate the sales volume at the most appropriate prices to provide what is thought to be the relevant sales receipts over the forecast period.

The current level of sales (for each product at current prices) is very much the starting point for sales growth analysis. Any expected growth in sales volume from, for example, prior investment in fixed and working capital must be added. There may also be some adverse influences upon sales value, for example, as a result of a decrease in sales volume because of, say, divestment or even a lowering of prices.

As a starting point it can be quite helpful to think of the first driver of business value as being sales growth. If the enterprise does not sell anything, then it cannot really be said to be in business! However, it is important to be realistic in assessing sales growth potential. Current and prospective competition, when combined with actual and potential barriers to entry typically influence sales growth potential.

EBITDA margin

EBITDA is often used rather than other measures of earnings, such as operating profit to overcome many of the difficulties that may arise because of taxation and capital structure differences, particularly within a cross-border valuation context[6]. It can also be thought of as being closer to cash than other measures of profit, because the depreciation of tangible assets and the amortization of intangible assets are ignored in its calculation[7].

EBITDA reflects the earnings to be generated after the costs of doing business have been taken into consideration. Typically, once sales forecasts and more concrete sales plans are agreed, managers will need to consider the means of ensuring the supply of those sales to customers and the costs of doing so.
Such costs will relate to:

- The sourcing and costs of raw materials
- Employing and training an adequate labour force
- Establishing sufficient sales and distribution facilities
- Marketing of the product/service
- Ensuring adequate production facilities
- Creating a management team able to manage the business.

In a not for profit organisation, activities will also generate costs that have to be charged against income receivable. However, in some not for profit concerns, the income may not be linked to the service in quite the same way that costs are linked to sales in a commercial enterprise. For example, a charity in which the income from donations and grants is unrelated to the 'output' or activity of the charity. In this case, the not for profit undertaking has to ensure that the best use is made of its income by providing a cost effective service. It is arguably more difficult to manage this where one is measuring benefits against costs than in the commercial world where the amount of profit is a measure of the degree of success.

What this illustration also flags up is that very different approaches may need to be adopted in generating forecast cash flows depending upon circumstances. What drives cash flow is by no means common to all types of business operations. A sequence of events starting with sales growth may be difficult to apply in all circumstances.

---

[6] In some circumstances, EBITDA information may not be available in which case the operating profit will typically need to be converted to cash flow by adding back depreciation and any other non-cash items.

[7] Depreciation can be thought of as being an apportionment of the sum paid for a fixed asset over its useful economic life. The simplest way to understand this is with reference to an illustration. Imagine a piece of machinery bought today for £100,000, which is expected to last for 5 years and to be worth nothing at the end of this time period. If paid for by cash, there would be a cash outflow of £100,000 at the time of purchase. However, for accounting purposes it would be written-off over the 5-year period, such that only a proportion, say one fifth or £20,000, would be charged against profit each year.

It is important to realise that the EBITDA margin on sales also depends on the type of business. Generally, the principle is that the greater the need for investment in fixed assets and working capital, the higher the profit margin has to be on sales. For example, food retailers in the UK have relatively low amounts tied up in fixed assets and working capital. They may own some of their stores, but also rent others, and have very little tied up in working capital by way of stocks and debtors. Such companies work on lower sales margins than heavy goods companies, like those supplying plant and equipment to industry, that have to plan for much higher margins on sales value. Such companies have large factories to pay for and the net profit on each sale has proportionately to be much higher than the retailer.

Cash tax flows

Once EBITDA has been estimated, a forecast amount of tax to be paid will have to be taken into account. Tax is often more difficult to consider from a general managerial perspective than the other cash flow drivers because it is very much a specialist area. For this reason, general assumptions about the cash tax rate are often made when valuing a business; nevertheless, there are one or two issues that are important for you to understand.

First, tax payable upon profits is an income tax paid by a venture on its income (or net profit) in just the same way that individuals have to pay income tax on their income. Companies in many countries must also pay capital gains tax on any gain made from liquidating an asset or investment held over time. For example, if an office building were sold for £10m which had originally cost £4m, there would be tax to pay on the capital appreciation of £6m. However, in many countries the capital gains tax is not levied on the full capital gain because an allowance is made for the general rate of inflation. In this example, the allowance for inflation would mean that the £4m original cost would be indexed to a higher figure and the resultant gain would be lower.

Secondly, a charge, for what has become known as deferred tax, is made in each year's accounts for a number of adjustments, including the amount of capital gains tax that would have to be paid if the asset were sold at the date the accounts were drawn up. The main point about deferred tax is that it is irrelevant as far as free cash flow is concerned. The concern is with the amount of tax actually paid in any year, that is the year during which any tax is payable.

Thirdly, under taxation systems like that in the UK, interest payable is a tax deductible expense, whereas, as a general rule, interest receivable and investment income are taxable income. In other words, for a company with a net interest expense, the tax charge in the income statement account has been reduced by the tax shield effect of interest. To arrive at the true after tax profits from operations, the tax charge must first be adjusted to reverse this effect. This can be estimated by multiplying the net interest payable figure in the income statement account by the marginal rate of corporation tax. The adjusted tax charge effectively represents the tax payable by the company if it had been entirely equity financed and had no non operating income. If this adjustment is not made, the way in which a company has been financed will distort the calculated return.

Fixed and working capital investment

Using information about sales growth potential, the EBITDA margin and likely cash tax payments, operating cash flows can be estimated. However, for valuation purposes free cash flow estimates are required in the form of deductions from operating cash flow for investment purposes. In other words, the distinction between operating cash flow and free cash flow is that investment necessary to maintain existing cash flows and to support future cash flows both of which need to be taken into consideration in deriving free cash flow. Such investment will be concerned with:

- Fixed capital investment in the form of investment for the replacement of fixed assets to meet existing customer demands (RFCI) and investment in new assets to meet intended sales growth projections (IFCI – incremental fixed capital investment).
- Working Capital Investment (WCI) that is investment in working capital, such as stocks of materials.

Estimating these can be difficult in practice and many different approaches can be adopted. For RFCI, the objective is to assess how much a company needs to reinvest in its existing core business, at current prices, in order to maintain both the productive capacity and, where it is an issue, competitive position. In other words, how much should the company be charging against profits for the use of its fixed assets on a replacement cost basis? This number is often referred to as the 'maintenance capex' (capital expenditure) and its calculation forces an assessment of the real economic value of a company's assets. Companies tend to invest according to their free cash flow and so an analysis of free cash flow should give a reasonable guide to a company's future investment spending. This is because falling free cash flow is often followed by falling capital investment and vice versa. Since companies are not obliged to disclose the RFCI, any assessment of its value is bound to be subjective. However, in some industries, maintenance capex can be estimated with some degree of confidence by referring to the replacement cost of capacity, for example, airlines, car manufacturers and steel producers. In other industries, however, the figure may bear little relationship to the eventual cost of replacing fixed assets. More generally, an estimate of maintenance capex must be put in the context of both actual capex and historic cost accounting (HCA) depreciation figure. Actual capex over several years, relative to sales or fixed assets, gives a guide to how much a company has thought it necessary to invest in its assets though this must be offset by an assessment of the proportion of that capex that was earmarked for expansion rather than maintenance. HCA depreciation in most cases provides a baseline figure for maintenance capex, such that a frequently used assumption is that depreciation is a good estimate for RFCI.

For the other two types of investment, IFCI and WCI, there are many different forecasting approaches. One approach mentioned above, which will be illustrated in the next section, involves estimating the relationship between increased sales and increased fixed and working capital expenditure using historical data. It is important to note that this will very often need to be disaggregated substantially. For example, working capital investment will typically be analysed in terms of required expenditure on individual components, like stocks and debtors.

Perhaps the most difficult problem in this area arises when there are step changes in technology. If a competitor invents a new production process, which dramatically lowers cash operating costs, a company is obliged to decide whether to invest in the same technology or face a steady loss of competitive position. Even if it judges that the return on that investment will be inadequate, once a rival's capacity is in existence it will tend to drive industry prices down to new, lower, levels relative to input costs. In effect, this means that a decision not to invest is a decision to begin to leave the industry.

Whilst reference has been made to fixed and working capital requirements to support future growth, they are not the only type of investment that may be necessary. Expenditure on research and development, product development as well as other less tangible items may be required. The reality is that this is a cash flow approach which recognises that any cash outflow, however defined for accounting purposes, must be taken into consideration.

Illustration estimating free cash flow

To see how the five cash flow value drivers can be used to provide a free cash flow estimate, let us consider a hypothetical company called Kingsand plc with sales revenue today of £300m, a value driver profile and financial position as illustrated in Table 3.1:

Table 3.1: Value driver profile

Year	1	2	3	4	5	Beyond
	%	%	%	%	%	%
Sales Growth Rate (SGR)	5	5	5	5	5	0
EBITDA Margin	10	10	10	10	10	10
Cash Tax Rate (CTR)	30	30	30	30	30	30
IFCI	10	10	10	10	10	0
IWCI	10	10	10	10	10	0
Cost of Capital	10	10	10	10	10	10
	£m	**£m**	**£m**	**£m**	**£m**	
Depreciation	10	10	10	10	10	10
RFCI	10	10	10	10	10	10
Financial Position	**£m**					
Fixed Assets	100					
Current Assets	50					
Current Liabilities	25					
	125					
	£m					
Share Capital	100					
Reserves	5					
Long-term Loans	20					
	125					

Applying these value drivers gives the after tax operating cash flow shown in Table 3.2:

Table 3.2: After tax operating cash flows

Year		1	2	3	4	5	Beyond
	£m	**£m**	**£m**	**£m**	**£m**	**£m**	**£m**
Sales Receipts	300	315.0	330.8	347.3	364.7	382.9	382.9
EBITDA		31.5	33.1	34.7	36.5	38.3	38.3
less Cash Tax		9.4	9.9	10.4	10.9	11.5	11.5
Operating Cash Flow		22.1	23.2	24.3	25.6	26.8	26.8

As indicated in the preceding section, operating cash flow does not take account of important cash outflows that will need to be incurred to support the existing and the intended sales growth. In order to achieve the intended sales growth rates, fixed and working capital investment may need to be incurred. Replacement fixed capital investment (RFCI) is required to maintain the existing assets in a satisfactory form to meet existing customer demands, whilst incremental fixed capital investment (IFCI) needs to be incurred to meet the projected sales growth rates. As we have indicated, an estimate has to be made of the amount of incremental fixed capital that will be required to support incremental sales. One way to build this in is to assume that for every £1 of sales to be generated some fixed capital investment will need to be incurred. For example, this might well be expressed as a percentage of incremental sales, such that a rate of 10% would be interpreted as for every £1 of additional sales 10 pence of incremental fixed capital investment will be required. This has to be recognised as being a rather simplistic approach insofar as investment may not occur in even increments, but may be incurred in 'lumps', however, it does represent a starting point.

Typically, there will also need to be an investment in working capital since additional sales will be difficult to sustain without incurring incremental working capital. More stock may be required and it may only be possible to achieve a growth in sales by extending credit and increasing debtors. In common with incremental fixed capital it can be assumed that for every additional £1 of sales to be generated, some working capital investment will be required. In other words, any increase in sales can only occur by taking on more stocks of raw materials and, possibly, by increasing accounts receivable (debtors). As indicated in Table 3.1, it is assumed that incremental fixed capital investment (IFCI) and working capital investment (IWCI) will be 10% over the five year assumed planning period.

All of this can now be pulled together to estimate prospective free cash flows. These are illustrated in Table 3.3.

Table 3.3: From operating cash flow after tax to free cash flow

Year		**1**	**2**	**3**	**4**	**5**	**Beyond**
	£m	**£m**	**£m**	**£m**	**£m**	**£m**	**£m**
Sales Receipts	300	315.0	330.8	347.3	364.7	382.9	382.9
EBITDA		31.5	33.1	34.7	36.5	38.3	38.3
less Cash Tax		9.4	9.9	10.4	10.9	11.5	11.5
Operating Cash Flow		22.1	23.2	24.3	25.6	26.8	26.8
less RFCI		10.0	10.0	10.0	10.0	10.0	10.0
less IFCI		1.5	1.6	1.7	1.7	1.8	0.0
less IWCI		1.5	1.6	1.7	1.7	1.8	0.0
Free Cash Flow		9.1	10.0	10.9	12.2	13.2	16.8

Relationship between the different drivers of free cash flow

The relationship between the cash inflows and outflows is important to recognise. To achieve sales growth, expenditure will have to be incurred, the amount of which will depend upon the magnitude of the sales growth and the capacity of the business to expand. The interrelationship between these cash flow drivers is vital to understand. This can be seen to be so particularly in the case of the sales growth rate and incremental fixed and working capital investment. Without adequate fixed assets and working capital it may be impossible to achieve a target growth rate, let alone sustain it. However, one problem with fixed capital investment is that it may often be 'lumpy'. Beyond a certain level of production it may be impossible to produce more without investing in completely new plant and equipment. Thus, the assumption of a linear relationship between sales growth and investment is one that may not always be realistic.

The identification of key value drivers is vital and it is important to recognise that they may vary over the life cycle of a business and by type of business. In the case of the life cycle, which is illustrated in Figure 3.1, in the start up phase, sales growth will often play a dominant role. However, with the development of the market and the increased participation of competitors, attention to profit margins may well be more important. This is because there will often come a point beyond which increased sales will result in value destruction, that is additional sales revenue might well be outweighed by the costs associated with generating it.

Figure 3. 1: Value drivers over the life cycle

	Stage of life cycle			
	Launch	**Growth**	**Maturity**	**Decline**
Value Drivers				
Sales Growth	Nil/high	High	Zero	Negative
EBITDA /Margin	Low/High	High	Medium	LOW
Cash Tax Rate	LOW	LOW	Standard	Depends
Fixed Capital Investment	High	High	Medium/Low	Low/Reducing
	>>>	>>	= or <<	<<
	Depreciation	Depreciation	Depreciation	Depreciation
Working Capital Investment	High	High	Low	Reducing
Cost of Capital	Very High	High	Medium	Low
(linked to level of business risk)				
Planning Period	Short	Medium/Long	Long	Short/Medium
Continuing Value	Large	Large	Medium	Medium

As indicated, not only will the stage of development have an impact upon the value drivers but also the type of business. An example of this is provided in Figure 3.2 for a systems solutions company reveals that work undertaken to identify the impact of the value drivers within four different businesses yielded very different results.

Figure 3.2: Impact of value drivers within a systems solutions company

Business	**1**	**2**	**3**	**4**
Value Drivers:				
Sales Growth Rate	Medium	High	High	Medium
EBITDA/Margin	High	Medium	High	High
Cash Tax Rate	Low	Low	Low	Medium
Fixed Capital Investment	Medium	High	Low	Medium
Working Capital Investment	High	High	Medium	Medium
Cost of Capital	High	High	High	High
Planning Period	Medium	Long	Long	Long

A business like that characterised under Business 2 is dependent upon substantial fixed and working capital investment to generate sales growth. In fact, this value driver profile can be likened to a start up situation in which fixed and working capital expenditure will be essential for stimulating future growth. It is also worth noting that in some businesses such expenditure will be directed at intangible rather than tangible items. Future growth may be driven by research and development in industries like pharmaceuticals, whilst in others expenditure on branding of products and product development may be the key.

Estimating strategic value and free cash flow

To estimate strategic value free cash flows must be discounted at the Weighted Average Cost of Capital (WACC), which is the subject of a later chapter. Strategic value is typically estimated by determining the value over the planning period and that from continuing period (the terminal value), which often represents the largest part of total value.

Value of the planning period

In the case of Kingsand plc, the WACC is assumed to be 10% after tax and when appropriately adjusted for inflation. This WACC represents the average return required by the providers of both debt and equity finance. With knowledge of this WACC, the present value of the cash flows for the five year planning period can be calculated, which is shown in Table 3.4 as being £41.2m.

Table 3.4: Estimating strategic value

Year		1	2	3	4	5	Beyond
	£m	£m	£m	£m	£m	£m	£m
Sales Receipts	300	315.0	330.8	347.3	364.7	382.9	382.9
EBITDA		31.5	33.1	34.7	36.5	38.3	38.3
less Cash Tax		9.4	9.9	10.4	10.9	11.5	11.5
Operating Cash Flow		22.1	23.2	24.3	25.6	26.8	26.8
less RFCI		10.0	10.0	10.0	10.0	10.0	10.0
less IFCI		1.5	1.6	1.7	1.7	1.8	0.0
less IWCI		1.5	1.6	1.7	1.7	1.8	0.0
Free Cash Flow		9.1	10.0	10.9	12.2	13.2	16.8
Discount Factor		0.909	0.826	0.751	0.683	0.621	
Present Value (Free Cash Flow)		8.2	8.3	8.3	8.2	8.2	
Cumulative Present Value		8.2	16.5	24.8	33	41.2	

Estimating terminal value (TV)

A planning period of five years was used, but the issue now arises of how to estimate a Terminal Value (TV) for the continuing period beyond year 5. Assume that this company has a share price of £1 and 100 million shares. This implies a market capitalisation of £100m, while the value calculated for the five year forecast period is £41.2m, a substantial difference. In fact, the value calculated represents only 41% of the market implied value and therefore the question arises of how this difference can be accounted for. One commonly used way of estimating TV involves the calculation of a perpetuity value by dividing the assumed perpetuity cash flow by the cost of capital. For this company, the free cash flow in the continuing period beyond year 5 is £16.8m (see Table 3.4), which when divided by the assumed cost of capital of 10% produces a value of £168m. However, what is required is the present value of the perpetuity and not the value at the end of five years. This present value is substantially lower than £168m and is approximately £104.3m (£168m : 10% x 0.621). This is obtained by discounting the £168m in five years to a present value (see Table 3.5).

Table 3.5: Present value of the planning period and TV

Year	**1**	**2**	**3**	**4**	**5**	**Beyond**
	£m	**£m**	**£m**	**£m**	**£m**	**£m**
Free Cash Flow	9.1	10.0	10.9	12.2	13.2	16.8
Discount Factor	0.909	0.826	0.751	0.683	0.621	
Present Value (Free Cash Flow)	8.3	8.3	8.2	8.3	8.2	
Cumulative Present Value	8	16	25	33	41	
Present Value of Residual Value					104	
Business Value					145	

Business value, corporate value and strategic value

To calculate a business value, the present value of the planning period has to be combined with the present value to be derived from the business beyond it. In the case of our example company, assuming a five year planning period and a cost of capital of 10%, the result is a total business value of £145.6m (£41.3m + £104.3m), as illustrated in Table 3.5. This value is now substantially higher than the market implied value of £100m, but the difference can be explained.

The business value that has been calculated is not the same as strategic value. Business value represents the value generated by the free cash flows against which all providers of funds have a claim, but strategic value is concerned with that part of business value, which is attributable to the shareholders. To understand how to arrive at this it is necessary to recall that business value was estimated by discounting the free cash flows at a cost of capital which took account of the benefit of both borrowed funds and funds provided by shareholders. To estimate strategic value the present value of borrowed funds needs to be subtracted in order to find the claim on the value of the business attributable to just the shareholders. It may also be the case that investments are held in other businesses, the benefits of which are not captured in the business valuation process. Any such benefits have to be added to determine corporate rather than business value. In fact, two adjustments are required to calculate strategic value, which take the following form:

Business value

+ Marketable securities or investments[8]

= Corporate value

- Market value of debt and obligations

= Strategic value

÷ Number of ordinary shares

= Strategic value per share

Assume that the market value of Kingsand's debt – long term loans in Table 3.1 – is £20m. For this company, the result of the calculation outlined above is shown in Table 3.6.

[8] Surplus cash invested in marketable securities (non operating assets) are assumed to create no additional value, that is, their net present value is zero

Table 3.6: Strategic value per share

Year	1	2	3	4	5	Beyond
	£m	£m	£m	£m	£m	£m
Free Cash Flow	9.1	10.0	10.9	12.2	13.2	16.8
Discount Factor	0.909	0.826	0.751	0.683	0.621	
Present Value (Free Cash Flow)	8.3	8.3	8.2	8.3	8.2	
Cumulative Present Value	8.2	16.5	24.8	33	41.2	
Present Value of Residual Value					104.3	
Business Value					145.5	
add Marketable Securities					0	
Corporate Value					145.5	
less Market Value of Debt					20	
Strategic Value					125.5	
Number of Shares (m)					100	
Strategic Value Per Share					£1.26	

The estimated business value is £145.5m, there are no marketable securities (that is, interest earning deposits) and the value of debt is assumed to be £20m. Debt and obligations are ducted from corporate value resulting in £125.5m. The number of ordinary shares (assumed to be 100 million) then divides this and a strategic value per share of £1.26 is obtained.

How might the figure for strategic value be interpreted? The company has a current share price of £1.00. As implied earlier, this share price can be compared with the publicly quoted price determined by the forces of demand and supply to see if a value gap exists. This is the term applied to the difference between the publicly quoted share price and estimates of its value using specific company information. For the company, there is a value gap of £0.26 at a 10% cost of capital (£1.26 - £1.00).

What does this strategic value per share represent? It is the estimated value per share and it is very dependent upon the assumptions made about the key value drivers. Change any of these and so too does the value. For example, an increase in the EBITDA margin, ceteris paribus, will result in a higher strategic value per share. By way of illustration, in one company that was analysed using this framework, an increase in the EBITDA margin to the levels currently achieved by peer group companies had the effect of doubling the strategic value per share and formed part of the rationale for it becoming an acquisition target.

Let us pause at this point and reflect upon the figure for strategic value estima company. It represents the value derived from a fairly simplistic view of the company. In it would be reasonable to expect that estimates used in a full valuation would have to invo considerable detailed analysis. For example, many businesses provide multiple services and/or produce multiple products. For them, a more realistic process of valuation would be to calculate the cash flows relevant to, say, each business unit using planning periods that reflect the different distinctive capabilities of each and then to discount them at a required rate of return relevant to each unit. All of these individual values could then be aggregated and the strategic value estimated. The ability to be able to go into such detail depends upon information being available. Obtaining information can often be difficult but a guide as to what may be available is provided in Figure 3.3.

Figure 3.3: Possible sources of available information

	Internal		**External**	
	Past	**Future**	**Past**	**Future**
Numeric	Management Accounting	Budgets and Forecasts	Competitors' Results	Brokers' Forecasts
Financial Text	Results Narrative	Five Year Plan	Brokers' View	Press Opinion
Numeric	Operating Performance	Capacity Planning	Market Share	Market Research
Non-financial Text	Performance Commentary	Strategic Goals	Trade Media	Technology Forecasts

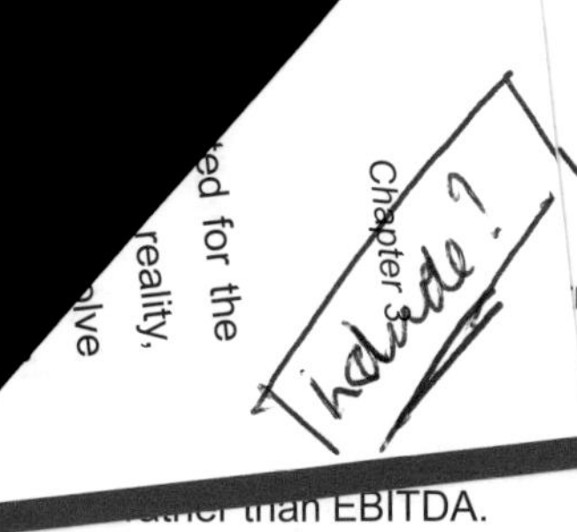

ration – RWM plc

nnual accounts and notes (see Appendix Chapter 1) plus the een used to calculate a strategic value using operating cash than EBITDA.

Historical Data Relating to RWM plc

	2004	2005	2006
	£m	**£m**	**£m**
Revenue	187.4	199.6	210.6
Profit Before Interest and Taxation	20.2	14.7	12.1
Taxation	5.0	2.7	2.4
Tangible Fixed Assets	66.9	76.2	86.7
Depreciation for year	4.4	5.2	5.9
RFCI	6.1	6.9	7.9
Working Capital	20.5	16.8	9.3

Operating Cash Flow for RWM Plc

	2005	2006
Operating Profit	14.7	12.1
add Depreciation (see Table 12.5)	5.2	5.9
Operating Cash Flow before tax	19.9	18.0
less Taxation	2.7	2.4
Operating Cash Flow after tax	**17.2**	**15.6**

Using this information we can calculate the five cash flow drivers for 2005 and 2006 as illustrated in Table 3.6:

Calculating Value Drivers for 2005 and 2006

	2005		2006	
Cash Flow Driver	**%**	**Calculation**	**%**	**Calculation**
Sales Growth Rate	6.5	$\frac{(199.6-187.4) \times 100}{187.4}$	5.5	$\frac{(210.6-199.6) \times 100}{199.6}$
Operating Profit Margin	7.4	$\frac{14.7 \times 100}{199.6}$	5.7	$\frac{12.1 \times 100}{210.6}$
Tax Rate	18.4	$\frac{2.7 \times 100}{14.7}$	19.8	$\frac{2.4 \times 100}{12.1}$
IFCI[9]	62.3	See 12.7	77.3	See 12.7
IWCI	-30.3	$\frac{(16.8-20.5) \times 100}{(199.6-187.4)}$	-68.2	$\frac{(9.3-16.8) \times 100}{(210.6-199.6)}$

Calculating Incremental Fixed Capital Investment (IFCI) for 2005 and 2006

		2005	2006
		£m	**£m**
Net Tangible Fixed Assets at end of year		76.2	86.7
add Depreciation for the year		5.2	5.9
Tangible Assets before depreciation		81.4	92.6
less Net Tangible Assets at beginning of year		66.9	76.2
Increase/(Decrease) in Tangible Assets		14.5	16.4
less Asset Replacement (RFCI)		6.9	7.9
Increase in Tangible Fixed Assets	(a)	7.6	8.5
Increase in Sales	(b)	12.2	11.0
IFCI	(a ÷ b x 100)	62.3%	77.3%

These values for the cash flow drivers, based upon an historical review, represent just the starting point. As we indicated earlier when we reviewed each of the cash flow drivers, a good deal of research is required to ensure meaningful forward looking free cash flow estimates.

Let us assume that research has been undertaken for RWM which has been used to produce the following cash flow driver estimates for 2007 to 2009:

[9] The calculation of the percentages for IFCI is often more complicated because depreciation and RFCI can differ. They should be calculated as shown to deal with situations where RFCI and depreciation values differ.

Cash Flow Drivers

	2005	2006	2007, 2008 and 2009		
Sales Growth Rate	6.5%	5.5%	9.0%	–	External analyst
Operating Profit Margin	7.4%	5.7%	9.0%	–	Improved cost control
Cash Tax Rate	18.4%	19.8%	20%	–	Conservative
estimate					(in need of review)
IFCI	62.7%	77.3%	20%	–	Minimum necessary to satisfy growth targets
IWCI	-30.3%	-68.2%	20%	–	External analyst

With knowledge of these cash flow drivers and estimates of depreciation and RFCI, we can produce free cash flow estimates by following a similar procedure as the earlier illustration. The result is as shown below:

Free Cash Flow Estimates

	2006	2007	2008	2009	
	£m	**£m**	**£m**	**£m**	
Sales	210.6	229.6	250.3		272.8
Operating Profit Before Interest and Tax		20.7	22.5		24.6
Taxation		–4.1	–4.5		–4.9
Operating Profit After Tax		16.6	18.0		19.7
Depreciation		7.0	7.0		7.0
Operating Cash Flow		23.6	25.0		26.7
RFCI		–8.0	–8.0		–8.0
IFCI		–3.8	–4.1		–4.5
IWCI		–3.8	–4.1		–4.5
Free Cash Flow		**8.0**	**8.8**		**9.7**

To express these future cash flows in present value terms we need to discount them at the required rate of return (cost of capital). Let us assume that the cost of capital of RWM after tax and when appropriately adjusted for inflation is 12%. With knowledge of this cost of capital we can calculate the present value of the cash flows of RWM plc for the three-year planning period as being £21.06m:

Present Value of Free Cash Flows

	2007	2008	2009	
Free Cash Flow £m	8.0	8.8	9.7	
Multiply by: 12% Discount Factor	0.893	0.797	0.712	
Present Value £m	7.14	7.01	6.91	
Total Present Value				21.06

A planning period of three years was selected consisting of 2007 to 2009 inclusive and, given this, we can assume that 2010 and beyond corresponds with the continuing period. A breakdown of the components of free cash flow for both the planning period and the years comprising the continuing period are:

Free cash flows for the planning and continuing periods

			PLANNING PERIOD			CONTINUING PERIOD	
	2006	**2007**	**2008**	**2009**	**2010**	**2011**	**2012**
	£m	**£m**	**£m**	**£m**	**£m**	**£m**	**£m**
Sales	210.6	229.6	250.3	272.8	272.8	272.8	272.8
Operating Profit Before Interest and Tax		20.7	22.5	24.6	24.6	24.6	24.6
Taxation		–4.1	–4.5	–4.9	–4.9	–4.9	–4.9
Operating Profit After Tax		16.6	18.0	19.7	19.7	19.7	19.7
Depreciation		7.0	7.0	7.0	7.0	7.0	7.0
Operating Cash Flow		23.6	25.0	26.7	26.7	26.7	26.7
RFCI		–8.0	–8.0	–8.0	–8.0	–8.0	–8.0
IFCI		–3.8	–4.1	–4.5	0	0	0
IWCI		–3.8	–4.1	–4.5	0	0	0
Free Cash Flow		**8.0**	**8.8**	**9.7**	**18.7**	**18.7**	**18.7**

Because sales growth is assumed to cease at the end of the planning period, sales and hence operating profit remain the same in each year of the continuing period as in 2009. Similarly, with depreciation assumed to be unchanged, operating cash flow remains the same in 2009 as in each year of the continuing period. However, where there is a noteworthy change is in the level of investment. Whilst RFCI remains unchanged because such investment will need to be undertaken to maintain the quality of existing assets, IFCI and IWCI fall off to zero. These you will remember were forecast upon the basis of sales growth – no sales growth, no IFCI or IWCI!

If we assume the 2009 free cash is received into perpetuity its value as we discussed earlier may be calculated as follows:

Value of Perpetuity	=	Free Cash Flow ÷ k
	=	£18.7m ÷ 0.12
	=	£155.83

However, this assumes that the perpetuity is measured at the end of the planning period in 2009. It is not the present value of the perpetuity, that is, its value in 2007. What its value is will depend on the cost of capital. Given that we know this to be 12% we can calculate the present value of the perpetuity by discounting it at the relevant discount factor, that is 12% at the end of year 3. Thus, the present value of such a perpetuity is calculated as follows:

PV of Perpetuity	=	(Payment ÷ k) (1 ÷ (1 + k))n
	=	(£18.7m ÷ 0.12) (1 ÷ (1 + 0.12))3
	=	£110.95m

Seen another way, £110.95m compounded for the next three years at 12% per annum produces £155.83m. To be more precise, £155.83m is the future value and £110.95m is its present value.

Now, the implication of this is that to calculate a business value where there is a given planning period, the present value of the planning period has to be combined with the present value to be derived from the business beyond it. In the case of RWM plc assuming a three year planning period and a cost of capital of 12%, the result is a total business value of £132.01m (£21.06m + £110.95m).

The size of the value from the continuing period, often known as the residual (continuing or terminal) value, is the largest contributor to total value. In fact, in this case the residual value represents 84% of the total value, hardly surprising when one considers that it represents a period of infinity, less the three years accounted for by the planning period.

The value we have discussed so far and calculated for RWM is what is known as business value and is not the strategic value. Business value can be defined as the value generated by the free cash flows in which all providers of funds have a claim.

The concern within Shareholder Value Analysis is with the determination of that part of business value (and any other value) generated which is attributable to the shareholders. How do we find this?

To arrive at business value we discounted free cash flows at a cost of capital that took account of the benefit of borrowed funds. Now we need to remove the present value of any such funds in order to find the claim on the value of the business attributable to just the shareholders.

It may also be the case that investments are held in other businesses, the benefits of which are not captured in the business valuation process. Any such benefits have to be added to determine corporate rather than business value. In fact, two adjustments are required to calculate strategic value that take the following form:

Business Value
add Marketable Securities or Investments
Corporate Value
less Market Value of Debt and Obligations
Strategic Value
Number of Ordinary Shares
Strategic Value Per Share

In terms of RWM plc we have estimated a business value of £132m, there are no marketable securities (for example, interest earning deposits) and the notes to the accounts for 2006 show creditors amounts falling due after one year of £20.1m. If we take such creditors as being a proxy for the market value of debt and obligations we can calculate strategic value as follows:

	£m
Business Value	132.01
add Marketable Securities	0
Corporate Value	132.01
less Market Value of Debt and Obligations	20.10
Shareholder Value	**111.91**

The number of shares for RWM plc for 2006 is 139 million and with knowledge of the number of shares this shareholder value can be converted into a strategic value per share.

Shareholder Value	£111.91m
Number of Ordinary Shares	139m
Shareholder Value Per Share	81p

What does this strategic value per share represent? It is the estimated value per share which is very dependent upon the assumptions made about the seven key value drivers. Change any of these seven and so too does the value. For example, changing only the cost of capital to 11% produces a business value of £145.72m, a strategic value of £125.62m and a value per share of 90p.

CHAPTER 4
STRATEGIC VALUATION ISSUES

Chapter Preview

This chapter will enable you to understand:

- **The principles and potential application of the three different ap proaches that can be used to calculate Terminal Value (TV):**

  1. **Discounted Cash Flow (DCF).**
  2. **Market relative valuation.**
  3. **Asset valuation.**

- **The contribution that the perpetuity approach can make in chal lenging valuation assumptions.**
- **The important interrelationship between the TV and the planning period chosen.**
- **The critical issues involved in estimating over what period of time (planning period) cash flows should be forecast.**
- **The link between the value of a business captured during this planning period and beyond it (the continuing period).**
- **The use of strategic frameworks as a starting point to ensure that the right questions are asked in relation to the length of the plan ning period used.**
- **How the planning period may be estimated in practice by first looking at a Price Earnings interpretation and, secondly, by using the concept of the market implied duration.**
- **The dynamic interrelationship between the planning period, the competitive advantage period and the terminal value.**

4.1 Introduction

The Terminal Value (TV) and some of the approaches, like the perpetuity method, that can be used in its estimation were introduced in the last chapter. This value which arises from the continuing period is often a source of considerable concern because it accounts for a significant proportion of total value.

In view of the potential significance of the TV in any decision, the structure illustrated in Figure 4.1 can be used to guide the assessment and selection of an appropriate method and its estimation.

Figure 4.1: Selecting an appropriate TV method

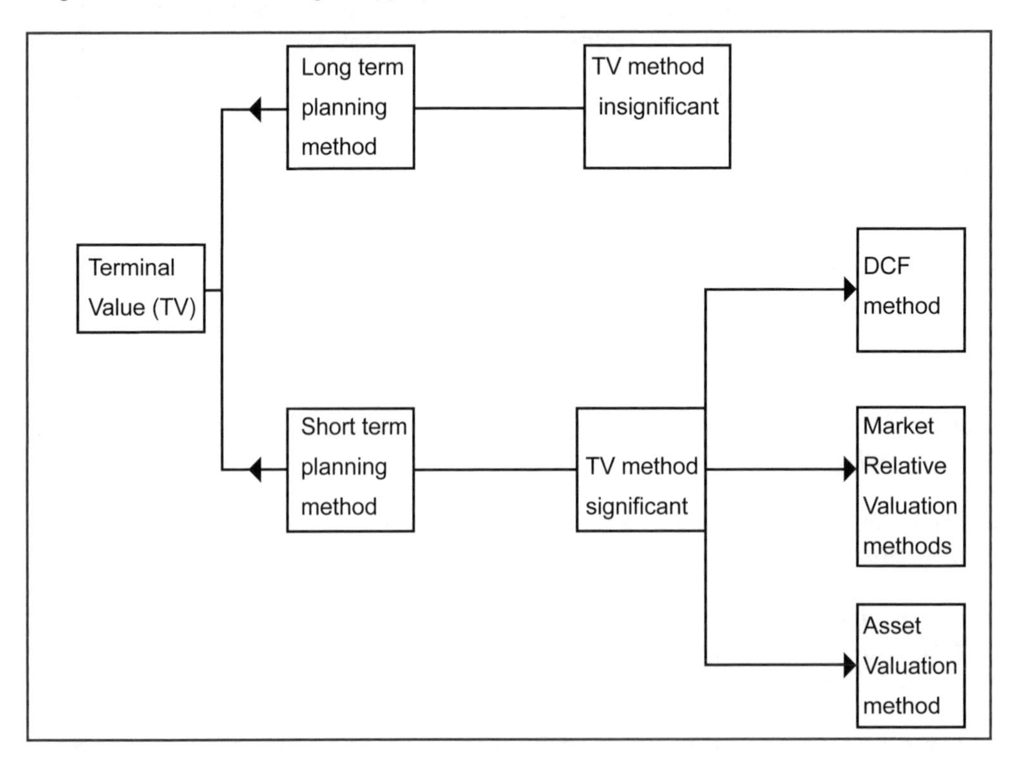

The starting point illustrated in Figure 4.1 is consideration of the time period. If the time period under consideration is very long, say in excess of 20 years, as may be the case of valuing a concession, then the TV estimation is relatively insignificant. For example, the value of £1 in year 20 is 0.149, assuming a discount rate of 10%. This means that the relative importance of the TV to the total value becomes insignificant over such periods, by comparison with frequently used short term time periods, like five years. In year five at 10% the discount rate is 0.621, meaning that every TV £ counts substantially towards the total value.

In the case of a short term time horizon being used, TV and the choice of a method for its calculation become important. Methods that can be used for estimating TV when a short term view is taken are shown in Figure 4.1 as:

- Discounted Cash Flow (DCF)
- Market Relative Valuation Method
- Asset Valuation Method.

4.2 Discounted Cash Flow (DCF) Methods

As illustrated in Figure 4.2, a number of issues have to be taken into consideration in estimating a TV using DCF analysis.

Figure 4.2: Issues in estimating TV using Discounted Cash Flow methods

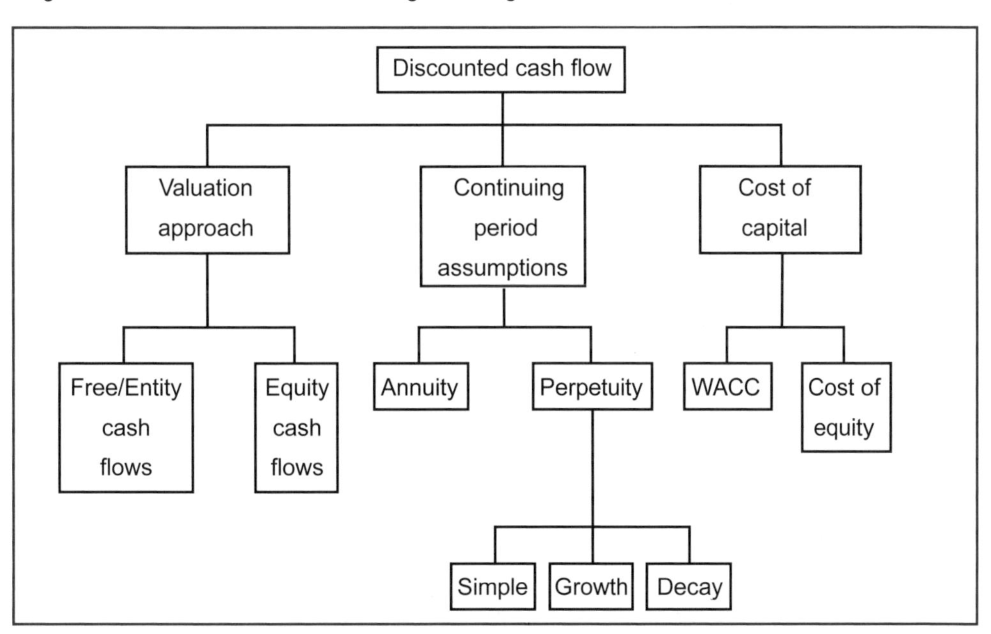

The way in which a DCF TV is estimated will be influenced by the:

- Valuation approach(es) adopted
- Continuing period assumptions
- Cost of capital.

Perpetuity TV Valuations

As illustrated in the last chapter, many proponents of DCF valuation methods use perpetuity TV calculations. There are different perpetuity methods that can be used which, in simple terms, assume that:

- Only the cost of capital can be earned in the continuing period, or
- More can be earned than the cost of capital, or
- Less can be earned than the cost of capital.

To correspond with these choices, the following TV calculations could be used:

- Simple perpetuity
- Perpetuity with growth
- Perpetuity with decay.

Simple perpetuity

The simple perpetuity approach is often represented as assuming constant cash flows beyond the planning period. It can be thought of as being reliant upon the same principles as those associated with calculating an annuity, but instead we consider a special case in which constant free cash flows are assumed to be received for an infinite rather than a finite period[10].

The simple perpetuity TV is typically calculated as follows:

$$\text{Terminal Value} = \frac{FCF_{T+1}}{ACC}$$

[10] The simple perpetuity can be derived from the growing free cash flow perpetuity formula (discussed in the next section). For now, it is important to stress that the simple perpetuity does not mean that growth will necessarily be zero; rather it indicates that any growth will add nothing to value, because the return associated with growth will equal only the cost of capital. In other words, it reflects the fact that the cash flows resulting from future investments will not affect the value of the firm because the overall rate of return earned on them will only equal the cost of capital hence the method is often referred to as the 'convergence formula'.

Where,

FCF_{T+1} = Normalised free cash flow for the continuing period
WACC = Weighted Average Cost of Capital

For Kingsand plc, the free cash flow in the continuing period beyond year 5 is £16.8m (see Table 3.4). Assuming this to be the normalised free cash flow and when divided by the assumed cost of capital of 10%, the result is a value of approximately £168m. However, this is not the value required for purposes of undertaking most valuations. Typically what is needed is the present value of the perpetuity and not the value at the end of five years. This present value is substantially lower than £168m and is in fact £104m (£16.8m /10% x 0.621), that is, £168m to be received in five years discounted to a present value.

Perpetuity with growth

There may be circumstances like the valuation of a telecommunications business in which it is believed that it will be possible to earn a return above the cost of capital in the continuing period. In such circumstances the perpetuity with growth approach is often argued as being more appropriate. It can be calculated as follows:

$$\text{Terminal Value} = \frac{FCF_{(T+1)}}{WACC - g}$$

Where,
FCF (T+1) = Normalised free cash flow for the continuing period
WACC = Weighted Average Cost of Capital
g = Expected growth in free cash flow into perpetuity

Assuming a growth in free cash flow into perpetuity of 2% results in the following TV estimate:

= £16.8m/ (0.10 0.02)

= £210m

Assuming a perpetuity growth rate of 2%, the resulting TV is £210m, 25% higher than using the simple perpetuity. Clearly, the growth rate used has a significant impact upon the TV and overall value and it is important to be able to justify the rate selected.

This approach has to be used cautiously because of the impact of growth assumptions on total value. In the case of a belief in real growth opportunities existing in the market, a reality check is essential. This reality check could be as simple as calculating what volumes would be say 10 to 20 years ahead, based upon such a growth rate and making comparisons with the total potential market, competitive forces and the like. It is also worth noting that perpetuity with growth calculations are sometimes used to take account of inflation. The assumption is that the cash flows in the continuing period should grow at a rate in perpetuity that reflects the inflation rate. Essentially, the logic of this is that if the free cash flow used in the continuing period calculation is not assumed to grow at the rate of inflation, it represents a real number that should be discounted at a real number. Given that WACC in the formula is expressed in nominal terms, conversion to a real rate is achieved by deducting expected inflation as g from the denominator. Opinion is divided about such practice in its use. Those who favour it do so because it is consistent with general principles, that is, real cash flows should be discounted at a real rate. Those who dislike it argue (amongst other points) that it is more realistic to assume that any growth will probably require at least additional working capital expenditure and that replacement (maintenance) fixed capital investment is likely to exceed depreciation.

Perpetuity with decay

This is a very conservative approach, which can be thought of as a special case of the perpetuity with growth method, that is, growth is negative in perpetuity. It assumes that after the planning period the company will be unable to earn even its cost of capital and in terms of the perpetuity with growth formula discussed earlier, it is calculated as follows:

$$\text{Terminal Value} = \frac{FCF_{T+1}}{WACC - (\ g)}$$

Assuming a negative growth in free cash flow into perpetuity of 3% results in the following TV estimate for Kingsand plc:

= £16.8m/(0.10 (0.03))

= £129m

Assuming a decay rate of 3% the result is a substantial reduction in the TV from the simple perpetuity. However, by implication the circumstances under which such conditions would prevail would suggest an exit strategy as being appropriate, in which case, an asset based valuation basis would often be argued as being more appropriate.

4.3 Key Issues in Estimating Terminal Value Using the Perpetuity Approach

TV is often the largest contributor to total value when using a perpetuity calculation and a relatively short planning period. The further into the future that the planning period extends, the lower is the relative contribution made by the continuing period. For example, over a five year planning period results similar to Kingsand plc are not uncommon, on average, where TV represents 60-¬70% of total value. Over a ten year period this will often switch, with 30 40% of total value coming from the TV. The underlying message is that it is desirable to project as far forward as possible with the planning period, but this is often counter to the planning period culture within many companies. This tends to mean the adoption of relatively short planning periods and perpetuity TV calculations are common. However, there may be good justification for using the perpetuity approach even under such circumstances. The reason is best understood with reference to the following questions that can be used with executives involved in reviewing the strategic value of their business for the first time:

1. 'Do you believe your business has a life in excess of the planning period you adopt?' The response to this is typically yes

2. 'Would it not be a good idea to use a period longer than your current planning period?' The answer is typically yes, but it would not be worth the effort because of the highly speculative nature of forecasting over long time periods

3. 'Do you have faith in your planning period assumptions and numbers?' The result is typically a reserved yes, with greatest confidence being felt with earlier rather than later numbers.

Given such "yes" responses there is a good case for using the perpetuity approach as a starting point, based upon their numbers from the planning period. The advantage of this approach is that it relates long term value to assumptions about business potential based upon managerial judgement and insight. In fact, reflection upon this approach by managers usually prompts the observation that the TV according to this approach is dependent upon their assumptions about the time period in which they have greatest comfort and the other value drivers, not least of which is the cost of capital.

Important Considerations in Applying DCF Approaches

1. All DCF methods are heavily dependent upon expected future cash flow estimates and estimates for the cost of capital. Given this, the approach is easiest to accept for companies where cash flows are currently positive and can be estimated with some reliability for future periods and for which a proxy for risk that can be used to obtain discount rates is available. The problem is that they often represent the only practical alternative for companies with quite the opposite characteristics

2. DCF TV calculations should really reflect a company's business cycle. With this in mind it is important to forecast far enough out to capture a complete business cycle and to use normalised figures as the input into the TV formula. Industry dependence on macroeconomic conditions typically differs in different stages of the business cycle and it is important to recognise that TV estimates are particularly sensitive to the phase of the cycle on which the estimates are based

3. In considering use of the perpetuity with growth method, it needs to be recognised that few companies can expect to exceed the cost of capital for long periods of time. As a guideline caution needs to be exercised in adopting a high growth rate and, for purposes of realism, assessment of the feasibility of key assumptions, like the sales growth rate against the market potential, should be undertaken over a limited time horizon. One alternative to the perpetuity with growth that we have found used in practice involves estimating a growth rate corresponding with expected economic (for example, GNP) growth plus inflation in a second time period of say five years beyond the assumed planning period, followed by a third time period using a simple perpetuity assumption.

Figure 4.3: Phasing growth rates over time

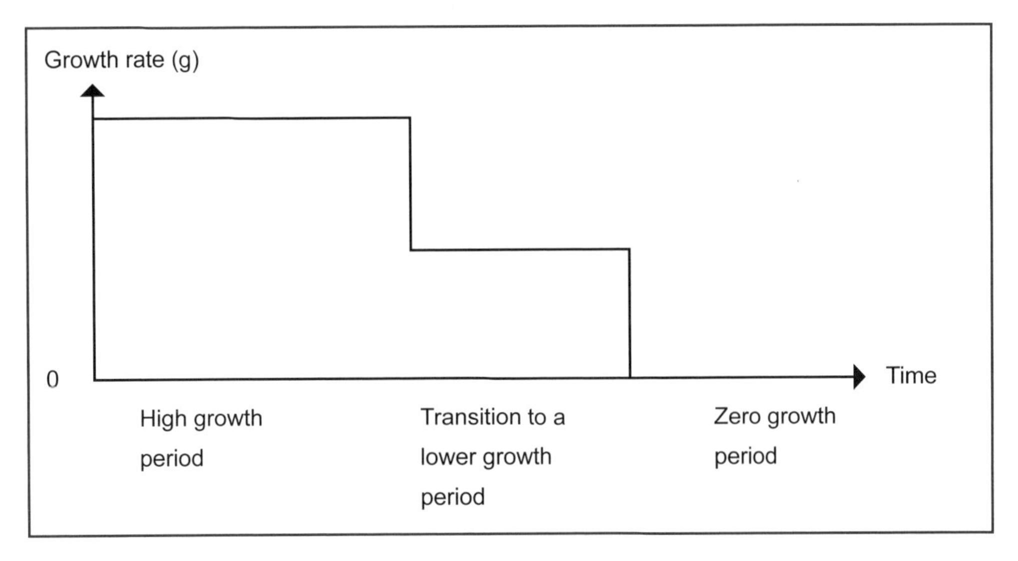

So, in many cases the largest proportion of total value is generated from the continuing period. For this reason, many practitioners also look to other methods, but DCF methods have much to offer, because they can be interpreted and applied to support user judgement. In fact, they can be invaluable in terms of trying to understand the underlying issues involved in a valuation, although their acceptance in the market place for the specific case under consideration may be limited. For example, this is particularly the case for new issues where the use of Price Earnings (PE) multiples and the like have long been accepted practice.

4.4 Market relative valuation methods

Market relative valuation methods can be used in valuing the whole business and not just the TV. They are often used in Initial Public Offering (IPO) valuations, with the most popular method being the Price Earnings (PE) ratio. However, other ratio methods like Enterprise Value: EBITDA, Price:Sales and Market:Book are used that are reckoned to give the most consistent results for steady, organically growing companies. For companies in periods of change and restructuring, these techniques have several shortcomings.

All of these methods seek to determine the value of a business by making a comparison between the financial characteristics of similar peer group companies, for which there is also a stock market valuation, and the company to be valued. The basic premise is that the relationship between the market value and some measure of financial performance for a number of peer group companies represents an appropriate basis for inferring the market value of the company to be valued.

Peer group comparators

A poorly selected peer group will make any relative valuation tenuous and great care needs to be exercised to ensure that companies for inclusion are realistic from an investor's perspective. Even if a satisfactory peer group has been selected, care should be taken not to exaggerate the effects of supply and demand on the underlying share price of some of the peer group's constituents particularly the less liquid ones. Further, one has to ask how to use the peer group data that is collected. For example, in terms of a PE relative valuation should the average ratio, the highest or the lowest be used? For example, imagine a sector with 20 companies and published PEs where the highest was 65, the lowest 8 and the average 18! This may be yet further complicated by the need to take account of the level of premium generally expected for acquiring control of a company.

As regards TV estimates using relative valuation methods there is one further major problem. The multiple(s) required are those for five years, 10 years or even longer and not today. Predicting such multiples is a minefield! Reflection upon various emerging markets crises paints a simple but vivid picture of this, where plunging share prices have been reflected in substantially deflated PE ratios. Predicting what these will look like in five years time is anyone's guess!

4.5 Asset value analysis

In addition to DCF and Market Relative Valuation Methods, analysts commonly look at the realisable value of the underlying assets as well. Asset valuation analysis (AVA) methods measure the economic value of assets as if they are sold. Such methods are a reasonable approach for companies that deal predominantly in assets that are relatively easily valued, like property companies. However, they represent a real problem for companies dealing with intangible assets, for example, drugs companies involved with patents, trademarks and brands.

If the collective use of assets within the business conveys a benefit greater than the sum of the individual assets, then realisable values will be irrelevant because they will always be lower than the economic value. However, calculating realisable values is useful for many reasons. It is useful at least to check that any realisable value is not greater than the economic value. A second reason is the inherent uncertainty of economic values. The advantage of considering realisable values is that it gives some indication of the extent of the loss if expectations about the earnings of the firm are disappointed. However, the relative importance of realisable values depends upon the control the shareholder has over the firm. Shareholders will only be in a position to enforce the sale of the firm's assets or their redeployment if they are planning to own a controlling interest in the firm.

Realisable values are not easy to calculate in practice because the information typically available in the published financial statements is expressed in terms of historic cost, sometimes adjusted upwards following a revaluation. Furthermore, such a valuation only reveals the values of individual assets and not what value might result from them being grouped together.

Asset value analysis is often considered to be most suitable for:

- Asset rich companies, especially after prolonged asset appreciation
- Situations where cash flows are unpredictable or negative
- Situations where asset revaluation has not been conducted for many years
- Turnaround situations
- Break up situations (unbundling).

4.6 Competitive Advantage Period (CAP)

In our experience, the most important challenge in creating value is to understand that it is about having and maintaining a competitive advantage. What the shareholder value methods like free cash flow permit is the measurement of value, making it happen is quite another matter. As we will illustrate, the challenge is to be better than the competition in some way, such that the goods and services provided have a higher perceived value to customers. The same is also arguably true for the perceived value of the shares to shareholders.

How the value of a business can be estimated using the free cash flow approach focusing upon a number of key value drivers was demonstrated in Chapter 3. This value consisted of that from the planning period and an assumed period beyond, known as the continuing period. In the illustration in Chapter 3, the value from the continuing period, the terminal value, represented

72% (£104 /£145) of the total corporate value and, as such, the size of this proportion typically represents a major cause for concern. If the time horizon is extended this proportion falls, but it then raises the 'million dollar question' ' how far out is it relevant to go?' The length of the planning period, together with the issue of competitive advantage and the Competitive Advantage Period (CAP), that period over which a firm enjoys a competitive advantage, is the subject matter of the remainder of this chapter. Before this discussion, it is useful for us to try and define competitive advantage and to put it into context with the other main area for consideration in the next chapter, the cost of capital.

One simple starting point for understanding competitive advantage is that it is achieved when the economic return on capital is greater than the cost of that capital. Imagine you run a successful business that has achieved a competitive advantage because of the reputation you have developed. The result should be that you will be achieving an economic return on the capital invested over and above the cost of that capital. New entrants will be attracted to your market, such that if you do not sustain the achieved returns your competitive advantage will be eroded. Without effort to sustain this competitive advantage, your return could fall such that you only achieve an economic return equal to the cost of the capital invested or, even worse, below. As you will see, this thinking is developed in terms of trying to assess the CAP, but information is also required about the cost of capital. The cost of capital can be seen as a benchmark against which to assess the economic return on capital invested, hence we need to have some understanding of its estimation.

4.7 *Relationship between CAP and Terminal Value (TV)*

As will be illustrated, there is often confusion between the planning period and the CAP, and the two are not necessarily the same. In reality, most valuation models use a planning period over which it is assumed that a return on capital is earned in excess of the cost of capital.

Figure 4.4: Relationship between planning period and terminal value

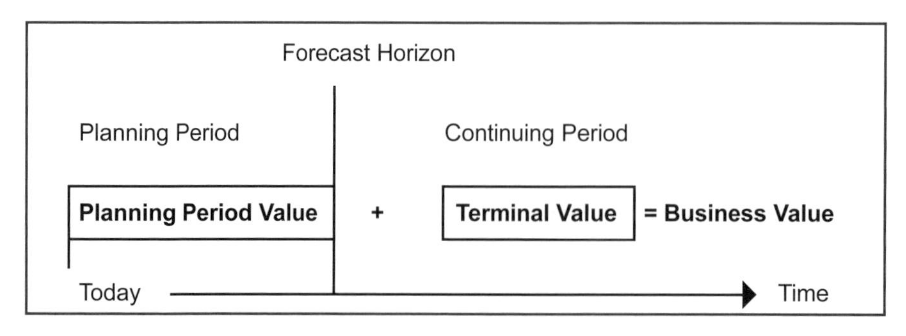

As illustrated in the example in the last chapter, a common approach is to forecast over a finite time period, like five years, and then to capture any remaining value assumed to arise in a perpetuity calculation. The logic behind this is that once the market has been established, cash receipts can be viewed as being potentially indefinite, as long as necessary replacement investment in fixed assets or other areas, like marketing or research and development expenditure, is undertaken to maintain an existing position. The use of a perpetuity calculation is convenient because it means that cash flows do not have to be estimated forever. However, blind reliance upon a standard period for assessing free cash flows and the adoption of a perpetuity calculation to capture value thereafter is inadequate. It is essential to look for ways of capturing future value as realistically as possible and to recognise that different business units may well have different time horizons over which they need to consider their long term strategic plans. The CAP is yet another variable in any valuation and can be considered to be a vital issue to assess. Unfortunately, whilst the principle underpinning its importance is understood, its estimation in practice is not. Quite simply, this is because its assessment is based upon a good deal of qualitative judgement and it is difficult to be accurate in its determination. Often less energy is expended in its determination than with other issues, which fall more readily within the financial specialist's comfort zone and, unfortunately, there are no easy answers to this issue about what is an appropriate CAP. Certainly, this chapter does not suggest a simple solution, but it does offer some guidelines based upon both theory and practice.

4.8 The Competitive Advantage Period (CAP) and strategic theory

As indicated, the CAP is the time during which a company is expected to generate returns on incremental investment that exceeds its cost of capital. Economic theory suggests that competitive forces will eventually drive returns down to the cost of capital over time. In other words, if a company earns returns above the cost of capital, it will attract competitors into the industry, the consequence of which will be a reduction in industry returns.

The concept of CAP is not new and has existed in the finance literature for many years, although not necessarily under that name. It has been labelled variously, examples of which are 'value growth duration' and 'T'. For example, it was formalised by Miller and Modigliani (1961) through their seminal work on valuation.

A number of strategic approaches that will be reviewed in the following sections have been developed that can, in principle, be applied to determine the length of the competitive advantage period.

Understanding the external context

One approach commonly quoted within the context of business valuation is that associated with the 'five forces' framework developed by Michael Porter (1980). The competitive period can be explained using five forces identified by Porter and illustrated in Figure 4.5.

Figure 4.5: Porters' five forces

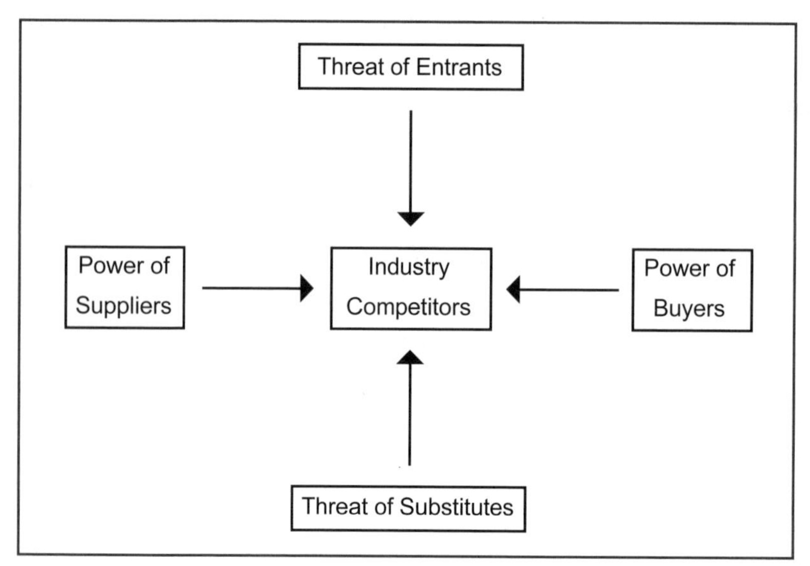

A company's competitive advantage may be threatened by potential entrants on the one hand and the possibility of substitute products on the other. It will also be affected by the relative power of suppliers and buyers and by the degree of competitive rivalry within the industry in which it exists.

In establishing the length of the competitive advantage period, a company's management needs to be aware of these forces. It may be aware of certain potential entrants to the market but it may also know that the barriers to entry are such that it will take a new entrant to the industry four or five years before it becomes a serious threat. Similarly, it may be aware that in the market from which it buys its most important raw materials, mergers and takeovers are taking place, which will make the suppliers' market less competitive and raw materials more expensive. Again, it is a question of judging the length of time over which the suppliers' prices will rise.

Although the contribution by Porter has been invaluable, there has been considerable interest in terms of what makes firms that operate within the same industry different. There is evidence to suggest that the performance achieved by an organisation depends more upon its relative performance within an industry rather than the industry sector in which it operates. For example, one analysis of the returns of a large sample of American firms by reference to their profitability in different industries produced the results summarised in Table 4. 1.

Table 4.1: Contributions to variance of profits across business units

	%
Corporate ownership	0.8
Industry effects	8.3
Cyclical effects	7.8
Business unit specific effects	46.4
Unexplained factors[11]	36.7
Source: Rumelt, 1991	

By far the largest contributor to explaining differences in profits is business unit specific effects, which account for 46.4% of the contribution to variance of profits. In other words, there are no systematically successful firms or industries, but there are systematically successful business units. These are the businesses that enjoy competitive advantages and outperform their competitors year by year.

The evidence, therefore, suggests that the performance achieved by an organisation depends more upon its relative performance within an industry than the industry itself. In other words, good relative performance within an industry translates into the generation of superior returns. Further work in this area has stimulated the view that this relative performance relates to core (distinctive) capabilities that can give businesses an edge.

Analysis of the internal context

Porter also outlined a framework for value chains, the underlying principle of this framework being that all tasks performed by a business organisation can be classified into 9 broad categories:

[11] Sometimes referred to as the X-factor.

- Five primary activities: inbound logistics, operations, outbound logistics, marketing, sales \ and service, plus
- Four support activities: firm infrastructure, human resource management, technology development and procurement.

Many adaptations of the value chain framework have emerged over time. One potentially useful variant is illustrated in Figure 4.6.

Figure 4.6: Value chain

Upstream	Midstream	Downstream	Final Custom
Suppliers of basic inputs raw materials, energy, parts. Research and development	First intermediary final manufacturing stages. Different stages of assembly and up to finishing.	Primary customers in distribution-branders, wholesalers, stockists, retailers.	Final customer or end user.

Since the value chain is composed of the set of activities performed by a business, it provides an effective way to diagnose the position of a business against its major competitors. Using the approach, it is possible to define the foundation for actions aimed at sustaining a competitive advantage, as opposed to the forces which determine industry attractiveness to the business. The latter are largely external and uncontrollable by the firm, whereas the activities within the value chain framework constitute the foundation of the controllable factors to achieve competitive superiority.

Kay (1993) has identified the following four types of distinctive capability:

1. Reputation
2. Architecture
3. Innovation
4. Strategic assets.

Reputation

Reputation enables a company to charge higher prices, or gain larger market share at a competitive price, for a functionally equivalent product. Examples of companies quoted by Kay for whom reputation is important are Lloyds TSB and Sainsbury's, the UK food retailing supermarket chain.

Architecture

Architecture can be viewed in terms of a unique structure of relationships in or around the company that is between the company and its suppliers. Via the development of a strategic architecture, an organisation should be able to commit the technical and production linkages across business units which will build upon distinct skills and capabilities that cannot be matched or easily replicated by other organisations. Examples of companies held as having strategic architecture as a distinctive capability are Marks and Spencer and Benetton.

Innovation

Innovation is seen as being a very strong source of competitive advantage, but one that is difficult to sustain because of the potential for replication. Patent protection can play an important part in reaping the benefits from innovation, but may be difficult to achieve in practice. One noteworthy exploiter of this approach has been the pharmaceuticals industry.

Strategic Assets

The ownership of strategic assets differs from the others because it is the product of the market or regulatory environment rather than of a company's distinctive achievement. An example is a concession to exploit a resource or an exclusive right to supply as a product of the market, or regulatory environment [12].

These four distinctive capabilities can also be seen in terms of the core competency approach associated with Prahalad and Hamel (1990). This focused upon the development of a strategic architecture to identify and commit the technical and production linkages across business units so as to build upon distinct skills and capabilities that cannot be matched or easily replicated by other organisations.

These competencies can be thought of as being the collective learning of the organisation, particularly how to coordinate diverse production skills and integrate multiple streams of technology. Because of diversified information systems, patterns of communications, managerial rewards and so on, there will be an inevitable fragmentation of core competencies

[12] Associated with this grouping may be many distinctive capabilities often overlooked, like those associated with the skill of the workforce

and an impetus for learning will be required.

In principle, Kay's four distinctive capabilities should enable an organisation to achieve what are often regarded as being major sources of competitive advantage size, market share, market selection and market position. However, they will continue to add value only if their capability and distinctiveness are sustainable. In fact, one key issue Kay considered was the sustainability of these four distinctive capabilities. On the basis of his research, Kay suggested reputation as generally being the easiest to sustain, strategic assets as being sustainable over long periods only if there are no changes in regulation or market conditions and innovation as being the most difficult. In fact, specific sources of sustainable competitive advantage have been identified in academic research. One example of such research was by Aaker (1989)(see Table 4.2), which although a little dated, provides a useful illustration. Aaker considered what the managers of 248 distinct businesses oriented towards service and hi-tech businesses thought were the sustainable competitive advantages of their businesses. He found that sustainable sources of competitive advantage varied from business to business and arose from more than one source. This indicates that it is not sufficient for a business to base its strategy on a single source of competitive advantage and that the challenge for both management and investors is to be able to identify the sources for any given business. What is more, and is so often overlooked, is that identifiable sources of competitive advantage do not necessarily translate into a CAP for valuation purposes. For there to be a CAP for such purposes, there has to be sustainability. If a firm cannot sustain its competitive advantage, then by definition it will be unable to generate future returns in excess of the cost of capital, quite simply because others will be able to enter the market and erode excess returns.

The somewhat dated nature of this research also illustrates one other very important point, competitive advantage is not static! What is a source of competitive advantage at one point in time may well be a prerequisite at a later date. For example, today would you regard a reputation for quality to be a competitive advantage or a prerequisite for survival? This is a debatable point, but that is part of the challenge – being quite clear about what is a source of competitive advantage and striving to take advantage of it!

Table 4.2: Sustainable competitive advantages in 248 businesses

	Hightech	Service	Other	Total
1 Reputation for Quality	26	50	29	105
2 Customer Service/Product Support	23	40	15	78
3 Name Recognition/High Profile	8	42	21	71
4 Retain Good Management & Engineering Staff	17	43	5	65
5 Low Cost Production	17	15	21	53
6 Financial Resources	11	26	14	51
7 Customer Orientation/Feedback Market Research	13	26	9	48
8 Product Line Breadth	11	25	17	47
9 Technical Superiority	30	7	9	46
10 Installed Base of Satisfied Customers	19	22	4	45
11 Segmentation/Focus	7	22	16	45
12 Product Characteristics/Differentiation	12	15	10	37
13 Continuing Production Innovation	15	20	10	35
14 Market Share	12	14	9	35
15 Size/Location of Distribution	10	12	13	34
16 Low Price/High Value Offering	6	20	6	32
17 Knowledge of Business	2	25	4	31
18 Pioneer/Early Entrant in Industry	11	11	6	28
19 Efficient, Flexible Production/Operations Adaptable to Customers	4	17	4	26
20 Effective Sales Force	10	9	4	23
21 Overall Marketing Skills	7	9	7	23
22 Shared Vision/Culture	5	13	4	22
23 Strategic Goals	6	7	9	22
24 Powerful Well Known Parent	7	7	6	20
25 Location	0	10	10	20
26 Effective Advertising /Image	5	6	6	17
27 Enterprising/Entrepreneurial	4	3	6	11
28 Good Co ordination	3	2	5	10
29 Engineering Research Development	8	2	0	10
30 Short term Planning	2	1	5	8
31 Good Distributor Relations	2	4	1	7
32 Other	6	20	5	31
Total	**322**	**552**	**283**	**1157**
Number of Businesses	**68**	**113**	**67**	**248**
Average Number of Sustainable Competitive Advantages	**4.73**	**4.88.**	**4.22**	**4.65**

4.9 Introducing the dynamic of time through life cycles

Many other sources of the potential underpinnings of CAP can also be found in the literature. For example, Williams (1985) has extended the Porter framework by incorporating the time dimension into value chain analysis. He has classified industry environments into three types:

- Class I industries, characterised by competitively stable value chains, which over time are relatively unchanged
- Class II industries, characterised by smoothly evolving value chains, which are reinforced through scale based learning
- Class III industries, characterised by dynamic and unstable value chains, which accelerate rapidly to maturity.

In an alternative view of the product life cycle Ansoff (1984) argued for an approach that considers the need provided by a product rather than the product itself. This equates with looking at a demand life cycle, capturing ongoing, changing levels of need. Such needs are satisfied by technology and Ansoff used 'calculating power' as an example of a need that has existed for thousands of years. The changing level of need is represented by a demand life cycle, so in terms of calculating power, the need was initially met by using fingers (as reflected in the Arabic numeric system); then by abacuses; later by slide rules; then mechanical adding machines; electronic calculators; and currently by computers. Each technological development offered enhanced benefits such as speed, cost, capacity or increased facilities. Ansoff suggested these to be demand technology cycles, with an 'S' shaped format suggesting emergence, rapid growth, slower growth, maturity and finally decline.

Within each demand technology cycle there will be a succession of Product forms that satisfy the specific need at the time. Ansoff used the hand calculator as an example. Initially, it took the form of a large plastic box with a small screen and numerical operating keys. Its performance was limited to four tasks addition, subtraction, multiplication and division. This was soon superseded by smaller hand held calculators performing many more mathematical and scientific functions. These in turn were succeeded by yet smaller versions and at much lower costs.

These cycles in the development of calculators suggests some interesting implications. If a company concentrates its product development, research and development and marketing efforts in a narrow aspect of the overall cycle, it may miss the opportunity to expand its market base. What is more, it may also overlook the fact that the demand technology cycle may be facing obsolescence. Companies need to decide in which demand technology to invest and when to move into a new technology. For some companies in some industries the choice is difficult as the demand technology cycles tend to have very short effective life spans, while others may become obsolescent very slowly and merge with the next generation. This means that in reality, CAP decisions may be very complex.

Whilst it is widely acknowledged that products go through cycles, it is not well recognised that business designs also go through cycles and reach obsolescence. A business design refers to the totality of how a company selects its customers, defines and differentiates its offerings, defines the tasks it will perform itself and those it will outsource, configures its resources, goes to market, create utility for customers and captures profit. Slywotzky (1996) has adopted the term value migration to illustrate that a business design can exist in only one of three states: value inflow, stability and value outflow. These states emphasise the importance of relative value creation power, with a view to satisfying customer priorities better than competitors, thereby earning superior returns. More specifically, these three states are:

- Value inflow. In the initial phase, a company starts to absorb value from other parts of its industry because its business design proves superior in satisfying customer priorities. Microsoft and EDS are among companies currently reckoned to be experiencing the value inflow phase
- Stability. This is characterised by business designs that are well matched to customer priorities and by overall competitive equilibrium. Companies such as Dupont are considered to be in this phase
- Value outflow. In the third phase, value starts to move away from an organisation's traditional activities towards business designs that meet evolving customer priorities more effectively.

The analysis of value migration can be very useful and can be thought of in terms of the three stages illustrated in Figure 4.7.

Figure 4.7: Three stages of value migration

- Between industries, for example, telecommunications, entertainment and computer
- Between companies in the same industry, for example, BT, Energis, Vodaphone, Cellnet and so on
- Within a single company, for example, fixed lines, mobile, multimedia.

Focusing upon value migration at the industry level is a useful first step because it creates a context in which to evaluate individual business designs. It is not that value disappears, but that it moves rapidly at times towards new activities and skills and towards new business designs whose superiority in meeting customer priorities makes profit possible. To meet the challenge of value migration, managers must ask - 'Where in my industry can a profit be made? How is that changing? What is driving that change? What can my organisation do about it?' Beneath these questions lies a more fundamental inquiry 'What is the changing pattern of what customers need, want and are willing to pay for and what business designs respond most effectively to this changing pattern?' In every industry there is a limited set of key moves that allows advantage to be taken of the next cycle of value growth. Every business design has a limited value creation life cycle. Managers must act to create the next viable business design. The key questions are 'Which move should I make? What future business design element will be most important? What future competitors do I have to worry about most? This is where scenarios can be a very useful tool for helping to answer these questions.

Figure 4.7: Summary of strategic perspectives relevant to the CAP

Three broad areas of focus	Strategic tools
Understanding the external context within which a business operates, and performance relative to others within the industry.	Porter's Five forces for industry analysis.
Analysis of the internal activities that comprise businesses and sources of sustainable competitive advantage.	Value chain of activities, distinctive capabilities and core competencies.
Synthesis of the external and internal perspective through the introduction of the dynamic of time and business as a game in a constantly evolving landscape and changing rules.	Life cycle analysis of products and technology. Three stages of value migration for industries and businesses.

4.10 Estimating CAP in practice

In determining CAP in practice, the assumption used about the time horizon will have a significant impact upon the size of any Terminal Value (TV). TV, that value arising from beyond the assumed CAP, known as the 'continuing period', is often a source of considerable concern in many valuations. This is important because it frequently accounts for a significant proportion of total value. In fact, in some circumstances, like a start up or a development in a new market, it may account for nearly all of the total value. This was confirmed by Copeland, Koller, Murrin (1994), which demonstrated that over an eight year forecast period the terminal value in four industries accounted for anywhere between 56 percent to 125 percent of total value.

Research has revealed that five years is popular as a planning period estimate for many UK companies. When compared crudely alongside market PE multiples that are much higher using current after tax earnings attributable to shareholders, there is the potential for a 'value gap'. One way of preventing a value gap is for a longer term planning period to be used, but this raises the immediate concern that planning for just five years can often be difficult enough. The fact that management looks typically only to a limited future period, say five years, is the real problem and there should be explicit recognition that the continuing period and the terminal value associated with it as being something directly within management's control. It is not a residual, but one of the most critical parts of the 'value future'. As such, it needs to be owned and actively managed, even though it may deal with a time horizon too distant to analyse prescriptively. If the valuation of this time period is seen to relate to the selected planning period, it is much more than a passive residual. In fact, it can be looked upon as being the consequence of actions taken over the time period falling within the comfort zone of management action.

Approaches for dealing with the CAP (and hence the terminal value) rely upon estimating Market Implied CAP (MICAP) and applying scenario thinking. Scenario thinking tries to ensure that short and long term pressures upon the business environment are not overlooked. While this approach is invaluable in freeing thinking, the all important question arises - 'Is it possible to estimate CAP empirically? This will now be considered with reference to the estimation of MICAP.

4.11 Market Implied CAP (MICAP)

This approach can be thought of as involving the following steps. First, a proxy for unbiased market expectations of six value drivers (other than CAP) is required, assuming use of a seven value driver model, that is, sales growth rate, operating profit margin, cash tax rate, fixed capital needs, working capital needs, cost of capital and CAP. Second, a valuation model is built, including a terminal value calculation based upon an assumed perpetuity. Last, the time period over which the forecast is undertaken is 'stretched' as many years as is necessary to achieve the company's current market price for its shares, that is, the period over which the return on new investment stays above WACC is stretched to achieve the market capitalisation. The resulting time period is the assumed CAP.

Think about the calculation of MICAP another way. In Chapter 3, we demonstrated how the share price for a business could be estimated using the 7 value driver approach. In effect, we assumed one unknown, this being the share price. Quite simply, the mathematics can be reversed. If the share price of a competitor is known and estimates can be obtained for all value drivers except time, the equation can be solved to identify how far out the planning period must be extended to determine it.

There is a belief that lengthening the CAP in this way can help to explain the X factor and a good illustration of this has been provided by Mauboussin and Johnson (1997)[13]. Based upon a study of a selection of companies within the packaged food industry in the September 1982 to August 1989 period, they found using the approach described above that the CAP for this group roughly doubled in the seven year period. In fact, this time period corresponded with most companies streamlining their business portfolios, cutting costs, increasing vital marketing expenditure and increasing cash flows.

Whilst this approach is useful as a practical tool, particularly from the perspective of the external analyst, it does have some limitations that may be summarised as follows:

- It presupposes that the market price of the share is an appropriate reflection of future prospects, but there may be a radical shift in prospect that has not been detected by the market. Many acquisitions have been concerned with business transformations not reflected in the share price until the occurrence of a predatory move

[13] Unexplained factors in Rumelt's research, see Table 4.1

- What happens when there is no share price, for example, for a private company or division/business unit? In this case there is no share price against which to 'stretch'. In our experience this can be dealt with effectively by undertaking market implied duration stretch on a carefully selected set of peer group companies, combined with scenario analysis.

An illustration of MICAP and its application is provided in Chapter 8, Section 8.17 relating to the initial public offering of shares in Jordan Telecom in 2002.

4.12 Interrelationship between the planning period, the CAP and the terminal value

As mentioned earlier in this chapter there are no easy answers to what is an appropriate CAP, in fact any decisions concerning the CAP cannot be taken in isolation. As Figure 4.8 shows, the planning period adopted is related to the CAP which, in turn, is related to the terminal value calculation. Similarly, the terminal value calculation used makes certain assumptions regarding the CAP that, in turn, influences the planning period chosen.

Figure 4.8 Dynamic interrelationship between planning period, CAP and terminal value

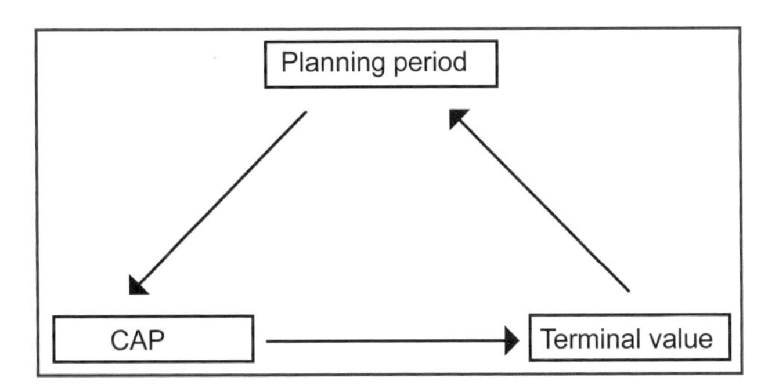

Two practical possibilities exist for the relationship between the planning period and the CAP:

- First, the planning period is equal to the CAP, which implies that there is no new value created beyond it because the returns on new capital have fallen to the cost of capital
- Second, the planning period is less than the CAP and hence there is new value being created beyond it that needs to be captured by the valuation. As will be illustrated in the next chapter, there are alternative possible approaches that can be used to take account of this additional value.

CHAPTER 5
ECONOMIC PROFIT AND PERFORMANCE MEASUREMENT

Chapter Preview

This chapter will enable you to understand:

- **The calculation of Economic Profit approaches such as Econom ic Value Added (EVA®) and Economic Profit and how they can be linked to conventional measures of performance.**
- **The use of Economic Profit as a performance measure and its linkage to the calculation of the value of a business.**
- **The distinction between the accounting perspective, as ex pressed in traditional financial statements, and the economic perspective used in ascertaining value and value creation.**
- **Performance metrics used to ascertain the value being created by a business.**

5.1 Introduction

In previous chapters it has been shown how by using value drivers a free cash flow forecast can be estimated and the total value generated from such a free cash flow estimate for the planning period and beyond can be calculated. However, this is by no means the only way in which strategic value can be expressed or calculated. While the measurement of value is an essential starting point for developing a truly effective value based management approach, it does not have to be calculated using free cash flow analysis. A number of alternative measures are available, of which economic profit is a good example. The advantage of using measures like economic profit is that they can be linked to performance measurement and executive compensation. However, do be aware that it is not the case that one must select either free cash flow or economic profit.

While the different measures can be shown to produce the same result in principle, whether this is the case in practice will be dependent upon the assumptions made. Often differences do arise for many reasons we will explore later, not least of which is the purpose for which the measure is used.

5.2 Economic Profit and Economic Value Added (EVA®)

EVA® is used to analyse a business in terms of the economic profit earned in a given time period after deducting all expenses, including the opportunity cost of capital employed. In other words, a business is only 'truly' profitable in an economic sense if it generates a return in excess of that required by its providers of funds, that is, shareholders and debt holders.

Economic profit is not a new idea and Alfred Sloan, the patriarch of the General Motors Corporation, is reckoned to have adopted the principles of economic profit in the 1920s and the General Electric Co. coined the term 'residual income' in the 1950s, which it used to assess the performance of its decentralised divisions (Mills, Sawers 1999).

Economic profit recognises that the one major cost that the conventional income statement account does not take into account is the cost of the capital used in generating profit. Consequently with economic profit, from the net operating profit after tax (NOPAT) a capital charge is deducted based on the product of the capital invested in the business and the cost of capital.

Economic Profit = NOPAT (Invested Capital x Cost of Capital)

For example, given a NOPAT of £1m, Invested Capital of £10 m and a cost of capital of 5%, the Economic Profit = £1m £500,000, that is, £500,000. Alternatively, it can be expressed as Economic Profit = (NOPAT% - WACC%) x Invested Capital that is, the spread approach, where NOPAT% = (NOPAT/ Opening Invested Capital) x 100. As shown in Figure 5.1 NOPAT can be equivalent to free cash flow under certain circumstances.

Figure 5. 1: NOPAT as cash flow

NOPAT can be equated with cash flow when it represents the constant level of cash that is generated by the business after making only replacement investment (but NOT growth investment). This is the investment necessary to maintain the cash flow generating capability of the existing assets. NOPAT equivalence with free cash flow can be shown to be so using the example in Table 3.3 in Chapter 3. We start with EBITDA as follows:

	Year 1
EBITDA	31.5
less Depreciation	-10.0
EBIT	21.5
Add back Depreciation	10.0
Less Cash tax	-9.4
Operating Cash Flow after tax	22.1
Less Replacement investment (Depreciation used a proxy)	-10.0
Maintenance Free Cash Flow after tax	12.1

NOPAT is calculated as EBITDA less depreciation less cash tax that is, £31.5m - £l0m - £9.4m = £12.1m. Thus the maintenance free cash flow after tax for year 1 is exactly the same figure as NOPAT for year 1. Of course, this is only so if replacement investment is the same as depreciation.

What may be the attraction of using economic profit type approaches? There are arguably many, but there is one that seems to be particularly noteworthy. Many organisations have developed performance assessment approaches that relate the profit generated in a given time period to the asset base or capital employed in generating it.

As illustrated in Figure 5.2, and as discussed earlier in Chapter 1, this Return on Assets approach can be developed as a framework for assessing company performance along a number of dimensions. Relatively poor performance in terms of the Return on Assets generated in a given time period can be viewed in terms of margins (Return on Sales) and asset utilisation (Sales Generation). This Return on Assets can also be linked to capital structure (Gearing or Leverage) and the markets perception of performance (Price Earnings and Market Book).

Figure 5.2. Hierarchy of ratios

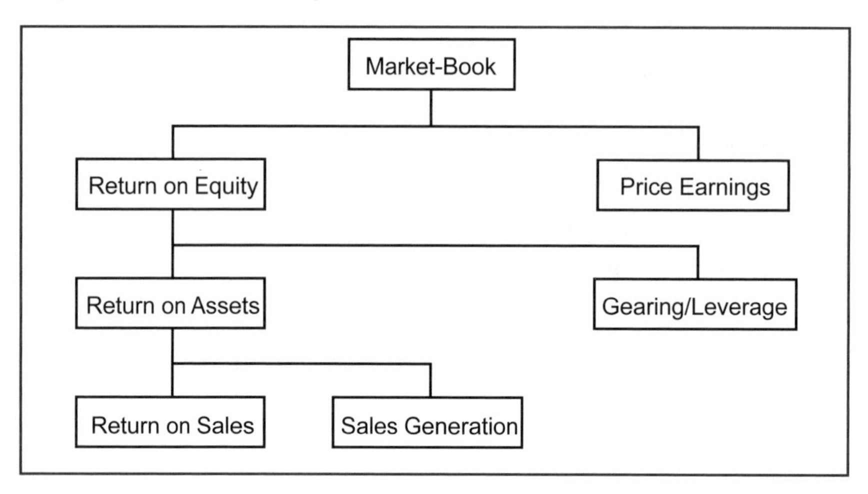

It can take a long time to implement performance assessment measures within companies, a point that may so often be under-estimated. As illustrated in Figure 5.3, the advantage of economic profit type approaches is that they can be linked to such conventional performance assessment frameworks.

Figure 5.3: Linkage between conventional financial ratios and economic profit approach

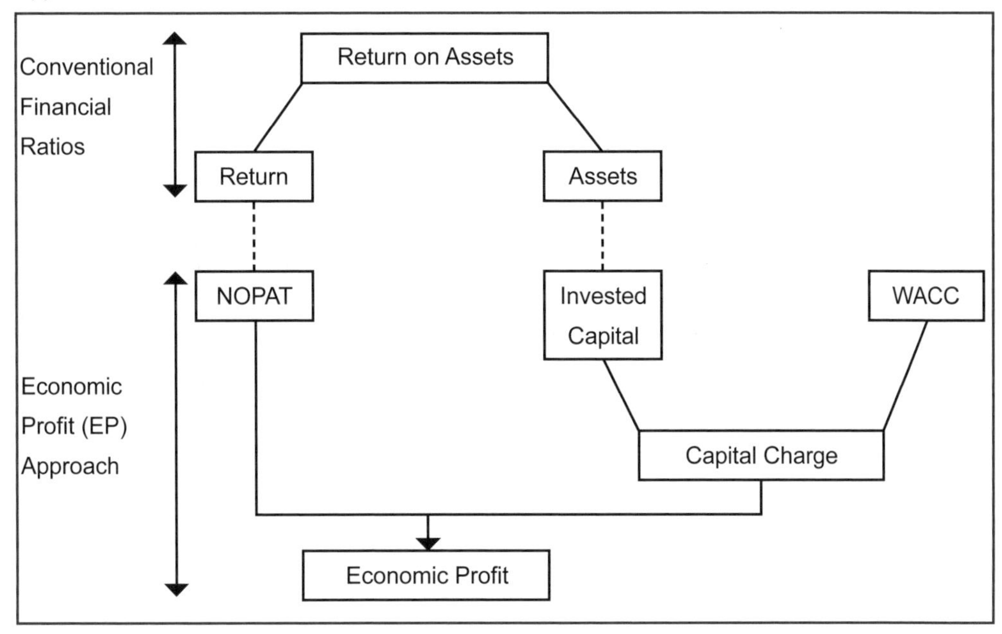

5.3 Linking economic profit and valuation calculations

Economic profit can be used not only to assess period by period performance but also for purposes of valuation. Economic profit is typically calculated over a specified time period, such as a year, with a positive economic profit figure signalling to management that value has been or will be created during the period in question, while a negative economic profit figure is indicative of value destruction. Economic profit (EP) can also be used for purposes of valuation as follows:

$$\text{Value} = \frac{\text{Invested}}{\text{Capital}} + \frac{EP_1}{(1+r)} + \frac{EP_2}{(1+r)^2} + \frac{EP_3}{(1+r)^3} + \frac{EP_n}{(1+r)_n}$$

In simple terms, to link economic profit with value, the economic profit for each time period is estimated in the manner shown earlier, discounted at r (typically the weighted average cost of capital) and added to the Invested Capital. The actual mechanics of this calculation are illustrated in Table 5.1, which draws upon the data provided in Table 3.3 from Chapter 3.

Table 5. 1 : EP Calculation

Year	1	2	3	4	5	Beyond
	£m	£m	£m	£m	£m	£m
Opening Capital	125.0	128.0	131.2	134.6	138.0	141.6
IFCI	1.5	1.6	1.7	1.7	1.8	0.0
IWCI	1.5	1.6	1.7	1.7	1.8	0.0
Closing Capital	128.0	131.2	134.6	138.0	141.6	141.6
EBITDA	31.5	33.1	34.7	36.5	38.3	38.3
less Depreciation	10.0	10.0	10.0	10.0	10.0	10.0
less Cash Tax	9.4	9.9	10.4	10.9	11.5	11.5
NOPAT	12.1	13.2	14.3	15.6	16.8	16.8
NOPAT/Opening Capital %	9.7	10.3	10.9	11.6	12.2	11.9
Cost of Capital %	10.0	10.0	10.0	10.0	10.0	10.0
Performance Spread %	- 0.3	0.3	0.9	1.6	2.2	1.9
Economic Profit (EP)[15]	- 0.4	0.4	1.2	2.1	3.0	2.6
Cost of Capital %						10.0
Perpetuity						26.0
Discount Factor	0.909	0.826	0.751	0.683	0.621	0.621
Present Value of SVA	-0.4	0.3	0.9	1.4	1.9	16.4
MVA[16]	20.5					
Opening Capital	125					
Business Value	145.5					
add Marketable Securities	0					
Corporate Value	145.5					
less Market Value of Debt	20					
Strategic Value	125.5					
Number of Shares (m)	100					
Value Per Share	£1.26					

The calculated value per share above - £1.26 – is the same as the value calculated from free cash flows in Table 3.6.

In Table 5.1 there is an initial negative EP because of the negative performance spread, that is, NOPAT/Opening Capital(%) is lower than the Cost of Capital (%). Thereafter, the EPs are

[15] Economic Profit = (NOPAT% - WACC%) x Invested Capital, that is, for year 1 (9.7% - 10.0%) x 125 = -0.4

[16] MVA is the sum of all EPs and equivalent to the Net Present Value (NPV)

positive over the five year period, resulting in a cumulative EP over years 1 through to 5 of £4.1m. In the period 'Beyond', the EP has been valued as a perpetuity providing a value of £16.4m (£2.64m/10% x 0.621), by far the largest contributor to total value; the sum total of the Present Value of EP numbers including the perpetuity results in what is known as the Market Value Added, or MVA.

To use the EP approach as a valuation method that can be readily compared with the free cash flow model we have developed, the Opening Capital must be added to the MVA, the result representing the Business Value. In the absence of any marketable securities, this also represents the Corporate (Enterprise) Value. An estimate of the Strategic Value of the equity is found by deducting the market value of debt. If the resulting £125.5m of Strategic Value is divided by the 100m ordinary shares in issue, the result is a value per share of £1.26.

5.4 The economic versus the accounting perspective

There is an important difference between the economic profit perspective and the traditional accounting perspective portrayed in financial statements that needs to be considered at this point. The traditional accounting perspective can be traced back to the 1300's and focuses on stewardship reporting. It explains to investors what has been done with their money and is principally backward looking. In particular, it assesses how much of the wealth created by the business has been realised in the form of tangible assets. It can be viewed as being a static model, concerned with the allocation of costs and revenues between relatively short time frames that draws upon accounting concepts. By comparison, economic profit type measures are more often concerned with the future economic profits that are likely to be generated over the life of a business and the risk associated with them.

The importance of the economic perspective becomes very clear within the context of ensuring that the opportunity cost of capital is achieved, that is what return would have been achieved on their investment in their next best use. Investors of all kinds require that at least their opportunity cost of capital is returned and this cannot be known unless economic returns are related to some notion of economic value. The need for such adjustments can be seen by looking at the market value versus the book value of companies listed on the stock market. For example, research in 1996 carried out by the Securities and Exchange Commission in the USA revealed that most companies going through mergers and acquisitions in the US during the period 1981 1993 were valued at between 2 9 times their book value. Software, communications and pharmaceutical companies were particularly highly valued, while banks, utilities and car companies were valued at the lower end of the range. Differences between the two groupings were attributable to their respective growth prospects at this time.

The EP calculations that have been undertaken for the example company were based upon the accounting perspective. However, it is possible to move from the accounting to an economic perspective by making adjustments to the accounting statements to produce estimates of the economic returns and the economic capital associated with their generation. Figure 5.4 illustrates the linkages between the two views of the value of a business. The underlying economic transactions of a business, that is, in cash flow terms are converted into accounting terms through the application of Generally Accepted Accounting Principles (GAAP).

Figure 5.4: The linkages between the accounting and economic perspective

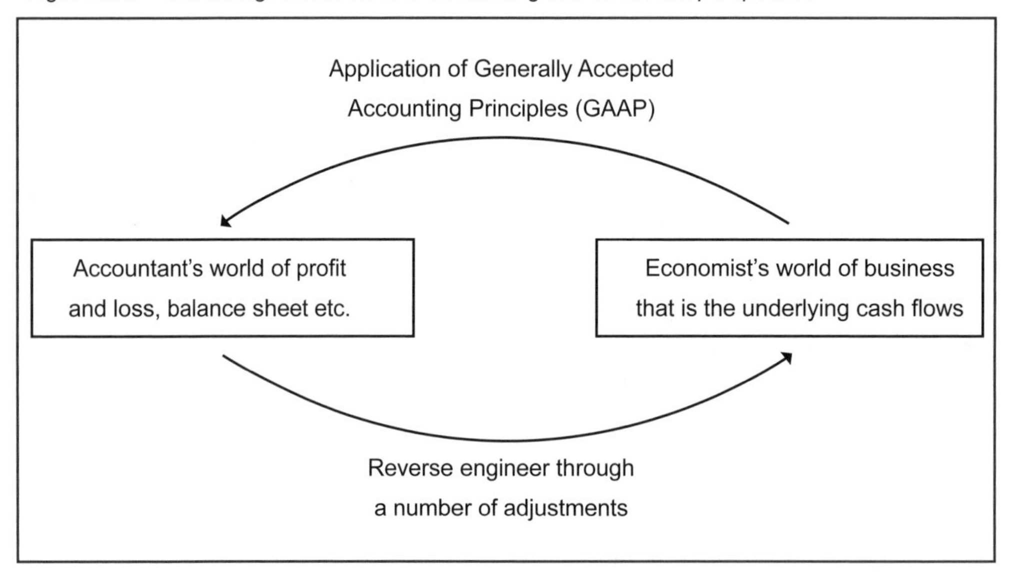

There are numerous potential adjustments that can, in principle, be made to convert accounting statements into their underlying economic form. These adjustments are often referred to as value based adjustments. In practice, a handful of adjustments may be sufficient and some of the more noteworthy adjustments are shown in the Figure 5.5.

Figure 5.5: Adjustments from an accounting to an economic perspective

Goodwill	Cumulative value of previously written off goodwill is added back to the assets and depreciated.
R&D expense	Capitalised as a long term asset and depreciated.
Cumulative unusual losses/gains after tax	Treated as an asset to be written off over the future periods that are expected to benefit.
Operating leases	The present value of non capitalised operating leases are added back to fixed assets and depreciated.

To be more specific about the effect of such value based adjustments, let us consider the effect in our example of a land revaluation. The advantage of considering such an adjustment is that it will impact only upon the balance sheet and not the income statement account. This is because land is not depreciated, only any property built on it. For the sake of simplicity, we will assume there is no such property and the Fixed Assets represent land. The impact of a revaluation of this land upon EP is illustrated in Table 5.2.

Table 5.2: Calculation of EP assuming a land revaluation

Year	1	2	3	4	5	Beyond
	£m	£m	£m	£m	£m	£m
Original Opening Capital	125					
Add: Land revaluation	25					
Opening Capital	150.0	153.0	156.2	159.6	163.0	166.6
IFCI	1.5	1.6	1.7	1.7	1.8	0.0
IWCI	1.5	1.6	1.7	1.7	1.8	0.0
Closing Capital	153.0	156.2	159.6	163.0	166.6	166.6
EBITDA	31.5	33.1	34.7	36.5	38.3	38.3
less Depreciation	10.0	10.0	10.0	10.0	10.0	10.0
less Cash Tax	9.4	9.9	10.4	10.9	11.5	11.5
NOPAT	12.1	13.2	14.3	15.6	16.8	16.8
NOPAT/Opening Capital (%)	8.1	8.6	9.2	9.8	10.3	10.1
Cost of Capital %	10.0	10.0	10.0	10.0	10.0	10.0
Performance Spread %	-2.0	-1.4	-0.8	-0.2	0.3	0.1
Strategic Value Added (SVA)	-3.0	-2.1	-1.2	-0.3	0.5	0.14
Cost of Capital %						10.0
Perpetuity						1.4
Discount Factor	0.909	0.826	0.751	0.683	0.621	0.621
Present Value of SVA	-2.7	-1.7	-1.0	-0.3	0.3	0.9
MVA	-4.5					
Opening Capital	150.0					
Business Value	145.5					
add Marketable Securities	0					
Corporate Value	145.5					
less Market Value of Debt	20.0					
Strategic Value	125.5					
Number of Shares (m)	100					
Strategic Value Per Share	£1.26					

The effect of a £25m land revaluation is to increase the capital invested. Given that the profit does not increase, this results in a lower NOPAT/Opening Capital (%). The cost of capital remains unchanged because it is calculated with reference to market values and not the information provided in the financial statements. The net result is a negative performance spread in Years 1 through 4 and very modest spreads thereafter. When the EPs are calculated and accumulated, the result is a negative MVA of £4.5m. How then can the same Strategic Value per share result? The answer is that the higher initial capital value is added. However, let us stand back and reflect upon the implications of this. Despite the changing profile of the EPs, the value of the business remains unchanged. This has important implications for managing the business, in that the original profile of EP numbers could prompt management to take one set of actions that would be diametrically opposite to those actions taken under the revised profile of EP numbers. Apparent management performance differs under the two scenarios and, it can be seen that in terms of providing a signal about the economic performance of the business, the figure for Invested Capital plays a significant role.

From a business valuation perspective, the value of a business appears to be independent of the opening amount of Invested Capital. This statement has to be accompanied by a word of caution in that the components that make up the value of the business are very different. For example, as Table 5.3 shows, while the total value is the same for both the base case and the adjusted base case, its composition is very different. Again, the signals for potential management action as a result of these differing components could be interpreted very differently.

Table 5.3: Comparison of valuation components

Base case			**Base case adjusted for revaluation**	
	£m	**%**	**£m**	**%**
Opening Invested Capital	125	86	150	103
Value of SVA for Years 1 - 5	4.1	3	-5.4	-4
Value of SVA beyond Year 5	16.4	11	0.9	1
Total	**145.5**	100	**145.5**	**100**

5.5 *Applying Economic Profit Principles Asia Hotels Limited*

The case of the Asia Hotels Limited can be used effectively to illustrate the use of EP. Asia Hotels Limited, is a listed company, but is closely held by its Directors and major shareholders who hold approximately 50% of outstanding shares. Initially limited to properties in Hong Kong, it diversified and embarked on an oversees expansion program and now has interests in projects in the United States, Australia, Indonesia, Thailand, the People's Republic of China, the Philippines and Vietnam. Its principal business comprises the ownership and management of prestigious hotel, commercial and residential properties in key destinations in Asia, Australia and the US.

A crisis in the SE Asia region had a major impact upon the company with its share price falling to HK$5.50 at the end of 2006. The company's reported financial position at that time was as is shown in Table 5.4.

Table 5.4: Asia Hotels Limited Summary of reported financial data

Balance Sheet as at December	**2006**	**2005**	**2004**	**2003**	**2002**
HK$ millions					
Net Assets	16,981	24,108	25,887	20,262	19,629
Shareholders' Equity	10,267	18,166	21,671	16,416	16,053
Ordinary Shares	578	581	586	539	539
Revaluation Reserves	8,210	14,211	16,762	13,189	13,155
Net Debt	6,689	5,406	3,873	3,597	3,398
Other data					
HK$ millions					
Sales	2,140	2,779	2,674	2,318	1,785
Share Price at period end [HK$]	5.50	6.40	14.60	11.20	8.95
Market Capitalisation at BS date	6,364	7,441	17,100	12,084	9,657
Number of Shares at BS date (millions)	1,157	1,163	1,171	1,079	1,079

At the point in time under review, the value of the business in 2006 looked at in terms of the market value of the equity, outside equity and other balances and net debt totalled HK$13,053 million, while net assets were HK$16,981 million. This corresponds with a negative Market Value Added (MVA) and indicates that the business is destroying value.

The equity (strategic) value of the business of HK$5.50 per share in free cash flow terms is summarised in Table 5.5.

Table 5.5: Strategic Value of Asia Hotels Limited

Period	**Free Cash Flow HK $millions**	**Present Value Factor**	**Present Value of Free Cash Flow HK $millions**
2007	746,976	0.9117	681,055
2008	915,424	0.8313	760,980
2009	1,110,824	0.7579	841,922
2010	1,337,488	0.6910	924,255
2011	1,600,418	0.6301	1,008,349
Beyond	14,280,777	0.6301	8,997,658
Business Value			13,214,220
Net Debt			- 6,689,000
Other Balances			- 162,000
Strategic Value			6,363,220
Number of Shares (m)			1,157,000
Strategic Value Per Share ($HK)			5.50

As demonstrated earlier, this strategic value can also be calculated using the Economic Profit (EP) approach as illustrated in Table 5.6.

Table 5.6: Economic Profit of Asia Hotels Limited

Period	Economic Return on Capital %	WACC %	Spread %	Capital Invested HK$ Millions	SVA HK$ millions	Present Value Factor	Present Value of SVA HK$ millions
2007	3.69	9.68	-5.99	16,981,000	-1,017,137	0.9117	-927,375
2008	4.60	9.68	-5.08	16,860,520	-856,305	0.8313	-711,835
2009	5.67	9.68	-4.01	16,720,763	-669,738	0.7579	-507,612
2010	6.94	9.68	-2.74	16,558,645	-453,322	0.6910	-313,263
2011	8.44	9.68	-1.22	16,370,589	-202,278	0.6301	-127,446
Beyond	8.56	9.68	-1.12	16,152,443	-1,871,666	0.6301	-1,179,250
MVA							-3,766,780
Opening Capital							16,981,000
Business Value							13,214,220
Net Debt							-6,689,000
Other Balances							-162,000
Strategic Value							6,363,220
Number of Shares (m)							1,157,000
Strategic Value Per Share ($HK)							5.50

This EP analysis demonstrates how the company is destroying value by generating an economic return on capital lower than the cost of capital. As indicated earlier in this Chapter, we need to ask whether the capital base is a realistic reflection of the economic capital invested. As indicated in the summary of financial performance in Table 5.4, the company has made substantial property revaluations. If you will recall from earlier, the effect of a revaluation upwards was to reduce the performance spread and EPs, while the value of the business remained the same. In this case the effect of revaluation downwards has been to decrease and, therefore, improve a negative MVA.

Key value drivers were identified for the company as being prices, investment in plant, property and equipment (PPE) and volumes (occupancy). There are likely to be major challenges in raising prices and volumes relative to PPE rationalisation. This might offer some potential for improving the negative performance spread, assuming of course that there is no expectation that property prices will rise again in the near future! Other action that might be contemplated is considered in Chapter 10.

5.6 Other performance measures

The importance of Invested Capital must be well understood in interpreting EP type calculations. As we have illustrated, the profile of EP numbers can vary substantially without the overall strategic value changing. The implications of this can be profound and could be political dynamite, particularly in a situation where the allocation of capital between business units is required. EP results might evoke quite the opposite reaction to that intended if there is a lack of belief or acceptance in the Invested Capital upon which they are based.

There has been some criticism of EP type measures on the basis that they discourage growth. The argument goes as follows. Except for the rare cases where an investment has an immediate payback, growth oriented managers can take a short term EP 'hit'. If this is the case it might encourage managers to milk the business because the easiest way to improve EP, at least in the short term, is by reducing and depreciating assets faster than earnings decline. Pursued for long enough, say three to five years, this can create a trap. Lack of investment can leave managers with such a depreciated asset base that any new investment will have a huge negative impact on EP. With this being so, the long term result of adopting EP can be one of delivering enhanced returns but not long term growth in the capital base.

EP is not the end of the story as far as measuring performance is concerned. Other alternatives do exist in the form of Cash Value Added (CVA) and Total Shareholder Return (TSR) /Total Business Return (TBR). These metrics can be split into two groups; those that are used by investors looking from outside who want to evaluate the performance of their investment in the company and those that are used by the companies themselves to evaluate their performance (see Figure 5.5).

Figure 5.6: Users of the other metrics

User	Investor	Company Management
Metric	TSR, MVA	TBR, EVA, SVA, EP, CVA

CVA is the simpler approach in which EP is adjusted to a cash and replacement cost basis by adding depreciation and amortisation back to net operating profit and accumulated depreciation is added back to the capital base. By eliminating the worst of Economic Profit's anti growth or reinvestment bias, CVA takes an important step, but may still remain inadequate because CVA still measures performance on the margin.

The alternative is to evaluate performance in much the same way as investors look at a share or executives size up a potential acquisition. This approach is called Total Shareholder Return (TSR) at the company level and Total Business Return (TBR) when extended to business unit level. By comparing the beginning value of a business with its ending value, plus free cash flow over the period, TBR effectively replicates total shareholder return inside a company at the level of the individual business unit see Figure 5.7.

Figure 5.7: TSR and TBR

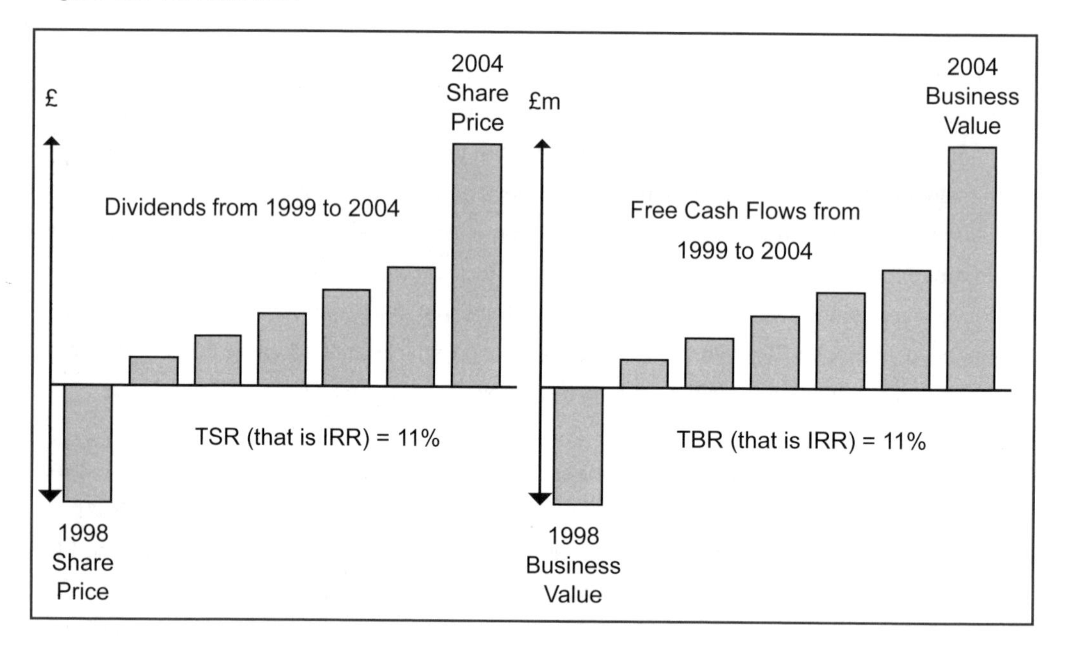

CHAPTER 6
COST OF CAPITAL AND CAPITAL STRUCTURE

Chapter Preview

This chapter will enable you to understand:

- The importance of the Weighted Average Cost of Capital (WACC) as the benchmark to be used to assess whether value is created or not for the providers of capital to a business
- How to calculate the WACC using a three step process, which involves calculating the cost of equity, the cost of debt and estimating the target capital structure
- How to calculate the cost of equity using the Capital Asset Pricing Model (CAPM) and how to calculate the cost of debt
- Issues involved in estimating the cost of capital from a business unit perspective

6.1 Introduction

How can a business evaluate whether a potential investment is really worthwhile? In every day life it is common practice to answer this question with reference to the rate of return that will be earned on funds invested. If money needs to be borrowed to undertake such a potential investment then there will be a cost associated with it, typically expressed as the percentage return required by the lender. Common sense would dictate that the return required from an investment should at the very least cover the cost of funds needing to be raised to finance it. What applies in everyday life also applies in corporate life. Organisations have to ensure that the opportunities in which it invests are those that will at minimum satisfy the returns required by the providers of funds. In other words, the cost of capital should equate with the opportunity cost of the funds tied up; that is, the return which would be achieved from their next best use.

The cost of capital is important to understand for many reasons. As indicated previously, only if a return is generated in excess of the cost of capital will shareholder value be created. It is also important to view it in terms of its impact on business value. This can readily be understood by recalling the free cash flow valuation approach reviewed in Chapter 3 and subsequent discussions about the perpetuity terminal value calculation. Small changes in the cost of capital denominator can have a very significant impact upon the resulting terminal value.

The importance of understanding the role of the cost of capital in value creation may be simple, but in practice its estimation is far more problematic, as will be seen in this chapter. One source of complication is that the providers of funds to a company are not typically a homogeneous group with identical requirements and expectations from their investment. At one extreme they may comprise long-term debt-holders seeking a secure and fixed rate of interest, while at the other they may be ordinary shareholders who accept that the return received is most likely to be contingent on the company's performance. Somehow the requirements of all providers have to be captured and there are different ways of achieving this that have been encountered in earlier chapters. One commonly accepted way is via the Weighted Average Cost of Capital (WACC) in which the requirements of all providers of funds are expressed in one percentage rate of return. Alternatively, costs associated with borrowed funds may be taken out of the cash flows resulting in equity cash flows, which are then discounted at the return required by the providers of equity. Whichever method is used, determining the cost of capital is a real challenge. This is for many reasons, not least because there are different views about the methods to be adopted for calculating the cost of equity.

Apart from the issues associated with estimating the cost of capital for the company as a whole, there is one other important consideration. This relates to the need by many businesses to have capital allocation procedures delegated to parts of the overall business. In large organisations it is unsatisfactory and makes sense to delegate the authority for making such decisions. However, such procedures may also need to recognise that different parts of the overall business will need to generate different returns, dependent on the degree of risk involved.

Understanding the cost of capital is one of the major challenges for management. Those who understand it should be able to ensure that their organisations benefit. However, as will be seen from what follows, its estimation requires a good deal of tough analysis and the exercise of sound judgement. It is also important to recognise that it is all too easy to become side-tracked by some of the issues relating to the determination of the cost of individual components that make up a corporation's capital structure. Nowhere is this more the case than for the cost of equity for which a number of approaches have been developed to try and capture the rate of return required by shareholders. These approaches in themselves are challenging, but there is one important issue to acknowledge, any approach is only as good as the data on which it is based.

6.2 Weighted Average Cost of Capital (WACC)

Opinions differ about the size of the cost of capital. To understand the source of such differences we will review the cost of capital, which is often referred to as the weighted average cost of capital, by considering three steps involving estimation of the:

1. Cost of equity
2. Cost of debt
3. Capital structure.

These three steps and the building blocks associated with them are illustrated in Figure 6.1.

Figure 6.1: Three steps for estimating WACC

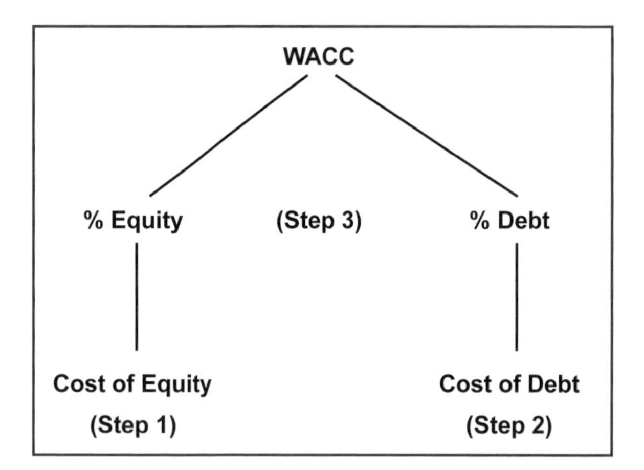

Of the three steps, the most difficult and controversial issue concerns the estimation of the cost of equity.

6.3 Cost of equity

Among the approaches available for calculating the cost of equity are the Capital Asset Pricing Model, Arbitrage Pricing Theory and the Dividend Valuation Model.

Capital Asset Pricing Model (CAPM)

Modern financial theory suggests that the cost of equity can be estimated from analysing what return investors require when buying a share. Their requirement can be estimated using the Capital Asset Pricing Model, known as CAPM. The underlying premise of the approach is the more risk an investor is required to take on, the higher the rate of return that will be expected. It is in a class of market models called risk-premium models which rely on the assumption that every individual holding a risky security will demand a return in excess of the return they would receive from a risk-free security. This excess return is the premium to compensate the investor for risk that cannot be diversified away.

The CAPM cost of equity can be estimated using the following formula:

Cost of equity = Risk-free rate + (Beta x Equity risk premium)

For example, the WACC for RWM plc in the Appendix to Chapter 3 was assumed to be 12 per cent. As will be demonstrated, this was firstly calculated using the CAPM to determine a cost of equity of 13.1 per cent. (This is combined with the cost of debt to calculate the WACC of 12% - see later in this chapter). The cost of equity of 13.1 per cent was calculated assuming a risk-free rate of 4.4 per cent, a beta of 1.3 and an equity risk premium of 6.7 per cent. In terms of the CAPM cost of equity formula, this can be shown as:

$$\text{Cost of equity} = 4.4\% + (1.3 \times 6.7\%)$$

$$= 13.1\%$$

Within the CAPM the variable specific to the type of business is the beta. Both the risk-free rate and the equity risk premium are assumed to apply to all companies within the market. The beta, risk-free rate and equity risk premium will now be examined in turn.

Beta

Beta is a relative measure of volatility that is determined by comparing the return on a share (stock) to the return on the stock market. In simple terms, the greater the volatility, the more risky the share, which will be reflected in a higher beta.

The type of risk that beta in the CAPM measures is called systematic, market, or non-diversifiable risk[17]. This risk is caused by macroeconomic factors like inflation or political events, which affect the returns of all companies. If a company is affected by these macroeconomic factors in the same way as the market is, then the company will have a beta of 1 and will be expected to have returns equal to the market. Similarly, if a company's systematic risk is greater than the market, then the company will be priced such that it is expected to have returns greater than the market. For example, if a share has a beta of 2.0, then on average for every 10 per cent that the market index has returned above the risk-free rate, historically the share will have returned 20 per cent[18]. Conversely, for every 10 per cent the market index has returned below the risk-free rate, historically the share will have returned 20 per cent below.

Beta values are widely available to investors in printed publications and on Internet websites, making the need to estimate them very unlikely. However, it is important to be aware that care

[17] It is important to note two types of risk are accounted for within CAPM thinking. In addition to the market-related risk captured in the beta, there is the risk which can be indetified with a specific business. This is known as unsystematic, specific or diversifiable risk and can be eliminated through individual investor action to carry diversified portfolios. Investors who choose not to be fully diversified will not be compensated for the total risk of their holdings, because the only risk which is priced and compensated for in the market is the systematic part.

[18] Beta is often measured by using standard regression techniques to analyse monthly returns historically over a five year time horizon.

needs to be exercised in using such betas . Four key inputs that have been found to impact on the value of the beta calculation are:

1. The market indicator used to regress the stock price against
2. The data to be regressed
3. The time horizon
4. Selected time interval.

On the first of these, most providers were found to use the S&P 500, whereas others were found to use the NYSE Composite Index. By all accounts, the impact of selecting one rather than another should have minimal impact. As regards the second, differences were found as to whether the stock price was regressed with or without an adjustment for dividends.

The third of these issues, the time horizon, has a greater impact on beta's value. Many providers offer betas with five years of data, including London Business School Risk Measurement Service, Value Line, Media General, Market Guide, Standard & Poor's and Argus. Although the traditional approach involves using five years of monthly data on returns to measure the firm's exposure, some doubt has been expressed about this time horizon. Small deviations in the time horizon used to estimate the beta have been found to cause wide and inexplicable fluctuations in the result. In fact, only with about eight years of monthly data was a respectable degree of stability in the estimates of beta found.

Finally, the selected interval is an important issue. Beta sources do vary in terms of the interval used with some using monthly intervals, others weekly or daily data. There is also an interval issue brought about by non-synchronous trading – stocks not trading at consistent intervals. As beta calculations require closing prices, a stock trading less frequently may show a closing price that reflects market information published days prior to the resulting trading activity. Equities trading more frequently may absorb market news within the trading day and produce a closing price more accurately reflecting market conditions.

The use of betas is a very controversial and often emotive issue. Some consider that the use of betas is not justifiable because the past is not a strong enough indicator of future market activity to warrant heavy use of beta. It is true information flow makes today's market significantly more volatile than the market of five years ago and market data for five years past may offer little insight into today's security movements. However, those who find beta useful should be aware of the differences in the inputs and the resulting impact on its value, but leaving even these differences aside some further care needs to be exercised in interpreting betas. Other statistics, like the standard deviation associated with the beta, may be all too readily overlooked. For example, a standard deviation of 0.33 on a beta of 1.0 indicates that, with 99 per cent confidence (assuming a normal distribution), the beta lies somewhere between 0.01 and 1.99. For this reason, reference may often be made in practice to the betas of comparable peer group companies.

Care also needs to be taken in interpreting betas for companies with unusual capital structures. For example, two companies identical except for their capital structure may be perceived very differently by the market. If one is all debt financed and the other is all equity financed, it is reasonable to expect greater volatility in the returns and the share price of the all debt financed company. This is because in prosperous times the debt will be an advantage, but the converse will apply in periods of economic downturn. In other words, there is a financial risk that will be captured in historical measurement of the beta that will be reflected in a higher number, despite the fact that the companies are identical in all other respects. In effect, the historical measurement is picking up noise relating to the capital structure which needs to be removed. This is achieved by a process known as ungearing and regearing the beta (or unlevering/ relevering the beta in US terms). The calculation necessary to ungear the beta is:

Ungeared (Equity) Beta = Published Beta / (1 + (1 – Tc) (D/E))

Where,

Tc = corporate tax rate;

D/E = debt/equity ratio.

This ungeared beta then needs to be regeared at the target debt/equity ratio using the following formula:

Regeared (Asset) Beta = Ungeared Beta x (1 + (1 – Tc) (D/E Target))

Where,

Tc = corporate tax rate;

D/E Target = target debt/equity ratio.

The basis of the first part of this calculation, that is, ungearing the beta, can be seen with reference to the example in Figure 6.2 in which we assume that we are trying to find the beta for a business that is not quoted on the stock market, for example a private company or the division of a publicly traded company. One comparable publicly traded business has been identified and both it and the company for which a beta is sought have the same 30% tax rate. Our comparable business has a very high beta of 2.0 and a correspondingly high target debt to equity ratio of 3:1, whereas the company for which a beta is sought has a much lower target debt to equity ratio of 1:1.

Figure 6.2: Ungearing the beta of the comparable

Ungeared Beta	=	Published Beta / (1 + (1 – Tc) (D/E))
	=	2.0 / (1 + (1 – 0.3) (3 / 1))
	=	0.65

Once ungeared, the beta needs to be regeared at a 'target' debt equity ratio based on a long-term substantial capital structure.

Regeared Beta	=	0.65 x (1 + (1 – 0.3) (1/1))
	=	1.11

Caution needs to be exercised in using and interpreting this approach. Definitions used in calculations may vary and it is a good idea to check that the calculation is really warranted, that is, that the beta calculation has really been influenced by the capital structure.

An alternative to using a published beta is the use of a predictive, or fundamental beta. This type of beta uses company-specific data (income statement account and balance sheet) to arrive at a multiple-factor beta, which is based on risk indices like company success, size and growth. The company specific data are regressed against systematic portfolios of risk indices, which results in a single factor weighted beta .

Risk-free rate

The risk-free rate represents the most secure return that can be achieved. From a UK perspective, anyone wishing to sleep soundly at night might invest all available funds in government bonds which are largely insensitive to what happens in the share market and, therefore, have a beta of nearly zero. The risk-free rate within CAPM is hypothetically the return on a security or portfolio of securities that has no default risk whatsoever and is completely uncorrelated with returns on anything else in the economy. Theoretically the best estimate of the risk-free rate would be the return on a zero beta portfolio. This means a perfect proxy for the risk-free rate would be a security with a beta equal to zero and no volatility. To find a perfect security is empirically impossible so a proxy is used that meets these requirements as closely as possible.

One of the issues that must be dealt with alongside the search for possible proxies is the maturity of the proxy. In developed economies, government securities tend to be the best candidates for the risk-free rate, since the government in many countries guarantees payment. However, government securities may have different maturity dates and different yields. For example, in the USA very long-term bonds with 30 year maturity dates exist, as well as short-term and medium-term bonds of ten years. Preference for a medium-term rate is not uncommon because it often comes close to matching the duration of the cash flow of a company being valued. A current Treasury-bill rate, because of its short-term nature, does not match duration sufficiently well. In order to use such a rate it would be necessary to apply rates expected to relate to each future period, not just today. In effect, the ten-year rate is a geometric weighted average estimate of the expected short-term Treasury-bill rates over the time period to be evaluated.

Equity risk premium

The equity risk premium is the excess return above a risk-free rate that investors demand for holding risky securities. The risk premium in the CAPM is the premium above the risk-free rate on a portfolio assumed to have a beta equal to 1.0. If an individual security is more or less risky, then it will have a higher or lower risk premium. The risk premium can be estimated in a variety of ways, which will be discussed under the headings of ex post (historical) analysis and ex ante (forward-looking) analysis.

(a) Ex post analysis

Ex post, or historical analysis is a popular way to estimate the risk premium, the rationale being that history is a good predictor of the future. When history is used the first question to be answered is, 'How should the return be calculated?' Returns over time can be calculated by a simple arithmetic or compound (geometric) average, each of which can be interpreted differently. A geometric average implies that investors use a buy and hold strategy with dividends reinvested. This is an appropriate performance measure if investors hold for more than one period. The arithmetic average measures the average one-period performance and is appropriate if investors buy and sell every period. The choice depends on the perceived holding period of the investor. For example, if the holding period is assumed to be ten years, then the appropriate measure would be the average of a series of ten-year geometric returns. Dimson, Marsh and Staunton (2000) of the London Business School in a 'Century of Investment

Returns' studied the performance of UK equities back to early 1900s. Their review of the indices of total returns for 16 countries confirmed that shares beat bonds and in every country in their study. The authors measured the equity-risk premium and found that whereas overall equities have beaten bonds this did not necessarily occur over long periods, say 20 years. In the 80 years or so since 1926, it is possible to measure only three distinct 20-year periods where this trend was found to hold. Yet earlier, there were periods when shares lost out to bonds. This 20-year rule also does not hold for other countries. Dimson et al found four stock markets — the Netherlands, Germany, Sweden, and Switzerland — where at times 40 years of market exposure were needed to ensure that shares outperformed bonds.

There have been concerns that some studies may have overestimated absolute equity returns, for example, because they relied upon inadequate data. For instance, during the First World War, for which data is hard to find, returns were generally lower. Also, earlier studies look at the historical share-price performance of companies that survive today, rather than examine the performance of now-extinct shares that would have been in a past investor's portfolio. Dimson et al correct for these factors, as well as using a full century of data to give a more comprehensive view of equity-risk premiums. This placed Denmark at the bottom of the league and Germany at the top. Dimson et al provide a global historical average equity premium, over bonds, of 4.6 percentage points, which is nearly half the widely received forward-looking estimate of 8.8 percentage points from Ibbotson Associates, a consulting firm, and the 8.5 percentage points frequently taught on finance courses. Furthermore, Dimson et al reckon that this estimate may also be too generous. Some stock markets, such as those of China, Russia and Poland are not included in the study, since they were closed down under communist rule. If these markets were taken into account, the historical equity premium would be even lower.

The true level of the equity premium is not merely an academic debate; it has consequences for individuals' everyday lives and for business decisions. As regards the first of these, pension funds, for example, have to take it very seriously. At present, many of their fixed liabilities in the form of the money owed to pensioners are held in the form of shares, which means that too much optimism about expected equity returns could have painful consequences. Participants in pension schemes with defined contributions rather than defined benefits would face substantial difficulties if lower returns than expected left them with a deficit at retirement. What is more, rich countries can expect a surge in the numbers of retired people, thereby placing great importance on having a good understanding of the equity risk premium.

(b) Ex ante analysis

The most common 'ex ante' approach uses the dividend valuation model. Such a model relies on knowing the current dividend yield for shares and an estimate of the growth rate for dividends in the future. The expected growth rate to be used as an input to the dividend valuation model may be estimated in several ways. The most direct way is to conduct a survey of investors about their expectations. There are also some regularly produced forecasts of earnings growth, which are available for both individual companies and for market indices.

An alternative way of using something like the dividend valuation model is to make less extreme assumptions than those conventionally used. For example, the assumption of a constant growth rate for dividends is unsatisfactory and one alternative draws on the discounted cash flow (DCF) approach. This starts from the current share price of the company under consideration and makes specific dividend forecasts for that company. The required rate of return is the discount rate that makes the present value of these dividends equal to the current share price.

The conclusion that can be drawn about the equity risk premium is that there are differing views about its calculation, each of which can be justified. Very often the basis used for its calculation in practice appears to depend to a large extent on the perspective taken.

The appropriateness of CAPM for estimating the cost of equity

Like all models, CAPM abstracts from reality by making a series of simplifying assumptions. Many of the assumptions behind CAPM may not hold in the real world, but that does not necessarily mean that the model is not valuable. Even simple models can yield useful results with practical applications. For example, Thomas Edison understood very little of what we now know about electricity, yet he was able to harness it and produce the light bulb.

A simple test of the risk return relationship measured by CAPM betas was performed by Sharpe and Cooper (1972). They separated all NYSE common stocks into deciles based on their betas and measured the returns that would have been achieved by holding each decile for each year during the period 1931 to 1967. The deciles were recalculated yearly to account for firms moving from one decile to another. Over the period of the study, stocks with higher betas generally produced higher future returns, as predicted by CAPM.

However, other studies have indicated that the CAPM does not adequately describe the risk return relationship. Various researchers have identified groups of stock with some common characteristics that consistently achieve higher or lower returns than would be implied by

CAPM. These anomalies would indicate that stocks with these characteristics have a greater or lesser exposure to systematic risk than that measured by CAPM. These characteristics are known as 'market anomalies' and the best known is the 'size' effect. Research has shown that an investor would have realised returns in excess of those predicted by CAPM (positive abnormal returns) by investing in low capitalisation (small company) stocks over the period 1936 to 1977 (Banz 1981). Both the magnitude and the statistical significance of the abnormal returns were large.

Another anomaly is known as the 'year end' or 'January' effect, which refers to the tendency for all stocks to earn excess returns in the month of January. Evidence provided has shown that this effect may also be linked to the small firm effect and, so far, no 'satisfactory' explanation of this anomaly has been advanced (Keim 1982).

In fact there has been severe criticism of the CAPM approach, with considerable doubt being expressed about the linear relationship between beta and expected returns (Roll 1982). Research has shown only a weak relationship between average return and beta over the period 1941 and 1990 and virtually no relation over the shorter period 1963 to 1990. Firm size and market-to-book ratios were found to be far more important in explaining differences, although such findings are still the subject of considerable academic debate (Fama and French 1992).

Arbitrage Pricing Theory (APT)

An alternative risk premium approach to CAPM known as Arbitrage Pricing Theory (APT for short) has been developed. The principle which underpins APT is that two assets that have identical risk characteristics must offer the same return, or an arbitrage opportunity will exist. APT attempts to measure the various dimensions of market related risk in terms of several underlying economic factors, such as inflation, monthly production and interest rates, which systematically affect the price of all shares. In a nutshell, regression techniques are used to estimate the contribution made by each APT factor to overall risk. However, this approach is more complex than CAPM and not without many difficulties in terms of its application. This is recognised in the USA where, for example, the monthly production figures published by the government are only estimates of true US industrial production. This means that they are 'noisy' (contain random errors) and inaccurate (contain biases introduced by the data-gathering procedure and the government smoothing or adjustment process). Error thus arises because high quality data in the form of share prices are regressed against lower quality data.

Arbitrage Pricing Theory (APT) requires less stringent assumptions than CAPM and it is reliant on the 'law of one price' which is used to replace the assumption that investors evaluate investments on the basis of the mean and variance of returns. The 'law of one price' simply states that in an efficient market identical products of any kind will sell for the same price. If two identical products existed at different prices, an arbitrageur could buy the cheaper product, sell it to those who wanted the more expensive product and earn a risk free return in the transaction. Further, this process would continue until the increased demand for the less expensive product and the decreased demand for the more expensive product caused the two prices to become the same. It is from this arbitrage condition that the APT gets its name.

The accuracy of any implementation of the APT cannot be evaluated until factors have been chosen. Research that has been undertaken has found the following factors to be of importance (Chen, Roll, and Ross, 1986):

- monthly industrial production
- interest rates
- investor confidence (measured by the spread between low grade and high grade bonds)
- long term inflation
- short term inflation.

Operational APT models have been developed in the USA using US data. As such, this means that its application outside the USA requires conversion to reflect the conditions in the market under consideration.

Dividend valuation model

The Dividend Valuation Model considers that the return shareholders require (hence the cost of equity to a business) can be determined with reference to the future dividend stream they require. At its simplest, this approach takes the view that the cost of equity to a company is only the dividend it has to pay which is derived by assuming that a company's dividend per share grows at a constant rate and that the company's risk will remain unchanged. If we call Ke the cost of equity, the model is:

$$K_e\,\% = \frac{d\,(1 + g) + g}{P} \times 100$$

Where,

K_e	=	Cost of equity
d	=	Current dividend
P	=	Market price
g	=	Expected dividend or price growth rate provided that investors expect dividends to grow at a constant rate in perpetuity.

Thus, if a company had a current dividend per share of 4p, a market price of £1.00 and an expected growth rate of 10 per cent, its cost of equity would be:

$$K_e\ \% = \frac{4p\ (1 + 0.10) \quad + \quad 0.10}{100p} \quad x \quad 100$$

$$= \quad 14.4\%$$

This measure of the cost of equity is fairly popular, particularly for valuing preference shares where g reduces to zero. In this case, the calculation of a cost of equity is quite straightforward if the shares are irredeemable, that is, if the dividend is paid in perpetuity. For example, a 10 per cent irredeemable preference share with a nominal value of £1 and a market value of £2 would have a cost (Kpref %) using this approach of:

$$K_{pref}\ \% = \frac{\text{Annual dividend}}{\text{Market price}} \quad x \quad 100$$

$$= \frac{10p}{200p} \quad x \quad 100$$

$$= \quad 5\%$$

If the preference share is redeemable, such that the dividend is not paid into perpetuity, then an internal rate of return calculation is required. This is necessary to find the percentage that equates all future cash flows from dividend payments and the redemption payment with the current market value of the share. This is known as the yield to redemption, yield to maturity or yield, for short. (The calculation of a yield for an irredeemable financial instrument is demonstrated shortly with reference to the cost of debt.)

However, for calculating the cost of equity relating to ordinary share capital the dividend valuation approach has to be used with care. First, the growth rate g is a long-run growth rate over an infinite horizon and as such is a difficult parameter to conceptualise. It relies on accurate estimates of growth rates that can be reliably projected into the future - a daunting task given that few businesses have a history of constant growth. Second, the long-run growth rate must, by definition, be strictly less than the cost of equity, Ke. Third, the parameters of the model are interdependent. It would seem that a higher growth rate implies a higher cost of equity. However, this is not true because the higher rate of growth will imply a higher current share value (P). The net effect will reduce the cost of equity but, if one estimates a higher growth rate, how much greater should P become? The answer is unclear. Finally, the model provides no obvious answer to the question - what cost of equity should be applied when the company is considering projects of different risk than its current operations? For this, approaches like CAPM are required.

It is not uncommon to find earnings being used in one form or another in cost of equity calculations. Common approaches are to calculate Earnings Yield (earnings as a percentage of the market value of equity) and Return on Equity (earnings as a percentage of the book value of equity).

6.4 Cost of debt

The second step in calculating the cost of capital is to calculate the cost of debt, which is the rate of return that debt-holders require to hold debt. To determine this rate the yield to maturity (YTM) has to be calculated, often by drawing on the principles of discounted cash flow analysis and particularly the internal rate of return. For example, consider a non-redeemable debenture with a nominal value of £100 that pays 10 per cent, or £10 per annum in perpetuity. What this represents as a return to the investor will depend on the value of the debenture in the stock market. If the value has fallen from £100 to £92, then the return or yield will be 10.87 per cent ([£10 ÷ £92] x 100). However, this may not tell the full story. First, the debenture may have a redemption date such that it may return £10 for a fixed number of years, at the end of which a sum of money will be paid by the company to redeem it. For example, if the debenture is to be redeemed after ten years at its face (par) value of £100, then the yield is the percentage that equates an annual interest payment of £10 up to the point of redemption together with £100 redemption payment in year ten, having its present value of £92. This percentage, represented by "i" in the following formula, is 11.38:

$$\frac{£10}{(1 + i)} + \frac{£10}{(1 + i)^2} + \frac{£10}{(1 + i)^3} + \ldots\ldots\ldots + \frac{£110}{(1 + i)^{10}} = £92$$

Second, the impact of taxation has to be taken into consideration as follows:

Cost of debt after tax = Cost of debt before tax x (100 – Marginal tax rate)

The marginal tax rate is the tax rate applied to the company's last earned pound of income, that is, the rate that applies to the highest 'tax bracket' into which the company's income falls. Marginal tax rates can differ from the statutory tax rates due to different income thresholds and net operating loss carry-forwards, which act to reduce the tax rates.

The marginal tax rate should not be confused with the average tax rate, which is the company's total tax liability divided by its total taxable income. Because the tax rate changes with the amount of taxable income under current laws, the marginal tax rate is often different from the average tax rate. In any event, before the marginal tax rate for an unquoted business can be estimated, it is necessary to first estimate its taxable income. Once this is known the current tax schedule can be used to determine the appropriate tax rate.

The cost of debt generally increases with financial leverage. Therefore, a change in target capital structure will change the cost of debt. The cost of debt must also follow the matching principle. The cost of debt must match the risk of the cash flows being discounted. While the basic calculation for estimating the cost of debt has been illustrated, in practice the way to calculate the cost of debt depends on information available:

- If the firm's capital structure is not expected to change and yields and market values of the relevant debt instruments are known, then the average yield to maturity of those instruments is used as the cost of debt.
- This can be done in two steps:
  1. Find or calculate the current yield to maturity for each instrument
  2. Use market values of each instrument to weight each instrument's yield and produce an average.

For public debt instruments, the yield to maturity can be found from market data because bond prices are quoted in financial journals. As indicated previously, the yield to maturity can be calculated as the interest rate that equates the present value of a bond's cash flows to its current market value. Whenever a bond's market value is less than its face value (that is, the yield to maturity is greater than the coupon rate), the bond is said to be issued at a discount. Whenever a bond's market value is greater than its face value (that is, its yield to maturity is less than the coupon rate), the bond is said to be issued at a premium.

When the cost of debt of non-publicly traded companies or divisions of publicly traded companies is required, peer analysis can be used in which the focus of attention is on peer instruments as distinct from peer companies. The objective is to try and find peer instruments for publicly quoted businesses where the characteristics are similar. In terms of the yield calculation we discussed previously, what is not known for a non-publicly traded company or the divisions of publicly traded companies is the market value of debt. In this situation, there are several other ways to estimate the cost of debt, such as:

- Find similar debt instruments that have known yields
- Find similar firms and use their bond rating to estimate the cost of debt. Good peers should have similar operations and debt structures (short term versus long term duration and so on)
- Calculate a synthetic bond rating for the firm, identify yields on bonds of similar rating and duration and use that yield as the cost of debt
- If similar instruments are not available, as a last resort divide interest expense by the book value of debt to estimate the cost of debt.

A problem often arises in determining the cost of debt in markets where the public trading of debt is not common practice. This is so in most emerging markets and also in some well developed markets in Western Europe. In such circumstances one method of estimating the cost of debt is to:

- Estimate the local risk free rate
- Identify the spread for a company with a similar debt rating where debt is publicly traded, this spread being the difference between its cost of debt and the risk-free rate
- Add the spread to the local risk-free rate.

Of course, as with any method of estimation this is not perfect and there are other issues that may need to be considered, for example, should a premium be added for illiquidity. Nevertheless, in some circumstances it may be the only available option.

One key point to recognise is that for purposes of estimation, reality checks should be used. For example, one invaluable cross-check is reference to the views of the commercial banker.

Dealing with more than one source of debt

Typically businesses have more than one source of debt financing. In this case the overall cost of debt can be calculated by taking the weighted average of the individual instruments based on market values. This involves multiplying the yield to maturity of each instrument by the percentage of the total market value of the portfolio that each instrument represents and summing the products. This is illustrated in Figure 6.3, where the approach was used to find the cost of debt for a large US buy out:

Figure 6.3: Calculation of weighted cost of debt

Type of Debt	**£m**	**Weight** **A**	**%** **B**	**Yield** **%** **A x B**
Short-Term Debt	13,600	0.5199	11.27	5.86
Existing Long-Term Debt	5,262	0.2011	9.75	1.96
Subordinated Increasing-Rate Notes (Class I)	1,250	0.0478	13.00	0.62
Subordinated Increasing-Rate Notes (Class II)	3,750	0.1433	14.00	2.01
Convertible Debentures	1,800	0.0688	14.50	1.00
Partnership Debt Securities	500	0.0191	11.20	0.21
Total	**£26,162**	**1.0000**		**11.66 %**

Once the weighted cost for all debt has been estimated before tax, the effect of tax needs to be considered as follows:

Cost of debt after tax = Cost of debt before tax x (100 – Marginal tax rate)

= 11.66% (100 – 35.5)

= 7.52%

It is important to note that it has been assumed there are tax advantages associated with debt. However, this may not always be the case. Where a business has large tax losses carried forward, the position may be much more complex; there is always a need to review each situation on a case by case basis.

6.5 Capital structure

The third step in the WACC calculation involves the estimation of the capital structure and to understand the issues involved here. Let us consider the following formula:

WACC = Ke + (E/V) + Kd (1 – Tc)(D/V)

Where,

V = debt (D) + equity (E)

D/V = the proportion of total value (V) claimed by debt (D)

E/V = the proportion of total value (V) claimed by equity (E)

K_d = the required rate of return on debt capital

K_e = the required rate of return on equity capital

T_c = the marginal corporate tax rate.

As regards the D/E ratio used in the WACC calculation, there is the question of whether book (balance sheet) values or market values should be used. Market values are conceptually superior, despite their volatility, because the firm must yield competitive rates of return for debt-holders and shareholders based on the respective market values of debt and equity. For example, suppose shareholders invested £5 million of initial capital in a company ten years ago and that over the ten year period book value grew from £5 million to £7 million. Suppose that a reasonable return in light of present market conditions is 20 per cent. Would the shareholders be satisfied with a 20 per cent return on the £7 million book value, based on the firm's historical costs, or would they expect to earn 20 per cent on the current market value of £20 million, based on current economic value? Clearly, the investors will expect returns based on current market value because they could liquidate their investment for £20 million and find other opportunities yielding 20 per cent. Thus, book value is not relevant to current investment decisions.

Despite the preference for market values, there are many difficulties associated with the determination of the market value of debt and equity. In very simple terms, the market value of equity can be determined for a quoted firm by multiplying the current stock price by the number of shares outstanding. For an unquoted business, the task is more difficult. In the case of the market value of debt, for a quoted company it is its price in the market multiplied by the volume of traded debt. In the case of an unquoted company it could be computed by discounting the future cash flows of each instrument at an estimated current yield to maturity, as described in the previous section on the cost of debt. If this information is not available, the book value of debt may have to be used as a proxy for the market value of debt. However, very often the difficulties associated with the estimation of actual market values for equity and debt encourages the use of a target capital structure, that is, a target D/E ratio. This target will be either based on judgement or benchmarked against peer group companies.

In the case of RWM plc (see earlier in Section 6.3), the WACC of 12% may be calculated from the cost of equity (13.1%, calculated earlier) and the cost of debt (assumed here to be 6%)

.

If the balance sheet in the Appendix of Chapter 1 is considered, the debt (creditors falling due after one year) consists of a number of long-term liabilities, amounting to £20.1m at the end of 2006. We shall make two assumptions: firstly, that the weighted cost of all the debt is 6.0% and, secondly, that the market value of this debt is equal to its book value - £20.1m.

The strategic value of the equity was calculated in the Appendix of Chapter 3 to be £111.9m. So the weighted average cost of capital from RWM plc is:

$$\text{WACC} = 13.1\% \times \frac{111.9}{111.9 + 20.1} + 6.0\% \times \frac{20.1}{111.9 + 20.1}$$

$$= 12.0\%$$

6.6 Is there an optimal capital structure?

The potential tax related benefits of debt capital and 'gearing up' on the one hand and the disadvantages of increased risk on the other has given rise to the view of there being an optimal, or ideal, capital structure. That is, there is some mix of debt relative to equity at which the tax advantage can be maximised before the perception is reached by debt and equity providers that the risk needs to be compensated for by a higher return.

Many believe that it is difficult to determine a single truly optimal capital structure in practice but that it is more valuable to see it as corresponding with a limited range of possible debt and equity mixes. Irrespective of the exact characteristics of the capital structure, the real challenge is to locate where it potentially lies when taking a forward-looking view. This is because in terms of undertaking a valuation, the real concern is typically to find the required rate of return or cost of capital to apply in valuing a potential opportunity from a series of estimated future cash flows. This means that the cost of capital should relate to the future, which is achieved by attempting to identify the most beneficial blend of debt and equity over the planning period. Attention will have to be paid to the most appropriate debt structure, which will have to take into consideration conditions relating to both the economy and the business. For example, we know that perceptions and the reality of borrowing can change given different economic conditions. In times of recession a massive change typically occurs in views about what constitutes an acceptable level of borrowing. Individuals and corporations often see the upside of borrowing from boom-time turn into a very real downside as interest rates rise at a time when effective demand and confidence are falling.

In addition to what is regarded as an acceptable level of gearing from a broad economic perspective, there is a need to consider specific business/industry characteristics since different types of business have different types of asset and repayment structure. Those with more to offer as security, or with more robust cash flows, should be able to gain most benefit from debt financing. The same is also the case for businesses with a good track record, even though their tangible sources of collateral may be limited.

The addition of debt has two opposing effects on a firm's cost of capital. First, since the after-tax cost of debt is normally less than the cost of equity for a firm, replacing debt with equity allows the firm to use a less expensive source of financing. This acts to reduce the overall cost of capital. However, additional debt increases both the cost of equity through financial leverage and the cost of debt through increasing risk of default. This acts to increase the cost of capital.

There is some debate concerning the extent to which these two effects counterbalance each other. Some have argued that there is no 'optimal capital structure'. According to this view, a firm's value is determined by its assets and its total value does not change when the cash flows from those assets are split into streams that go to different investor groups. This is equivalent to saying that the two effects of debt cancel each other out at all ratios of debt to equity. The alternative view favours the concept of an 'optimal capital structure'. According to this view, capital structure does make a difference because of imperfections in the capital markets, such as the tax deductibility of interest and transaction costs. If this is the case, the two effects will cancel only when the firm is at its 'optimal capital structure'. At that point, increasing the percentage of debt in the capital structure will increase the cost of capital, as will decreasing the percentage of debt in the capital structure. If an additional unit of debt causes the overall cost of capital to decline, the first effect predominates and the firm is below its optimal debt/equity ratio. This means that the firm can create value for its shareholders by adding more debt. If an additional unit of debt causes the cost of capital to rise, the leverage effect predominates and the firm can create value by reducing the amount of debt in its capital structure.

The problem lies in understanding where these most desirable blends of debt/equity are located. Optimal gearing models have been developed based on the relationship between bond ratings and ratios, like interest-coverage. However, such relationships may serve as useful screening tools, but our preference is to seek the most desirable debt/equity mix by taking a business unit perspective, which is covered in the next section.

6.7 Cost of capital - a divisional business unit perspective

The approach outlined in this chapter enables a cost of capital for the whole company to be estimated, but it has some very real shortcomings. Often it is important to understand the value of the individual business units which, together, make up the whole company.

Companies can be thought of as consisting of a number of component businesses each of which has a different risk return relationship. However, the calculation of the divisional cost of capital is by no means a simple task. The cost of capital is, in fact, the weighted average of the costs of the separate sources of capital, in terms of equity and debt. In other words, when estimating the cost of capital for divisions of quoted companies, financial managers need to determine the cost of equity, the cost of debt and the capital structure for each of the divisions.

The main problem with the calculation of divisional discount rates is the availability of information. For publicly quoted companies finance theory provides an established existence of a relationship between risk and return. Risk is measured through the returns of a security, but the market data required does not exist for a non-traded firm or for a division of a publicly traded firm. However, there are two main approaches that can be used in such circumstances:

1. the analytical approach (sometimes known as the "cross-sectional" approach
2. the analogous approach.

1. The analytical approach

This involves working from revenue, margins, asset saleability and other operating and structural characteristics. Data are developed from history or simulation and connected to market estimates of systematic risk and debt capacity via some linking mechanism. The analytical approach seeks to develop a relationship between accounting and market risk measures. If a stable relationship can be observed, divisional accounting data can be used to estimate the market risk of the division. However, although there is theoretical support for the analytical technique, there is no evidence that accounting and market linkages are stable. In other words, conflicting results from empirical studies illustrate that accounting returns fail to account for market risk.

2. The analogous approach

This method involves finding firms that have market histories, as well as a restricted set of products very similar to the product line being examined. Analogous approaches differ from the analytical approach in that market data are utilised as a measure of risk. A series of analogous approaches have been developed, the most notable being the pure-play approach. This method is based on the premise that a proxy beta derived from a publicly traded firm, whose operations are as similar as possible to the division in question, is used as the measure of the division's systematic risk. The pure-play approach attempts to identify firms with publicly traded securities that are engaged solely in the same line of business as the division . Once the pure-play firm is identified, its cost of equity capital is determined and then used as a proxy for the required divisional cost of equity capital. The presumption, of course, is that the systematic risk and capital structure of the pure-play are the same as those of the division.

Another analogous approach, the full-information approach, is based on the theoretical premise that a firm is simply a portfolio of projects; therefore the beta of a firm is the weighted average of the betas of its projects. This approach assumes that the beta of a division is the same, no matter which firm owns the division. The estimation of the cost of equity for a division is then a relatively simple process. Suppose a company has four business segments; the starting point would be to look for a number of quoted companies that have similar business segments in their portfolio and to calculate their equity betas. In addition, sales for each business segment are necessary to estimate the divisional betas, as these represent the weights for each business segment. Segment betas are then extrapolated by applying regression analysis assuming that the beta of a firm is the weighted average of its divisional betas.

The implication of analogous approaches varies in the degree of complexity, but the main strength of these techniques lies in the fact that market data are utilised as a measure of risk, thus validating their use in divisional cost of equity estimations.

Once cost of equity estimates have been undertaken for business units they can be fed into business unit cost of capital calculations. However, questions often arise about the appropriate debt:equity mix to use. In fact, careful consideration must be given to the question of the balance between both the parent company and the business unit's capital structures. A good case can be made for not basing the target capital structure for a business unit on the existing capital structure of the corporation as a whole, but on the debt capacity it could support as a stand alone company. Corporate raiders have often taken advantage of managements' failure to consider this fact.

One way of estimating stand alone debt capacity and leverage is to ask: 'What would the business unit's target capital structure be after a leveraged buyout?' This requires a thorough analysis of its financial position, the degree to which its assets are specialised (and therefore of lower collateral value in the event of bankruptcy) and its industry and competitive position. Another way of determining a business unit's target capital structure is by comparing its present structure to that of its peer group companies and adjusting the structure according to its competitive position. This method assumes that the average company in a given peer group has reached its optimal capital structure, which may not be the case.

6.8 Country Risk and the Cost of Capital

The risk premium for particular company's equity is estimated by multiplying the company's beta by the market risk premium. Beta is a measure of the degree of systematic risk of the company. But both the systematic risk and the market risk premium are measures of factors calculated from national data – that is, from within the country which is the host of the equity. If a company invests abroad it may be that an additional risk needs to be considered – country risk. Country risk premiums reflect the additional volatility in business returns from investing elsewhere than in the home country.

Specific country risk premiums are discussed in the next chapter in Section 7.4. Chapter 7 is a chapter dealing with the whole question of risk in financial management and the adjustments that should be made for country risk are dealt with in that context there.

CHAPTER 7
CORPORATE FINANCE AND RISK MANAGEMENT

Chapter Preview

This chapter will enable you to understand:

- **The importance of risk management within corporate finance.**
- **The importance of derivatives in managing risks.**
- **The principles of international financial risk management.**
- **The issues associated with measuring country risk and its incorporation in financial analysis.**
- **The importance of integrated risk management.**
- **The reason for the 'revolution' in corporate risk management.**
- **The changing function of risk management.**
- **The link between Value Based Management (VBM) and risk management.**
- **Enterprise-wide Risk Management (ERM) and the essence of the frameworks developed to support its implementation.**
- **Three stages for managing risk and uncertainty in the valuation of capital projects, that is:**

  1. **Risk identification**
  2. **Risk assessment**
  3. **Risk management action.**

- **The impact that risk can have on project appraisal.**
- **How to undertake sensitivity analysis in capital project appraisals.**
- **How the options approach might facilitate managerial decision making.**

7.1 Introduction

Corporate finance and risk have strong links with one another and a case has been made for what is referred to as 'integrated risk management' that involves the identification and assessment of the collective risks that affect firm value and the implementation of a firm-wide strategy to manage them. This enterprise focused perspective is reviewed alongside other views that have been expressed on the links between finance and risk, such as that which challenges traditional boundaries between capital and insurance markets. There are key links with other issues relating to corporate finance that have been reviewed in earlier chapters, but prior to reviewing these we will review the traditional financial risk perspective.

7.2 Managing financial risk

A common feature in managing financial risk is the use of derivatives. A derivative is a device which passes all or some of the risk of holding an asset on to another party. There are three areas where they are most prominently used:

- currencies – where the rate of exchange between one currency and another changes over time
- interest rates – where the level of interest rates change over time
- commodities – where the market price of goods changes over time.

Derivative markets have grown up in each of these three areas so that holders of currencies, debt instruments (paying interest) or commodities can avoid losses that would be incurred from changing exchange rates, interest rates or commodity prices. Some of the risk of holding those assets is passed on to another party who is willing to take some of the risk. The risk we are considering here is essentially the financial risk – rather than the business risk:

For example, a British company may have sold goods to an American customer who will pay for the goods in dollars in three months time. The currency derivative will take from the supplier any risk that the £:$ exchange rate will change over the three months; it will not take away the risk that the American customer defaults and does not pay the account.

You may ask why another party would be willing to take on the risk that the holder of currency, debt or commodities is avoiding. The reason is that, whilst the holder of an asset is able to avoid the risk of loss through price changes by using derivatives, the holder also loses the possible gain from holding the asset. 'Prices' of currencies, interest rates and commodities can go up as well as down. By making the offer of a derivative, the other party accepts the risk of loss but also has the right to any gains.

A key axiom of risk management is that risks are best taken by the person with the greatest knowledge, understanding and hence ability to control the risk but do be aware that there might also be natural hedges, that is particular risks that may offset each other. Often these natural hedges are discovered by accident. For example, during the US hurricane season in 1998 a telecoms company discovered that the loss of telephone traffic due to destruction of its telephone masts was outweighed by additional revenues from worried families starting to call relatives. The purchase of hurricane futures on the Chicago Board of Exchange would have been an unnecessary expense.

Types of derivatives

There are a number of different kinds of contracts that are used to pass on the financial risk from one party to another. These can be categorised as follows:

- Forward contracts
- Options
- Futures
- Swaps

We shall look at each of these in turn.

Forward contracts

In a forward contract, the offer is made by another party to the holder of an asset to acquire the asset at some time in the future at a price which is agreed now. The other party hopes that the price of the asset will be higher than the price that has been agreed in advance – so that the asset can be bought and sold on the agreed date at a profit. The holder of the asset loses the right to this possible gain, but avoids the possibility of the loss if the price of the asset should fall.

Currency and commodity forward contracts are agreements to pay an agreed rate for the currency or the goods at an agreed date in the future. This allows the business expecting a foreign currency in the future, or a grower, for example, of a commodity, to be sure now of the price that it will receive for the currency or for the goods in question. A forward interest rate agreement fixes the rate now that will be paid on a loan that is to be taken out sometime in the future.

Options

Options allow the holder the right to buy (or sell) an asset at a given price but the holder is under no obligation to do so. The holder has the option of not taking up the contract. If the price is favourable when the time comes to sell the asset, the option price can be ignored and the holder can 'walk away' from the deal. The option contracts are more expensive than forward contracts because the holder of the option can take the gain, if any, whilst being able to avoid the loss from changing prices.

The use of option contracts is best explained by an example or two.

Currency options are used by suppliers to set a maximum exchange rate for the currency that is to be converted into the supplier's home currency. They are used by companies purchasing abroad to set a minimum rate of exchange for the currency that they will require to make the payment to their supplier:

- For example: A plc in the UK sells €10,000 of goods to a German customer who is expected to pay in three months time. A plc takes out a currency option to sell Euros at a maximum of €1.50:£1.00 in three months time – that is, producing £6,667 (€10,000/1.5). If the exchange rate is €1.45:£1.00 in three months time, A plc will ignore the option contract and convert for £6,897 (€10,000/1.45). If the exchange rate is €1.55:£1.00, the option contract will be called upon and the Euros will be converted at €1.50:£1.00.

- For example: B plc in US purchases €10,000 of goods from a German supplier who expects payment in 90 days. B plc takes out a currency option to buy Euros (with which to pay the German supplier) at a minimum of €1.00:$1.00. If the exchange rate in three months time is, say, €1.10:$1.00, B plc will acquire the Euros for $9,091 (DM10,000/1.10) and walk away from the option to buy the Euros at €1.00:$1.00. If the exchange rate falls to €0.90:$1.00, the option will be used to acquire the Euros at €1.00:$1.00.

Interest rate options are arranged to fix a maximum interest on a loan to be taken out in some months time. If a corporate treasurer is of the opinion that the interest rate may rise in the next month or two an option could be purchased to take up loan facilities within, say, six months at no more than 9%.

The options contracts discussed above are specific and relate to one deal at a time and are arranged through brokers, that is, the Over the Counter (OTC) market. An alternative form of the currency option contract or the interest rate option contract is the traded option, which is provided by an exchange. Contracts are of a standardised size, with fixed delivery dates, which make them less flexible than the customer specific option, but are cheaper to arrange.

Futures

A financial futures contract is an agreement to buy or sell a standard quantity of a specific financial instrument at a future date at a price agreed between the parties. Although there are financial instruments in the futures markets for currencies, futures markets are used mostly to hedge interest rate movements. Interest rate futures contracts involve purchasing (or selling) a number of 'futures' on which a profit or loss will be made, depending on the movement of interest rates associated with an underlying financial instrument – such as the interest rate on Eurodollars. The profit or loss made on the contract will counteract the cost or benefit from any change in the interest rate on loans arranged earlier. The hedge may not exactly match the cost (or benefit) from changes in interest rates, because the available size of futures contracts is fixed – and it may not be possible to match exactly the size of a loan with the size of futures contracts.

Swaps

Currency swaps and interest rate swaps have developed to assist in the management of loans –particularly loans made abroad – against interest rate changes and changes in the currency exchange rates involved. The market developed from one-off arrangements made by two companies swapping loans in their individual countries. Banks soon realised that they could act as 'warehouses' for such arrangements. The home party to a currency swap could go to its bank and obtain a foreign currency loan. The bank would match this as best it could and hedge any residual position in the forward or futures market.

Currency swaps work as follows:

- A UK company wishing to invest in South Africa (SA) borrows in the UK
- A South African company wishing to invest in the UK borrows in South Africa.

Loans are swapped, making rand available to the UK company in SA, pounds available to the SA company in the UK. In, say, five years' time, the cash flow from the UK subsidiary's investment in SA will provide rand to repay the SA company's loan in SA. The UK company's loan will be repaid from the cash flows of the SA subsidiary's investment in the UK. Both parties are fully hedged against currency fluctuations and both may have access to cheaper loans because the loans will each be raised in their home country, where they are known.

The market for interest rate swaps developed from the realisation that the spread between the rates offered to high and low credit rated companies for fixed interest borrowings is wider than for floating-rate borrowings. So each borrower raises funds in the market where they have relative advantages and swap loans.

Some companies avoid the use of complex derivatives because they are outside the company's core business. You could say the same about IT. With IT you make sure you understand it, control it and use it. It is the same choice with derivatives. You cannot use what you cannot control, but if you have an adequate control system, derivatives can add value.

7.3 International financial management and exposure management

From the point of view of financial management, some risks from having multinational interests can be reduced; some simply have to be managed as best one can. Risks arising from potential currency exchange rate changes and possible interest rate changes – particularly in the short term – can be reduced by using the kind of instruments listed in the previous section. Other risks from trading on the international scene are much more difficult to control. These risks involve the exposure to economic factors and political risks.

Transaction exposure

Most companies trading internationally take a totally risk averse attitude towards exposure to foreign exchange risk. There are too many examples where corporate treasurers have taken a view about the currency markets, have not hedged the future cash flows and have incurred heavy losses for their company as a consequence. Such 'transaction exposure' can, for the most part be hedged. It may be more difficult in some currencies to hedge than others, but one or other of the methods described earlier can usually be employed to determine, in advance, the future cash flows with certainty.

Economic exposure also known as translation exposure

Economic exposure is the possibility that an unexpected change in exchange rates or interest rates will cause a change in the future cash flows of a firm active in a particular country. The cash flow will be affected because of the effects the change in exchange rates or interest rates will have on the economy of the country in question. The value of the firm (measured as the present value of expected future cash flows) will change because more or less business will be expected following the change in exchange rates or interest rates. Such 'economic exposure' is not easily measurable, but in the longer term is vastly more important than transaction exposure. It will determine whether or not a multinational company will choose to maintain its investment in a particular country.

Theoretically, the effect of factors which affect economic exposure should cancel out. To take a very simple example, if a country raises its interest rates (through action by its central bank), the exchange rate should, in theory, strengthen. Consequently the higher costs of borrowing are offset by the cheaper imports that are now available. But there may be a time lag before such benefits of a high exchange rate are felt. In the meantime, the local economy will be slowing down, exports will be more expensive and profits may fall. The best strategy for managing such economic exposure in any one country is to diversify operations and financing internationally.

Political risk

Political events might interfere with a foreign subsidiary's cash flows and, in severe cases, with its very existence. When facing balance of payments difficulties and pressure on its currency's value, for example, a host country's government might resort to controls on the conversion or transfer of its currency abroad. Other actions a host country may take that will affect the cash remittances by a multinational include changes in the local tax rules, requirements for a larger local content in the production of goods or services supplied by the multinational, the imposition of quotas and even the expropriation of assets.

The objective of multinationals in this regard is to manage this 'political risk' as best they can. Multinationals will seek to estimate the chance of political actions affecting their cash flows. Many countries will provide insurance for companies that have invested abroad against losses from political events which lead to controls on currency convertibility, expropriation, wars and revolutions. Such insurance is often available from a government agency in the parent's country when the country wants to encourage direct investment in developing countries.

7.4 Country Risk and the Cost of Capital

Country risk relates to the likelihood that changes in the business environment will occur that reduce the profitability of doing business in a country, such changes potentially affecting operating profits adversely as well as the value of assets.

Many country risk service providers analyse country risk in terms of several components, often classified as being economic and non-economic, which after the application of 'appropriate' weights provide a value capturing country risk. However, a fundamental question for anyone considering making an investment overseas is how can country risk be taken into consideration?

If it is accepted that country effects will remain significant in spite of apparent convergence, it raises the question, how can country risk be measured. One approach starts with the basic proposition that the risk premium in any equity market can be written as:

Equity Risk Premium = Base Premium for Mature Equity Market + Country Premium

As such, the country premium should reflect the extra risk in a specific market, but formulating it in this manner raises the questions:

- What should the base premium for a mature equity market be?
- Should there be a country premium and, if so, how do we estimate the premium?

To answer the first question, it is often argued that because the US equity market is a mature market and there is sufficient historical data it is possible to make a reasonable estimate of the risk premium. However, the same approach could be used for any market for which there is sufficient historical data to determine a base premium. It is important to note that following this approach does presuppose that any appraisal will be undertaken in the currency associated with the base premium. In other words, the cash flows relating to the investment appraisal will be converted in US dollars, such that US dollar cash flows for the prospective opportunity will be discounted at a US dollar denominated discount rate that captures the systematic country risk.

Once the base premium has been selected alternative approaches have been proposed for estimating the country premium that involve the use of:

- Default risk spreads
- Default spreads plus relative standard deviations
- Relative volatility.

Default spreads are one of the simplest and most easily accessible approaches that can be used. Default spreads are obtained from the rating assigned to a country's debt by a ratings agency (S&P, Moody's and IBCA all rate countries). These ratings measure default risk (rather than equity risk) but they are affected by many of the factors that drive equity risk – for instance, the stability of a country's currency, its budget and trade balances and its political stability. The other advantage of ratings is that they come with default spreads over the US Treasury bond.

While ratings provide a convenient measure of country risk, there are costs associated with using them as the only measure. First, ratings agencies often lag markets when it comes to responding to changes in the underlying default risk. Second, the ratings agency focus on default risk may obscure other risks that could still affect equity markets. What are the alternatives? There are numerical country risk scores that have been developed by some services as much more comprehensive measures of risk. The Economist, for instance, has a score that runs from 0 to 100, where 0 is no risk and 100 is most risky, that it uses to rank emerging markets. Alternatively, country risk can be estimated from the bottom-up by looking at economic fundamentals in each country. This, of course, requires significantly more information than the other approaches.

One view is that the country risk measure captured in the default spread is an intermediate step towards estimating the risk premium to use in risk models. The default spreads that come with country ratings provide an important first step, but still only measure the premium for default risk. Intuitively, it can be argued that we would expect the country equity risk premium to be larger than the country default risk spread. To address the issue of how much higher the volatility of the equity market in a country relative to the volatility of the country bond can used to estimate the spread. This yields the following estimate for the country equity risk premium:

Country Equity Risk Premium =

$$\text{Country Default Spread} \quad \times \quad \left(\frac{\text{Standard Deviation} \quad \text{Equity}}{\text{Standard Deviation Country Bond}} \right)$$

To illustrate, assume country B has a default spread of 4.83% and the annualised standard deviation in country B's equity index over the previous year was 30.64%, while the annualised standard deviation in the country B's dollar-denominated country bond was 15.28%. The resulting country equity risk premium for country B is as follows:

Country B's Equity Risk Premium = 4.83% x (30.64%/15.28%) = 9.69%

The third alternative is to assess country risk using a relative volatility approach. For example, the modified US $ CAPM approach has been used by major investment banks and starts from the perspective that the results of beta analysis for emerging markets often gives results contrary to common sense. For example, based upon the analysis of equity returns of individual countries against a world portfolio Godfrey and Espinosa (1996) found that:

- All developed countries have betas higher than 0.5
- 15 of 26 emerging market countries have betas below 0.5
- 4 such countries have negative betas, implying costs of equity below risk-free rates
- Risk premium in emerging market countries is lower than the risk premium for the US.

By comparison, Godfrey and Espinosa found that the volatility of the emerging markets from the analysis as measured by the standard deviation of mean equity returns revealed a picture far more in keeping with expectations. This, together with other reasoning, led to the proposed use of the modified US $ CAPM (Credit Suisse First Boston 1997). According to this approach adjustments to the risk-free rate are made for country risk by the addition of a credit spread and to the beta for the volatility of the market in relation to a US reference point, as measured by the relative standard deviation, that is,

$$Ke = (Rf_{US} + \text{Credit Spread}) + (\text{Adjusted } ß \times RpUS \times \alpha)$$

Where,

Ke	=	Estimated cost of equity
Rfus	=	Risk-free rate in US
RpUS	=	US Market Risk Premium
Adjusted ß	=	σ_i/σ_{us}, that is, the standard deviation of stock market returns in the country of the prospective investment divided by the standard deviation of the US stock market.
α	=	Adjustment for the interdependence between the risk free rate and the market risk premium.

This approach makes a number of important and questionable assumptions. Firstly, that the equity risk premium in the US market is an important performance benchmark; second, the equity risk premium (ERP) demanded by investors in local markets can be inferred from the

ERP of the US, adjusted for the volatility of the local markets relative to US; and, third, that there is an interrelationship between the risk-free rate and ERP.

As to which approach is to be preferred or if there is a better alternative is still the subject of research and you may encounter a number of different methods being used in practice. Certainly, it is important to recognise that a most fundamental issue is whether to adjust the discount rate or the cash flows. The approaches described focus on the former and take a different stance on the basis for the adjustment for which further research is required to identify what should be preferred. Alternatively, the cash flows could be adjusted, and although this has merits in principle, practitioners often prefer discount rate adjustments. The distinction between the two main alternatives does raise a fundamental issue relating to time. Many valuation approaches make use of perpetuity assumptions and there is a danger in the use of such an approach with a country risk adjusted discount rate, because it implies the risk will last forever. It seems reasonable to believe that country risk premiums will decline over time such that just as companies mature and become less risky over time, countries can mature and become less risky as well. This has been confirmed by Gangemi et al. (1999) who examined the 25-year period from 1970 to 1994 consisting of monthly data on 18 countries drawn from the Morgan Stanley database. This analysis included running mean reversion-based regressions of one period's beta estimate on the immediately prior period's beta estimate. Their research drew upon earlier work by Blume (1971) who found asset betas to have a 'regression' tendency; that is, over time, the estimated betas tended to regress toward the grand mean of unity. For instance, an asset whose beta is estimated to be extremely low in one period will tend to have a less-extreme beta estimate closer to unity in the next period. Blume's results have been widely accepted to the extent that a literature has developed on the application of Bayesian techniques to beta estimation so as to adjust for mean reversion.

In Gangemi et al's research, the basic Blume approach was directly applied to a sample of country-level data, thereby allowing an assessment of the mean reversion properties of beta from an international investor's perspective. Generally, the results revealed a degree of mean reversion in country betas, quite similar to that documented for individual company betas.

Assuming the Morgan Stanley country indices to be good proxies for the investment opportunity set facing the internationally focused investor, then the following are the practical implications of these results for their portfolio decisions that arise from the study:

- mean-reversion models should be used for assessing international beta risk
- the potential effect of major market movements such as the crash of October 1987 in the analysis should be acknowledged in any analysis, and
- a simple "50/50" weighting scheme should be considered whereby a half weighting is applied to the global unity prior and the other half weighting is applied to the previous period estimate of beta.

It must be stressed that there is a real need for substantial research to test the different approaches. This is further confirmed by Fernández (2003) with reference to 75 common and uncommon errors in company valuation'. As he points out with reference to Ukrainoil:

'How to calculate the cost of equity is far from clear. There is not consensus in the finance literature.'

Fernandez illustrates eight formulae that have been developed for estimating the cost of equity in emerging markets, including two of those reviewed earlier. None of these yields identical results and this is a good illustration that we are a long way from having established a scientific method for determining the cost of equity in emerging markets and further flagging an area that is need of substantive research.

From Country Risk to Project Risk

If the foregoing was not enough, while assessing the country risk is a challenge, there is yet another very real problem in terms of evaluating how individual companies in that country are exposed to country risk. Damodaran (2002) illustrates three alternatives:

1. Assume that all companies in a country are equally exposed to country risk. Thus, for Brazil, with its estimated country risk premium of 9.69%, each company in the market will have an additional country risk premium of 9.69% added to its expected returns. For instance, the cost of equity for Aracruz Celulose, a paper and pulp manufacturer listed in Brazil, with a beta of 0.72, in US dollar terms would be (assuming a US Treasury bond rate of 5% and a mature market (US) risk premium of 5.51%):

   Expected Cost of Equity = 5.00% + 0.72 (5.51%) + 9.69% = 18.66%

   Damodaran recognises that the biggest limitation of this approach is that it assumes all firms in a country, no matter what their business or size, are equally exposed to country risk.

2. Assume that a company's exposure to country risk is proportional to its exposure to all other market risk, which is measured by the beta. For Aracruz, this would lead to a cost of equity estimate of:

   Expected Cost of Equity = 5.00% + 0.72 (5.51% + 9.69%) = 15.94%

3. Allow for each company to have an exposure to country risk that is different from its exposure to all other market risk as follows:

   Expected Return =
   Rf + Beta (Mature Equity Risk Premium) + k (County Risk Premium)

Using this rationale, Aracruz, which derives the majority of its revenues in the global paper market in US dollars, should be less exposed than the typical Brazilian firm to country risk. Assuming a k of 0.25, the resulting cost of equity in US dollar terms for Aracruz is:

Expected Return = 5% + 0.72 (5.51%) + 0.25 (9.69%) =11.39%

Three different expected returns are the result of applying the three different approaches. The higher the percentage, the greater is the assessment of country risk and the lower would be the resulting net present value in a discounted cash flow analysis. Yet again, there is no definitive answer as yet as to which approach is preferred. Research is under way with the intention of providing appropriate guidance.

7.5 Integrated Risk Management

From a broader perspective, firms can be argued as having three fundamental ways of implementing risk management objectives:

1. the firm's risk profile modifying operations
2. adjusting capital structure, and
3. employing targeted financial instruments.

As such, integration requires these three to be combined, with the goal being to maximise value by shaping, necessarily involving the removal of some risks and the retention of others.

The emphasis is strategic rather than tactical and the distinction is made with reference to an example involving the hedging of contracts for the purchase of goods or services from a foreign country at some future date. The focus in this instance is specific to the transaction, whereas a more strategic approach would be directed at questioning how exchange rate fluctuations would affect the value of the entire firm.

It is important to recognise that integration means both the integration of risks and integration of ways to manage risks. Integrated risk management evaluates the firm's total risk exposure, instead of evaluating each risk in isolation and this is important because it is the total risk of the firm that typically matters to the assessment of the firm's value and its ability to fulfil its contractual obligations in the future.

There is an interesting challenge associated with having integrated risk management as an objective and it is one that has parallels with the developments associated with Value Based Management (VBM). One of the major challenges with VBM is to have a conceptual framework for management to understand the key influences upon the value of the business, in terms of the key 'value drivers'. These value drivers vary from business to business and over time. What is important to a property company may well be very different than for a financial services business. Equally, the relative importance of the drivers of value in the start up phase of an operation will be very different to those in maturity. Understanding these value drivers is very important in thinking about an optimal risk policy. It is vital that managers understand how the degree of uncertainty about these value drivers can potentially affect firm value. In other words, to set risk targets, managers have to understand the channels through which risk can affect firm value.

Given that the fundamental goal of risk management is to maximise shareholder value, the question arises, how? There are some fairly well documented methods of risk management that include:

1. Systematic risk management. According to financial theory, total risk consists of systematic (market or beta) risk and specific (unsystematic) risk. In a world with widely available diversification opportunities, systematic risk is the only risk for which investors require compensation. Whilst systematic risk cannot be diversified away by investors or management, exposure to it can be mitigated by adjusting holdings of risky assets and cash or by hedging with futures, forwards or swap contracts. Although in principle such exposures could be managed by investors, it is argued that in practice they will not have sufficient understanding of the firm's exposures, thereby making this a rich potential area for sound corporate level risk management.

2. Capital structure management. Optimal capital structure is a much publicised but poorly understood concept in finance. The principle that via careful management and structuring of debt and equity, an optimal capital cost can be found that avoids financial distress is well founded. However, in practice, estimating such an optimal position is a real challenge and not well covered in the literature. However, techniques are available for trying to understand this, not least of which is the use of cash flow stress testing against disaster based scenarios associated with the impact of problems relating to the core value drivers of the business.

7.6 The Revolution in Corporate Risk Management

There has been a revolution in corporate risk management over the last decade. Innovations in risk management have occurred, from risk management as a process to risk management products, demonstrating a confluence of risk management and corporate finance. Until the 1990s different perspectives on risk management seemed to have co-existed to all intents and purposes as independent spheres of theory and practice. Forces of convergence have worked together to unify these disparate risk management perspectives and practices in the last ten years.

Risk management appears to be on an inevitable course of convergence with the modern theory of corporate finance and companies today can focus selectively on risk finance or risk transfer, use features like triggers to control the cost of capital acquired through risk management products, integrate their financing and risk management decisions through the use of enterprise-wide products and replace expensive paid-in capital with cheaper sources of contingent capital that provide an infusion of funds only when truly necessary. Such expanded products are likely to be beneficial, however, only if a company has the right risk management process in place, one in which corporate financial and risk management decisions are no longer made separately but in a fully integrated way that is clearly informed by the goal of increasing firm value. Therefore, key within the risk management revolution is 'convergence' which relates to various perspectives on risk management once divided by extreme differences in vocabulary, concepts and methods; convergence of organisational processes for managing an extraordinary variety of risks; convergence of risk management products offered by hitherto completely separate industries like insurance and capital markets; and, finally, convergence of risk management with the quest for the corporate holy grail of an optimal capital structure.

At the heart of this revolution is what has emerged as 'alternative risk transfer' (ART) which is defined as the large and growing collection of 'contracts, structures and solutions' provided by insurance and/or reinsurance companies that enable companies to transfer or finance some of their risks in non traditional ways . ART represents the foray of the insurance industry into the corporate financing and capital formation processes that were once the near exclusive domain of commercial and investment banks. The view taken here is that not taking account of risk management opportunities in a corporate finance context is quite likely to lead to serious inefficiencies in how a firm manages risk or raises funds — if not both.

A comprehensive approach to corporate finance must begin with a risk management process and strategy that aims explicitly at maximising the value of the firm. Then, in executing that strategy, management must consider the full range of available risk management products, including new risk finance products such as 'contingent capital' and 'finite risk' contracts along with well-established risk transfer instruments like interest rate and currency derivatives – covered in an earlier section. Given that this range today encompasses both new and established products provided by insurance companies as well as commercial and investment banks, a comprehensive approach to corporate finance means taking account, and full advantage, of the convergence accomplished in the last decade.

7.7 The Changing Function of Risk Management

The revolution in corporate risk management may have important implications for roles and responsibilities . The risk manager and treasurer are typically entrusted with managing operational and financial risks within the framework of a given capital structure, but the composition of the risk is the responsibility of the CFO. Besides avoiding or reducing risk, the risk manager has traditionally had recourse to the insurance markets to transfer risk to third parties and the treasurer has had recourse to the capital markets to transfer risk and (separately) to obtain financing. The CFO has often viewed the capital markets as the primary vehicle for maintaining or transforming capital structure.

As capital and insurance markets converge, progressive organisations have started developing risk management tools that incorporate features of both. For example, one 'new' integrated risk management product provides a single block of insurance capacity that protects against a broad set of risks, both those that are traditionally insured and those that are hedged in the capital markets. The rationale is that it may be inefficient to purchase insurance and financial loss protection separately, because the corporation may be over-protected on the financial side and under-protected on the insurance side, or vice versa. By purchasing an integrated cover that protects both insurance and financial exposures, the corporation is assured that capacity will be available no matter what the source of the loss is. The consequence is that no matter what the source of the loss is, the ultimate effect on the bottom line is the same. Another consequence of the convergence of insurance and capital markets is the development of tools that combine risk transfer and financing. For example, finite risk reinsurance products combine financing and risk transfer in a way that allows corporations to achieve in a single transaction the benefits of both insurance and debt financing.

This revolution in risk management techniques has implications for the CFO as well. Any policy regarding capital structure configuration is predicated on an assessment of the risks confronting the corporation. In fact, a company's risk profile may change as a result of the implementation of new risk management instruments, with a consequent change in the corporate capital needs. Instead of simply optimising the balance of debt and equity, the CFO now has at least three instruments to use: debt, equity and insurance. In addition, there are techniques that directly address the capital structure issue. Given that equity capital is an expensive source of long-term financing and that the risk profile of a firm determines its required amount of equity capital, substitutes for paid-up equity capital have the potential to offer significant economies. Contingent capital products, for example, promise to infuse the company with capital precisely when it is needed in the event of a catastrophic loss. These products eliminate the need to hold expensive on-balance-sheet equity capital for those rare events that may inflict severe financial harm on a corporation. An off-balance-sheet contingent capital facility (almost insurance, but not quite) can be cost effective.

If taken to a logical conclusion, the days of clearly defined boundaries between capital markets and insurance arenas are over. Newer specialty insurance products are emerging to insure financial risks not traditionally covered by insurance and new worlds are opening up for the specialty insurance markets. Where traditional insurance is reluctant to go, specialty insurance now stands, firmly securing a foothold in the financial risk arena. Specialty insurance can be seen as a vehicle to free up capital that is otherwise reserved for potential losses, as well as having a positive effect on the balance sheet and giving customers more options to protect their businesses.

Taken to a more extreme view, traditional methods like loss portfolio transfers, transferring future claims payment obligation, and credit insurance, which have been around for some time, may be supplemented with new insurance programs to cover financial risk. Furthermore, some corporations looking for ways to use insurance could use it to free up capital that sits dormant on the balance sheet as reserve capital.

Organisations using these solutions could potentially be very broad, for example, they could 'range from banks to energy companies, from tyre manufacturers to grain growers'. The reasons are as varied as the companies themselves and range from reducing balance sheet risk to giving collateral value to transactions, as well as integrating hazard risk into one financial cover. This 'insurative' approach is in its relative infancy, but there are examples of its application:

- Royal Bank of Canada (RBC) that signed a deal with Swiss Re to guarantee the bank up to $200 million (Canadian) should the bank's loan portfolio experience exceptional losses. The deal allowed RBC access to otherwise reserved capital without the risk of a loss crippling the bank and for Swiss Re, it is an investment, as well. The heart of the argument about this deal was that it is far more efficient for Swiss Re to take in the premium, reinvest the premium and be standing by ready to cover the risk should (a significant loss) happen.

- United Grain Growers of Canada (UGG) deal in 1990. The deal, which was worth $250 million (Canadian), integrated the hazard risk that UGG faced with the risk to the balance sheet from a fluctuation in grain volume. Swiss Re acted as advisor and structured the deal. It turned out that the major source of risk was weather-related, but on closer examination, it was not explicitly the weather. The explicit part seemed to be more closely related to the volume of grain. UGG was able to construct, with an index that would help them to track what was going on in the industry in volume. In other words, it was an insurance policy with deductibles and limits that combined hazard risks and the grain volume risk. The result was that it gave UGG an additional lever to optimise its capital structure.

7.8 Risk and VBM

One key question that needs to be answered is 'what is the appropriate level of risk for a company to take'? Every company has a different appetite for risk depending on sector, strategy, size and maturity as well as a wide range of external and internal factors, however, all risks should be identified, prioritised, aligned with strategic goals and then evaluated. If risk appetite can be defined and applied to the business, there is a far greater chance that risks within the business can be more fully understood and communicated. As a consequence, the extent to which a company can manage each of its key risks should become clearer, leading to far more efficient capital allocations and fewer surprises for the CEO and shareholders.

Value Based Management (VBM), has traditionally focussed upon growth and the improvement of performance. More recently, the darker side of managing for value has attracted much attention, not least because of studies undertaken which have revealed very significant declines in share prices in relatively short time periods. For example, one study by Deloitte found that over the last decade almost half of the 1000 largest global companies suffered declines in share prices of more than 20 percent in a one-month period, relative to the Morgan Stanley Capital International (MSCI) World Index. By the end of 2003, roughly one-quarter of these companies had still not recovered their lost market value. Another one-quarter took more than a year for their share prices to recover.

Significant value shifts through deterioration of the stock price can have a disastrous impact on a company. Two major questions on the minds of all CEOs and Boards of companies are:

1. What are the most important risks to focus upon? (That is, what factors could bring about a deterioration?)
2. What can be done to manage and mitigate them and, associated with this, will any particular framework really help?

Research by Ernst and Young and Oxford Metrica (2003) identified the significant positive and negative shifts in shareholder value across the largest 1000 companies globally over a five-year period, regardless of the root cause of the shift. The events underlying these value shifts were then identified and classified into a conceptual framework that provides a taxonomy of the drivers of value and risk. In broad terms, the research indicated that within a five-year period, it is quite likely that a CEO will experience a sudden jump or precipitous fall in value while he or she is at the helm. Moreover, the impact on value tends to be sustained. What is most important, however, is that CEOs have a detailed understanding of the particular value drivers for their individual businesses as well as an understanding of how those drivers may change over time.

More specifically, the study showed that most Chief Executives will experience at least one of these major shareholder value shifts during their tenure, that is,

- 75% chance of experiencing a positive shareholder value shift of over 30% (relative to the market) in a five-year period.
- 40% chance of experiencing a negative shareholder value shift of over 30% (relative to the market) in a five-year period.

There is no pattern for the timing of these shifts; for example, around annual reporting or the issue of quarterly results. Moreover, these shifts in shareholder value tended to be sustained. Management of the underlying events tended to be 'destiny determining' for the company — not only did they define the likely future shareholder value performance but they also had a significant and usually negative effect on the reputation of incumbent CEOs.

While the majority of sudden positive value shifts were driven by strategic alliances, mergers and acquisitions, confidence in management's ability to execute core business processes and investment in research and innovation, the majority of sudden negative value shifts were driven by a failure to adapt to changes in the business environment, customer mismanagement and poor investor relations.

Since there is currently no associated engineering or financial instrument, like insurance or derivatives to hedge these critical value events, it is up to senior management and the CEO in particular, to own and actively manage risks and opportunities. Several common underlying risk factors that resulted in a negative effect on value have been identified, illustrating that companies must:

- Manage critical risk interdependencies
- Proactively address low-frequency, high-impact risks
- Foster a strong ethics and control culture
- Provide timely information on control factors.

Manage Critical Risk Interdependencies

The vast majority of companies that suffered the greatest losses in value were found to be exposed to more than one type of risk, but equally firms were found to fail to recognise and manage the relationships among different types of risks. The problem is that actions taken to address one type of risk, such as strategic risk, can often increase exposure to other risks, such as operational or financial risks and companies should implement an integrated risk management function to identify and manage interdependencies among all the risks facing the firm. Unfortunately, most firms manage risk in 'silos,' often leaving them blind to relationships between risks. For example, in a 2003 survey of financial services executives by the Global Association of Risk Professionals, more than half said their firm used disparate systems for operational risk and credit risk, while only 10 percent said that they had integrated technology that covers both sets of risks.

This raises a key question, 'How can managers gain a comprehensive view of risk interdependencies?' The essential first step identified is to build an integrated risk management function, championed and supported by senior management that is positioned above all divisions and departments. The purpose of this group is to identify the key risks across the corporation, understand the connections between them and develop a risk-management strategy that takes into consideration the organisation's appetite for risk . By all accounts one exemplar is Bank of America, which integrates risk management at the time business strategies are developed, rather than planning for risk after a strategy has been established. Central to its approach is looking at risks holistically, rather than in isolation. For instance, when considering risks in the underwriting process, the bank assesses how its business strategy, sales practices, and business development practices affect the risk profile of what is underwritten.

Once again there is scope for the 'insurative' approach discussed earlier to support the comprehensive approach. This not only helps the organisation reduce overall risk but can also lower the costs of risk management. One company that has pursued this approach is Honeywell which formerly bought product liability, property and foreign exchange insurance policies separately. By understanding the risk interdependencies of these products, it developed a comprehensive insurance contract with American International Group that bundled several different kinds of policies. By all accounts, this has enabled the company to cut its overall risk abatement cost by more than 15 percent (Meulbrook 2001).

Proactively Address Low-Frequency, High-Impact Risks

Some of the greatest value losses have been found to be caused by exceptional events such as the Asian financial crisis, the bursting of the technology bubble and the September 11th terrorist attacks. However, many firms apparently fail to plan for these rare but high-impact risks and they should employ 'stress testing' to ensure that their internal controls and business continuity plans can withstand the shock of a high-impact event. Companies should proactively plan and acquire the strategic flexibility to respond to specific scenarios.

Foster a Strong Ethics and Control Culture

Corporate cultures and incentive systems that set high premium for returns without complementary controls can lead to major value and brand losses and senior management needs to create a culture emphasising the central importance of ethical behaviour, quality control and risk management. Compensation incentives should be aligned with long-term value creation and brand protection.

Provide Timely Information on Control Factors

A number of organisations lacked access to current information required for senior management to respond quickly to emerging problems and firms need to improve their internal information systems and communication mechanisms to ensure that senior management and boards of directors receive accurate, near real-time information on the causes, financial impact and possible solutions of control problems.

Given the frequency of sudden and dramatic drops in share prices, even the largest companies need to take a serious look at current risk management practices. Companies that go beyond traditional methods to take a more integrated and comprehensive approach to risk management may reduce the likelihood of suffering major losses in value.

7.9 Enterprise -wide Risk Management (ERM)

One view is that the challenges and threats to a loss of value can be met via the measurement and coordination of the management of all of a company's major risks in a manner consistent with the fundamental business objectives of the firm. To accommodate this we have seen the emergence of Enterprise-wide Risk Management, or ERM.

There is little doubt that the need for a comprehensive system of risk management is critical because of today's business environment and the case for an ERM system to measure and coordinate the management of all of a company's major risks in a manner consistent with the fundamental business objectives of the firm is very strong. As indicated, ideally an ERM would aim to consolidate and integrate both the process by which a firm manages its risks and the risks that are targeted in that process, but at least one study has shown that ERM has many different interpretations (Deloitte Development LLC 2005). That there are so many different interpretations is probably a consequence of the fact that ERM has been widely discussed for more than a decade and despite this long gestation period it has taken root in only a few, primarily larger organisations. Interest built slowly since the mid-1990s, when the Economist Intelligence Unit created an extensive ERM framework. From such roots, professional associations from internal audit groups to business risk managers to chief financial officers have been discussing the potential of ERM at conferences, in papers and in trade publications for several years. However, until relatively recently, corporate interest was driven primarily by intellectual curiosity and internal audit experimentation. Whilst ERM has been argued by its proponents as providing a solid foundation upon which companies can enhance corporate governance and deliver greater shareholder value, there is little or no evidence of these objectives having been achieved.

While ERM definitions vary, there seems to be fewer disputes about its goals which may be summarised as to:

- Enable the board and senior management to understand how the risks for which they are ultimately responsible are being managed on a day-to-day basis
- Aggregate and integrate/correlate significant risk information up through the firm to create an enterprise-wide view of the firm's risk profile and its 'in control' status
- Equip business and corporate areas with the capabilities to proactively identify, assess and report on the control of their significant financial and non-financial risks at any time within the context of the firm's business objectives.

With broad objectives defined, an organisation can then move toward a more detailed description of ERM that enables definition of current and target risk management capabilities. At this stage, discrete projects and initiatives can be defined to close the gaps and move the company toward its goals.

There are differences between ERM and other less formal, more ad hoc approaches (Culp 2002). First, ERM seeks to consolidate exposure types not just across financial risks but also across non-financial perils and hazards. In so doing, ERM seeks to differentiate between core risks and non-core risks and, as part of that process, between those risks in which the firm has some perceived comparative informational advantage and those where it views itself as no better informed than other market participants.

A second distinguishing feature of ERM is that it involves viewing all risks facing a company through some form of common lens, but at a more general level, ERM implies the ability of management to transform the chaotic variety of financial instruments into an orderly array of related and in some respects interchangeable tools for accomplishing the firm's overarching risk management goals. From this vantage point, what matters is not whether a risk is best managed through 'swaps,' 'insurance' or 'trading limits,' but whether the company's resulting enterprise-wide risk exposure conforms to the risk tolerances of its security holders and, in the process, enables the firm to minimise its cost of capital.

A third characteristic of ERM is its attempt to consolidate the risk management process organisationally across systems, processes and people. In other words, the 'enterprise-wide' in ERM refers not just to a company's view of the risks it is facing, but also the degree of coordination and consolidation with which the firm manages those risks.

Finally, ERM managers are constantly looking for more integrated risk management products and solutions. Capital and insurance markets have been converging over the last decade on both the demand and supply sides. On the supply side, an investment banker might solicit a once-unheard-of meeting with the head of a corporation's captive insurance company instead of its chief financial officer (CFO). At the same time, several reinsurance companies now boast of relationships with corporate CFOs that are deeper than those most CFOs now have with their derivatives dealers.

On the demand side, corporations with a growing ERM focus are increasingly seeking one-stop shopping for their risk management solutions, prompting insurance and reinsurance companies like AIG and Swiss Re to offer earnings per share insurance and derivatives participants like Goldman Sachs and Lehman to set up licensed reinsurance subsidiaries.

To the staunch proponents of ERM it represents an aspiration to coordinate and concentrate the raw materials of strategic risk management, to distinguish 'core' (that is, strategic) from non-core risks, and makes it an imperative for the highest levels of management to engage systematically in these efforts. They argue that it makes exacting and stringent demands for the coordinated comparison of risks and their means of mitigation considered as a whole, which go beyond those of previous approaches. However, it prescribes an approach or a framework rather than providing specific leads as to what are the key elements in strategic risk that must be checked. It promises a rich harvest of results, but much else as to how to analyse strategic risk has to be left open to the user. For a more penetrating and potentially practicable approach into the realities of strategic risk, it seems that great benefit can be derived from examining other aspects of the relationship between strategic risk and value.

Enterprise-wide Risk Management Frameworks

Until recently, there has not been a standardised framework for approaching enterprise-wide risk management (ERM) that organisations could use to establish benchmarks and best practices. To address this void and as a consequence of regulatory and legislative pressures, the Committee of Sponsoring Organisations of the Treadway Commission (COSO) has developed an enterprise risk management framework: 'Enterprise Risk Management - Integrated Framework' (COSO 2004). COSO's framework defines ERM as follows:

'Enterprise Risk Management is a process, effected by an entity's board of directors, management, and other personnel, applied in a strategy setting and across the enterprise, designed to identify potential events that may affect the entity, and manage risks to be within its risk appetite, to provide reasonable assurance regarding the achievement of entity objectives.'

Implementing the COSO Framework

The COSO ERM framework can appear to be intimidating upon first review because the report is very comprehensive and consists of two volumes: one volume presents the framework and the other offers helpful guidance for implementing it.

Arguably, one of the drawbacks with introducing such a comprehensive framework is that it requires a significant investment of time and resources to fully implement within an organisation. Further complicating this challenge is that effective ERM requires ownership by executives, careful oversight by directors and a cultural shift at most organisations. That makes the initial implementation of the framework the biggest challenge before the process can reach its potential.

Practical approaches to implementing the framework have started to emerge designed to help organisations become comfortable using an entity-wide portfolio approach to risk management. For example, one approach (Ballou and Heitger 2005) consists of:

1. Implementing the ERM framework on a limited basis across each of the COSO framework's eight interrelated components:

   - Internal environment
   - Objective setting (in four areas: strategy, operations, reporting and compliance)
   - Event identification

- Risk assessment
- Risk response
- Control activities
- Information and communication
- Monitoring

2. Placing initial emphasis on entity-wide risks across all four risk categories identified by the COSO framework - strategic, operations, reporting and compliance.

The ERM framework can be expanded, including an eventual cascading of the framework throughout other levels of the organisation as senior management becomes comfortable with the culture the framework creates. Part of that cultural change requires that people throughout the organisation take ownership of risk management.

There are several claimed benefits associated with using a building-block approach to implementing the COSO ERM framework that have much in common with the implementation of some other initiatives, like Activity Based Costing. These include:

- size does not matter
- culture shifts take time
- better allocation of resources

However, there are also pitfalls to avoid when using a building-block approach to ERM that can occur if an organisation is not careful to emphasise the cultural shift. Two of the more important challenges they recognise are:

- **Simplification of the Framework.** Over time, the initial ERM framework becomes too simplified for an effective understanding of entity-wide risks and making management decisions. Thus, organisations need to invest a sufficient amount of time and resources to implement an effective ERM framework culture and establish a foundation for managing risks not only at the entity level but also at other levels of the organisation as the framework evolves. Sufficient time and resources should be invested in each component of COSO's framework to help avoid oversimplification.

- **Sceptical Perceptions Associated with Implementing a Framework.** When an organisation opts to roll out new initiatives slowly, sceptics within the organisation often will assume that there is an ulterior motive. For example, even if the initial rollout of an organisation's ERM framework emphasises ownership of risk management only within pockets of the organisation, executives and directors should try to create a risk management culture across the entire organisation. This will demonstrate their commitment to the ERM initiative to all employees and curb scepticism. Furthermore, if the organisation only introduces a skeletal risk management framework, stock market analysts might see it only as a signal that an organisation is following trends to meet shareholder expectations. Thus, executives should ensure that a firm-wide risk management culture is developed, even though initial rollouts of the framework might not involve every aspect of the organisation.

Pressure for the implementation of the new COSO ERM Framework was provided by a series of high-profile business scandals and failures where investors, company personnel and other stakeholders suffered tremendous losses. In response, the US Congress passed the Public Company Accounting Reform and Investor Protection Act of 2002 (better known as Sarbanes-Oxley, or SOA). Section 404 of SOA mandated that companies use a suitable, recognised control framework for evaluating the effectiveness of internal controls. COSO's framework for internal control had existed for a decade without generating great enthusiasm, but SOA requirements in the past two years elevated dialogue about the framework. The original model, which looks like a colourful Rubik's Cube puzzle, was not a simple concept to grasp or implement and this might explain its slow uptake before 2002, when SOA became law. Ironically, COSO's new ERM framework adds even more rows and columns and is inherently complex. Doubtless this complexity will create work for consultants to help organisations implement the model and realise the potential benefits because a comprehensive management approach that covers the entire organisation's ERM strategy will never be a quick fix. However, the COSO ERM framework, despite its limitations, is arguably a major step in the right direction and may well become the standard for ERM frameworks: only time will tell.

7.10 Managing Risk and Uncertainty

In everyday terms we often think of risk as the 'What can go wrong with something we are committed to doing?' Such a view just looks at the downside aspect of risk. Risk can also be viewed as an upside opportunity which needs to be managed, for example, developing new products and services to push forward the frontiers of customers experiences and so get ahead of the competition. So, risk arises as much from the likelihood that something good will not happen as it does from the threat that something bad will happen.

Typically risk and uncertainty are viewed synonymously and the words are often used interchangeably. However, there is a useful distinction, when we take a risk we are betting on an outcome that will result from the a decision we have made, in that for the risk we take there exists some basis upon which to estimate outcomes whilst for uncertainty there is very little basis. So, the distinction is one of the levels of information and/or knowledge we have to estimate possible outcomes and our degree of commitment to those outcomes.

There are three stages to any risk management process:

1. Risk identification
2. Risk assessment
3. Risk management actions.

1. Risk Identification

Critical to any project evaluation is the identification of the risks that will affect it. In identifying risks it is useful to take a number of different perspectives:

- Internal versus external risks, for example, risk from lack of skilled people versus competitor risk
- Risks as threats and as opportunities, for example, risk of explosion and risk of developing new competitive advantages
- Soft versus hard risks, for example, risk from cultural change versus interest rate risk.

In the identification of risk it can be useful to use a checklist such as the one shown in Figure 7.1. However, one must bear in mind that risks are by their very nature are a function of the particular situation being looked at.

Figure 7.1 Risk Identification Checklist

Environmental Risks

Product risk, market risk, industry risk, competitor risk, technological risk, regulatory risk, legal risk, political risk, social risk, financial market risk and so on.

Operational Risks

Supplier risk, input price risk, capacity risk, health and safety risks and so on.

Financial Risks

Interest rate risk, foreign currency risk, liquidity risk, credit risk and so on.

People Risks

Risks arising from; employee and management fraud, leadership and management capability, employee competence and skills, authority limits and so on.

Technology Risk

Design risk, completion risk, infrastructure risk, engineering risk and so on.

Organisational Risk

Risks arising from culture, structure, processes and so on.

2. Risk Assessment

This stage may usefully be thought of as comprising two parts:

1. Tracing project risks through to the project cash flows
2. Risk prioritisation by assessing the significance of each risk using the likelihood versus impact matrix.

Tracing Project Risks

By using a typical Income statement account, one can trace each risk identified for a project to the appropriate cash flow line of the project and hence assess the impact of each risk. This is show in Table 7.1.

Table 7.1 Examples of Risk Impacting on Cash Flows

Calculation of Cash Flows for a Project	Examples of Risks Impacting Cash Flow Line Items
Revenue	Competitor, Foreign currency and Regulatory risks
less: Cost of Sales	Operating, Supply and management risks
Gross Margin	
less Other Operating Costs	Operating and Environmental risks
Profit Before Interest and Tax (PBIT)	
less Interest	Financing and Project Completion risks
Profit Before Tax (PBT)	
less Cash Tax	Political risks
Profit after tax (PAT)	

add back: Depreciation	
add back: Interest	Political and Project Completion risks
Operating Cash Flow After Tax	
less Capital Investment	Design and Regulatory risks
less Working Capital Investment	Supply risks
Free cash flow to the Firm (FCFF)	
less Interest After Tax	
less Debt Repaid/Raised	Financing and Project Completion risks
Free Cash Flow to Equity (FCFE)	

Note 1: See Chapter 12 for an explanation of calculation of FCFF and FCFE.

Risk Prioritisation

Prioritisation of each project risk into one of four categories using the matrix, shown in *Figure 7.2,* to assess the significance of the risk in terms of its likelihood of occurrence and the severity of its impact should it occur. In this way the matrix enables a management team to focus on the vital few risks that must be managed.

Figure 7.2 Project Risk Categories

Impact \ Likelihood	Low	High
High	Transfer/Share with Others	Avoid if Possible
Low	Retain and Finance	Control Through Risk Management

3. Risk Management Actions

Each quadrant in the above matrix has an associated implication in terms of the management actions that may be taken to manage the risk. With each management action there are a number of key issues to be addressed:

- Retain and Finance: Retain the risks and finance them as and when they arise using the firm's own internal resources. Key issue: How much should be set aside as a contingency for these risks?
- Control: Control risks through organisation wide risk management processes. Key issues: Who will be responsible and accountable for risk management within the organisation and how will the risk management process be implemented?
- Transfer and/or share: Transfer and or share the risks with other parties who are willing to take on the risks for a price. Issue: Need to identify who will take all or part of the risk and at what cost?
- Avoid: Avoid the risk in its entirety. Issue: Is it possible to completely avoid the risk?

A common rule of thumb in risk management practice is that the person, organisation or group most able to handle and manage a risk is the one who should bear it.

4. Approaches for the Treatment of Risk in the Appraisal Process

In general we have two main approaches open to us for the treatment of risk within the project appraisal process.

- First, is to test the robustness of the analysis and evaluation by changing the assumptions and examining the effects of these changes on the conclusions. Techniques for doing this include sensitivity analysis, scenario analysis and simulation analysis each of which is summarised below.
    - **Sensitivity Analysis:** Examines the sensitivity of the decision rule, for example, NPV, IRR and so on, to changes, one at a time, in the assumptions of the key variables underlying the project
    - **Scenario Analysis:** Specific scenarios are developed for the future of the project and the viability of the project is examined under each scenario. These scenarios tend to be based on macroeconomic and industry factors
    - **Simulation Analysis:** Applies statistical sampling in an attempt to use the information in the entire distribution of the variables rather than just the expected value to arrive at a decision.

- Second, is to factor the risks into the discount rate or the expected cash flows and see the impact on the performance measures such as NPV and IRR used to evaluate the project.

As regards the second approach we need to separate the total risks of a project into two parts, namely the risks specific to the project itself and the macroeconomic risks affecting the project. Specific risks are best dealt with through the cash flows of the project which are adjusted to take account of the impact of such risks whilst macroeconomic risks which affect all projects are best dealt with by adjusting the discount rate. Figure 7.3 summarises this distinction and the treatment of risks within the appraisal process.

Figure 7.3 Distinction and Treatment of Risks within the Appraisal Process

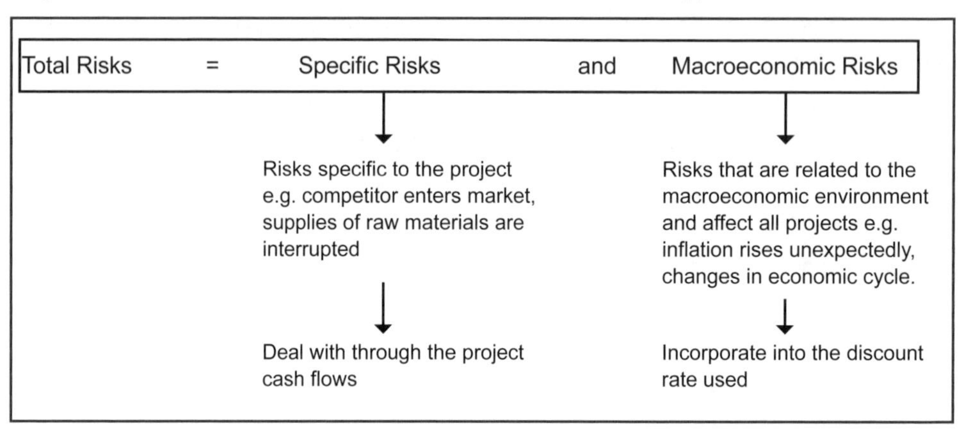

5. Risk and Strategic Decision Making

One aspect that is often missed from any risk assessment exercise is that of the decision maker themselves and the impact they have in terms of their role as the decision maker. Figure 7.4 shows the pivotal role played by the decision maker between the external and the internal environment of a firm for which a project decision is about to be made.

Figure 7.4 External and Internal Environment of a Firm

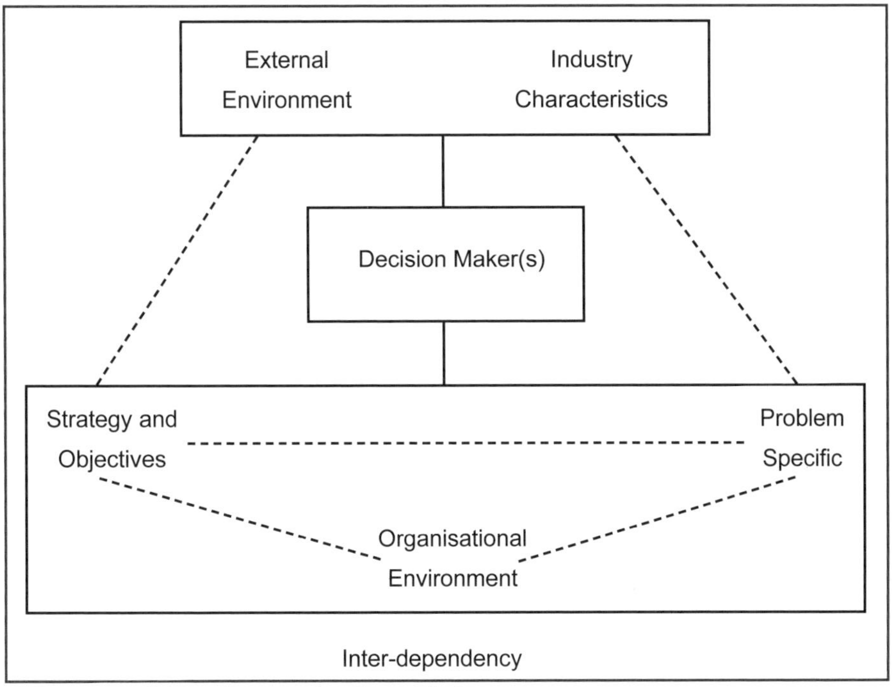

The areas of risk not covered so far relate to:

Problem Specific Risks

These arise from the organisation's ability or otherwise to formulate and resolve a specific strategic problem or issue. For example, the following issues may prove difficult and expose the organisation to risk:

- Identification of the problem and its consequential effects
- Structuring the problem, understanding the key variables and their interrelationship
- Identifying alternative solutions to the problem and their respective implications
- Complexity of the decision task.

Risks Arising From the Decision Maker

These risks relate to:

- Experience of previous problems and projects and their solutions
- Degree of aversion to taking risk
- Bias in decision making resulting from level of knowledge, political allegiance, incentives, beliefs and values.

7.11 *Sensitivity Analysis*

One important management tool available for questioning both potential benefits and risks associated with a project is sensitivity analysis. In essence, the assumptions surrounding a project can be input to computer software or a programmable calculator to produce a base case net present value and internal rate of return, from which changes in assumption can easily be made to gauge the effect upon them. The mechanics of such an application are now considered within the context of a simple example. The data to be used in our example concerns a project with the following features:

- Capital Outlay £5,000,000
- Life 10 years
- Sales Volume 80,000 units
- Selling Price £85 per unit
- Labour Costs £22 per unit
- Material Costs £40 per unit
- Fixed Costs £660,000 per annum
- Cost of Capital 12%

In practice the data would be far more detailed and important factors like taxation and inflation should be included if the resulting net present value is to be calculated at a company cost of capital. However, we have deliberately made the example as simple as possible to show the advantages of such an application.

Steps:

1. Determine the cash flow and calculate the net present value before making any adjustments to the input variables
2. Adjust each of the input variables adversely by a fixed percentage, in this case we will use 10%
3. Determine the alternative cash flows and calculate revised net present values
4. Rank each of the input variables according to the sensitivity of the net present value.

1. Determine the cash flow and calculate Net Present Value (NPV)

a. Determine the Cash Flow

(Sales volume x Contribution per unit) – specific fixed costs

= (80,000 x £23.00) – £660,000

= £1,180,000

Calculation of Contribution Per Unit:

	£
Selling price	85.00
– Labour cost	22.00
– Material cost	40.00
Contribution per unit	23.00

ii. Calculate the net present value

(Cash flow x Annuity factor) – Capital cost

= (£1,180,000 x 5.630) – £5,000,000

= £1,667,000

2. Adjust the input variables adversely by 10%

Table 7.2 Input Variables Varied Adversely by 10%

Capital Outlay	£5,000,000	x 1.10	£5,500,000
Life (years)	10	less 1	9
Sales Volume (units)	80,000	/ 1.10	72,727
Selling Price	£85.00	/ 1.10	£77.27
Labour Costs per unit	£22.00	x 1.10	£24.20
Material Costs per unit	£40.00	x 1.10	£44.00
Fixed Costs per annum	£660,000	x 1.10	£726,000
Cost of Capital	12%	x 1.10	13.2%

Calculation of the sales volume and selling price is as follows:

a. Vary the sales volume adversely by 10%:
   80,000 units divided by (1 plus 0.10) = 72,727 units
b. Vary the selling price adversely by 10%:
   £85.00 divided by (1 plus 0.10) = £77.27

Alternative calculation of sales volume and selling price:

For simplicity, it is possible to take 10% of the sales volume, that is, 80,000 times 10% which equals 8,000 units. The net figure would be 72,000 units. Similarly, the selling price would be reduced by £8.50 to give a net of £76.50. It is important to realise that this method is not technically correct and will not produce a consistent movement in each of the variables.

3. Determine alternative cash flows and calculate revised NPVs

Table 7.3 Determine the Alternative Cash Flows

	A Sales Volume Units	B Contri-bution P.Unit	C Fixed Costs	D Cash Flow (A*B–C)
		£	£	£
Capital Outlay	80,000	23.00	660,000	1,180,000
Life (years)	80,000	23.00	660,000	1,180,000
Sales Volume (units)	72,727	23.00	660,000	1,012,721
Selling Price	80,000	15.27	660,000	561,600
Labour Costs per unit	80,000	20.80	660,000	1,004,000
Material Costs per unit	80,000	19.00	660,000	860,000
Fixed Costs per annum	80,000	23.00	726,000	1,114,000

Example calculations of the revised contributions per unit above - with a 10% adverse change in:

	Selling Price £	Labour Cost £	Material Cost £
Selling price	77.27	85.00	85.00
– Labour cost	22.00	24.20	22.00
– Material cost	40.00	40.00	44.00
Contribution per unit	15.27	20.80	19.00

Notes for calculations in Table 7.3

1. Column A. For each variable must determine the volume; these are all at 80,000 units except for the reduction in sales volume to 72,727 units
2. Column B. For each variable must determine the contribution per unit. These are all at £23.00 per unit except for the adverse changes in selling price, labour costs and material costs; revised calculations are shown above - that is, £15.27, £20.80 and £19.00
3. Column C. These are the fixed costs and are all at £660,000 per annum except for the increase in fixed costs line to £726,000
4. Column D. This shows the revised cash flows for each of the elements within the project. The calculation is Column A times Column B minus Column C.

In Table 7.4 we calculate the revised net present values using annuity tables, (taken from Appendix B).

Table 7.4 Calculate NPVs (Using Annuity Tables)

	A Cash Flow	B Annuity Factor	C Present Value of Cash Flow (A x B)	D Capital Outlay	E Net Present Value (C – D)
	£		£	£	£
Capital Outlay	1,180,000	5.650	6,667,000	5,500,000	1,167,000
Life (years)	1,180,000	5.328	6,287,040	5,000,000	1,287,040
Sales Volume	1,012,721	5.650	5,721,874	5,000,000	721,874
Selling Price	561,600	5.650	3,173,040	5,000,000	–1,826,960
Labour Costs p.u.	1,004,000	5.650	5,672,600	5,000,000	672,600
Material Costs p.u.	860,000	5.650	4,859,000	5,000,000	–141,000
Fixed Costs p.a.	1,114,000	5.650	6,294,100	5,000,000	1,294,100
Cost of capital	1,180,000	5.382	6,351,940	5,000,000	1,351,940

Notes for calculations in Table 7.4

1. Column A. We take the revised cash flows from Table 7.3, Column D
2. Column B. For ease of calculation we are using annuity factors to arrive at the present value of the cash flows. For most of the elements we will use the annuity factor for a 10 year life at 12%, that is, 5.650. The second element, the life, we use the annuity factor for a 9 year life at 12%, that is, 5.328. The last element, the cost of capital, we use the annuity factor for a 10 year life at 13.2%, that is, 5.382. For this last annuity factor we used a standard spreadsheet program to determine the value of 5.382
3. Column C. Column A (revised cash flow) times Column B (annuity factor)
4. Column D. This is the capital outlay. For most of the elements the capital outlay is £5,000,000. The only exception is the capital outlay element which is adversely adjusted by 10% to £5,500,000
5. Column E. Column C (present value of cash flows) minus Column D (capital outlay).

4. Rank each of the input variables

The final stage in the sensitivity analysis is to rank each of the elements of the project in descending order based on the revised net present values. Here we take the output from Table 7.4, Column E starting with selling price with a negative net present value of –£1,826,960 through to cost of capital with a net present value of £1,351,940.

Table 7.5 *Input Variables in Decreasing Order of Sensitivity*

	NPV £
Selling Price	–1,826,960
Material Costs	–141,000
Labour Costs	672,600
Sales Volume	721,874
Capital Outlay	1,167,000
Life	1,287,000
Fixed Costs	1,294,100
Cost of Capital	1,351,940

The analysis highlights the variables which will have the greatest impact on the net present values of a project. By amending the original data by 10% negative, two sensitive variables to the project are found, that is, the selling price and the material costs. If the selling price were not £85.00 per unit but only achieved £77.27 per unit, then the project would generate a negative NPV of £1,826,960, while a 10% increase in material costs would generate a negative NPV of £141,000.

Given that the company's cost of capital is 12% then a £7.73 reduction in selling price could be a potential disaster. With knowledge of this potential problem area, an investigation could be undertaken by the marketing department to establish whether difficulties in achieving a selling price of £85.00 are likely. If so, then despite the initially favourable NPV, the project is not acceptable on economic grounds. This, of course, assumes there to be no sales volume/ selling price relationship such that a reduction in price to £77.27 might well be associated with an increase in sales volume. This is one other area of investigation readily considered by using a computerised model.

In summary, such analysis permits project proposals to be evaluated and the analysis can be used to identify sensitive variables without having to input any additional data. In practice, the analysis would be extended much further than in the example so as to explore changes in a number of variables and any interrelationships between them.

7.12 The options approach to facilitate managerial decision making

Research undertaken in the last two decades has shown that managers in diverse fields tend to make the same kind of decision-making mistakes. Of these, the single most common decision trap is what is referred to as 'frame blindness': setting out to solve the wrong problem because a mental framework has been created for a decision that causes the best option to be overlooked. In fact, the word 'option' is extremely relevant because in recent years, practitioners and academics have argued that traditional discounted cash flow models do not capture the value of options embedded in many corporate decisions. These options need to be considered explicitly because their value can be substantial.

Figure 7.5: New economic and financial theories are challenging Net Present Value

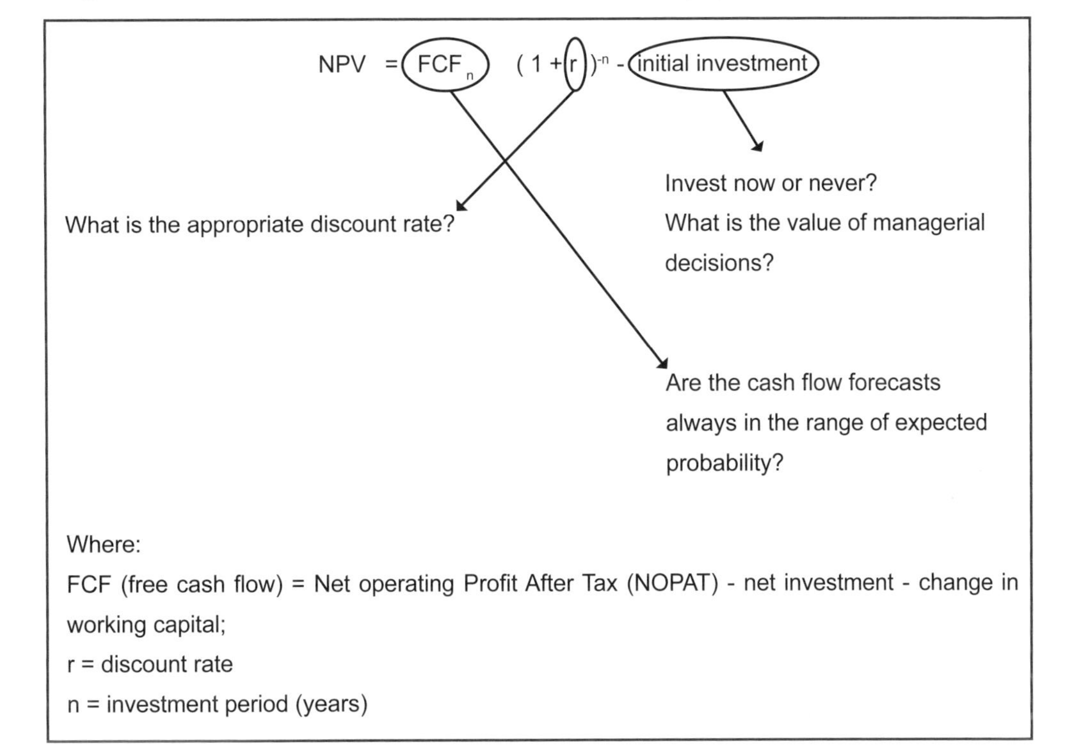

Companies in every type of industry have to make investment decisions, to allocate resources to competing opportunities. They have to decide whether to invest now, to take preliminary actions to preserve the right to invest in the future, or to do nothing. For such purposes they use investment appraisal techniques. The theoretical underpinnings for the use of investment appraisal techniques were drawn from the economic theory of the firm which contends that corporate investment decisions should be guided by the rule of net present value (NPV) maximisation. This gave rise to the widely accepted capital budgeting tool of discounted cash flow (DCF) analysis, which measures a project's desirability on the basis of its expected NPV. However, the DCF model has not been without criticism and two particular defects of DCF analysis are important. First, it tends to overlook the strategic reasons for an investment, such as investing in a not-so-profitable project in order to acquire future growth opportunities. For example, in conditions where technology is changing rapidly, investments may be made for competitive reasons alone and such investments may well fail the DCF test. The second important criticism of DCF analysis is that it fails to take account of the value of active management. Such management might decide to wait for major uncertainties, say, over future market conditions, to unfold in order to avoid losses, or to undertake specific R&D expenditure intended to lead to new patents. Such options and the calculation of their potential value would not be included in the usual NPV reckoning. Active management aims to produce valuable information thereby reducing uncertainty over the future. Furthermore, subsequent to making an investment, management can revise operating plans that underlay an original cash flow forecast, like altering input and output mixes or shutting down plant temporarily, in order to maximise operating cash flows. Quite simply, active management can affect a project's value but it is not accounted for in conventional DCF analysis.

Researchers have examined the shortcomings of the conventional DCF and have shown that not only is it incomplete, but also it may lead to costly errors. These errors arise from two sources. First, investments guided by the positive NPV criteria may be made too hastily. This is a problem because most capital investments are irreversible and thus justifiable only if the expected profit margin is sufficiently large. Secondly, conversely, worthwhile investments, based on the same criteria, may be rejected inadvertently. As a consequence, any theory of investment needs to address the question: how should a corporate manager facing uncertainty over future market conditions decide whether to invest in a new project? (Mills, R.W., Weinstein, W.L., Favato, G. 2006).

Management has to decide when to invest, how operating plans should be modified during the life of the project, and whether to abandon a project in midstream. By guiding a project/

investment from beginning to end, management may be able to squeeze its cash flow distribution towards a higher rate of return. This has led to the development of the idea that because management control can impact upon a project's payoff in terms of potential profits and losses, control opportunities can be seen as being analogous to 'call' and 'put' options and, therefore, may be analysed using options pricing theory. This theory has its origins in the valuation of stocks and shares, where a stock option is an explicit contract conferring certain rights upon the holder, who exercises the option only when it is profitable to do so. In fact, an option is a contract that creates an opportunity, but not an obligation, to buy (a 'call' option) or sell (a 'put' option) at an agreed price at a future date.

As previously indicated, the options approach can be and has been extended in principle to capital projects, so that the opportunity inherent in a capital project can be viewed as Real Options like implied contracts that allow management to choose only those actions that have positive cash flow effects. Indeed, during the 1990s, finance researchers generated a plethora of Real Options models and statistical applets, with much of this work advancing the use of technical tools (differential equations, dynamic programming and Monte Carlo simulations) for pricing Real Options.

Like NPV analysis, the Real Options approach involves projecting future cash flows and choosing an appropriate discount or probability rate. However, unlike NPV analysis, the Real Options perspective assumes managers can influence the outcome by interventive actions that add value over time. For example, the purchase of a computer software company entitles the owner to the company's free cash flow, but the assets acquired in place are not the only opportunity purchased. Along with the assets there may also be the chance to acquire less tangible benefits, for example, to learn about other software companies that might be for sale. The company may also include highly skilled individuals who could be used to produce extra at little cost but with high value. Because such follow on investment opportunities are relatively intangible and speculative, their expected cash flows are rarely examined directly. Nevertheless, these opportunities may have important value. This perception places Real Options on the interface between strategy and finance, albeit initially without quantification.

One Real Options approach, known as the Black-Scholes algorithm, has attracted particular attention. In this approach the following five factors are used to determine the project's option value:

1. Exercise price
2. Stock price
3. Time to expiration
4. Project volatility
5. Risk-free rate.

A specific illustration of the options approach using this approach can be seen with reference to a pharmaceuticals company. This company wanted to enter a new line of business that required the acquisition of a number of appropriate technologies from a small company. Under the terms of the proposed agreement, it would pay $2 million over a period of 3 years. In addition, it would pay royalties to the company should the product ever come to the market. The company had the option to terminate the agreement at any time if dissatisfied with the progress of the research.

To use the approach it was necessary to provide inputs for the five factors which were:

1. Exercise price. This represented the cost of a capital investment to be made approximately two years hence
2. Stock price. This represented the value of the underlying asset or the present value of the cash flows from the project (excluding the capital investment to be made and the present value of the up-front fees and development costs over the next two years)
3. Time to expiration. This ranged from two, three and four years, with the option being exercisable in two years at the earliest. The option was structured to expire in four years because the company thought that competing products, making market entry unfeasible, would exist by then
4. Project volatility. This was represented by a sample of the annual standard deviation of returns for typical biotechnology stocks obtained from an investment bank
5. Risk-free rate. A US Treasury rate of 4.5% was used over the two to four year period referred to in the time to expiration of the model.

Despite the apparent relevance of Real Options to business decisions, it has had limited impact generally. For example, in a survey by the consulting company Bain (2000), forty six percent of firms that experimented with Real Options analysis gave up . One problem frequently expressed is that options theory is regarded as being notoriously arcane and many discussions that go beyond the conceptual level get trapped in the mathematics. This may be a real problem because in the author's experience many managers have only a passing acquaintance with the subtleties of the Net Present Value calculation and potentially stand little chance with more complex approaches like the Black-Scholes pricing model. This is unfortunate because Real Options are best understood as a way of thinking and need to be positioned correctly alongside an approach that creates coherent stories about possible future outcomes, which is the territory of scenario analysis, that is reviewed later.

CHAPTER 8
VALUATION APPLICATIONS – MERGERS AND ACQUISITIONS, JOINT VENTURES, INITIAL PUBLIC OFFERINGS (IPOS) AND EMERGING MARKETS.

Chapter Preview

- Why target shareholders are often most likely to gain from a merger or acquisition by way of financial returns.
- How to apply the Strategic Value Analysis framework to acquisition opportunities to assess the potential sources of benefit to the acquirer.
- How to apply the Strategic Value Analysis framework to joint venture opportunities to assess the potential sources of benefit to the different parties involved.
- How to structure the potential sources of benefit into those gained from operational changes, changes in the financial structure and tax benefits.
- How options thinking can assist in evaluating joint venture opportunities.
- How to apply the tools of corporate finance in emerging market and IPO valuations.

8.1 Introduction

The challenge for the board of directors in a publicly quoted company is not only to ensure that the goods produced and/or the services provided satisfy the requirements of the market, but also to satisfy the other stakeholders of the business. For publicly quoted companies a failure to provide for the relative claims of debt holders as well as to provide value to the shareholders means there is a market for corporate control with the share price a key consideration. Directors have to ensure value is provided. A failure to provide value to the shareholders may result in a loss of control by the board and a drastic change in the management of the business as it stands. It is important to realise that there is no single view of value. The value of a business is what someone is prepared to pay for it and, unless their intention is to liquidate it and sell off the assets, its value will relate to what a potential acquirer is able to do with it. The value of the Rover car company to BMW was undoubtedly different to the view of value as part of British Aerospace. A means is required of evaluating any advantages (synergies) potentially available from combining two businesses.

In this chapter how the analysis of strategic value can be used to value a company's shares before and after an acquisition will be reviewed, with a view to trying to identify the existence of any substantial value gap between different perceptions based on the dynamics of business activities. How a large complex business with multiple divisions can be valued in principle using strategic value analysis, where the information about the detail of its activities is very limited, will also be illustrated.

Let us be quite clear at the outset that what follows is based on publicly available information which we have shown to be limited in its comprehensiveness. This means that any valuation might differ substantially from that based on expert knowledge of specific business segments and information known to the company and not in the public domain.

When undertaking a valuation one should recognise that not only would the likely values of each value driver change over time, but also the composition and breakdown of each. For example, over the course of time the range of products or services produced or provided by a business are likely to change and it is, therefore, desirable to disaggregate the sales growth rate to reflect this. Similarly, over the course of time the cost of capital may change to reflect the different expectations of the providers of funds.

The starting point in valuing a company is available published information such as the contents of its annual report and accounts, which can be used to obtain an historical picture of past value drivers. This historical picture can then be used as an important base from which to make future projections. This approach was adopted in producing the case study covered in this chapter which provides an opportunity to understand some important issues surrounding the acquisition and to view the acquisition from the seller's and buyer's perspective.

8.2 Boom in Merger and Acquisitions (M&A)

In recent times in a climate of relatively loose credit standards and cash rich strategic and financial markets, buyers have competed aggressively for acquisitions thereby giving sellers the ability to negotiate very attractive terms. Recent years have been characterised by a booming M&A market which raises the all-important question, what are the factors influencing it? Those that are important include:

- Favourable debt markets
- Market forces – supply and demand
- Development of mega-funds
- Hedge fund growth and activity
- Dispersion of deals
- Capital structure

Favourable Debt Markets

The reliance upon debt financing increased and in the US the proportion of bank debt to profit, referred to as bank debt multiple, rose steadily from an average of 3.7 times EBITDA (earnings before interest, tax, depreciation and amortization) in 2001 to 4.3 times in 2005, a level that had not been seen since 1999 according to S&P/Leveraged Commentary and Data. This relaxing of credit standards was supported in a survey by the US Federal Reserve (2005), which reported the percentage of banks loosening their credit standards was at its highest level in 10 years. Default rates continued to decline and were at their lowest level in 2005 for a decade according to PricewaterhouseCoopers (2005).

Market Forces – Supply and Demand

Quite simply there has been an increased demand from all potential players, with corporations, private equity firms and hedge funds all actively seeking deals. Favourable equity market conditions have favoured the use of equity. For example, in 2005, more than $172 billion was raised, according to Standard & Poor's (2006).

Development of Mega-funds

The advent of mega-funds, some more than $10 billion, has also contributed to the increase in M&A volume. Funds of this magnitude by private equity sponsors are a relatively new phenomenon and, as a consequence, buyout firms are positioned now to compete with corporations for any transaction. Deals have become larger and according to Dealogic, nine of the 10 biggest private equity transactions ever were announced in 2005. In addition, there has been an increase in 'clubbing,' which allows private equity firms to team up to pursue exceptionally large buyouts with a 'safety in numbers' mentality. Clubbing gives private equity firms access to more diversified experience to help win the deal while allowing them to spread the risk.

Hedge Fund Growth and Activity

Hedge fund activity within M&A activity has also been very important[19]. Although hedge funds have traditionally been regarded as being short-term oriented, today they seek returns wherever they can find them and locking up money for longer periods of time is not regarded as a barrier. They have become active in leveraged buyouts, often as the lead lender and they have also been observed buying equity at auctions when a member of a private consortium is looking to exit but is not able to find a bidder at the right price.

Hedge funds typically have the ability to provide their own acquisition financing giving them a competitive advantage over most other buyers and they may not be limited in terms of industry concentration or investment size. As such they are quickly offering formidable competition to some private equity firms, which inevitably places pressure on M&A pricing and the auction process as a whole.

Dispersion of Deals

M&A activity is no longer concentrated among just a few industry segments. Unlike the late '90s, when the activity centred on media, telecom and technology, activity is now distributed across a wide variety of industries including energy, utilities and financial services. Activity is also distributed more broadly geographically. At more than $1 trillion in 2005, European M&A volume was 49 percent higher than the $729.5 billion reported in 2004, according to Dealogic. As in the US, telecommunications was the most active sector in 2005. Furthermore, Asian-Pacific M&A activity hit a record $474.3 billion, a 46 percent increase from $324.5 billion in 2004. Such geographical dispersion has helped to spread national and international M&A across sectors, for example, steel, pharmaceuticals, hotels and commercial property.

---

[19] A hedge fund generally refers to a lightly regulated private investment fund characterised by unconventional strategies (for example, strategies other than investing long only in bonds, equities or money markets).

Not only has the M&A playing field expanded, the speed in which deals are completed has accelerated. For instance, institutional investors such as hedge funds now simply buy a whole company, take it off the street and then 'parse' out the deal later rather than arranging the financing with four or five partners before closing the sale. Another factor that is speeding the time involved is staple financing. During the '90s, lenders typically would not provide financing without knowing who was going to own the enterprise, but this has changed and because competition is so intense, investment banks that represent the seller often arrange financing for any buyer up to a certain level. This so-called 'staple financing' is attached to the agreement and enhances the sale by giving sellers a ready idea of how much leverage a buyer can put on the table. Previously a sponsor would look at a deal, evaluate it and then bid on it before arranging the financing, but with staple financing, the deal already has been reviewed by a lender.

Capital Structures

Today, there are numerous different financing alternatives such that the final structure for any given transaction may often become a mixture of capital layers. To minimise financing costs, deals often start with a senior-secured loan, for example against the assets of the business and because it is secured it has the advantage of being cheap. This senior debt is then followed by other layers, each becoming increasingly more expensive as it necessitates riskier funding, with equity at the bottom.

8.3 What is Private Equity?

As indicated, the resurgence in the M&A market has been fuelled by private equity, but what actually is it? Whereas the principle of private equity is quite straightforward, one of the challenges is that it may be encountered under different labels.

In principle, private equity is medium to long-term finance provided in return for an equity stake in potentially high growth unquoted companies. Some sources use the term 'private equity' to refer only to the buy-out and buy-in investment sector, but others, in Europe (not the USA), use the term 'venture capital' as an alternative. This can be quite confusing because in the USA 'venture capital' refers only to investments in early stage and expanding companies. To avoid confusion, the term 'private equity' is used by the British Venture Capital Association (BVCA) to describe the industry as a whole, encompassing both 'venture capital' (the seed to expansion stages of investment) and management buy-outs and buy-ins.

Private equity arguably provides long-term, committed share capital, to help companies grow and succeed without some of the hindrances of a stock market listing. It can be applied to companies at all stages of development from a start-up to mature established companies with a stock market listing. For a business start up, expansion, a buy into a business, a buy out of a division of a parent company or a turnaround or the revitalisation of a company private equity may well help. However, private equity is very different from raising debt or a loan from a lender, such as a bank. Whereas lenders have a legal right to interest on a loan and repayment of the capital, irrespective of success or failure, private equity is invested in exchange for a stake in the company and, as shareholders, the investors' returns are dependent on the growth and profitability of the business.

Almost invariably there will be a planned exit for the private equity investor, which can take many forms, from an eventual stock market listing from the reshaped business to a secondary sale to another private equity investor. An example of the former is that a unit of Kohlberg Kravis Roberts & Company (KKR), the private equity giant that came to fame with the $25 billion buyout of RJR Nabisco in 1989, and went public in a $5 billion offering in Amsterdam . Demand was high with the offering raised more than three times what was expected, although its first-day performance was lacklustre.

Taking such a fund public may seem like an oxymoron because private equity funds typically buy public companies listed on exchanges, take them private, turn them around and cash out. They operate on a schedule of years and avoid the demands that regulators and shareholders make on public companies every quarter. However, for KKR, which remains a private firm, a public unit gives it access to permanent capital, instead of raising money for a fund with a limited shelf life.

The KKR offering is a flash point for private equity because of its size and because of the status of KKR, but this is nothing new. Hundreds of publicly traded private equity funds are listed on global markets and together control an estimated $80 billion in capital. The majority of these funds are based outside the United States and do deals in Britain and Europe and comprise private equity firms like Wendel Investissement and Eurazeo, both of France, and 3i in UK. In fact in Europe some well-established companies have transformed themselves from manufacturing or industrial companies into private equity investors, like Ratos of Sweden, and just kept their public listing. By all accounts, such funds make it easier to attract cash because it makes it straightforward for shareholders to exit.

Whilst having an exit appeal it is important to understand that it may be a while before investors in the IPOs of listed private equity funds see much return on their money. For example, Apollo Management followed KKR with a fund of its own, a $1.5 billion offering on Euronext Amsterdam. Like KKR's issue, which traded down after the IPO, the Apollo offering has been argued as being likely to suffer from the infamous private equity 'J curve' (Meyer et al 2005). The J curve effect is where start-up expenses - such as the costs of the offering itself - reduce the net asset value of the fund at the outset such that only later do returns become positive. Since shareholders in the listed funds have put in their capital up front and they will not necessarily be getting cash distributions or dividends from the proceeds of exits, their only real upside is gains in the share price. At first glance it does not seem as though the general partners of the sponsoring firms have much reason to worry about share price levels, since they get their management fees in any case, the capital is perpetual and their 'carry,' or incentive fees, are based on the performance of the underlying private funds, not the listed one. In the case of Apollo, some portion of the carry will be put back into the listed fund and members of the KKR general partnership have put $72 million into the KKR Private Equity Investors fund.

Listed private equity funds have rather a chequered history. By all accounts such listed funds were not uncommon from about 1940 through the 1960s, but they suffered from very volatile share prices, shareholder dilution with subsequent capital raising and, ultimately, some traded at such a large discount to net asset value that they became vulnerable to takeovers.

In the late 1990s, listed venture capital funds ran into similar difficulties. The KKR and Apollo funds, however, are structured more like funds of funds in that investors do not own regular shares, but instead, units of a limited partnership based in Guernsey that itself chiefly owns limited partnership stakes in the underlying funds. By all accounts, the fund is pretty much immune to takeover and the structure also shields KKR and Apollo from having to make much in the way of disclosure about returns on individual portfolio investments, although they will have to make quarterly earnings reports. In the US, the issue was a private placement from a foreign issuer to qualified buyers only, which means the filing requirements are not very onerous.

Despite a chequered history, these publicly traded private equity funds are part of a growing asset class and in 2004 the first index for publicly traded private equity funds was developed by the Swiss company LPX GmbH/Ltd. in Basel. The LPX50, which comprises the top 50 listed private equity funds, had a market capitalization of 46 billion euros ($58 billion) at the end of March 2006. Banks started introducing financial products linked to it.

From a UK perspective, private equity originated in the late 18th century, when entrepreneurs found wealthy individuals to back their projects on an ad hoc basis. This informal method of financing became an industry in the late 1970s and early 1980s when a number of private equity firms were founded. Private equity is now a recognised asset class. According to the BVCA there are over 170 active UK private equity firms, which provide several billion pounds each year to unquoted companies, around 80% of which are located in the UK.

As indicated, in recent years, private equity investment has become very significant, but while much can be found in the academic literature on early stage venture capital investment, little attention has been paid to the recent developments in leveraged buy out (LBO) and private equity, which mostly affect established (non-entrepreneurial) firms. These trends have important implications for the private equity market and also more generally, for the governance and performance of corporations.

What are the benefits of private equity? Some private equity backed companies have been shown to grow faster than other types of companies. This is made possible by the provision of a combination of capital and experienced personal input from private equity executives, which sets it apart from other forms of finance. Private equity can help a company achieve its ambitions and provide a stable base for strategic decision making because the private equity firms may only seek to increase a company's value to its owners, without taking day-to-day management control. Although the company may have a smaller 'slice of cake', within a few years the 'slice' could be worth considerably more than the whole 'cake' was before.

Private equity firms may need to adopt strategies to secure attractive deals without engaging in the public auctions that have become prevalent. While private equity transactions have often been associated with cost-cutting to improve efficiency, there may need to be stronger emphasis on entrepreneurial activity to realise the upside potential of these firms. Changes in the stock market and the market for corporate control also raise issues concerning the ability of private equity firms to realize the gains from their investments (especially for modest sized deals in mature sectors) while at the same time meeting investors' significant return expectations within a particular time period. Private equity firms have developed new forms of exit, such as the widespread growth in secondary buy-outs and these secondary buyouts raise questions concerning the returns that can be generated and the willingness of limited partners to invest in the same deal a second time through a follow-on fund at a higher price. In fact, the growth of the private equity market has raised many other critical questions, not least of which is how private equity transactions increase value.

Last, but not least, high risk-adjusted returns from private equity transactions have attracted new types of entrants and, in particular, hedge funds. This has raised further concerns given the transaction-oriented nature of hedge funds and their ability to add real value (in a managerial sense) to enterprises.

8.4 Hedge Funds and Private Equity

Hedge funds have attracted much attention recently and, as indicated, have been linked very strongly with private equity and the rise in M&A activity, but what is the difference and how are they linked?

A hedge fund generally refers to a lightly regulated private investment fund characterised by unconventional strategies (for example, strategies other than investing long only in bonds, equities or money markets). They are primarily organised as limited partnerships and previously were often simply called 'limited partnerships' and were grouped with other limited partnerships such as those that invested in oil development.

The term hedge fund dates back to the first such fund founded by Alfred Winslow Jones in 1949. Jones' innovation was to sell short some stocks while buying others, thus some of the market risk was hedged. While most of today's hedge funds still trade stocks both long and short, many do not trade stocks at all.

For US-based managers and investors, hedge funds are simply structured as limited partnerships or limited liability companies. The hedge fund manager is the general partner or manager and the investors are the limited partners or members. The funds are pooled together in the partnership or company and the general partner or manager makes all the investment decisions based on the strategy it outlined in the offering documents.

In return for managing the investors' funds, the hedge fund manager will receive a management fee and a performance or incentive fee. The management fee is computed as a percentage of assets under management and the incentive fee is computed as a percentage of the fund's profits. A 'high water mark' may be specified, under which the manager does not receive incentive fees unless the value of the fund exceeds the highest value it has achieved. The fee structures of hedge funds vary, but the yearly management fee may range from 1-2% of the assets under management and the incentive fee is usually in the range of 10-20% of the profits of the fund. Certain highly regarded managers demand higher fees.

Research by Elton, Gruber, and Blake (2003) has shown that incentive fees correlate to higher returns in mutual funds, perhaps suggesting the attractiveness of hedge funds, where incentive fees can be much higher and restrictions on trading are less.

Offshore hedge funds are usually domiciled in a tax haven and, for US-based fund managers, are designed to allow the manager to manage the assets of foreign investors and tax-exempt US investors. In this structure, the manager will receive a management and incentive fee as in an onshore fund.

The typical hedge fund asset management firm includes both the domestic US hedge fund and the offshore hedge fund. This allows hedge fund managers to attract capital from all over the world. Both funds will trade 'pari passu' based on the strategy outlined in the offering documents[20].

Hedge funds are similar to private equity funds, such as venture capital funds, in many respects. Both are lightly regulated, private pools of capital that invest in securities and compensate their managers with a share of the fund's profits. Most hedge funds invest in very liquid assets and permit investors to enter or leave the fund easily. By comparison, private equity funds often invest in very illiquid assets such as early-stage companies and so investors are 'locked in' for the entire term of the fund.

The amount of hedge-fund money flowing into public companies in the US skyrocketed in the recent past, thanks to a financing mechanism known as PIPE, or 'private investment in public equity'. PIPE investments, which involve the issuance of large chunks of new stock to a qualified investor, rose 20 percent in the first quarter, to $6.03 billion, according to PlacementTracker, a unit of Sagient Research Systems of San Diego, which provides data on private placement.

PIPE offerings cost less than public offerings and require minimal regulatory oversight, making them attractive for small companies. The companies typically agree to discount the shares by anywhere from 5 percent to 20 percent, with the agreement that they cannot be resold to the public for two months or more.

[20] Pari passu is a Latin phrase that means 'at the same pace' and, by extension also 'fairly', 'without partiality'. In finance this term refers to two or more loans, bonds or series of preferred stock having equal rights of payment, that is, have the same level of seniority.

8.5 Criteria for successful acquisitions

Studies have been undertaken to identify how companies approach M&A deals by analysing how successful the transactions were in creating shareholder value. One study conducted the research in two parts: main board directors who had been closely involved in their company's deal were asked about the process adopted and their view of the success of the transaction. Then, for each deal, a relative measure of change in equity price was taken pre-deal and then a year later. This was compared with the overall trend in the relevant industry segment to arrive at an assessment of whether or not shareholder value had been created.

Of the companies in the survey, 30% were found to create value as a result of the transaction. This marked a significant improvement on the position reported in the previous KPMG (1999) survey where only 17% of deals added value. Similarly the percentage of deals which destroyed value had fallen from 53% to 31%. 24% of companies in Europe and 35% of companies in the US were found to have created shareholder value from M&A transactions.

No significant correlation was found between experience and success. Those companies that were involved in a high number of transactions did not necessarily have a better track record in creating shareholder value, which is consistent with the findings of other studies. Evidence has been found for both positive and negative effects of acquisition experience. First, in the majority of cases, when a firm's current acquisition was dissimilar to its prior acquisitions, acquisition experience had a negative influence on acquisition performance (for slightly and moderately experienced acquirers). When experience across all acquirers was examined, the effect of acquisition experience was U-shaped. The best performers appeared to be either those without experience who, therefore, did not make an inappropriate generalisation error or those who had a significant amount of experience and appropriately discriminated. Second, in the minority of cases, when a firm's current acquisition was similar to its prior acquisitions, acquisition experience had a positive influence on acquisition performance. The results suggest that those firms that make multiple acquisitions within the same industry benefit by generalising past acquisition knowledge. Hence, even though it is possible to apply past experience inappropriately, poor outcomes might be avoided if firms apply experience to similar acquisitions.

A gap was found to persist in a KPMG 2001 study between the objective results and the respondents' subjective assessment: 75% believed that their deal had been successful in achieving its objective. The most likely explanation for this discrepancy given in the study is the way respondents defined their objectives. While it can be assumed that the ultimate objective of all corporate activity is to enhance shareholder value, it was clear from the survey that respondents often had other, more immediate, goals in mind when embarking on a transaction. In this context, 29% of respondents referred to increasing market share and 28% to expanding into new geographic markets, as opposed to only 23% who cited maximising shareholder value. Furthermore, when measuring the success of the transaction, only 25% of respondents evaluated its effect on shareholder value and most failed to measure implementation against their original objectives.

Six factors have been found to be critical in creating shareholder value (KPMG 1999):

1. Synergy evaluation
2. Integration project planning
3. Due diligence
4. Selecting the management team
5. Resolving cultural issues
6. Communications.

Transactions were found to be more successful in creating shareholder value where:

- there is a robust and well managed process
- priorities are allocated to the activities to be carried out
- clear decisions are taken about how and by whom the activities should be handled.

The survey indicated that certain key practices were likely to have a significant bearing on the outcome of a transaction.

1. Early action - Process management and other key activities tackled at an early stage in the transaction
2. Main board leadership - A main board member responsible for M&A policy and activity, resulting in leadership and buy-in to achieve transaction goals
3. Pre bid value assessment - Rigorous assessment of the target company and the deal, including understanding the drivers of value and the price range which will enable the purchaser to create value
4. Formal transaction process plan - A formal transaction process plan setting out clear roles and responsibilities, prepared before the detailed investigation into the target. This to be formally reviewed and approved, addressing any variations to the original assumptions arising during the process

5. Process manager involved throughout - Appointment of a dedicated process manager, with appropriate skills, involved from an early stage
6. Process manager empowered with wide ranging role - Process manager with responsibility for key activities, including risk and issue management, deal assessment, negotiations and implementation
7. Independent assessment of post deal implementation - The use of external advisers to provide independent evaluation of the implementation process and measurement post completion.

However, it was found to be not the individual practices themselves but rather their combination which leads to successful transactions. The more that are adopted, the more likely it is that the deal will increase shareholder value. Furthermore, successful companies undertook nearly all the practices earlier than those that failed to create value, although there were significant differences in the adoption of key practices by respondents in Europe and the US. European companies were more likely than those in the US to have a main board director responsible for the transaction and a formal plan in place at the earliest stages. However, process managers in US companies were more heavily involved than those in Europe and more emphasis was given to pre-bid value assessment and issue management.

8.6 Shareholder Value in merger and acquisition analysis

While the evidence suggests that only target shareholders gain, it does not mean that acquisitions do not rest on sound value creation logic. The result of an acquisition may be increased cash flows for the newly combined business, as compared to the sum of the cash flows of the two pre-acquisition firms. However, if the acquiring company shareholders are overgenerous to target shareholders they may see none of the benefit.

A useful example of the application of a free cash flow approach like Strategic Value Analysis for evaluating an acquisition was provided by the Glaxo-Wellcome take-over. In a report by James Capel, analysts estimated a base case value for Glaxo with Wellcome of approximately 575p per share pre-acquisition, compared to Glaxo's existing share price of 732p . This illustrates that the value of a company can be shown to depend on the perspective taken. The same company in the hands of another owner may be able to create substantially more value. The value to be created can be visualized with reference to the following framework:

Value of Combined Companies	=	Stand Alone Value of Acquirer	+	Stand Alone Value of Target

Furthermore, this framework can be applied by valuing the acquired and target companies on a stand alone basis and then comparing the sum of the two values obtained with their estimated value as a combined entity, making due allowance for all potential synergistic benefits. To be meaningful in managerial terms, such valuations require the identification of the key value drivers so that the potential sources of benefit can be understood and analysed. Unfortunately, the research from the KPMG 1997 survey introduced previously revealed that 32 per cent of the respondents were unaware of which key performance measures financial markets use to value their organisation's shares .

One important technique that can be used to understand the various perspectives and sources of benefits is value mapping. Such value mapping is illustrated in Figure 8.1, where the sources of synergies resulting from an acquisition were 'mapped' in conjunction with the value to acquirer and target shareholders.

Figure 8.1: Value mapping synergies

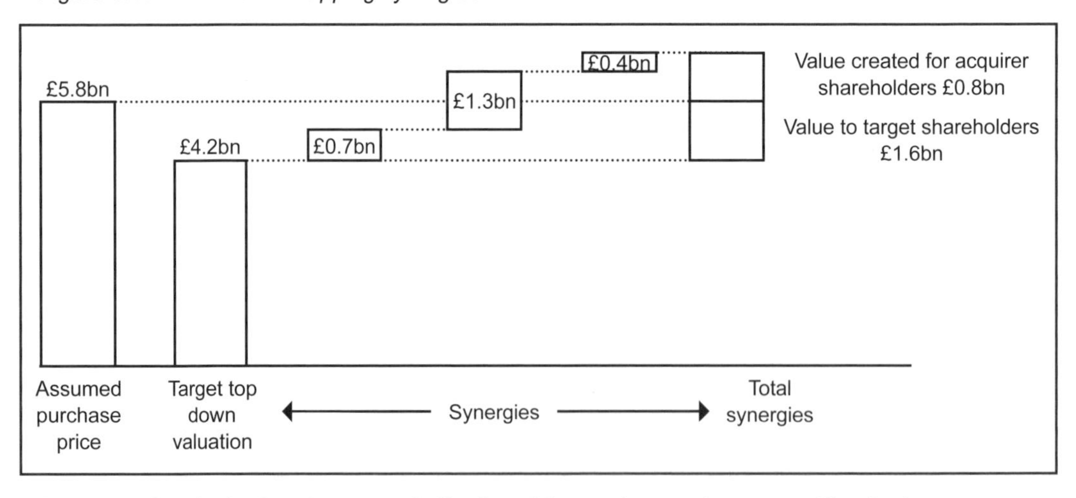

This type of analysis also gives some indication of the maximum price to pay. Clearly, the name of the game from the acquirer's perspective is to pay less than the value created, otherwise value to the acquirer's shareholders will be destroyed .

8.7 The Depar Group

Background and the sellers' perspective

In 2007, the Chairman of the Depar Group, Mr Andrew Simon, faced the prospect of having to mount a credible defence of his company against a hostile bid from the mini conglomerate Wardle. The Depar Group was a small multi-national organisation that had experienced considerable growth since the second half of the 1990s through acquisition. For example, its turnover grew from £95.8 million in 2001 to £279 million in 2005, but declined to £239.9m in 2006. Depar's businesses were broadly grouped in the speciality and industrial chemicals sector and organised in five divisions:

- Adhesives and sealants
- Industrial coatings
- Polymer compounds
- Plastics
- Footwear materials and components.

The Depar Group had been in some difficulty since it had announced the 2005 results at the beginning of 2006. It had reported a turnover performance, down 6 per cent from 2004 and profit before tax down 52 per cent to £7.3 million (£15.2 million 2004) which, after tax, extraordinary items and dividends payments, resulted in a loss of £1.8 million.

Depar's poor position had resulted from a number of factors:

- over exposure to the recession – white goods and construction sectors in the UK being badly affected
- its international markets, primarily the USA and EU, were affected by the world-wide economic down turn
- overpaying for a major acquisition in 2002
- the burden created by a high level of fixed payment capital to finance the acquisition
- poor management, which saw reasonably high gross margins reduced to an average operating margin of around 2 per cent on 2005 figures.

All this left Depar's management with little credibility. Depar's share price had slumped to a low of 43p in August 2006 but was beginning to climb again following successful rationalisation, cost cutting and marketing initiatives.

8.8 Valuation from target's perspective

This view of the company's share price can be compared alongside a valuation undertaken using strategic value analysis in Table 8.1. This shows a valuation of 46p, relatively close to the current market price of 43p.

Table 8.1: Strategic value of Depar's cash flows

	2006	2007	2008	2009	2010	2011	Beyond
	£m	£m	£m	£m	£m	£m	£m
Sales	239.90	241.34	243.27	249.35	258.08	267.63	267.63
Operating profit		20.03	23.60	23.69	24.52	25.42	25.42
– Cash taxes (33%)		6.61	7.79	7.82	8.09	8.39	8.39
+ Depreciation		7.10	7.50	7.90	8.40	8.90	9.50
Operating cash flow		20.52	23.31	23.77	24.83	25.93	26.53
– RFCI		5.00	5.50	6.10	7.30	8.70	9.50
– IFCI		0	0	0	0	0	0
– WCI		0.32	0.42	1.34	1.92	2.10	0
= Free cash flow		15.20	17.39	16.33	15.61	15.13	17.03
x Discount factor		0.895	0.801	0.716	0.641	0.574	
Present value of free cash flows		13.60	13.93	11.69	10.01	8.68	
Cumulative present value of free cash flows		13.60	27.53	39.22	49.23	57.91	
+ Present value of residual value						83.01	
Corporate value						140.99	
– Market value of debt and preference shares						107.51	
Strategic value						33.48	
Strategic value per share (divided by 72.71m)						£0.46[21]	

[21] *To calculate the incremental fixed capital investment, multiply the forecast percentage (see Table 8.3) by incremental sales. The incremental fixed capital is in fact zero. Replacement fixed capital is required to cover the cost of maintaining the existing plant and equipment.
To calculate the working capital investment, multiply the forcast percentage by incremental sales.
To calculate the residual value, take the residual period free cash flow (that is, where there is no sales growth) and divide by the cost of capital. Then use the discount factor for 2011 to calculate the present value of the residual value (17.03 ÷ 0.1176 x 0.574).

Table 8.2: Estimation of Depar's cost of capital pre-acquisition

Cost of equity = Rf + (B x ERP)	15.38%
Cost of debt	8.14%
Cost of preference shares	11.06%
Weighted Average Cost of Capital (WACC)	11.76%

Other than the cost of capital, the following value drivers in Table 8.3 were used in estimating the shareholder value shown in Table 8.1: sales growth; operating profit margin; IFCI and WCI. They were calculated from information which has been summarised in Table 8.4.

Table 8.3: Forecast percentages

Year	**2007**	**2008**	**2009**	**2010**	**2011**
Sales growth (%)	0.6	0.8	2.5	3.5	3.7
Operating profit margin (%)	8.3	9.7	9.5	9.5	9.5
IFCI (%)	0	0	0	0	0
WCI (%)	22	22	22	22	22

Figure 8.2: Summary of commentaries relating to value drivers

Sales Growth Forecast – 2007 figures suggests some signs of the recession lifting and in particular strong growth in the North American polymer compound sector. In general sales growth will tend to be slow to flat until the recession ends and even then the effect may be lagged until core markets themselves grow. In 2007, Depar divested its footwear components business thus reducing its UK originated turnover by £31.6 million.

Operating Profit Margin Forecast – average margins had improved to 5.7 per cent in 2007 results. Divisional analysis suggests that the polymer business already has margins in double figures and adhesives and sealants have high gross margins, which are being eroded. So Depar's turnaround strategy must seek to achieve a target industry average of 10-12 per cent medium term. In the industrial coatings division, Depar will be forced to keep margins low by the intense competition and depressed state of the market.

Fixed Capital Investment Forecast – fixed capital for the next five years will be only for replacement purposes and has been estimated at £5 million, £5.5 million, £6.1 million, £7.3 million and £8.7 million, respectively. Replacement capital expenditure in the continuing period has been estimated as being £9.5 million. Depreciation over the five year period has been estimated at £7.1 million, £7.5 million, £7.9 million, £8.4 million and £8.9 million, respectively. It is assumed to equal replacement capital expenditure in the continuing period.

Working Capital Forecast – this is another area which may benefit from tighter financial controls. However, the effect of new marketing initiatives and a severe competitive environment may force Depar into looser credit policies and higher than desired stock levels to maintain a good service which would force working capital expenditure up.

8.9 Sources of value creation

The objective in undertaking strategic options like mergers and acquisitions is to add value. Of course, additional value may not result immediately and it may take time to capture. This is where an approach reliant on assessing future cash flows conveys distinct advantages over more traditional measures that focus on the shorter term. However, there will still be a major challenge to meet in ensuring that the additional value actually occurs!

How is value added from a merger or acquisition? Potential synergies may result, the benefits of which can be related to their impact on the seven value drivers of the Shareholder Value Analysis approach. For example:

1. Sales growth may improve because of being able to use the distribution channels of each organisation to sell the products of both
2. Reductions in operating profit margins may be possible because of being able to use production facilities more efficiently
3. Cash taxes may be saved by being able to plan the tax position of the new combined organisation. This area may be particularly beneficial for certain types of cross-border deals
4. Fixed capital requirements may be lowered by being able to use available spare capacity for increased sales activity. There may also be an impact on replacement capital requirements, a good example of this being the decision to merge by two high street clearing banks. It may be possible to provide service to both sets of customers in the new organisation by cutting the number of branches

5. Working capital requirements can be reduced if the two businesses have a profile of cash flows opposite in effect to one another. There may also be potential benefits arising from better debtor, creditor and stock management
6. The planning period may be lengthened because, for example, the new larger venture increases barriers to entry
7. The cost of capital may fall if access is obtained to cheaper sources of finance.

A second, and very important, source of value may also come from stripping out some activities/businesses. In this way the net costs associated with a merger or acquisition can be substantially reduced and the real benefits drastically improved.

What makes mergers and acquisitions particularly challenging is that obtaining good quality, robust financial information may be very difficult for an acquirer. On the other hand, for the organisation being acquired, a major difficulty may arise in understanding the basis for the value placed on the organisation by an outsider whose rationale might be based on a totally different view of its future potential.

8.10 The potential acquirer's perspective: Mardel's bid

On 20 November 2006 Mardel launched a hostile bid for Depar with an offer of 80p per share (£58.2 million). Mardel was run by three ex-Hanson men under the chairman Chris Miller and recently had successfully acquired two other companies in the sealants and adhesives sector. Mardel saw Depar as a basically sound organisation, with strong market shares in UK adhesives and coatings and US plastics, which would benefit from both being unhampered by gearing and by the introduction of a strong management team.

Analysts had forecast profits of £8.9 million and earnings of 3.2p for Depar in 2006 and this confirmed Mardel's view that the company would be in a poor position to fund new capital expenditure, meet redemption obligations, repay bank debt and pay preference and ordinary dividends. In contrast its offer valued Depar at more than 25 times earnings and left Andrew Simon with little room to mount his defence. (On the announcement of the offer, Depar's shares jumped to 91p.).

In his defence document, presented to shareholders on 4 January 2007, Mr Simon claimed that Depar was back on the mend and announced a 40 per cent rise in pre-tax profits to £10.2

million for 2006. However, many feared the worst as the document omitted to include a profit forecast for the current year. Depar's shares rose to 103p and Mardel announced that it was not willing to overpay for any acquisition. As regards views about such a bid one analyst commented:

A range of 100p (realistic) to 120p (maximum) would appear to be the right ball park.

8.11 An alternative buyer's perspective: Kassal's rival bid

On 6 January, Mardel revised its bid to 95p per share and on the same day Kassal, the UK's second largest chemical group, bought 6.1 per cent of Depar's shares at 100p and announced its intention to make a bid above 100p. Kassal's announcement effectively out-manoeuvred what many thought would be Mardel's winning bid and allowed Depar to reject the 95p offer as inadequate.

Kassal's impending bid provided Depar with the opportunity of offering shareholders a good exit route. But first Kassal had to come up with a new bid price, one that Depar would be able to recommend and which would be acceptable to Kassal's investors.

Kassal's appearance was no sudden move as CEO Ken Hinton had reportedly been tracking Depar for seven years, first approaching Andrew Simon in 1996 and again in January 2006 following Depar's bad results.

Kassal had a strong management team and had experience in transforming a low margin bulk operation into a speciality chemicals company. Mr Hinton and his team had a reputation for ruthless cost cutting, especially in non-core businesses and had overseen the rise in Kassal's margins from 10 to 15 per cent since 1996.

Kassal had five core businesses – organic chemicals, absorbents, metals and electronic chemicals, construction chemicals, and hygiene and process chemicals. Clear potential synergies were seen between some of these businesses and Depar. In fact, Ken Hinton described the adhesive and polymer businesses as a 'classic fit'. (Figure 8.3 provides an anecdotal record of Kassal's assessment of Depar's businesses).

As a result of detailed sector knowledge, it was reckoned that the management of Kassal should be able to ensure that benefits from synergies could be achieved. Furthermore, it was believed that purchasing Depar need involve no dilution of earnings in the first year following acquisition.

Kassal offered and subsequently paid 120p per share for Depar, but was not prepared to assume any additional debt and, therefore, its offer consisted mainly of paper. Kassal's shares fell 27p to 583p on announcement of the terms of the offer, having fallen 10 per cent since the announcement of its intention to bid.

Figure 8.3: Kassal's assessment of Depar's businesses

Adhesives and polymer compounds provide 'classic fit':
Ken Hinton, Kassal's CEO, was reported to have claimed that Depar's two largest business sectors provided great potential for synergies from incorporation into Kassal's businesses.

Adhesives and sealants
Depar's operations have sales of £85 million from the construction and automotive sectors. Kassal already sells different adhesives to the construction sector and uses an alternative distribution network.

Polymer compounds
Kassal had no direct experience in this area. With sales of £85 million the products all involved formulating chemicals; one of Kassal's strengths and also a good fit.
The US operations were supplying high quality plastics to the food, medical and electronics sectors at good margins. The UK and Italian operations were in lower margin markets and required repositioning.

Question marks remain over other businesses:
Powder coatings
This area was outside Kassal's expertise and its potential for margin improvement limited. Therefore it would be under immediate divestment consideration.

Mr Hinton said of the business, 'When I have to compete with big boys like these (ICI and Courtaulds), I start getting nervous.'

Plastic fabrication

Five operations with sales of £20 million were also less attractive to Kassal. Three operations - in the USA, UK and Italy – provided reasonable margins, but the other two businesses required a complete turnaround.

Miscellaneous

Depar's remaining businesses, of which the vinyl coatings for wallpaper accounted for the majority of £40 million sales, provided no fit at all for Kassal.

8.12 Acquisition must enhance Kassal's earning in the first year

Ken Hinton was committed to immediate returns from Depar and promised to tackle their margins as his first priority. In the 1990's Mr Hinton had improved Kassal's margins from 10 per cent to today's level of nearly 15 per cent.

The improvement at Depar would probably come from:

- better pricing policies
- extending product ranges
- reducing raw material costs
- improved manufacturing
- cutting overheads
- better marketing
- significant job losses.

Mr Hinton denied that the cost of rationalisation would affect earnings. Kassal had plenty of experience of cost-cutting and there would be few environmental costs.

8.13 Value of the acquisition to Kassal

In reviewing the potential value of Depar to Kassal it is important to recognise that benefit can be derived from a number of sources. One useful classification is under three main headings: operating, financing and tax.

Operating benefits

These can be thought of in terms of what the acquirer, Kassal in this case, can do with the operations of the business that Depar has not done. One way of understanding any potential operating benefits is by reviewing the cash flow value drivers for Depar against the potential strategic fit of the two companies. For example, using the strategic value approach and sensitivity analysis on the base case reveals that the business is very margin sensitive. Given Kassal's track record for margin improvement identified a significant benefit could be unleashed if similar results could be achieved from Depar. For example, margin improvement to 10 per cent, 11 per cent, 12 per cent, 14 per cent and 15 per cent for the five years of the assumed CAP, with this margin being maintained in the period beyond, results in a strategic value of £1.37 per share. However, it must be recognised that such improvement is very unlikely to be achievable in all parts of the business. In fact, given the assessment of the fit of the Depar businesses in Kassal it might well be regarded as reasonable to assume the divestment of poorly fitting businesses with the achievement of this revised margin profile on the parts remaining. If, for the sake of illustration, we assume that businesses with revenues of £80 million are sold for £80 million after tax, the resulting share price is £1.54, although this is obviously heavily dependent on the assumed disposal value.

This line of analysis could be continued to incorporate different scenarios. The advantage it conveys lies in illustrating potential from asking 'what if' questions that can be readily analysed using a spreadsheet model. However, the potential results may be very different from reality and any such speculative analysis would need to be supported by a more rigorous interrogation.

Financing benefits

Operating benefits are not the only consideration. Some acquisitions take place simply to capture the benefits of a changed capital structure, often involving the replacement of equity funding with long-term debt.

However, whether this is the result will depend on the current proportion of debt. If it is perceived as being too high the result will be that attempts to drive WACC down by substituting debt for equity will fail. This is because the demands by the providers of funds to be compensated for a higher rate of return will at least offset the benefits from the substitution of debt for equity.

Tax benefits

Our preference is to review tax benefits after operating and financing benefits have been considered. Tax is very much a specialist area, which can have an important impact on a decision. However, a major problem with tax issues is that they vary from country to country and typically require specialist expertise once the operating and financing benefits have been reviewed thoroughly.

In reality, to make a full assessment of the potential of the acquisition to the acquirer it is necessary to go beyond the simple spreadsheet screening approach considered so far. Issues relating to potential operating, financing and tax benefits would be best looked at in terms of both the acquirer and the target. In its most detailed form, pursuit of this approach would involve calculating the cash flows corresponding with each business unit for both the buyer and the seller, discounting the cash flows by the relevant cost of capital for each business and then summing the results.

As already indicated, a significant part of Depar offered little fit with Kassal and could be disposed of. If estimated cash flows from such disposal is factored in together with the consequential potential impact on the other value drivers, the result is attractive, but that is not the end of the story. When the operational restructuring opportunities to Kassal are factored in together with the potential from refinancing the Depar business, a value in excess of £2 may be obtained per Depar share. Of course, the secret as with any acquisition is in making this actually happen!

8.14 Evaluating joint ventures

In the case of a joint venture the basic procedure is the same but there will be concern that the joint venture parties will each benefit from the newly formed enterprise. This involves a second step in terms of attributing the resulting synergies. In the case of a joint venture there are therefore two steps, each of which requires estimating:

- the benefit in the form of the value that will be created by the joint venture; and
- whether the respective sharing of any value created will meet the requirements of each partner.

The primary concern in this section is with demonstrating in principle how the analysis of strategic value can be applied in evaluating a joint venture opportunity. This is quite straightforward in principle and requires the valuation of the:

- existing organisation on a stand-alone basis; and
- newly formed joint venture.

8.15 Case study - joint venture in People's Republic of China

The Chinese partner involved in this joint venture occupied a factory within a large industrial complex owned by a municipal government. The other partner was a large Hong Kong based company with multiple share listings. The factory was one of the larger producers of lubricants for the motor industry and it enjoyed a good reputation for its brand name, especially in North China. In view of the rapid growth in the automobile industry in China, the organisation was positioned to perform exceptionally well in the foreseeable years.

The factory produced two families of products. Current demand for the new but more expensive product was about 35 per cent of the total demand for lubricants, but was expected to rise to 55 per cent by the year 2001. However, as the Chinese factory was built some 20 years ago it was not designed for manufacturing this new product which enjoyed higher profit margins than the older product. There was also the added difficulty that the facilities were outdated and the production cost was no longer competitive.

In addition to the outdated equipment and poor product mix, the factory was heavily burdened by the overhead being charged by the parent organisation. The parent organisation had been experiencing financial difficulties for the past few years, mainly because of the problems of accounts receivable and the demand for new capital for new infrastructure projects. This situation had been getting worse, such that the factory had no alternative but to struggle along with this burden and with its existing operational structure, unless there was an injection of fresh capital from external investors. With this view in mind, a foreign partner was invited to look at the possible opportunities and serious negotiation followed the initial investigation. The potential foreign partner understood the potential of the automobile industry in China, had experience in Chinese projects and was interested in producing auxiliary products to serve this important and growing industry.

The existing production facilities meant that there was very limited freedom to improve the product mix or increase the production volume. Using the information relating to the existing production facilities resulted in a strategic value of approximately 1.5 RMB million. This was calculated by first estimating the free cash flows for a five-year planning period using the five value cash flow drivers. The free cash flows for these five years and beyond, together with the value drivers for the first year, are summarised in Table 8.4.

Table 8.4: Free cash flows for the existing factory being run by the Chinese partner

Year		**1**	**2**	**3**	**4**	**5**	**Beyond**
	RMB m	**RMB m**	**RMB m**	**RMB m**	**RMB m**	**RMB m**	**RMB m**
Sales receipts	14.20	14.91	15.66	16.44	17.26	18.12	18.12
Operating profit		0.15	0.31	0.66	0.69	0.72	0.72
– Cash tax		0.00	0.00	0.11	0.11	0.12	0.24
Profit after tax		0.15	0.31	0.55	0.58	0.60	0.48
+ Depreciation		0.40	0.40	0.40	0.40	0.40	0.40
Operating cash flow		0.55	0.71	0.95	0.98	1.00	0.88
– RFCI		0.40	0.40	0.40	0.40	0.40	0.40
– IFCI		0.00	0.00	0.00	0.00	0.00	0.00
- WCI		0.21	0.23	0.23	0.25	0.26	0.00
Free cash flow		-0.06	0.08	0.32	0.33	0.34	0.48

Note: At this time the exchange rate was US $1 = 8.56 RMB

In determining the cost of capital to use for valuing this joint venture, the question of risk needed to be addressed carefully. The basic principle applied to risk is that the greater its magnitude, the larger will be the reward or premium required to compensate for such risk. There are alternative approaches for estimating the premium for risk in developed financial markets, none of which are particularly helpful in China. There is one additional issue associated with risk. As we have indicated on a number of occasions in earlier chapters, financial theory urges making a distinction between that risk which is market related and that which is specific to the company. While the former should be built into the estimation of the cost of capital, specific risk should be taken into account in the estimation of annual cash flows. We know that it can often be difficult to distinguish between market and specific risks. In circumstances where it is extremely difficult to use the tools and techniques of corporate finance to estimate the risk premium to include in the cost of capital estimation, our preference is to build as many risks as possible into the cash flows using a scenario approach. Such risks include political, exchange rate, sovereign and commercial risks.

Not surprisingly, estimating the cost of capital of this Chinese organisation was a challenge. In fact, a range of values was actually used in the valuation process. Here, a cost of capital of 20 per cent after tax is assumed for purposes of illustration only.

Table 8.5 shows the calculation of the strategic value of the Chinese organisation on a stand-alone basis assuming a five-year planning period.

Table 8.5: Chinese organisation stand-alone value calculation

Year	**1**	**2**	**3**	**4**	**5**	**Beyond**
	RMB m	**RMB m**	**RMB m**	**RMB m**	**RMB m**	**RMB m**
Free cash flow	-0.06	0.08	0.32	0.33	0.34	0.48
Discount factor (20%)	0.833	0.694	0.579	0.482	0.402	
Present value (free cash flow)	-0.05	0.06	0.19	0.16	0.14	
Cumulative present value	-0.05	0.01	0.20	0.36	0.50	
Present value of residual value					0.96	
Strategic value					**1.46**	

The result is 0.96 RMB milllion. In using a simple perpetuity we are assuming that beyond the planning period the organisation can only earn returns equal to its cost of capital, hence there is no additional value creation beyond the planning period. This seems consistent with the fact that the Chinese organisation wanted to form a joint venture and then close down its existing plant.

8.16 Value of the joint venture

Having estimated the value of the organisation on a stand-alone basis, the next step required an estimation of the strategic value to be created as a result of the joint venture proposal. With additional contact and visits to the plant, the foreign investor became convinced that the factory had a reasonably strong management team and its brand name was quite valuable. More importantly, the two partners felt comfortable working with each other. With further due diligence analysis, which included a market study, the foreign investor made the following proposal for the median scenario of market demand:

- A new joint venture to be formed with the Chinese party (Party A) holding 40 per cent of the equity and the foreign party (Party B) holding the remaining 60 per cent
- Total investment to be 32.2 RMB million of which 13.92 RMB million would be the fixed capital with the balance (18.28 RMB million) to be the working capital
- The capital injection to be used to build a new factory with a capacity of 10,000 tons per year as compared with the 4,000 tons per year from existing operations
- The new factory to have a product mix to reflect the demand of the market
- The plant is to be designed to allow flexibility to change the capital injection and, hence, the scale of the plant in response to changing market demand, for which three scenarios emerged out of the market study, namely; low, median and high product mix in response to the changing customer requirements
- The old facility to be shut down as soon as the new plant is up and running, that is, in approximately a year's time.

Table 8.6 shows these strategic changes for the median scenario translated into free cash flows and value terms.

Table 8.6: Potential strategic value created by the joint venture

Year		1	2	3	4	5	Beyond
	RMB m	RMB m	RMB m	RMB m	RMB m	RMB m	RMB m
Sales receipts	14.20	42.60	48.14	56.81	65.33	75.13	76.63
Operating profit		5.96	6.74	10.23	11.76	13.52	13.79
–Cash tax		0.00	0.00	1.74	2.00	2.30	4.46
Profit after tax		5.96	6.74	8.49	9.76	11.22	9.33
+Depreciation		1.00	1.00	1.00	1.00	1.00	1.00
Operating cash flow		6.96	7.74	9.49	10.76	12.22	10.33
–RFCI		1.00	1.00	1.00	1.00	1.00	1.00
–IFCI		13.92	0.00	0.00	0.00	0.00	0.00
–WCI		8.52	1.66	2.60	2.56	2.94	0.00
Free cash flow		– 16.48	5.08	5.89	7.20	8.28	9.33
Discount factor		0.833	0.64	0.579	0.484	0.402	
Present value		– 13.73	3.53	3.41	3.47	3.33	
Cumulative present value		– 13.73	– 10.20	– 6.79	– 3.32	0.01	
PV of residual value (with 2% growth)						20.83	
Strategic value						**20.84**	

In calculating the residual value we have used the perpetuity with growth method on the assumption the joint venture will be able to earn returns in excess of the cost of capital beyond the planning period; this is in contrast to the Chinese organisation. The perpetuity with growth method takes the value of the free cash flow beyond five years of 9.33 RMB million and capitalises it by the product of the discount rate less the growth rate (0.2 – 0.02). It then converts the result to a present value by discounting it. The result is 20.84 RMB million.

The results are quite impressive with a strategic value of 20.84 RMB million being generated using a five year planning period. However, nearly all the contribution now comes from the residual value element. In fact, the residual value as a proportion of the strategic value is so high that many questions should be asked about it. Is it realistic? Could it be too large, or even too small? In fact, the valuation process would certainly not stop at this point. But the illustration shows that the value of the joint venture business may well be substantially above the stand-alone value. If we believe the calculations, the value created by the joint venture is approximately 19.38 RMB million (20.84 RMB million – 1.46 RMB million).

The fact that all the value is generated beyond the selected planning period could be taken as a fundamental flaw of the approach. However, it is important to recognise that joint ventures may take a considerable time before they are ready to be judged on traditional output measures. The need for patience is underscored by a study of Fortune 500 firms that started new (wholly owned) businesses with the intent of diversifying. The median start-up took seven to eight years to show a positive return on investment or positive cash flow and no ventures had positive cash flow in the first two years. In fact, many of the start-ups that turned positive early (in return on investment terms) failed to retain their profitability. Considering that joint ventures are often used in the riskiest of circumstances, the need for patience should be even greater.

8.17 Valuing in Emerging Markets—An IPO Case Study

The valuation and pricing of an initial public offer (IPO) always raises a difficult and contentious issue. Trying to gauge market sentiment and set a price that does not spell disaster in terms of the desired objectives is a real challenge. IPOs can be valued using a variety of methods, but there will generally be a discounted cash flow (DCF) estimate of some form, and great care should be exercised in terms of the implicit and explicit assumptions.

In very simple terms, the key components in a DCF valuation typically include assumptions about:

- the generation of the cash flows, both in the period for which explicit and detailed estimates are made as well as the period beyond—this latter component is often referred to as the continuing, terminal, or residual value;
- the discount rate or cost of capital;
- the method for valuing the cash flows over the time period beyond the explicit forecast; and
- the time horizon for the explicit forecast.

Academics and practitioners have identified many sources of error in DCF valuations, not the least of which is unrealistic assumptions about future cash flows. In particular, behavioral finance, with its roots in the pioneering research of psychologists Daniel Kahneman (recent winner of the Nobel Prize for his work) and his late colleague Amos Tversky, has traced human error in decision-making to several common causes that include self-deception arising from overoptimism and overconfidence. Overoptimism and overconfidence often characterize DCF valuations in terms of the growth in free cash flows within the explicit forecast time horizon, but can be even more pronounced in the period beyond.

As outlined in an earlier chapter, the conventional approach in estimating the value of businesses with long-term growth potential is to use a two-stage model. The first stage represents a finite period in which growth is assumed to be explicitly captured in the projected cash flows over that period. The second stage assumes a certain level of net cash flow in perpetuity that grows at an assumed composite rate, g, thereby avoiding the need to forecast individual cash flows. As a consequence, value from the second stage can be calculated very simply as follows:

$$\text{Terminal Value} = \frac{\text{FCF } (t+1)}{\text{WACC} - g}$$

where FCF (t+1) represents the estimated prospective perpetuity cash flow and WACC the weighted average cost of capital. In other words, the first stage of a conventional DCF valuation is typified by the use of explicit forecast assumptions about individual line items in the free cash flow projections, whereas g in the second stage generally represents a number that is designed to capture in some way the net total of expectations about individual line items.

Of course, the deduction of a growth rate in the denominator of the calculation has a significant impact upon the estimated value—the higher the growth rate, the higher is the value. As anyone who has worked with such models will know, a major concern typically arises about the impact of g on the resulting value and, therefore, how g might be estimated in any meaningful way. At the end of the day, the user of investment research needs to be able to establish confidence about the assumptions underlying the estimate of g. The problem is the lack of any readily available framework in corporate finance as normally practiced for "testing" the growth rate assumption.

The purpose of this case study is to outline a framework for formulating growth assumptions based upon the tools and techniques of corporate finance. The framework uses the analytical technique called Market Implied Competitive Advantage Period (MICAP) that was introduced in Chapter 4 to challenge conventional perpetuity-with-growth assumptions on the basis of market-derived information about comparable businesses. As with all such frameworks, this one has strengths and weaknesses, but the former outweigh the latter. The framework is introduced in the context of the Jordan Telecom initial public offering (IPO) in 2002, where a one-percentage-point change in the perpetuity growth rate altered the estimate of fair market value by nearly 10%, so it is clearly important to validate the growth assumption.

Proposed Framework for Challenging IPO Pricing

The five steps outlined below constitute the basic framework for evaluating the results of a DCF valuation for an IPO.

1) Choose businesses comparable to the IPO company being valued and obtain their relevant share prices, up-to-date financials, estimates for cash flow growth, and WACC. The objective here is to obtain estimates of all valuation inputs other than time, so that we can use Market Implied Competitive Advantage Period (MICAP) analysis to solve for the explicit time period impounded in the share price, assuming a simple perpetuity in the period beyond.
2) Find the time period for each comparable business that equates the "relevant" share price with prospective cash flows based on the assumptions. This time period represents the MICAP for the comparable company and will be used for defining the second time period in a three-stage valuation model.
3) Use this three-stage model to calculate three values: the first is the discounted value of the free cash flows in the original explicit forecast; the second represents the discounted value of free cash flows from the end of the explicit forecast period up through the MICAP

for the comparable business (with these free cash flows being estimated from the growth profile of the comparable businesses); and the third is the value calculated from a simple perpetuity for the period beyond the MICAP.[22]

4) Analyze the values from Stages 2 and 3 of this three-stage model using the perpetuity-with-growth model for each of the comparable businesses to establish what the perpetuity growth rate would have to be to justify the free cash flows in the perpetuity period beyond Stage 1 of a traditional two-stage model.
5) Apply the growth rates from Step 4 to the two-stage valuation model and iterate on share price as an input to the WACC calculation with the share price as an output.

This five-step framework provides a methodology for the fundamental assessment of the cash flow growth assumptions used in a DCF analysis—particularly for the terminal value, which typically represents the largest portion of the valuation. The framework focuses upon the analysis of comparable businesses to form a view about a reasonable perpetuity-with-growth estimate, based upon the experiences of similar businesses. In effect, Market Implied Competitive Advantage Period analysis asks the question: Using the value implied in competitors' share prices, for how many years is the return on capital expected to exceed the cost of capital? This question is posed with the assumption that free cash flows and the cost of capital can be reasonably well estimated, so that the number of years of explicit cash flows required to arrive at the current market price (consistent with a steady state in the terminal period) can be calculated as the only unknown variable. It is important to note that the terminal value method proposed here in the application of the approach is a simple perpetuity because all growth is assumed to be captured over the MICAP. The final stage reflects a steady state in which the business generates an economic return that is equal to the cost of capital.

To avoid concerns about the impact of perpetuity-with-growth estimates, then, the three-stage model captures the growth element more explicitly. The first stage involves a detailed forecast for all items constituting the free cash flow, so that assumptions about the envisaged growth characteristics of the company are captured explicitly for this time period. The second stage involves a growth forecast for just the net free cash flow over a finite time period that follows the explicit forecast period, possibly based upon perceptions of growth in the sector, and the third stage assumes that all growth has been captured and measures the valuation of a single cash flow into perpetuity (see Figure 8.4).

[22] Terminal Value = FCF (t=1) / WACC, that is, zero growth.

Figure 8.4: The three stages of caluation.

Explicit Cash flow Forecast Based Upon Detailed Company Projections	Net Cash flow Forecast Based upon Company or Sector Growth Characteristics	Simple Perpetuity Cash Flow
Stage 1	Stage 2	Stage 3

The time horizon of the second stage can be estimated using MICAP analysis and the results of this estimation provide a cross-check for the growth estimates in a standard two-stage valuation model. In addition to challenging the original perpetuity-with-growth rates, the results from the three-stage analysis can be used to produce a revised equity valuation for the company.

In the five-step framework, it would be unrealistic to assume that there is any definitive way to estimate a correct growth rate. To do so would be tantamount to suggesting that the future can be foretold! However, the framework can certainly be used to challenge growth-in-perpetuity assumptions, as will be illustrated below using Jordan Telecom.

Applying the Five-Step Framework to Jordan Telecom

In 1971, Telecommunications Corporation (TCC) was established as a state-owned corporation to provide and operate telecommunications services in Jordan (telephone, telegraph, and telex). In 1997 TCC was privatised and adopted the name Jordan Telecommunications Company (JTC). In January 2000, a 40% stake was sold to the Joint Investment Telecommunications Company (JITCO), thereby establishing Jordan Telecom. In September 2002 the Jordanian government wanted to sell 15% of its share capital (37.5 million shares) through an IPO.

The prospective IPO generated a flurry of research reports. The one drawn upon here was representative and offered the following evaluation:

Using the discounted cash flow (DCF) method, we arrived at an estimated fair value for Jordan Telecom in the range of JD618.8-671.9 million (Jordanian dinars), which translates into JD2.48-2.72/share.

The report provided a two-stage discounted cash flow valuation model based on a seven-year explicit forecast period and two terminal value scenarios based on growth in perpetuity of 5% and 6%. The analyst estimated free cash flows over the seven-year forecast period (see Table 8.7) and then discounted them to a present value of JD272.4 million as the value of Stage 1. Based on a 5% perpetuity growth rate, the terminal value was JD428.5 million (61% of total enterprise value) and it was JD489.5 million with the 6% perpetuity growth rate (64% of total enterprise value). The analyst then subtracted the market value of debt and preferred stock (JD82 million) to arrive at an equity market value for Jordan Telecom in the range of JD618.8–671.9 million, or JD2.48–2.72 per share based on 250 million shares outstanding.

Table 8.7: Analysts' Free Cash Flow Estimates (millions of Jordanian dinars)

STAGE 1							
Year	**2002**	**2003**	**2004**	**2005**	**2006**	**2007**	**2008**
Free Cash Flow	43.10	55.70	59.60	70.20	73.90	76.00	78.70

The critical issue is that the terminal value, whether based on 5% or 6% growth, accounted for more than 60% of the total value even with a seven-year explicit forecast period. With such a large proportion of the total value affected by these assumed growth rates, it is critical to understand their validity. Since much of the analysis was based upon comparisons with selected peer group companies, the validity of the two perpetuity-with-growth estimates can be reviewed by applying the five-step model outlined earlier.

In the case of Jordan Telecom, the peer group comparables were from Central and Eastern Europe which, according to the analyst, offered the closest match with the Jordanian market situation in terms of penetration levels, per capita GDP, credit ratings, and the standing of their mobile subsidiaries. The more geographically proximate Gulf operators were judged to be in a more advanced stage of development than Jordan Telecom.

Once the comparable businesses have been identified, the next step is to obtain up-to-date financial information, generate prospective cash flow forecasts, and estimate their cost of capital (WACC). Financial information is usually available; and WACC estimation, while challenging, is not normally a major problem. Estimating free cash flow growth rates is a little more difficult because consensus estimates for the future may not be available, although the initial use of historical trend analysis balanced against an assessment of the prospective strategy is probably a good starting point.

The projected free cash flow profile from Step 2 is extended until the current share price is reached and a simple perpetuity terminal value is obtained for the continuing period. This can be viewed as a steady state period in which the business generates an economic return that is equal to the cost of capital; there is no economic incentive to invest other than to replace assets that have worn out or become obsolete. Nonetheless, there is no incentive to exit the business, because in principle all costs including those relating to capital are covered and economic theory would suggest that a normal profit is being earned. The time period up until steady state is an estimate of the MICAP, or the period of competitive advantage implied in the share price.

As regards Jordan Telecom, one of the peer group companies cited in the analyst's report was the Polish telecom company Telekomunikacja Polska SA (TPSA), which was trading between 11.40 and 11.50 Polish zloty at the time of the analysis. Using a mid-range share price of 11.44 zloty as the reference point, projected cash flows based on a historical trend analysis resulted in a MICAP of ten years, which reflected annual free cash flow growth rates of 18.6%, 17.1% and 15.9% (based on historical trend analysis) for the three years beyond the seven-year forecast period used in the Jordan Telecom analysis—that is, in Years 8, 9 and 10.[23] In other words, the only way to obtain a value close to the mid-range share price of 11.44 zloty was to extend the explicit cash flow forecast period to ten years, after which point a simple perpetuity resulted. Table 8.8 summarises these calculations.

Table 8.8: MICAP analysis for TPSA (millions of zloty)

Year	**8**	**9**	**10**
PV of Future Cash Flows	14.3	16.4	16.4
Terminal Value	48.1	55.8	60.8
PV Terminal Value	14.3	14.5	15.8
Total Market Value	28.6	30.9	32.2
Less: Net Debt	16.2	16.2	16.2
Equity Value	12.4	14.7	16.0
Number of Shares	1.4m	1.4m	1.4m
Share Price (zloty)	8.89	10.52	11.44

[23] The annual growth in Jordan Telecom's free cash flow over the seven-year forecast period never reaches these levels, which further supports the five-step approach because, as we see later, even with these much higher annual growth rates in cash flows we do not get near the analyst's 5% to 6% perpetuity-with-growth estimate.

In terms of the three-stage model described earlier, if the growth profile for TPSA is applied to Jordan Telecom, then years 1–7 represent Stage 1, years 8–10 represent the Stage 2 balance of the MICAP period of ten years, and Stage 3 is represented by all years after year 10.[24]

If TPSA's growth in free cash flow for each year from the end of the seven-year period up to the end of year 10 is representative of the potential growth in Jordan Telecom for Stage 2, then the growth rates of 18.6%, 17.1% and 15.9% can be applied to the Jordan Telecom free cash flow forecast in estimating the cash flows in Stage 2 and also the simple perpetuity for Stage 3. This is illustrated in Table 8.9.

Table 8.9: Application of TPSA Free Cash Flow Growth Rate to Jordan Telecom (millions of Jordanian dinars)

	STAGE 2			STAGE 3
Year	**2009**	**2010**	**2011**	
Growth Rate from TPSA MICAP	18.6%	17.1%	15.9%	
FCF Forecast for Jordan Telecom	93.3	109.3	126.7	
Discount Factor	0.882	0.778	0.686	
Present Value (Free Cash Flow)	82.3	85.0	86.8	
Cumulative Present Value	82.3	167.3	254.1	
Terminal Value Without Growth				4647.7

The value of Stage 2 of 254.1 million Jordanian dinars is the cumulative present value (as of year-end 2008) of the discounted free cash flows for years 8, 9 and 10 (2009–2011 inclusive) using a WACC of 13.4%.[25] The value of Stage 3 of 647.7 million Jordanian dinars is the terminal value without growth, or the simple perpetuity of 2011 cash flow (assumed to equal t+1) discounted back to a present value as of year-end 2008 (86.8/0.134).

The original perpetuity growth estimates used by the analyst can now be assessed by drawing upon the information gathered from the peer comparison and applying it to the rearranged perpetuity-with-growth formula to find the growth rate associated with the sum of the values

[24] As indicated earlier, the difficulty with three-stage models is identifying where Stage 3 in particular starts, but the analysis of a comparable business allows this to be estimated. With regard to the start of Stage 2, the original seven-year estimate for Jordan Telecom was accepted on the grounds that only the growth rates used in perpetuity were being challenged in this instance.

[25] The 13,4% WACC is estimated from information provided in the analyst report: a risk-free rate of 9.5% (obtained using the stripped yield of a ten-year Brady bond), a beta of 0.96, an equity risk premium estimate of 6% for CEEMA markets, a cost of debt of 6%, outstanding debt of JD82 million, and a target equity-to-debt ratio of 4:1.

from Stages 2 and 3 of the three-stage model.

$$\text{Terminal Value (TV)} = \frac{\text{FCF (t+1)}}{\text{WACC-g}}$$

$$g = \text{WACC} - \left[\frac{\text{FCF (t+1)}}{\text{TV}} \right]$$

With a WACC of 13.4%, a perpetuity free cash flow of JD93.3 million, and a terminal value of JD901.8 million (equal to the sum of the Stage 2 present value of JD254.1 million and the perpetuity present value of JD647.7 million from Table 8.2), the implied perpetuity growth rate beyond Stage 1 using the formula is 3.1%.

This perpetuity growth rate is substantially less than the 5% or 6% used in the original valuation. Of course, it was derived from an assessment of one of Jordan Telecom's peer companies, but TPSA was one of the comparables used as the basis of the original analysis. Still, it is quite reasonable to ask what the result would have been had the other peer companies been analyzed similarly — and in point of fact, there would have been no perpetuity growth warranted at all, because the MICAPs of the companies for which such analysis could be undertaken did not extend even to seven years.

The final part of the analysis involves using the growth rate calculated from the analysis of the peer group in a traditional two-stage model to gauge the impact on equity value.[26] The 3.1% derived from applying the TPSA growth estimates to Jordan Telecom can now be applied to the two-stage model developed in the Jordan Telecom analyst report to "test" the implied IPO price.

In IPO pricing, of course, there is no established market equity value to use in the WACC calculation. In fact, within the WACC-based model used by the analysts, the market value of equity is both an input and an output; it is an input in terms of establishing the market-based target debt-to-equity ratio and it is also the output of the valuation exercise. One approach, therefore, is to iterate on the price, so that the IPO price and the price used in calculating the WACC are mutually consistent. Since the amount of debt and all other variables for undertaking the valuation are known, we can treat the market equity value as the unknown variable and

[26] The valuation can be undertaken within the three-stage model outlined; however, great user benefit has been demonstrated from relating the approach back to the original two stages.

solve for it accordingly. In effect, iteration is undertaken until the input market value of equity and the resulting output market value are the same. Of course, variation in the debt:equity ratio will affect the beta used to estimate the WACC, but we can apply the levering and unlevering formula (see Chapter 6, Section 6.1) in calculating the cost of equity to ensure consistency. Based on the information provided in the analyst report, the result is a WACC of 13.9% and a price of JD1.89, as illustrated in Table 8.10.

Table 8.10: IPO Price Iteration for Jordan Telecom

The unlevered beta is estimated from the levered beta of 0.96 in the analyst's report based on the debt-equity ratio associated with the price "guess," assuming a tax rate of 40%; for Round 1, the unlevered beta is 0.96/[1.0 + (1 – 0.4) x 82/620]. The initial price guess is the lowest price estimate from the analyst's report.

	Round 1	**Round 2**	**Round 3**
Unlevered beta	0.89	0.87	0.87
Price (guess)	2.48	1.85	1.89
Number of shares	2.5MM	2.5MM	2.5MM
Equity value	620.0	462.5	472.5
Debt/equity ratio	1/7.6	1/5.6	1/5.8
Levered beta	0.95	0.97	0.97
WACC	14.1%	13.9%	13.9%
DCF—Stage 1	261.3	263.0	262.9
PV of terminal value	282.9	291.2	290.6
Business value	544.2	554.2	553.4
Less: Debt	82.0	82.0	82.0
Equity value	462.2	472.2	471.4
Price	1.85	1.89	1.89

Conclusions

Based on the information provided by an analysis of a potential IPO valuation with respect to comparable companies, the estimates for perpetuity growth in the case of Jordan Telecom were overoptimistic. As a result, the originally estimated IPO valuation of JD2.48–2.72 per share was overstated. The MICAP analysis generated an implied share price of JD1.89, suggesting that there would have to be some very substantial changes in the projected cash flows to justify the original estimates.

Should we be surprised that the result of the analysis produced a share price different to the post-IPO price, which fell from JD 2.45 (closing value on 4th November 2002) to JD 2.17 (closing value on 7th August 2003)[27] The simple answer is no and there are a number of reasons for this. First, the analysis undertaken by the analyst drew upon the central and eastern European peer group, a perspective that might not have been shared by the market as a whole. Second, the analysis drew entirely upon the information provided in the research report and focussed principally upon the growth assumptions used in estimating the terminal value, with no attempt being made to question the other assumptions; for example, relatively small changes in the assumptions, particularly the WACC, could have a material impact on the value. Last, but by no means least the efficiency of the Jordanian stock market is an issue open to debate.

While this framework has been demonstrated on the Jordan Telecom IPO, it can be applied to any situation in which perpetuity growth estimates are used in free cash flow valuations. Of course, the selection of comparable companies is often a significant challenge insofar as there can be considerable debate about the criteria for comparability and whether there really are any comparable businesses at all. In the legitimate absence of comparable companies, an established company in the marketplace can still be a useful proxy because it will at least prompt the right questions about the plausibility of the growth assumptions. In essence, the real value of the 5-step framework is that it provides a systematic line of investigation for challenging perpetuity growth assumptions.

Postscript

Jordan Telecom's Performance during the Six Months after Listing

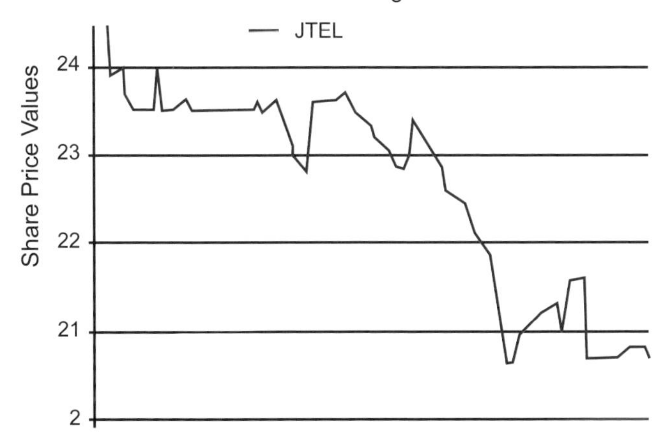

[27] See Postscript

The Jordan Telecom Company (JTC, Amman Stock Exchange code JTEL) began trading on the Amman Stock Exchange (ASE) on 4 November 2002. During the first six months since its listing on the market, JTC's share price has slipped into a definite downward trend losing a total of 14.28 percent from JOD 2.45 (closing value on 4th November 2002) to JOD 2.17 (closing value on 7th August 2003), trading habitually in shallow volumes. In the period of January–August 2003 JTC's price reached the highest value of JOD 2.37.

Source: Basel Khraisheh, Amer Mouasher, Talal Touqan, and Samer Sunnuqrot, Market Performance Report (3-7), August 2003, Jordan National Bank plc (www.arabfinance.com).

CHAPTER 9
INTANGIBLE ASSETS

Chapter Preview

This chapter will enable you to understand:

- **The importance of intangible assets.**
- **The problem in the provision of information about corporate performance and the information gap.**
- **The importance and challenges in measuring human resource value.**
- **The importance and challenges in brand valuation, including the different approaches that can be used to value brands.**

9.1 Introduction

A view that has attracted much attention in recent times is that successful companies of the twenty first century will not be able to rely simply upon the traditional value drivers associated with tangible assets, but rather they will have to manage these tangible assets along with intellectual assets. More specifically, they will have to focus upon intellectual property in the form of patents and trademarks.

As an illustration of the potential impact of intellectual capital, one only has to consider the growth in the market-to-book ratios of firms like Microsoft and Oracle. This market-book ratio is simply the market capitalisation of the business' equity divided by the book value of the equity found in the balance sheet. The growth in the market-to-book ratios is taken as being indicative of the intellectual capital in a company on the grounds that as the balance sheet accounts for all physical capital, anything remaining can only represent the intellectual capital.

A problem confronts businesses, users of business reporting information, standard setters and regulators in terms of how best to understand and communicate the difference between the market capitalisation of a company and its accounting book value. One approach is simply to attribute the entire difference to some ill-defined notion of 'intangibles', however, that approach provides little feedback information to users of financial and business reporting information.

Attempts to reconcile the accounting book value with the market capitalisation presents many difficulties as the following table illustrates:

1.	**Accounting book value**	**£XXXX**
2.	+ Market assessments of differences between accounting measurement and underlying value of recognised assets and liabilities	£XXXX
3.	+ Market assessments of the underlying value of items that meet the definition of assets and liabilities but are not recognised in financial statements (for example, patents developed through internal research and development)	£XXXX
4.	+ Market assessments of intangible value drivers or value impairers that do not meet the definition of assets and liabilities (for example, employee morale)	£XXXX
5.	+ Market assessments of the entity's future plans, opportunities and business risks	£XXXX
6.	+ Other factors, including pessimism and market psychology	£XXXX
7.	**Market capitalisation**	**£XXXX**

Items 2 and 3 can be difficult enough to measure, but items 4, 5 and 6 are often extremely difficult to identify and, therefore, measure. Their inclusion begs all sorts of questions about the definition of intangibles.

9.2 *What are Intangibles?*

Intangibles are defined by Lev (2000) as 'a non-physical claim to future benefits' arising from innovation, organisational practices and human resources. They differ from physical and financial assets because owners of such tangible assets can exclude others from enjoying the full benefits of investments. Non-owners can rarely be perfectly excluded from sharing the benefits of intangibles. Such partial or non-excludability gives rise to spill-overs (benefits to non-owners) and absence of control in the strict legal sense over most intangibles. These, in turn, create unique and significant challenges in managing and reporting on intangible assets, leading to a constant tension between the value creation potential of these assets (scalability) and the difficulties of delivering on the promise.

There is nothing new about intangible assets, but there has been a surge in interest in intangibles since the mid-1980s because of the unique combination of two related economic forces. The first of these forces is intensified business competition, brought about by the globalisation of trade and deregulation in key economic sectors (for example, telecommunications, electricity, transportation, financial services) and the second is the advent of information technologies (IT), most recently exemplified by the Internet. These two fundamental developments, one economic/ political, the other technological, have dramatically changed the structure of corporations and have catapulted intangibles into the role of the major value driver of businesses in developed economies.

9.3 *The Information Gap*

In one survey undertaken to determine exactly which measures are critical in assessing the value of a company, the respondents were asked to rank performance measures in order of importance and all three groups agreed on a Top Ten list that included just three financial measures - earnings, cash flow and gross margins and seven non-financial measures. Of the seven non-financial measures, three:

- strategic direction
- quality/experience of the management team and
- speed to market

came from internal company data and the remaining four required data not typically captured by internal systems. These four were:

- competitive landscape
- market size
- market growth and
- market share.

Corporate information systems often cannot produce sufficiently reliable information on the critical non-financial measures of performance. Not surprisingly, companies are reluctant to provide this information to the market place, which then creates a reporting gap. The implication for investors is a large information gap, because they do not get information on the measures they and the companies agree are important. To make matters worse it is argued that sell-side analysts, who are the experts with the skills and time to make sense of any information that does become available, are torn among serving the investors who rely on their recommendations, maintaining access to corporate managers and meeting the demands of their investment-bank employers. However, if the market receives relevant, accurate information almost continuously, investors will be able to form a clear picture of performance as each quarter progresses. Because current market prices will already reflect this information, quarterly earnings releases will simply document what the market already knows. Analysts' estimates, pre-announcements and whispers will no longer seem so important. However, the current failure to report non-financial information can be seen to have many important implications. Customers, shareholders and potential investors will talk about companies, whether they have any real information or not. Furthermore, if companies do not provide the information, someone else will somewhere online, whether on a Web site, in an e-mail message or in a chat room.

This raises the all important question of what information should a company report? One view by Eccles et al (2001) is that the needs of the investment community should be the focus, itself comprised of four interrelated elements, which taken together provide a comprehensive picture of a company's plans and performance. They are:

1. Market overview - management's view on the company's competitive position and external environment
2. Value strategy - an explanation of the company's strategy, including how it intends to create value
3. Managing for value - a summary of the company's performance targets and an assessment of how well it is meeting them
4. Value platform - the elements that underpin value and future financial performance, including people, innovation, supply chain, customers, brands and reputation.

Rather than simply report financial performance and assume that it completely captures the value the company creates, Eccles et al argue that managers should also provide information on its investment in the value platform and how that contributes to value creation. Also, within this model, companies should provide information on both hazard risk (the things that can go wrong) and opportunity risk (the things that they do to create value) and how they manage both.

This raises the interesting question of who should take responsibility for making these dramatic changes in external reporting? The accounting profession will play a critical role in value reporting and accounting firms will have to move beyond simply auditing financial figures and into the treacherous realm of non-financial measures, where they will have to identify key value drivers and risks, and set the standards by which they will be assessed and compared. This is not to ignore the role of corporate executives and boards of directors, who will have the responsibility of ensuring that all material information is disseminated as quickly as possible to everyone at the same time. Equally importantly, companies will have to develop sound measurement methodologies for the key non-financial value drivers and intangible assets that the market finds important and present resulting data in an organised and structured manner.

How and what form might such value reporting take? Wright and Keegan of PWC (1997) have proposed an approach that has seven core components :

1. Perform a preliminary evaluation of the financial drivers of the company - the levers of shareholder value
2. Determine how these drivers are embodied in the corporation's objectives and how the drivers are shaping business operations
3. Understand how management has developed the strategies currently in place to achieve these objectives

4. Determine whether the objectives and strategies are supported by performance measurements, and assess the quality of measurement data provided to management
5. Assess whether management processes foster value creation
6. Draw up the 'big picture' from all of the foregoing activities and select the most relevant points to communicate with the investing public about value-creating strategies, processes, goals and results
7. Review, on a rotating basis, how effectively the major processes of the company (such as capital planning and acquisitions, budgeting, strategic planning, product/service planning, management forums and executive compensation) are functioning and fix what needs to be fixed.

9.4 Human resource value

Although many companies publicly thank their employees for the skill and dedication that have contributed to the company's progress or success, there is little evidence of how this important asset contributes to the performance of the business or evidence of how companies effectively manage and develop their people to create value.

The value of a company is often considered to be the value of its assets and, although there has been considerable debate and discussion of the criticality of people as a vital asset in organisations, whether in the private or public sector, and a recognition that their skills and their knowledge are crucial factors in a business' competitive advantage and profitability, from a financial reporting perspective there has been no generally accepted procedure for measuring the quality and effectiveness of human capital. In accounting terms, human capital – people - are treated as costs except when they are 'purchased' on a contract, for example, football players. The move for corporations to classify the stock options they give to their employees as an expense means that there is a development towards identifying a 'truer' cost of people, that is, including all of their remuneration package, but it remains the case that there is more emphasis on cost than value.

Financial specialists, like Financial Directors, have voiced their frustration at their inability to measure the return on investment in employees and want a greater role in managing human capital One survey (CFO Research Services 2005) found that more than two-thirds recognised human capital as a major driver and that businesses spend 36% of their revenues on human capital – pay, benefits, training – but only 16% of financial managers understand the return they are getting or felt that they knew how to measure a return on investment. It identified that 'CFOs see the importance of human capital to business success but cannot apply ordinary financial discipline to what is often their company's largest investment'.

There are some real challenges associated with capturing the value of people and what seems essential is a framework that facilitates a meaningful dialogue. If we strip back to the basics of value based management, one of the initial prerequisites is to develop a valuation model demonstrative of potential value creation. Typically this is built with reference to the financial statements from which prospective free cash flow estimates can be derived. Interestingly, these statements are not very explicit about the real costs of people and the point can be well understood if the framework is stripped back to simple value drivers. In building a valuation model based upon a simple value driver framework that looks at the ability of the sales growth rate and the margin to be derived from the added sales revenue, provision has to be made for replacement and incremental fixed capital investment; the former is required to ensure that assets depleted over time are replaced to ensure that at least the current capacity can be maintained to provide the existing level of sales revenue and the latter is required to allow for growth in sales capacity. In the case of the replacement of fixed capital, the objective measurement of requirements should be relatively straightforward, but what about the human resource? Objective benchmarks exist to establish whether machinery is functioning adequately and its condition, but the same is not necessarily the case for people. There might also be additional cause for concern because according to a number of sources there is a potential population crisis with some interesting ramifications for the working population and maybe the ability to judge replacement human resource requirements!

Population projections to 2300 published on 9 December 2003 by the Population Division of the United Nations Department of Economic and Social Affairs show (medium scenario) that world population could age rapidly, with the median age of the world rising from 26 years today to nearly 50 years in 2300 as population stabilises to reach 9 billion in 2075, a level it would still be at in 2300 (World Population in 2300).

The rapid population growth of the last decade has added unusually large numbers of young people to the UK and the consequence of this will become apparent at mid-century as this younger generation grows older and lives longer. The number of people of pensionable age is now projected to rise from 11.1 million in 2004 to 17.5 million (pensionable at 65) by 2050. Young dependants (aged under 16) are projected to fall by 1.4% from 11.65m in 2004 to 11.48 million in 2031, and old dependants (pensionable age) to rise by 37.9% from 11.13m in 2004 to

15.34m in 2031, while the working age population is expected to rise 8.4% from 37.1m to 40.2m, becoming gradually older. There is no shrinking workforce but concerns have been expressed about it being 'inactive, overweight, spaced out and stressed'. In fact, the government's aim is to bring 80% of the working age population into employment. Although not stated as policy, this would improve dependency ratios[28] (to the working age population that supports it) and, along with higher retirement ages, remove the 'need' to raise birth rates or continue to allow excess immigration and settlement The new debate about the dependency ratio in Western Europe, where as little as 65% of the 'active, employable' population is thought to be in work in recent years, raises major questions about raising the qualifying age for state pensions, the level of income support for those without work as a disincentive to seek work and the alleged liberality in certain regimes, such as the Dutch at any rate until recently, in classifying adults as medically unfit for work rather than unemployed. What is clear is that the population changes have some interesting implications! Let us return to the analogy for developing a valuation model – with a higher rate of obsolescence, a sensible valuation model would have a stronger focus of attention upon the replacement fixed capital requirements to ensure that the existing level of demand could be satisfied. It is obvious that depletions to the capital base would have import ramifications for the ability to deliver against current targets.

Does the same analogy not hold for people? If the prognosis for this increasing working population is that it will be older and potentially more prone to illness and being less fit, is there not a corporate, as distinct from a state or individual, response? If people are really important there may well be a strong financial case to focus upon measures of the capability of the human resource to deliver. Such measures can be roughly distinguished into two parts. The first part, which would deserve attention in its own right on another occasion, is about productivity. The UK government has repeatedly called for increased productivity in the economy and recent studies have challenged this claim that it has been increasing either relative to the economy of a few years ago or foreign economies. According to the Conference Board (2006), the UK has been falling further behind the productivity of the US. Plainly there are issues of both public and private investment in those aspects of education and training which can affect the productivity of labour and capital. Furthermore, there are controversial assumptions as to the value in terms of costs and revenues produced when one worker replaces another, for example, an immigrant for an indigenous or a younger for an older. Embedded in this first factor concerning the value of people is the observation of The Conference Board that their figures show that British improvement relative to France and Germany is entirely due to an increase in working hours in the UK. That fact would refresh the long-standing debate as to whether Britain's longer working hours compared with those of pre-Accession EU countries reflects on British workers

[28] In demographic terms, the dependency ratio of a population is usually the ratio of its non-working age population (both young and old dependants) to the total population.

being healthier than their Continental counterparts – or on the contrary underlies the claim that the health of British workers is inferior because of the association with longer working hours.

Be that as it may, the focus here is on the second type of measure which might well be captured under the heading of 'wellness'. This could be even more compelling if it can be shown that it is worthwhile to invest in wellness programmes from an established financial perspective and for this it is useful to review developments in US.

9.5 A financial model for investing in people

In the US, a programme that improves the quality of care received by employees potentially can provide four benefits to an employer: reduced medical expenditures (for both employees and their families), reduced absences, improved on-the-job productivity and reduced turnover due to employees' perceptions of the total compensation package associated with the job. In countries with nationalised health insurance or health service programmes, like the UK, the last three of these benefits still apply. Relative to a healthy person, an employee in poor health is more likely to be absent from work and less productive when he or she is at work and a study has suggested that these indirect costs of poor health may actually exceed direct medical costs. To quantify the benefits to an employer of investing in their workers' health it is important that all sources of benefits should be considered, but a typical company estimates how a health-benefit or health-care quality-enhancing program will affect their bottom line by considering only the direct medical costs that they reimburse as health benefits. This leads to implementation of programmes where the investment return from the reduction in direct medical costs yields a positive benefit, for example, in the form of a positive Net Present Value (NPV). For example, according to Nicholson et al (2005) over 40% of employers have implemented disease management programmes for expensive and debilitating conditions such as diabetes, heart disease and asthma, where the evidence suggests that the NPV from direct medical savings alone may be positive . However, the same authors indicate that fewer than 25% of employers have implemented such programmes for lower back pain and obesity. The key problem is one all too familiar in issues relating to investing in people, the benefits of reduced absences and improved on-the-job productivity are not accurately measured for inclusion in NPV estimates.

It appears that where employers have attempted to measure the impact of programmes on workers' productivity, they have generally focused only on reductions in absenteeism. Even then, most analyses underestimate the benefit of reduced absenteeism by using an employee's wage as a proxy for the value of his/her time. This conventional method assumes, usually implicitly and often incorrectly, that employees are perfect substitutes for one another, that an absent worker or a worker with impaired productivity will not impact the productivity of his team-mates and that companies do not lose sales when a worker's productivity is diminished by poor health (Pauly et al 2002).

Nicholson et al propose and illustrate an approach that enables employers to more thoroughly examine all of the ways that an investment in the health of their employees could improve the bottom line, in the same fashion that companies analyse potential investments in other capital projects. They focus on how to measure the indirect, or productivity related, benefits.

Most studies that evaluate the financial benefit of reducing absenteeism assume that the value of each work day lost is equal to the employee's daily wage. In the neoclassical economic model, wage rates should be equal to the value of the incremental output produced by each worker. According to the typical method, if an employee misses one fewer day of work the company gains the value of his/her output, which is assumed to be equal to his/her daily wage. Traditional methods for assessing the financial impact of health-related absences are likely to underestimate the true gain to employers and employees from implementing policies that improve worker health and ability to work. This is because the cost of the absent worker is only one element and if a company loses revenue, for example, due to a worker's absence (for example, a commercial flight is delayed or cancelled when the pilot is sick), all of the rest of the team is affected and the cost of an absence is lost revenue, which will often exceed a single worker's wage.

Nicholson et al also examined whether the cost of an absence does indeed vary across jobs according to (a) the likelihood that a manager can find a perfect substitute for the absent employee, (b) the extent to which the employee functions within a team and (c) the extent to which the employee's output (or his team's output) is time sensitive. After identifying 35 jobs in 12 industries that involved different types of production functions, over 800 managers were interviewed to determine the extent to which the three characteristics were embodied in a given job, as well as the financial consequences of absences. They provided empirical support for the hypothesis that the cost associated with missed work varies across jobs according to the three key characteristics. Based on these manager interviews, the authors estimated wage 'multipliers' for each of the 35 different jobs, where the multiplier is defined as the cost to the firm of an absence as a proportion (often greater than one) of the absent worker's daily wage.

The mean multiplier for the 35 jobs included in the study is 1.61, and the median multiplier is 1.28. This implies that for the median job the cost of an absence is 28 percent higher than the worker's wage. To obtain an accurate estimate of the cost, the employee's wage is multiplied by the appropriate multiplier for that job or for a job with the same combination of job characteristics. This will yield higher, more accurate estimates of the financial return on health-related costs, if most workers are paid when they are absent (up to certain point), and the expected absence rate will be considered when determining the wage per day paid.

Until recently, most employers assumed that absences were the only source of health-related work loss. However, employees who come to work but are not feeling well may not be able to perform at their usual level of productivity. This is sometimes referred to in the literature as 'impaired presenteeism.' Burton et al. (1999) found that, as the number of health risks increases, an employee's productivity decreases; and that disease states that have produced disability events are also associated with work loss. Many of the findings of studies suggest that the costs of impaired on-the-job productivity are larger than the costs associated with absences and Stewart et al (2003) gauged the extent of 'lost productive time (LPT)' through a national, randomised telephone survey in 2001-2002. Using the wage rate as a measure of the cost of work loss, they estimated that health-related LPT costs employers $226 billion per year, or $1,685 per employee per year — 71% of which was explained by reduced performance at work.

It is likely that many of the same factors that produce multipliers for absenteeism also operate for impaired presenteeism, but these multipliers have not yet been estimated on a large scale. Measuring and monitoring all three drivers of health-related employer costs—direct health care costs, absence and impaired presenteeism—provides employers with a more complete picture of the financial impact of workforce health on a company's performance and helps employers prioritise programmes and evaluate the financial impact of those programmes. This management discipline places workforce health investment decision making processes on a par with that of other company assets.

Corporate application - The Dow Chemical Company

Is there any evidence of corporate applications of this approach? By all accounts, The Dow Chemical Company, a large employer headquartered in Michigan, surveyed over 12,000 U.S.-based employees in the summer of 2002 to develop a comprehensive understanding of the costs associated with chronic health conditions. Sixty-five percent of employees reported having one or more chronic condition, with the two most common being allergies and arthritis/joint pain or stiffness. They used a multiplier of 1.41 based on Dow's distribution of workers in nine different job categories and the job-specific multipliers developed in their own study. The survey provided Dow with an accurate estimate of the true prevalence rate of chronic conditions among their workers. By using the prevalence and the per-person cumulative costs (medical costs, absenteeism and presenteeism), Dow could calculate the total cost impact to the company by health condition. In addition, when analysing costs on a per worker basis, several conditions with large medical costs, such as diabetes, arthritis and circulatory disorders, were not in fact the most expensive conditions when productivity effects were included. Depression/anxiety was the most expensive condition (on a per worker basis) due in large part to substantial presenteeism costs. In fact, the estimated presenteeism costs exceeded medical costs for each of the nine conditions studied. These data helped Dow develop focused intervention strategies on specific conditions that may have been less well informed without the survey. The overall magnitude of these costs helped motivate a philosophical change from managing direct medical costs to an investment-based approach incorporating direct and indirect costs. As a result of this analysis, Dow's strategy is focusing more on prevention, quality of care and more sophisticated purchasing, such as pay for performance programmes.

9.6 Brand Valuation

Why Value Brands?

Many have acknowledged that capital has become less of a constraint on businesses and physical assets can be replicated with ease, with the result that there has tended to be a greater emphasis on how this capital can be used to creatively differentiate the organisation. It has been recognised that this differentiation (and increased shareholder value) will flow from intangible assets, like brands.

The benefit of ascertaining the correct brand value should ensure that resources are appropriately channeled to where they will deliver the greatest value to the organisation. However, there is a problem insofar as resources can only be channelled if it is understood where the best results can be achieved.

The financial concern with brand valuation has traditionally focused on the recognition of brands on the balance sheet, which has presented problems to the accounting profession due to the uncertainty of dealing with the future nature of the benefits associated with brands and hence the reliability of the information presented. The potential dilemma is that if the value of brands is not to be expressed on balance sheets then the 'full' value of a company is not being reported; but in the absence of a professional consensus there would ensue a free-for-all in the valuing of brands that would discredit the entire process. Further studies within finance have investigated the impact on the stock price of customer perceptions of perceived quality, a component of brand equity and on the linkage between shareholder value and the financial value of a company's brands. However, there is currently a more specific managerial concern with brand valuation often from an internal perspective in terms of effective resource allocation as much as external, for example, for acquisition purposes. In this regard, there are two critical issues . The first is to be quite clear about exactly what is being valued, that is whether it is the trademark, the brand itself or the branded business. Secondly, the purpose of the valuation is essential to understand and an important distinction must be made between technical and commercial valuations. Technical valuations are conducted for balance sheet reporting, tax planning, litigation, securitisation, licensing, mergers and acquisitions and investor relations. The primary purpose of technical valuations is to give a point-in-time valuation and frequently they relate to a valuation of the trademarks. Commercial valuations are more typically for internal management purposes and often relate to issues associated with market strategy, budget allocation and scorecards.

Irrespective of the ultimate purpose, the big problem is how to determine exactly what a brand is worth. In fact, the value of a brand is fairly straightforward according to modern financial theory and it is the cumulative value of all the cash flows the brand itself is expected to generate over time, discounted to the present at an interest rate appropriate to the riskiness of the cash flows. The problem is that the value of the branded business is made up of a number of tangible and intangible assets. Trademarks are simply one of these and brands are a more comprehensive bundle of trademark and related intangibles. In the case of Microsoft Windows, value is partly trademark-related or brand-related, but is also largely attributable to the patent and other marketing intangibles. There is a need to establish what are the intangible assets creating the value and usually there are a variety of these. There could be excellence in managing business processes, distribution rights or patents. Hence the concept of attributing cash flows to the brand itself is basically elusive and disputable.

Brand Valuation Methods

Value, like beauty, is in the eye of the beholder and has different meanings to different people and thus is not an objective concept. The valuation approach used is effectively the objective of the valuation. The objective of the valuation is determined by its use. Some of the more common valuation approaches can be classified into five categories:

1. Cost-based approaches
2. Market-based approaches
3. Economic use or income-based approaches
4. Formula-based approaches
5. Liquidation approaches.

1 Cost-based approaches consider the costs associated with creating the brand or replacing the brand, including research and development of the product concept, market testing, promotion and product improvement. The accumulated cost approach will determine the value of the brand as the sum of accumulated costs expended on the brand to date. This method is the easiest to perform, as all the data should be readily available. Unfortunately, this historic valuation does not usually bear any resemblance to the economic value. The replacement cost approach determines the cost that would be incurred to replace the asset. An advantage of this method is that it provides a better reflection of the true cost of the brand, but the cost does not bear a relation to the open market value. For example, over investing in that brand might result in not recovering the full investment if sold.

2 Market-based approaches are based on the amount for which a brand can be sold. The open market valuation is the highest value that a willing buyer and willing seller would be prepared to pay for the brand and should reflect the possible alternative uses; the value of future options as well as its value in existing activities; and realism rather than conservatism.

3 Economic use approaches, also referred to as income-based approaches, consider the valuation of future net earnings directly attributable to the brand to determine the value of the brand in its current use. There are different economic use valuation techniques:
(a) The first are the price premium or gross margin approaches that consider price premiums or superior margins versus a generic business as the metric for quantifying the value that the brand contributes. However, with the rise of private label it is often hard to identify a generic against which the price or margin differential should be measured.
(b) An alternative is to use economic substitution analysis, which assesses what the financial performance of the branded business would be and how would the volumes, values and costs change if the brand did not exist. The problem with this approach is that it relies on subjective judgments as to what the alternative substitute might be.
Because of the difficulties associated with the two economic use valuation approaches above, it can be particularly insightful to use either an earnings split or royalty relief approach.

(c) In the former case, earnings are attributed above a break-even economic return to the intangible capital. These excess earnings are split between the various classes of intangible assets, one of which is the trademark or brand.
(d) In the case of the royalty relief approach, it is necessary to imagine that the business does not own its trademarks but licenses them from another business at a market rate, where the royalty rate is usually expressed as a percentage of sales. Apparently, this is a frequently used method of valuation because it is highly regarded by tax authorities and courts, largely because there are many comparable licensing agreements in the public domain and it is relatively easy to calculate a specific percentage that might be paid to the trademark or brand owner. Having determined the slice of earnings attributable to the trademark or brand, now and for each year in the forecast period, it is necessary to discount them back to a net present value — the trademark or brand value.

One problem arises if intangible assets are valued separately without reference to one another because the sum of intangible assets may possibly be greater than the value of the branded business. In this case it is necessary to reconcile all asset values back to the branded business valuation initially calculated. It is then necessary to consider the value of each intangible asset in the context of the others and to apply a similar approach to each of the major intangible assets.

4 Formula-based approaches consider multiple criteria to determine the value of a brand. While similar in certain respects to income-based or economic use approaches, they are included as a separate category due to their extensive commercial usage by consulting and other organisations.

5 The liquidation value is the value that the asset would fetch in a distress sale. The value under a liquidation sale is normally substantially lower than in a willing buyer and seller arrangement. The costs of liquidating the asset should normally be deducted in determining the value of the asset.

These are by no means the only approaches and more commonly accepted now is the use of discounted cash flow methods, even though there is no straightforward way to translate theory into practical reality. The principal problem is that none of the key variables is directly measurable, as is evident if we consider the cash flows attributable to the brand. They are distinctly different from the cash flows derived from all products (or services) that carry a brand. A portion of those cash flows is properly attributable to the capital employed to create the products, while other portions may arise from a host of intangibles other than the brand. These include, but are not limited to, research and development, business processes and superior management expertise.

One other problem is that many conventional approaches to brand valuation start with an estimate of the total profits attributable to the branded business, but there is a real problem if multi-brand companies do not organise their reporting in a way that allows them to calculate profits by brand. In fact, what evidence there is suggests that the majority measure operating results by product lines or business units (Ehrbar et al 2002). Even if one accepts the estimate of profit by branded business, the problem of isolating the portion attributable to the brand itself remains. The conventional approach typically is to do this by calling on the opinions of 'industry experts.' In sum, the estimation of the first key variable, current profit attributable to the brand, is the product of subjective judgements and guesstimates. The other key element in conventional brand valuation usually is an equally subjective assessment of brand strength, which is used to discount future brand profits.

BrandEconomics, EVA® and Brand Valuation

BrandEconomics use a top-down approach of estimating the valuation framework combining two methodologies introduced earlier, Young & Rubicam's BrandAsset® Valuator (BAV) measure of a brand's consumer franchise and Stern Stewart's EVA® model for performance measurement and business valuation. Their brand valuation framework begins with an empirical calculation of the role of brands in driving business value in specific product and service categories. This enables an estimation of the value of individual brands based on the sectors within which they operate, their strength in those sectors and the scale on which a brand is employed.

BrandEconomics starts the valuation process by separating a company's total market or enterprise value (market value of equity plus book value of debt) into two components: tangible capital and what they call intangible value. Tangible capital is the book value of the assets on a company's balance sheet and intangible value is simply total market value minus tangible capital. This definition of intangible value reflects the presumption that tangible assets will simply earn a cost-of-capital return. Any return in excess of the cost of capital represents a return on intangible assets, which they define as including superior management. As a result, tangible capital always will be valued at book and any variation between market value and the book value of tangible capital reflects the expected profit contribution from all intangible assets. Relating this to the EVA valuation model, intangible value is equal to the present value of current and expected future EVA, which is mathematically identical to the net present value of forecasted free cash flows.

The empirical challenge in the top-down valuation approach used by BrandEconomics is to determine the degree to which differences in brand health, however measured, explain differences in intangible values. The key element in their modelling process is brand health as measured by BAV, the world's largest database on consumer perceptions of brands.

BrandEconomics argues that intrinsic brand values also can hold important keys to strategy, particularly for companies with portfolios of branded businesses. They distinguish between current operations value, or COV, which is the annuitised value of current profits, discounted at the cost of capital, that is, it is the value of the business under the assumption that current profits continue unchanged in perpetuity. Intrinsic future growth value, or FGV®, is the value of the business that represents opportunities for future profit growth based on the potential of all intangible assets in the business, including intrinsic brand value. If we consider branded businesses whose brand health, especially differentiation, has been in decline for the last 5 or 10 years, these typically are brands that enjoy huge, though possibly declining, operating margins, large market shares, high consumer awareness and seeming brand loyalty. Given the high current profitability, managers may be lulled into focusing too much attention on maintaining market share by price discounting (which only hastens the brand's decline) and maintaining operating efficiency. Unless drastic action is taken to reverse the erosion and revitalise the brand, the products often become commodities and operating margins ultimately will follow the downward trajectory of the brand's health. Arguably failing to exploit the full potential in these brands is like leaving large sums in non-interest-bearing demand deposits and the company's market value probably reflects the presumption that its brands will remain underexploited. Nevertheless, the company may receive unsolicited offers to buy the brands from others who may be better situated to realise their potential through geographic expansion, new distribution channels, brand extensions, partnering or co-marketing deals—that will get the value out of the demand deposit and put it to work for shareholders. Best practice according to this view is to identify the strategies that will realise existing growth opportunities and create new ones, communicate the strategies to key players so that the company receives proper credit in the stock market and execute well.

Focused management of the drivers of brand value can play a vital role in identifying, developing and exploiting the intrinsic potential in brand assets. The point is that in an environment in which innovation can quickly make many competitive advantages obsolete, brands can be among the most durable sources of market power. Around this point there is a convergence, not antagonism, between the concerns of marketing and financial analysis.

CHAPTER 10
VALUE BASED MANAGEMENT

Chapter Preview

- Value Based Management (VBM) as an approach for managing the value of a business
- Critical questions that VBM must answer
- Key issues implementing VBM
- Scenario analysis, supported by the adaptation of the free cash flow strategic valuation model, as a powerful tool for gaining a strategic focus to VBM
- Review of the four phases to implementing VBM together with associated issues
- The raison d'être of VBM as being the influence on behaviours throughout the organisation in line with value creation principles
- Identification that the exact recipe for implementing VBM will vary from organisation to organisation but there are a number of key issues that have been found to be important to address; these include timescales, role of champion, role of corporate centre, level of cascading, cost of capital and changes to reporting systems
- The successful implementation of a VBM programme in the long term is dependent on having in place a Value Direction' process that provides the organisational direction to enable the tenets of VBM to become part of the ongoing management and culture of an organisation
- The real benefits of a VBM programme are derived from viewing it as an organisational change process, not a one off finance initiative.

10.1 What is Value Based Management?

Value Based Management (VBM) is an approach that can be used for the management of a business that differs from traditional approaches to managing a business insofar as it is linked with the principles of Discounted Cash Flow (DCF). DCF principles are typically used to develop a value based strategy from which value based plans are developed and implemented as VBM. From a managerial perspective VBM draws upon all of the tools of Corporate Finance reviewed in the context of managing the business as an ongoing concern. It is the last chapter in this book because it can be seen as the managerial catalyst for Corporate Finance.

In the preceding chapters, we have focused upon the measurement of value and the assessment of performance. Attention has been directed at many technical issues to ensure that as realistic a vision of value as possible is obtained. In this final chapter we consider the issues associated with implementing Value Based Management (VBM) but it is important to recognise that a focus on value creation can benefit all stakeholders not just shareholders. Questioning whether the focus should be on shareholders or stakeholders is the wrong question. The right question is how can value be created so that all stakeholders benefit over the lifetime of the organisation?

The impetus to adopt VBM for managing the business is often associated with some external threat, like being a potential acquisition target. In some cases, businesses in the Western world live under a cloud of 'conglomerate discount' that exists when a conglomerate is worth less than the sum of its parts[29]. In such cases, a demerger may allow executives to concentrate on a narrower range of businesses and thereby stimulate greater value creation than might otherwise have been the case. For example, it was reported at the time of the demerger of ICI into ICI and Zeneca in the 1990s that the move was intended to allow ICI executives to release what were referred to as 'creative management energies' . By all accounts the company's focus upon profitability in the past was not as good as it should have been.

A second impetus to adopt VBM can be related to one of the most noteworthy adopters of the approach in the UK, Lloyds TSB a major retail bank. A major stimulus for focusing upon value came from poor past performance and prospects for the future if no corrective action was taken. The action taken by Lloyds involved a number of steps which, by all accounts included:

[29] Conglomerate discount is often driven by investor fears of poor allocation of resources and to the administrative cost burden incurred by the conglomerate.

- Ranking businesses on the basis of the shareholder value they had created. Each activity was viewed either as a creator or destroyer of value and businesses with a permanent negative cash flow became a target for divestment
- Making provisions for problem country debt. This produced accounting losses but no movement in cash and as a result the share price went up, not down
- Adopting higher value strategies such as expansion into life assurance and private banking which reduced the group's risk profile and increased its cash flow
- Recognising that in measuring performance, 'cash is king'. Earnings per share and other accounting variables should not be used exclusively to assess performance, because they ignore the time value of money and exclude risk. This approach involved the inherent assumption that long term cash flows are what determine market value
- Introducing performance related remuneration, thus linking the interest of its people more closely with those of the owners.

The key point about pursuit of a VBM approach is that focussing upon shareholder value gives clear discipline. The company's goal becomes to analyse every strategic decision in terms of its impact on shareholder wealth and also to focus upon shareholder value to evaluate acquisitions, divestments, capital investment projects and to assess alternative strategies.

Adopting a VBM approach provides the toolkit to manage companies better from a strategic and financial standpoint, but implementing the approach creates major challenges. In fact, there are different approaches to involvement with VBM and its implementation that can be seen in terms of those companies that:

1. Have adopted various value analytical techniques but not yet the broader managerial implications of the approach
2. Have embraced the underlying principles of a value based approach and have also embarked upon implementation
3. Do not appear to have experimented at all
4. Claim to be value oriented companies but whose actions do not support this impression.

There appear to be few large companies that have not claimed to have embraced some part of the shareholder value philosophy. There also appears to be a number of companies in pursuit of maximising shareholder value according to their annual reports but whose apparent interpretation of this would appear to be focused towards accounting based measures like earnings per share.

10.2 VBM implementation steps

Assuming the decision to proceed with implementing VBM has been taken and that there is strong corporate sponsorship for the process, the steps that need to be taken can be summarised as determining:

1. What is the managerial interpretation of your current value in the market?
2. What is influencing it, that is, what are the key value drivers?
3. What are the apparent managerial actions for improvement and what is their impact?

Addressing these questions will give rise to a subset of important questions, like:

- What is the Competitive Advantage Period (CAP)? How do you know?
- What is the cost of capital?
- How should the terminal value be estimated?
- Which measures of value should be used?
- What frameworks should be used to guide managerial and employee actions?

10 Step Approach Revisited

Implementation does not happen by itself. It is one thing to measure prospective value, but quite another to achieve it. Companies implementing VBM have adopted different approaches, however, before we proceed to review two of these approaches it is important to identify the overall framework of which these two can be seen to be a part. This framework can be viewed in terms of the following steps:

1. What is the managerial interpretation of your current value in the market?
2. What is influencing it, that is, what are the key value drivers?
3. What are the apparent managerial actions for improvement and what are their impacts?
4. In light of 3., what should be the new vision?
5. What is the value of the new vision?
6. How does the vision translate into customer, shareholder and other relevant perspectives for the organisation
7. How does the organisational vision look in terms of divisions /business units?
8. What is the divisional value?
9. What are the key divisional value drivers?
10. What do these divisional value drivers look like in terms of the micro drivers and key performance indicators (KPIs)?

While the specific implementation approach adopted by businesses may differ, we have found that these 10 steps capture the sequence of events that need to be followed. The first five challenge the current vision, value and potential for improvement for the whole business. However, in terms of implementing any changes that are identified as being warranted, approaches like the Balanced Scorecard and Business Excellence Model are invaluable – see later in this chapter. But those methods need to be related to a vision that has been clearly articulated and which can be related specifically to financial performance. Such approaches can not only be applied at the overall business level, but also within business units/ divisions.

In fact, it would be difficult to imagine successful implementation without driving change down through the business as a whole. The advantage of the 10 step approach outlined above is that it relates the use of such approaches to fundamental questions about value and performance in financial terms at the overall business and business unit levels.

The benefit of adopting a VBM perspective is best understood with reference to an example and in what follows we will draw upon the circumstances surrounding Asian Hotels Limited to illustrate many of its features.

10.3 The VBM approach

To illustrate the VBM approach we return to the case study of Asia Hotels Limited – see Chapter 5, Section 5.5 for the original data. We will draw on the following three questions that were introduced earlier:

1. What is the managerial interpretation of your current value in the market?
2. What is influencing it, that is, what are the key value drivers?
3. What are the apparent managerial actions for improvement and what are their impacts?

What is the managerial interpretation of your current value in the market?

The share price of Asia Hotels Limited at the end of 2006 was HK$5.50m making the market value of the equity HK$6,364 million. At the same time the value of net debt was HK$6,689 million. This is for a business whose net assets stood at the last full balance sheet date as HK$16,981 million. The implications of this are that the business is a value destroyer. Net assets of HK$16,981 million look from a market perspective as though they are being used to create a value of HK$13,053 million (HK$6,364 million plus HK$6,689 million). As such, this business could be seen as a potential acquisition target if it was not closely held.

What is influencing it, that is, what are the key value drivers?
As illustrated in earlier chapters, the starting point we recommend is to understand the current share price of HK$5.50 in terms of the key factors that drive it. These factors are known as 'value drivers' and, in our experience, they are important to understand because all too often businesses do not really know what is driving value. This can be for a number of reasons, not least of which is that the key factors may have changed. For example, a management college set up in the 1940s designed to provide non qualification experiential training to potential board members might have a prime countryside location as a key value driver for attracting potential customers. Sixty years on when the bulk of the income is driven from a distance learning graduate MBA programme for which students do not attend, location may not be such a key value driver. In the minds of such students and to the market if it was a publicly traded business, other factors, like the quality of communications, are likely to be far more important. There might still be those living in the past who believe location to be important, but the problem is that their perception of the allocation of resources into maintaining the quality of the premises in the UK as distinct from other choices, might actually destroy value. Alternatively, if the value drivers have not changed it may be the case that the relationship between changes in their value and the impact upon share price is not known. For example, in one acquisition in which we were involved it was evident that the potential acquirer would raise margins in the target business. While it was appreciated that such action would increase the share price, the extent of the increase was not appreciated until a simple financial model had been built.

What are the apparent managerial actions for improvement and what are their impact?
Having valued the business and identified the key value drivers, the next critical step is to understand how to translate them into measures of performance that are understood and can be implemented such that there is the incentive to take the necessary action.

10.4 The strategic perspective and scenario analysis

Our experience has shown that this VBM approach has also to be viewed from a strategic perspective. For example, the share price of HK$5.50 per share for Asia Hotels Limited might be shown to increase drastically as a consequence of completely refocusing of the business outside Asia. In the absence of testing this against the potential consequences of such a move it is pure speculation. That is where scenario thinking becomes particularly important and as a consequence of such analysis a number of critical issues can be addressed, that include:

1. What are the business' prospects according to your scenarios?
2. What is driving the prospects?
3. What is the value of these prospects?
4. Do these prospects make sense?
5. What should be the business response?

Scenario analysis

As indicated in an earlier chapter, scenarios start from the premise that there is more than one future and recognise the need to illuminate the major forces and trends driving a valuation, their interrelationships and the critical uncertainties. Scenarios need not be heavily driven by mathematical or statistical analysis. Shell, for example, when applying this technique does not assign probabilities to its scenarios for several reasons. First, it intentionally looks at several scenarios that are more or less equally plausible, so that none is dismissed out of hand. Second, by definition, any given scenario has only an infinitesimal probability of being right because so many variations are possible. Third, the reason to be hesitant about all scenario quantification is that there is a very strong tendency for people to clutch at the numbers and ignore the more important conceptual or structural messages. The value of performing this procedure is not so much the ultimate valuation number that it produces, but the insights discovered in the process of investigating the nature and existence of the opportunities available to management.

Specifically, the use of scenarios can help to avoid the shortcomings associated with traditional approaches to analysis, in which the assumptions used will often be extrapolated from the present situation with inadequate attention being paid to the impact of changes in the external environment of a particular business. With these traditional approaches, instead of a specific impact analysis there is an assumed vacuum, as if discontinuation and turbulence will not punctuate the external environment. Drawing upon scenario analysis can make considerable improvements. When linked appropriately, to free cash flow and strategic value calculations, it provides a distinctive way of grasping the key navigational questions about the future of a business. In terms of the CAP, the approach seeks to force questioning and thought about when the conditions signalling the end of the CAP might occur, that is, a return greater than the cost of capital cannot be achieved. This involves asking key questions like 'How can the free cash flow projections be validated for that period?' and 'Suppose the business under consideration is moving into a period of increasing turbulence?' To cope with that, it may become a significantly different business or it may fail to cope and as a result under perform relative to its original plan, which assumed little turbulence.

It is usually easy to imagine at least two different free cash flow projections and the benefit from going through more than one projection and discovering the linkages typically enhances managers' learning, not least because many predictions are often mistaken. Scenarios help to avoid mistakes and can be seen in quite simple terms as being long term 'stories' about possible future external environments, framed as two or three credible pathways.

Scenarios oblige the recognition of the dependencies that business performance has on external factors over which a firm has no control (like rain), but to which it might be able to respond in a timely manner (like an umbrella available before the next rainfall). They also encourage thinking through a welter of diverse speculations and the structuring of these into coherent pathways, which are relevant to a particular business. The pay off is that, in terms of the scenarios, the impact on the business of such external factors can be estimated. This enables an analysis of the potential value of the business to be undertaken, not with one straight line calculation, but with different higher and lower values.

The risk of unwittingly making the analysis of strategic value abstract occurs when it is detached from the real business environment. This can occur when the assumptions underlying the numbers in a business plan, when put through the strategic value model, are not challenged but implicitly treated as a matter of faith. The risk is that of being mesmerised by numerical calculations whilst overlooking the possibility that the plan itself assumes a single track extension of the current business into the future CAP.

By contrast, the link between strategy and scenarios forces attention on a wide-ranging search for developments in the external environment, favourable or not, which can help managers to anticipate and adjust for the potential impact on the value drivers of changes in the environment. It means surfacing and challenging the assumptions behind the numbers given for the value drivers. Developing scenarios does not mean mechanically changing business variables by a fixed percentage. Instead, it means developing a comprehensive set of assumptions about how possible futures may evolve and how they are likely to affect industry profitability and the company's performance.

Scenarios start from 'What if ... ? questions. By depicting future pathways which are different from the pathway assumed in a particular plan, adopted or proposed, the uncertainties about the plan can be highlighted. As scenarios express in a patterned way uncertainties about what external factors could impact on the value drivers, there should be at least two scenarios, preferably equally credible, to be posed against each other. Comparison of their respective impact on one or more value drivers would clarify the issues or challenges distinctive to each scenario which managers could confront in the future. Those issues would surface by grasping the impacts of each scenario on value drivers such as sales growth rate, operating profit margin and fixed and working capital requirements and the cost of capital. Thus the working out of different potential values for a business, based on scenarios, gives more flexibility, realistic relevance and 'navigational' value to the analysis of strategic value.

By means of scenarios the variables which could impact on a business' long term value may be identified. For example, for a manufacturing business which has outperformed rivals in the past, credible ideas as to what trends would constitute change, one scenario, which includes increasing customer power, loss of differentiation and more intense cost/price competition, would suggest that falling margins can be identified. All of these arise from a mix of factors, which range from the growth of international competition to the growing added value ability of distributors.

Focusing on say the first five years of the example at hand, the impact on the five cash flow drivers of external conditions beyond the immediate control of the company may be illustrated by means of different credible scenarios. Armed with scenario outcomes the firm can mentally and practically prepare to see the earliest signs of change in its external environment. In effect it can, on a hypothetical basis, perceive in advance that if it's key strategic challenges were to unfold very differently from the alternative what responses would be required. In other words, management can anticipate initially on a 'What if?' basis that to achieve, say, the sales receipts in the original plan, product and process technology changes would be required by a steep escalation in fixed and working capital investment needs.

Scenarios express and structure uncertainties about the future: of themselves they cannot resolve this uncertainty. But sharp and sensitive mental preparation by advance calculation of the value impact of alternative scenarios enables faster responses to be made. In this case, improved thinking about the substantive issues the business challenges raised by each scenario could lead to a planning process that enables an anticipated challenge, indeed a threat, to be converted by virtue of well timed and scaled company response into an opportunity.

The materials chosen for scenarios may be brief and prosaic, formulated without recourse to larger scale constructions about economic, political and other macro changes. But they are sufficient to illustrate the point that current assumptions used for estimating the future value of a business must be specified in credible speculations about the future and structured in such ways as to show how different future conditions can impact on the key value drivers.

The process of working out present value and CAP implications of different scenarios enables managers to make two important gains in their strategic thinking:

- They can see how the strategic value outputs derived from the inputs of their preferred or current plans depend on assumptions, which could be clarified and critically evaluated by comparisons made with the assumptions of credible alternative scenarios. Managers would therefore focus on the quality of their assumptions, about changes in the external environment, as a precondition of any confidence in the numbers subsequently generated through the free cash flow strategic valuation (Shareholder Value) model
- Wrestling with each scenario's present value and CAP implications should sharpen managers' sense of the range of options they could have in driving forward their business in one direction or another. It gives a mental grip on how to weigh up in advance the risk/gain possibilities under each scenario.

There is however a third benefit. Each scenario helps to clarify the dominant strategic challenges associated with it and how different (or similar) would the responses to each challenge have to be. Here is where the real and rapid advance in strategic thinking can occur. Consequences revealed through free cash flow analysis and strategic valuation help to clarify the first candidates for an effective strategic response. For example, these could be how an initial reactive response towards a threat might be converted into an opportunity, or how an attempt to respond to two different scenarios instead of wagering on one against another might yield a strategy aimed at resiliency against more than one possible future.

The scenarios developed can be used with publicly traded competitors or peers to ask the question, 'what time period is implied by the share price?'. This produces what can be thought of as a market implied duration CAP that can be viewed against the time horizons determined from a scenario assessment. Typically there are differences in the results which raise what we refer to as the terminal value issue. In very simple terms, the terminal value issue relates to the difference between the market implied duration value and the value of the scenario(s) and an analysis of the terminal value arising from this difference can be undertaken to see the assumptions implied. For example, a significant difference between the perpetuity value of the terminal value determined from scenario based calculations and the market implied terminal value can be examined in terms of the implications by way of prospective growth assumptions. For example, if the market implied duration is 10 years and the scenarios reveal 5 years, there is 5 years additional implied growth and a higher terminal value. A key question arises in terms of the feasibility of this extra 5 years of growth and the issue can be examined by way of an extension of the scenario activity, in which external financial observations are challenged in terms of their managerial implications for the value drivers within the free cash flow strategic value model. In other words, 'What rate of growth is implied by the difference and what would be necessary to make it happen?'

10.5 Key issues to consider in implementing VBM

There are some key phases that are essential in implementing VBM, which are the:

1. Introduction of concepts and gaining of corporate commitment
2. Establishment of policies and procedures
3. Integration of concepts into practice
4. Development and refinement of the approach.

Phase 1

The introduction of concepts and the gaining of commitment can take some time. We would expect it to take a minimum of six months. It will involve:

- Presentations to senior corporate and divisional management of the concepts and its potential benefits to the company
- Discussing key concerns and issues, for example value based executive compensation
- Obtaining commitment of the managing director and key corporate and divisional management.

Phase 2

Establishing policies and procedures will often require considerable time and effort. In our experience, quite how much time is often dependent upon the size of the organisation, but as a rough guide six months is manageable if ambitious. More specifically, this phase will involve the:

- Formation of a 'task force', for example, drawn from senior central management and divisions
- Identification of specific obstacles and issues, for example, how to relate the approach to the corporate financial management and reporting culture

- Determination of appropriate divisional costs of capital, terminal value frameworks, and planning periods
- Development of appropriate applications at corporate and divisional level
- Development of application guidelines
- Identification of education requirements of those employees who will perform or need to understand the approach
- Development of education programmes.

Phase 3

The integration of concepts into practice is the longest and probably the most critical part of the implementation process. Nine months is a rough and ready guideline, the actual length of time is heavily linked to the size of the organisation and how extensively the approach is to be introduced. In particular it typically involves the development of a framework that makes explicit recognition of the need to ensure a strong customer focus. Whilst the first two phases are important, the reality is that without explicit attempts to integrate principles with practice, the only deliverable will be a valuation shell. Achieving a strong customer focus may sound straightforward in principle, but the practice is more difficult. The aspiration to be customer oriented may be easily thwarted without recognition that it may have broader organisational ramifications. It is one thing to have the aspirations to be customer focused, but it is quite another to be able to meet such requirements. This will be particularly so in turbulent market conditions in which the areas in which internal excellence is required to achieve customer satisfaction may be difficult, to say the least. The ways in which such customer orientation will be attempted differ, but approaches we will review later, are the balanced scorecard and the business excellence model. Once these issues have been considered carefully, other initiatives that need to be undertaken include:

- Incorporation of the approach into performance measurement via financial and non financial performance measures
- Delivery of education programmes on the approach and how it links to current practices
- Use of the approach for evaluating capital expenditure plans, acquisitions, research and development expenditure and so on
- Provision of expert assistance when needed.

Phase 4

The last phase is very much an open book as regards the time involved. What it is likely to involve is the:

- Refinement of the approach and performance measurement
- Linking of the approach to incentive compensation schemes
- Development of the approach for investor communications.

The phases and underlying activities outlined above are by no means definitive but they a typically consistent from organisation to organisation. However, there will need to be some tailoring to particular circumstances of each organisation. So, whilst the basic building blocks of VBM are fairly consistent the exact recipe varies.

Balanced Scorecard

There has been increasing concern in many organisations about the way that performance is currently measured. The development of global markets accompanied by intense competition has necessitated a drive for quality and a search for continuous cost improvement. Accompanying this drive has been the questioning of whether established methods of measurement and analysis are still wholly appropriate.

In all areas of business it has become clear that the needs of both customers and shareholders have to be satisfied and that an emphasis upon one to the exclusion of the other will not be accepted. The challenge to meet these needs in a turbulent business environment means that businesses have to be able to respond to customer requirements with their internal delivery mechanisms and also be able to update and change them as necessary. The implications of this are profound. To be successful, companies will need a broad set of performance indicators and not just a set focusing upon financial indicators of performance. What is more these indicators will have to be appropriate and relevant. To take a personal health example, the benefits of prevention via diagnosis are well known. What we require is an understanding of those things that really matter to our future well being. Dwelling upon the past or what has happened is only relevant insofar as it helps us make future decisions.

The Balanced Scorecard was developed to broaden the scope of performance indicators away from a preoccupation with financial performance. This approach includes some financial measures, which are complemented by operational measures like customer satisfaction, internal process measurement and the organisational innovations and improvement to activities. All the latter require operational measures of strategy and represent the drivers of future financial performance.

As illustrated in Figure 10.1 the balanced scorecard allows managers to look at the business from four important perspectives:

- How do customers see us? (customer perspective)
- What must we excel at? (internal perspective)
- Can we continue to improve and create value? (innovation and learning perspective)
- How do we look to our shareholders? (financial perspective)

Figure 10.1: The balanced scorecard

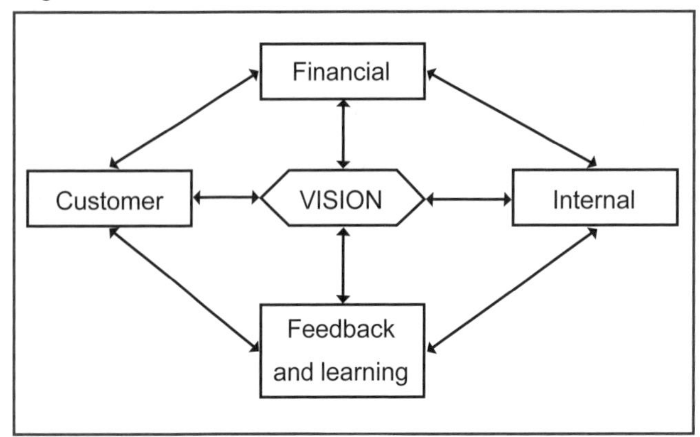

Each perspective considers important performance related issues in their own right. The customer perspective is seen as being particularly important. Meeting customer requirements has clear implications for the organisation's delivery mechanisms and the internal business perspective focuses upon the processes and actions that need to be undertaken within the organisation. The measures in the form of the resulting performance indicators will stem from the analysis of those features, which will have an impact upon customer satisfaction.

The innovation and learning perspective focuses on the dynamics of change. The contemporary business environment recognises that targets have to keep changing and need to be redefined: for example, continuous improvements to products and processes are of necessity. As a result this perspective focuses on such challenges and measures them in terms of innovation, improvements and learning.

Last, but by no means least, is the financial perspective, which relates to shareholders. Key indicators are typically adopted which cover profitability, liquidity and increasingly, value creation.

While valuation models of the type discussed in the preceding chapters are invaluable for understanding the sources of value and the potential action required to improve it, there has to be a means by which this action can be translated into specific managerial action to make it happen. In this respect, the Balanced Scorecard can be invaluable for linking the vision with the managerial action essential to bring about improvement.

One of the key benefits of adopting a Balanced Scorecard approach is that it offers the potential to align business goals throughout the whole organisation. In other words the scorecard can be a vehicle for translating higher level business goals into a level of specificity appropriate for each level in the organisation and in doing so makes them actionable. The mechanisms for making this happen are the organisations key management processes, that is, business planning, budgeting, performance reporting and incentivisation. Embedding the scorecard into these business processes ensures that alignment of goals is achieved throughout the organisation.
See Figure 10.2.

Figure 10.2: Driving VBM down the organisation via the key management processes

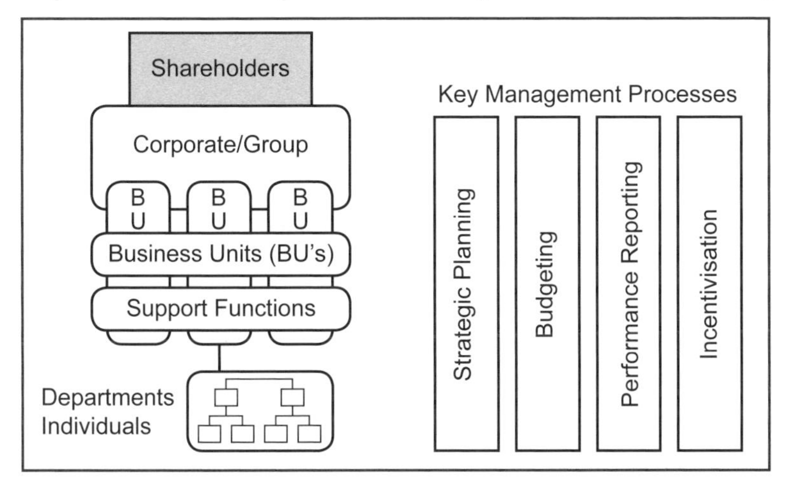

When used in this way the balanced scorecard becomes part of a businesses value based management system for understanding the dynamics of value creation. See Figure 10.3.

Figure 10.3: Value Based Management system

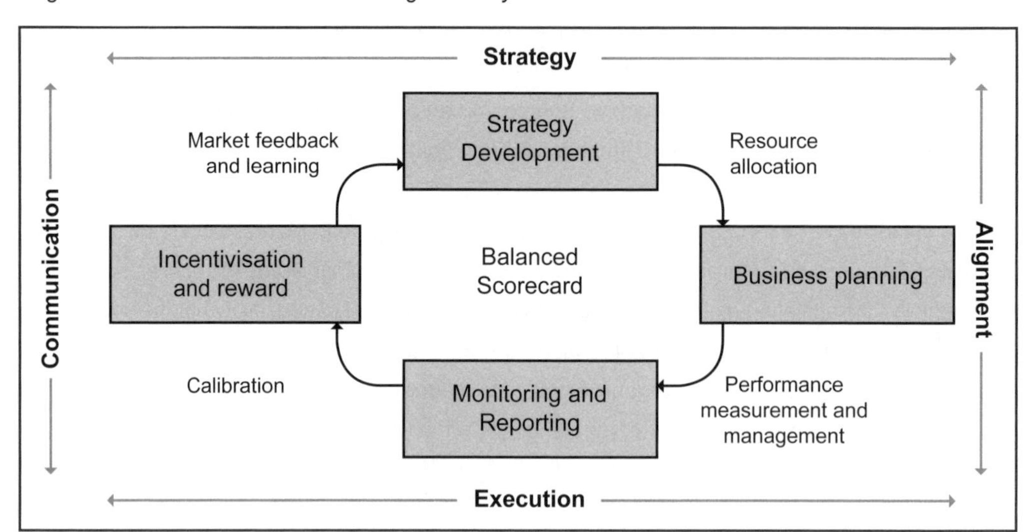

In Figure 10.3, there are four key processes to a typical value based management system, which are part of a self reinforcing circle:

1. Strategy development. This is concerned with articulating the organisation's vision and expressing it in terms of the specific strategic goals that need to be achieved from the shareholder, customer, employee and innovation perspective. Here the scorecard has a role as the mechanism for translating a vision into more tangible goals. In essence it is about deciding what should an organisation do and culminates in the allocation of resources to do it
2. Business planning is about how the strategy should be specifically carried out. In other words, what specific actions, activities and programmes need to be undertaken in order to achieve the organisation strategic goals. The role of the scorecard is to ensure that the execution is in alignment with the strategy
3. Monitoring and reporting is about measuring the organisation's performance in executing its strategy. Put another way, it answers the question: how well did the organisation do what it said it would do? Here again the scorecard has a role as the measurement framework for making this assessment
4. The incentivisation and reward stage concerns rewarding people for the attainment of the strategic goals and in so doing the role the scorecard performs here is that of a mechanism for communicating how successful or not the organisation was. Additionally, the scorecard functions as a tool for capturing the key lessons that the business has learned or must learn to achieve its vision.

Focusing upon a handful of measures that are the most critical components of the desired objectives is a feature of the approach. As a result of this, its implementation by organisations has been shown to have two major benefits:

1. It brings together in a single management report, many of the disparate elements of a company's competitive agenda
2. It helps to prevent decisions being made that are not in the interests of the whole organisation, even though it may benefit one particular part of the business. By forcing senior managers to consider all important operational measures together, the balanced scorecard lets them see whether improvement in one area may be achieved only at the expense of another.

Business Excellence Model

Many organisations that have adopted or are adopting the principles of value we have discussed in connection with Strategic Value Analysis have emphasised the achievement of business excellence, focusing upon the Business Excellence Model.

Figure 10.4: The Business Excellence model

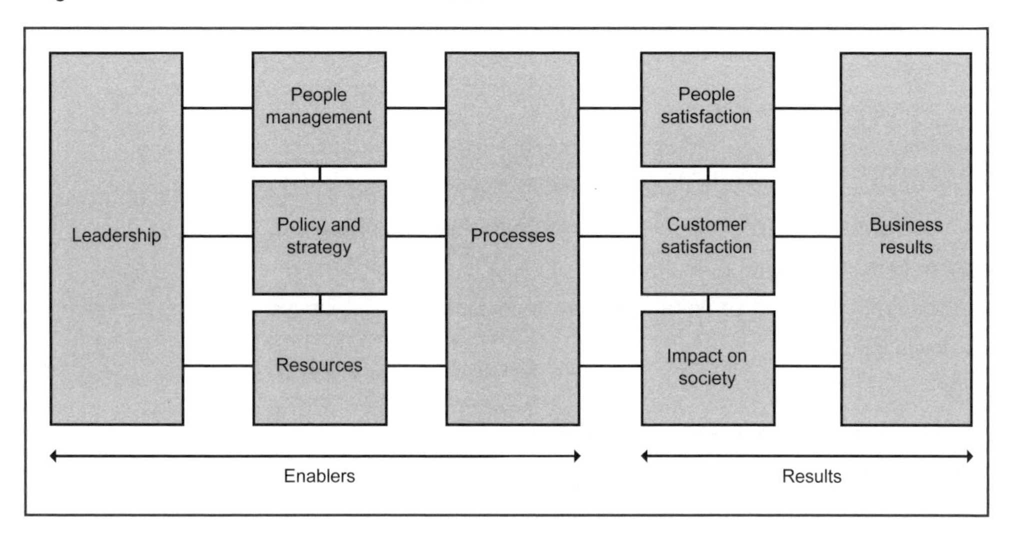

A standard European model has been developed which is used to measure an organisation's 'level' of excellence. This business excellence model is based on the principle that in order for an organisation or team to succeed, there are a number of key 'enablers' on which it should concentrate its efforts and it should measure its success through a number of key 'results' areas.

The key enablers by which organisations judge themselves are:

- How well the organisation is led
- How well its people are managed
- How far its policy and strategy are developed and implemented by its leaders and people
- How well it manages its resources and develops and manages its processes.

The key result areas by which the model then measures successes are those identified with reference to the balanced scorecard:

- How far it satisfies its customers
- How well motivated and committed its workforce is
- How the local and national community outside the organisation views its activities in terms of its contribution to society
- The key business results - profit, return on capital employed, shareholder earnings, achieving budgets

10.6 Implementing VBM The Evidence

This section provides evidence from some recent research into the implementation of shareholder value in large international companies. Summary findings related to those factors found to be key in successful implementation, their implications and some observations, on the benefits to be derived and the pitfalls to be avoided are presented. The study undertaken was an in depth analysis over a number of years in three large international companies. The findings are recognised as not necessarily generalisable and the need for further research is acknowledged.

Key features of successful implementation

Research into the adoption of shareholder value in large international companies found the following key features of successful implementation:

- Value creation is viewed as a key objective and not as another management initiative.
- Top management commitment to the shareholder value approach is essential, building on the research and understanding of the ideas underpinning the approach.
- The process needs to be championed at CEO/director level, with delegation for implementation.

- The importance of communicating the ideas and concepts of the discounted cash flow based, rather than accounting, view of future performance to the senior management of the business(es) involved is essential.
- A process of developing awareness is vital, followed by a more formal education process for the business unit/company heads, led by corporate centre, related to developing an understanding of the application of the concept within the company.
- The process of strategic planning is critical in implementing the approach. The preparation of realistic strategic reviews by business units, with alternative strategies evaluated using shareholder value concepts are a primary planning tool. These are an important key to success in maximising shareholder value and considerable effort is needed to establish an effective way of managing and enabling this. Of particular significance is the role of the corporate centre in challenging and coordinating this process.
- The development of the value based framework and management processes needs to be supported by the strategic planning process, and managed by the corporate centre. Although the value based approach may be adopted for strategic purposes, it is typically very difficult to integrate it into all the financial reporting systems. A step by step approach is often favoured, adopting the approach initially where the greatest benefit can be realised. It is important to recognise that to fully align the value based approach and financial reporting requirements will take considerable effort.
- The commitment of management to the process is critical for success and reward systems could play an important part in principle, but care needs to be exercised in the timing of the introduction of such schemes.

Key implementation issues

Companies intending to implement value based management need to be aware of a number of key issues identified in companies that have been involved in implementation:

Timescale/Speed

The process of implementation usually takes longer than anticipated. There needs to be a preparedness, and planning, to overcome resistance to the changed requirements, particularly implementing to manage the ongoing business, and making the measures meaningful at operational level. Companies determining to manage for shareholder value are committing themselves to a lengthy, and costly, process. Conversely, speed in being able to create value is seen as crucial, and an inability to hasten the process and enable speedy decisions can be frustrating. Management processes will need to be improved, and the use of external consultants can be a motivating force to speed up the process of change.

The Role of the Champion/Change Leader

Successful move to VBM needs a driving force someone who wants shareholder value to be the way the company is measured and who is prepared to take the lead. Recognition of the lengthy timescale of implementation and the need for a driver/leader of that change involves a considerable resource requirement to provide an effective leader of the change, who may be 'tied up' as a key resource for a number of years. During this time they will need to work and develop their own strategy and style to be effective in their role of influencing and enabling management in the implementation. Managements must be aware of and plan for such a considerable resource, and plan to ensure continuity and succession in this key role.

Role of the Corporate Centre

Leaders of the change are often part of the corporate centre, and the centre becomes a primary resource, in terms of education and training in the application of the concepts, providing support, guidance, feedback to enable and influence management and to coordinate and challenge management. The need for a good linkage between those teams working in the centre, who are usually competent and knowledgeable about value based concepts, who are familiar with the corporate language, and those who are out in the business units, in operational positions at the customer face is essential. Research has identified that the role of the centre in influencing the progression of the implementation, in manner and scope, has been identified as an important factor. There has been a need to 'gather in' the business units to communicate, educate and train in the new concepts by which they will be measured, which has strengthened the influencing role of the centre. If the role of the centre (parent) is critical to the implementation then also is an understanding of how the centre (parent) has achieved the outcome i.e. how it has itself added value is an important element, and what has it had to spend so much time and effort doing to achieve the outcome in multi-business companies, the corporate parent may be considered central to corporate strategy and decision making.

If accepted as the key corporate objective, the implementation of shareholder value techniques to create value in a business is a 'parenting opportunity'. One potential area of parenting opportunity concerns specialist expertise not possessed by the business that certainly fits the requirement for the implementation of the shareholder value concept at corporate level. The cascading of this expertise and the ability of the corporate centre to achieve this is seen as a significant issue and is closely linked to the parenting role and consideration of the value they add to the process.

Level of cascading throughout the company

Once the underlying concept has been 'bought into' by the top management, the next step is the transference /cascading of the concept in the development of value creating strategies and value creating processes undertaken with the business unit/operating company heads. Research has found that heads of the business units/operating companies had been involved fairly early in the process but the further transference into the management of the business units/ operating companies had not generally progressed very far, which was a reflection of the difficulty identified of making the approach meaningful at operational level. There had been significant commitment to making the approach visible and to promoting understanding within the companies, but providing tangible means of measuring and managing value for those working with customers, clients or in operations had not progressed as far as the companies would have liked.

The fundamental principle behind value based systems (whichever metric is adopted) is based on well established and accepted finance theory. However true this may be at corporate level, this is only likely to be the case further down the company if the 'shareholder value talk' is in terms that make sense to an individual's work. The primary objective of a value based system is to link the firm's strategies and management performance evaluation to the creation of shareholder value. Successful use of these approaches lies in their effective implementation throughout an organisation and this means ensuring that those involved in transferring the concepts are able to portray them in practical ways rather than as a complicated theory. The requirements for implementing the process at corporate level are likely to be different from implementation at lower levels in the company, and companies must recognise that they need to address such issues as resource implications for educating and training below business unit/operating company head level and the degree of cascading that would be necessary.

It has been shown that the principles underpinning shareholder value calculation are well established. They are found in use in project finance and in the evaluation of major investments; they are used to give insight into how the market values a business. They are used in decisions concerning restructuring, mergers and acquisitions which are seen as routes to value creation. The use of these techniques is part of the function of managing the portfolio. Although widely used at corporate level, research also shows that there are only a handful of companies who have progressed to the stage where a value based management approach is used throughout the company. Many use the approach at corporate level, where the need to understand which parts of the business deliver value, and which are using excessive amounts of capital without making sufficient returns is a vital.

The evidence is that good progress has been made in adopting the shareholder value approach as an effective strategic planning tool, and that this has produced a higher standard of strategy development at corporate and business unit level in determining the markets and businesses in which to operate and investments that are necessary to support those decisions. This has been the primary focus of the companies and there are differing views as to the timescale and the level of cascading that will occur in the future. However the need to establish shareholder value measures that are usable at operational level is accepted as an important issue, along with the recognition that this will require skill and commitment to manage and overcome any resistance to change, to prepare management to learn and anchor new behaviour.

Cost of capital

Estimating and understanding the cost of capital is a fundamental issue in shareholder value, and an area which poses some difficulty when attempting to address the issue of the cost of capital is its estimation for each business unit/ operating company. Often a simplistic view is adopted, whereby the total company cost of capital is used and applied to each of the business units/ operating companies, but it is recognised that this is not an accurate policy and considerable work is being undertaken to assess and establish different costs of capital for individual business units/operating companies. This is an area that has typically been managed at corporate level and there is some concern about the level of understanding of the issue below that level, which would need addressing in terms of communication and education in the future. Without an adequate assessment and understanding of the cost of capital it is not possible to determine how much or whether, value has been created or destroyed.

Change from established financial/management reporting systems

Moves to change the financial/ management reporting systems to a discounted cash flow basis are essential. The degree of development has been limited, and often the current reporting systems are not adequate ~ or always suitable for value reporting. This is an area where it is recognised that existing accounting systems which still form the basis of performance reporting need to be adapted to incorporate more fluidly operational value drivers to ensure that management and measurement are aligned operationally.

The ongoing nature of the approach

Maximising shareholder value is accepted as a key corporate objective by many companies; it is not viewed as another management initiative. The intention is that the company will be managed and governed to maximise value for its shareholders and stakeholders on a long term basis; the objective is to ensure that the company produces returns on its capital in excess of its cost of capital. There is a powerful sense that the process of implementation does not have a finite end; it requires continual review, feedback and the drive/momentum of top management to sustain the approach.

Observations on successful implementation of value¬ based management

To enable companies to achieve their objective of value creation, there appears to be a vital requirement for the company to be directing the value creation process. This is a requirement significantly greater than initial implementation. It requires accepting the long term responsibility for maintaining and retaining the processes and behaviours necessary to satisfy the key objective of achieving a return on capital greater than the cost of capital, and providing the direction to achieve it. For this, although initial championing is important, there is a need for the value direction process to become an integral, ongoing part of the management. Directing value to produce a return greater than the cost of capital influences the whole company and encompasses all functions of the company. An analogy could be drawn with the development of IT. Some years ago the role of IT was not recognised as spanning all functions and influencing the whole business in the way it is now accepted to do.

Value direction is not necessarily a finance led responsibility but a coordinating role, bringing a set of value direction skills, covering a number of functional areas and a set of prerequisites for the creation of value. The following list is not suggested as exhaustive but indicative of the types of skills necessary:

- developments of applied corporate finance
- financial culture
- cost of capital
- change management
- value performance measurement
- strategic planning
- value metrics
- value budgets
- value plans
- education and training
- investor relations
- information management/ technology
- internal audit
- executive compensation
- recruitment/ resourcing

A number of these prerequisites cover the development of value reporting systems, an important area for the management and measurement of value. Many of the current accounting systems are developed for the requirements of statutory financial reporting, and internal management accounting and performance reporting systems are drawn from these. A development would be to separate the financial reporting requirement entirely from the internal reporting system to allow these to be developed exclusively for value reporting which would better reflect the requirements at different levels in the organisation. Although financial information is necessary at certain levels, physical measurements, e.g. in terms of customers satisfied, are more relevant and appropriate at operational level, where accrual accounting is usually unhelpful for management and measurement. Value direction means ensuring that the necessary links are in place between building budgets and targets in physical value terms and enabling their transfer to financial data at higher levels, to enable everyone to 'get on with managing the business in meaningful terms for creating value'.

10.7 What can VBM facilitate?

- Strategic and financial planning at corporate and business levels
- Corporate investment decisions
- Evaluation of revenue expenditure programmes
- Corporate finance decisions with respect to dividend policy, investor relations, treasury management, and financial decisions
- Performance targeting, measurement and reward systems

The critical success factors found to enable the implementation of VBM include:

- Top management being visibly committed to, and actively interested in, VBM
- Value to shareholders being set alongside ambitions to satisfy other corporate values and not being seen as the sole objective of the organisation
- Inclusion of planning, control and reward systems
- Education in the use of cash based financial tools and exposure to strategic analysis tools
- Willingness to explore areas where value creation may be weak
- Early hand over of management of the process to management rather than be championed by external consultants
- Having a clear plan early on for a roll out programme throughout the organisation
- Management of expectations so that managers will realise that the lags will occur between investing in change and reaping the rewards.

On the other hand, in implementing a VBM programme a number of 'don'ts' include:

- Avoid degeneration into a number crunching exercise where modelling and measurement take a life of their own
- Avoid falling into the trap of playing the 'VBM game' through manipulating terminal values of business strategies which need to be tested against external assumptions
- Do not apply VBM only to a particular area of the management process or business e.g. capital investment decisions
- Avoid being 'bull-headed'. It is sometimes tempting to accept compromise in order to make headway, e.g. defer changes in reward systems.

The key benefits to be derived from VBM include:

- Development of a common framework for integrating long range strategic plans, capital programmes, acquisitions, short term budgets, etc.
- Rewards systems that align behaviour and motivation.
- Realisation that a trade off not only exists between large investment projects, but also between these and revenue programmes.
- Performance measurement has become much more outward focused and geared to achievements relative to competitors and also relative to market conditions.

10.8 Changing role of finance

For successful businesses and particularly those embarking on a shareholder value initiative, there will be many important issues to address, but three that are crucial, are:

- Strategy implementation: to ensure that the agreed strategy is proceeding according to plan. It is reckoned that financial managers have to keep the whole company under review; they have to ensure that the necessary control points are in existence, the milestones and responsibilities are mapped out and that everyone is aware of what they have to do
- Strategic change: financial managers and their information systems have to respond to present day pressures
- Strategic flexibility: finance has to be ready to respond fast to opportunities, which arise, for example, new investment opportunities in Eastern Europe.

Historically the finance function was considered an overhead and treated as such, but increasingly today it is reckoned to be an essential asset for driving business competitiveness and effectiveness. The modern finance function will need to focus on implementing global integration strategies, deploying cutting-edge technology and continuously working to upgrade the quality of its people and processes in order to adapt to changing business requirements. The reasons for this are that the finance function faces an important set of challenges in the form of having appropriately focussed analytical tools to manage for value from:

1. An internal perspective – managing for value
2. An external perspective – mergers and acquisitions.

Appropriately focussed analytical tools to manage for value from an internal perspective

It is up to the finance function to consistently provide 'better information for better business decisions'. Detailed information about the current performance of the business, factors affecting future growth and new business opportunities cannot be gleaned from internal analysis of operations and the balance sheet alone. The challenge is to implement world-class financial and business analysis tools, potentially providing a dashboard from which to monitor performance, in order to operate a proactive rather than a reactive business model.

Appropriately focussed analytical tools to manage for value from an external perspective

Merger and Acquisition (M&A) activity is no longer concentrated among just a few industry segments. Unlike the late '90s, when the activity centred on media, telecom and technology activity is now distributed across a wide variety of industries including energy, utilities and financial services. Such geographical dispersion has helped to spread national and international M&A across sectors, for example, steel, pharmaceuticals, hotels and commercial property. Furthermore, there are new players in the M&A market, like private equity structures, that can pose a threat to the continuation of even the most apparently secure firm in its current form.

Private equity can be applied to companies at all stages of development from a start-up to mature established companies with a stock market listing. For a business start up, expansion, a buy into a business, a buyout of a division of a parent company, a turnaround or the revitalisation of a company private equity may well help. However, private equity is very different from raising debt or a loan from a lender, such as a bank. Whereas lenders have a legal right to interest on a loan and repayment of the capital, irrespective of success or failure, private equity is invested in exchange for a stake in the company and, as shareholders, the investors' returns are dependent on the growth and profitability of the business.

Not only has the M&A playing field expanded, the speed in which deals are completed has accelerated. For instance, institutional investors such as hedge funds now simply buy a whole company, take it off the street and then 'parse' out the deal later rather than arranging the financing with four or five partners before closing the sale[30].

With such developments in M&A, both the enabling and the tracking of the value creation process frequently rest in the hands of the CFO. The CFO is required to play an active role in all phases, from strategic planning through opportunity identification and initial evaluation to execution and integration. In doing so, the CFO must lay the foundations for increased efficiency and productivity, which will underpin value creation.

10.9 The ascendancy of the general financial manager

Financial management within corporate finance in some form or another is increasingly being seen as the responsibility of virtually every person in the firm. For example, cost management is one such area and the importance being attached to it has significant implications for financial specialists like the management accountant. There is a view that business pressures will impact upon the financial specialist such that the demand for management accountants as specialists may fall, while the need for management accounting more broadly may rise. Such an outcome would reflect a move towards decentralisation, which will mean greater general managerial responsibility for much of the traditional domain of the financial specialist. Taking this view, the management accountants who survive the transition will need to be highly skilled and:

- will become a part of their organisation's value added team
- participate in the formulation and implementation of strategy
- translate strategic intent and capabilities into operational and managerial measures
- move away from being score keepers of the past and to become the designers of the organisation's critical management information systems, besides being knowledgeable about cost management and management accounting.

---

[30] A hedge fund generally refers to a lightly regulated private investment fund characterised by unconventional strategies (for example, strategies other than investing long only in bonds, equities or money markets). They are primarily organised as limited partnerships and previously were often simply called 'limited partnerships' and were grouped with other limited partnerships such as those that invested in oil development.

It seems that there will be pressure for some current responsibilities of the finance specialist to be driven down into the organisation, but there will also be a clearly defined role for central financial specialists. The responsibility for cost management will become increasingly the domain of all managers, but a breed of financial specialists will be required at the centre. The reason why the responsibility for cost management will become more general has been illustrated with reference to health service treatment protocols. These are standardised ways to treat a particular medical condition and are used in healthcare to reduce costs. The objective is to give physicians a concrete idea of the minimum cost procedure the average patient should receive to obtain effective treatment. The key point is that treatment protocols are developed and implemented by individuals with clinical knowledge, such that the management accountant becomes a key specialist with the responsibility for providing strategically critical information for managing costs.

The implications of these changes are that:

- As cost management becomes more important, so too does management accounting with the consequence that cost information currently not collected is required. This means that a firm's cost system often has to be upgraded. A key role of the management accountant will relate to the design of a system, but once designed the responsibility for its management will move to the workforce
- Empowering the cost management process requires the decentralisation of the management accounting function
- The management accounting function becomes one of supporting the broader workforce probably by way of being a member of a multi skill team rather than as a member of a functional team of specialists and also one of monitoring performance.

The overall implications are that finance and VBM will be the domain and responsibility of a broad based group of managers. While the financial specialists will be required to provide the guidance and direction, the implementation will be by general managers with business responsibilities that include financial management.

APPENDIX A

%	1	2	3	4	5	6	7	8	9	10
Period										
1	0.990	0.980	0.971	0.962	0.952	0.943	0.935	0.926	0.917	0.909
2	0.980	0.961	0.943	0.925	0.907	0.890	0.873	0.857	0.842	0.826
3	0.971	0.942	0.915	0.889	0.864	0.840	0.816	0.794	0.772	0.751
4	0.961	0.924	0.888	0.855	0.823	0.792	0.763	0.735	0.708	0.683
5	0.951	0.906	0.863	0.822	0.784	0.747	0.713	0.681	0.650	0.621
6	0.942	0.888	0.837	0.790	0.746	0.705	0.666	0.630	0.596	0.564
7	0.933	0.871	0.813	0.760	0.711	0.665	0.623	0.583	0.547	0.513
8	0.923	0.853	0.789	0.731	0.677	0.627	0.582	0.540	0.502	0.467
9	0.914	0.837	0.766	0.703	0.645	0.592	0.544	0.500	0.460	0.424
10	0.905	0.820	0.744	0.676	0.614	0.558	0.508	0.463	0.422	0.386
11	0.896	0.804	0.722	0.650	0.585	0.527	0.475	0.429	0.388	0.350
12	0.887	0.788	0.701	0.625	0.557	0.497	0.444	0.397	0.356	0.319
13	0.879	0.773	0.681	0.601	0.530	0.469	0.415	0.368	0.326	0.290
14	0.870	0.758	0.661	0.577	0.505	0.442	0.388	0.340	0.299	0.263
15	0.861	0.743	0.642	0.555	0.481	0.417	0.362	0.315	0.275	0.239
16	0.853	0.728	0.623	0.534	0.458	0.394	0.339	0.292	0.252	0.218
17	0.844	0.714	0.605	0.513	0.436	0.371	0.317	0.270	0.231	0.198
18	0.836	0.700	0.587	0.494	0.416	0.350	0.296	0.250	0.212	0.180
19	0.828	0.686	0.570	0.475	0.396	0.331	0.277	0.232	0.194	0.164
20	0.820	0.673	0.554	0.456	0.377	0.312	0.258	0.215	0.178	0.149

%	11	12	13	14	15	16	17	18	19	20
Period										
1	0.901	0.893	0.885	0.877	0.870	0.862	0.855	0.847	0.840	0.833
2	0.812	0.797	0.783	0.769	0.756	0.743	0.731	0.718	0.706	0.694
3	0.731	0.712	0.693	0.675	0.658	0.641	0.624	0.609	0.593	0.579
4	0.659	0.636	0.613	0.592	0.572	0.552	0.534	0.516	0.499	0.482
5	0.593	0.567	0.543	0.519	0.497	0.476	0.456	0.437	0.419	0.402
6	0.535	0.507	0.480	0.456	0.432	0.410	0.390	0.370	0.352	0.335
7	0.482	0.452	0.425	0.400	0.376	0.354	0.333	0.314	0.296	0.279
8	0.434	0.404	0.376	0.351	0.327	0.305	0.285	0.266	0.249	0.233
9	0.391	0.361	0.333	0.308	0.284	0.263	0.243	0.225	0.209	0.194
10	0.352	0.322	0.295	0.270	0.247	0.227	0.208	0.191	0.176	0.162
11	0.317	0.287	0.261	0.237	0.215	0.195	0.178	0.162	0.148	0.135
12	0.286	0.257	0.231	0.208	0.187	0.168	0.152	0.137	0.124	0.112
13	0.258	0.229	0.204	0.182	0.163	0.145	0.130	0.116	0.104	0.093
14	0.232	0.205	0.181	0.160	0.141	0.125	0.111	0.099	0.088	0.078
15	0.209	0.183	0.160	0.140	0.123	0.108	0.095	0.084	0.074	0.065
16	0.188	0.163	0.141	0.123	0.107	0.093	0.081	0.071	0.062	0.054
17	0.170	0.146	0.125	0.108	0.093	0.080	0.069	0.060	0.052	0.045
18	0.153	0.130	0.111	0.095	0.081	0.069	0.059	0.051	0.044	0.038
19	0.138	0.116	0.098	0.083	0.070	0.060	0.051	0.043	0.037	0.031
20	0.124	0.104	0.087	0.073	0.061	0.051	0.043	0.037	0.031	0.026

%	**21**	**22**	**23**	**24**	**25**	**26**	**27**	**28**	**29**	**30**
Period										
1	0.826	0.820	0.813	0.806	0.800	0.794	0.787	0.781	0.775	0.769
2	0.683	0.672	0.661	0.650	0.640	0.630	0.620	0.610	0.601	0.592
3	0.564	0.551	0.537	0.524	0.512	0.500	0.488	0.477	0.466	0.455
4	0.467	0.451	0.437	0.423	0.410	0.397	0.384	0.373	0.361	0.350
5	0.386	0.370	0.355	0.341	0.328	0.315	0.303	0.291	0.280	0.269
6	0.319	0.303	0.289	0.275	0.262	0.250	0.238	0.227	0.217	0.207
7	0.263	0.249	0.235	0.222	0.210	0.198	0.188	0.178	0.168	0.159
8	0.218	0.204	0.191	0.179	0.168	0.157	0.148	0.139	0.130	0.123
9	0.180	0.167	0.155	0.144	0.134	0.125	0.116	0.108	0.101	0.094
10	0.149	0.137	0.126	0.116	0.107	0.099	0.092	0.085	0.078	0.073
11	0.123	0.112	0.103	0.094	0.086	0.079	0.072	0.066	0.061	0.056
12	0.102	0.092	0.083	0.076	0.069	0.062	0.057	0.052	0.047	0.043
13	0.084	0.075	0.068	0.061	0.055	0.050	0.045	0.040	0.037	0.033
14	0.069	0.062	0.055	0.049	0.044	0.039	0.035	0.032	0.028	0.025
15	0.057	0.051	0.045	0.040	0.035	0.031	0.028	0.025	0.022	0.020
16	0.047	0.042	0.036	0.032	0.028	0.025	0.022	0.019	0.017	0.015
17	0.039	0.034	0.030	0.026	0.023	0.020	0.017	0.015	0.013	0.012
18	0.032	0.028	0.024	0.021	0.018	0.016	0.014	0.012	0.010	0.009
19	0.027	0.023	0.020	0.017	0.014	0.012	0.011	0.009	0.008	0.007
20	0.022	0.019	0.016	0.014	0.012	0.010	0.008	0.007	0.006	0.005

%	31	32	33	34	35	36	37	38	39	40
Period										
1	0.763	0.758	0.752	0.746	0.741	0.735	0.730	0.725	0.719	0.714
2	0.583	0.574	0.565	0.557	0.549	0.541	0.533	0.525	0.518	0.510
3	0.445	0.435	0.425	0.416	0.406	0.398	0.389	0.381	0.372	0.364
4	0.340	0.329	0.320	0.310	0.301	0.292	0.284	0.276	0.268	0.260
5	0.259	0.250	0.240	0.231	0.223	0.215	0.207	0.200	0.193	0.186
6	0.198	0.189	0.181	0.173	0.165	0.158	0.151	0.145	0.139	0.133
7	0.151	0.143	0.136	0.129	0.122	0.116	0.110	0.105	0.100	0.095
8	0.115	0.108	0.102	0.096	0.091	0.085	0.081	0.076	0.072	0.068
9	0.088	0.082	0.077	0.072	0.067	0.063	0.059	0.055	0.052	0.048
10	0.067	0.062	0.058	0.054	0.050	0.046	0.043	0.040	0.037	0.035
11	0.051	0.047	0.043	0.040	0.037	0.034	0.031	0.029	0.027	0.025
12	0.039	0.036	0.033	0.030	0.027	0.025	0.023	0.021	0.019	0.018
13	0.030	0.027	0.025	0.022	0.020	0.018	0.017	0.015	0.014	0.013
14	0.023	0.021	0.018	0.017	0.015	0.014	0.012	0.011	0.010	0.009
15	0.017	0.016	0.014	0.012	0.011	0.010	0.009	0.008	0.007	0.006
16	0.013	0.012	0.010	0.009	0.008	0.007	0.006	0.006	0.005	0.005
17	0.010	0.009	0.008	0.007	0.006	0.005	0.005	0.004	0.004	0.003
18	0.008	0.007	0.006	0.005	0.005	0.004	0.003	0.003	0.003	0.002
19	0.006	0.005	0.004	0.004	0.003	0.003	0.003	0.002	0.002	0.002
20	0.005	0.004	0.003	0.003	0.002	0.002	0.002	0.002	0.001	0.001

%	1	2	3	4	5	6	7	8	9	10
Period										
1	0.990	0.980	0.971	0.962	0.952	0.943	0.935	0.926	0.917	0.909
2	1.970	1.942	1.913	1.886	1.859	1.833	1.808	1.783	1.759	1.736
3	2.941	2.884	2.829	2.775	2.723	2.673	2.624	2.577	2.531	2.487
4	3.902	3.808	3.717	3.630	3.546	3.465	3.387	3.312	3.240	3.170
5	4.853	4.713	4.580	4.452	4.329	4.212	4.100	3.993	3.890	3.791
6	5.795	5.601	5.417	5.242	5.076	4.917	4.767	4.623	4.486	4.355
7	6.728	6.472	6.230	6.002	5.786	5.582	5.389	5.206	5.033	4.868
8	7.652	7.325	7.020	6.733	6.463	6.210	5.971	5.747	5.535	5.335
9	8.566	8.162	7.786	7.435	7.108	6.802	6.515	6.247	5.995	5.759
10	9.471	8.983	8.530	8.111	7.722	7.360	7.024	6.710	6.418	6.145
11	10.368	9.787	9.253	8.760	8.306	7.887	7.499	7.139	6.805	6.495
12	11.255	10.575	9.954	9.385	8.863	8.384	7.943	7.536	7.161	6.814
13	12.134	11.348	10.635	9.986	9.394	8.853	8.358	7.904	7.487	7.103
14	13.004	12.106	11.296	10.563	9.899	9.295	8.745	8.244	7.786	7.367
15	13.865	12.849	11.938	11.118	10.380	9.712	9.108	8.559	8.061	7.606
16	14.718	13.578	12.561	11.652	10.838	10.106	9.447	8.851	8.313	7.824
17	15.562	14.292	13.166	12.166	11.274	10.477	9.763	9.122	8.544	8.022
18	16.398	14.992	13.754	12.659	11.690	10.828	10.059	9.372	8.756	8.201
19	17.226	15.678	14.324	13.134	12.085	11.158	10.336	9.604	8.950	8.365
20	18.046	16.351	14.877	13.590	12.462	11.470	10.594	9.818	9.129	8.514

%	11	12	13	14	15	16	17	18	19	20
Period										
1	0.901	0.893	0.885	0.877	0.870	0.862	0.855	0.847	0.840	0.833
2	1.713	1.690	1.668	1.647	1.626	1.605	1.585	1.566	1.547	1.528
3	2.444	2.402	2.361	2.322	2.283	2.246	2.210	2.174	2.140	2.106
4	3.102	3.037	2.974	2.914	2.855	2.798	2.743	2.690	2.639	2.589
5	3.696	3.605	3.517	3.433	3.352	3.274	3.199	3.127	3.058	2.991
6	4.231	4.111	3.998	3.889	3.784	3.685	3.589	3.498	3.410	3.326
7	4.712	4.564	4.423	4.288	4.160	4.039	3.922	3.812	3.706	3.605
8	5.146	4.968	4.799	4.639	4.487	4.344	4.207	4.078	3.954	3.837
9	5.537	5.328	5.132	4.946	4.772	4.607	4.451	4.303	4.163	4.031
10	5.889	5.650	5.426	5.216	5.019	4.833	4.659	4.494	4.339	4.192
11	6.207	5.938	5.687	5.453	5.234	5.029	4.836	4.656	4.487	4.327
12	6.492	6.194	5.918	5.660	5.421	5.197	4.988	4.793	4.611	4.439
13	6.750	6.424	6.122	5.842	5.583	5.342	5.118	4.910	4.715	4.533
14	6.982	6.628	6.302	6.002	5.724	5.468	5.229	5.008	4.802	4.611
15	7.191	6.811	6.462	6.142	5.847	5.575	5.324	5.092	4.876	4.675
16	7.379	6.974	6.604	6.265	5.954	5.668	5.405	5.162	4.938	4.730
17	7.549	7.120	6.729	6.373	6.047	5.749	5.475	5.222	4.990	4.775
18	7.702	7.250	6.840	6.467	6.128	5.818	5.534	5.273	5.033	4.812
19	7.839	7.366	6.938	6.550	6.198	5.877	5.584	5.316	5.070	4.843
20	7.963	7.469	7.025	6.623	6.259	5.929	5.628	5.353	5.101	4.870

%	21	22	23	24	25	26	27	28	29	30
Period										
1	0.826	0.820	0.813	0.806	0.800	0.794	0.787	0.781	0.775	0.769
2	1.509	1.492	1.474	1.457	1.440	1.424	1.407	1.392	1.376	1.361
3	2.074	2.042	2.011	1.981	1.952	1.923	1.896	1.868	1.842	1.816
4	2.540	2.494	2.448	2.404	2.362	2.320	2.280	2.241	2.203	2.166
5	2.926	2.864	2.803	2.745	2.689	2.635	2.583	2.532	2.483	2.436
6	3.245	3.167	3.092	3.020	2.951	2.885	2.821	2.759	2.700	2.643
7	3.508	3.416	3.327	3.242	3.161	3.083	3.009	2.937	2.868	2.802
8	3.726	3.619	3.518	3.421	3.329	3.241	3.156	3.076	2.999	2.925
9	3.905	3.786	3.673	3.566	3.463	3.366	3.273	3.184	3.100	3.019
10	4.054	3.923	3.799	3.682	3.571	3.465	3.364	3.269	3.178	3.092
11	4.177	4.035	3.902	3.776	3.656	3.543	3.437	3.335	3.239	3.147
12	4.278	4.127	3.985	3.851	3.725	3.606	3.493	3.387	3.286	3.190
13	4.362	4.203	4.053	3.912	3.780	3.656	3.538	3.427	3.322	3.223
14	4.432	4.265	4.108	3.962	3.824	3.695	3.573	3.459	3.351	3.249
15	4.489	4.315	4.153	4.001	3.859	3.726	3.601	3.483	3.373	3.268
16	4.536	4.357	4.189	4.033	3.887	3.751	3.623	3.503	3.390	3.283
17	4.576	4.391	4.219	4.059	3.910	3.771	3.640	3.518	3.403	3.295
18	4.608	4.419	4.243	4.080	3.928	3.786	3.654	3.529	3.413	3.304
19	4.635	4.442	4.263	4.097	3.942	3.799	3.664	3.539	3.421	3.311
20	4.657	4.460	4.279	4.110	3.954	3.808	3.673	3.546	3.427	3.316

%	31	32	33	34	35	36	37	38	39	40
Period										
1	0.763	0.758	0.752	0.746	0.741	0.735	0.730	0.725	0.719	0.714
2	1.346	1.331	1.317	1.303	1.289	1.276	1.263	1.250	1.237	1.224
3	1.791	1.766	1.742	1.719	1.696	1.673	1.652	1.630	1.609	1.589
4	2.130	2.096	2.062	2.029	1.997	1.966	1.935	1.906	1.877	1.849
5	2.390	2.345	2.302	2.260	2.220	2.181	2.143	2.106	2.070	2.035
6	2.588	2.534	2.483	2.433	2.385	2.339	2.294	2.251	2.209	2.168
7	2.739	2.677	2.619	2.562	2.508	2.455	2.404	2.355	2.308	2.263
8	2.854	2.786	2.721	2.658	2.598	2.540	2.485	2.432	2.380	2.331
9	2.942	2.868	2.798	2.730	2.665	2.603	2.544	2.487	2.432	2.379
10	3.009	2.930	2.855	2.784	2.715	2.649	2.587	2.527	2.469	2.414
11	3.060	2.978	2.899	2.824	2.752	2.683	2.618	2.555	2.496	2.438
12	3.100	3.013	2.931	2.853	2.779	2.708	2.641	2.576	2.515	2.456
13	3.129	3.040	2.956	2.876	2.799	2.727	2.658	2.592	2.529	2.469
14	3.152	3.061	2.974	2.892	2.814	2.740	2.670	2.603	2.539	2.477
15	3.170	3.076	2.988	2.905	2.825	2.750	2.679	2.611	2.546	2.484
16	3.183	3.088	2.999	2.914	2.834	2.757	2.685	2.616	2.551	2.489
17	3.193	3.097	3.007	2.921	2.840	2.763	2.690	2.621	2.555	2.492
18	3.201	3.104	3.012	2.926	2.844	2.767	2.693	2.624	2.557	2.494
19	3.207	3.109	3.017	2.930	2.848	2.770	2.696	2.626	2.559	2.496
20	3.211	3.113	3.020	2.933	2.850	2.772	2.698	2.627	2.561	2.497

APPENDIX B
GLOSSARY OF TERMS

Absorption Costing

The practice of charging all costs, both direct and indirect to operations, processes or products.

Accounting

The process used to measure and report relevant financial information about the economic activities of a business to its stakeholders, e.g. shareholders, management and employees.

Accounting Period

The period of time between two reporting dates.

Accounting Policies

These are disclosed in the annual reports published by quoted companies and represent the interpretation of accounting principles and requirements adopted by the board of directors.

Accounting Principles

A number of generally accepted accounting principles are used in preparing financial statements. They are only generally accepted and do not have the force of law. You should note that sometimes they are referred to as accounting concepts and conventions.

Accounting Rate of Return

A method used to evaluate an investment opportunity that ignores the time value of money. The return generated by an investment opportunity is expressed as a percentage of the capital outlay.

Accounting Standards board (ASB)

The UK body responsible for producing accounting standards.

Accrual Accounting

The process of accounting which recognizes the incidence of income and expenditure, irrespective of the timing of associated cash flows.

Accruals

Charges made against profits for costs which have been incurred but for which invoices have not yet been received.

Accumulated Depreciation
The accumulation of annual depreciation charges which, when deducted from the value of fixed assets, yields what is referred to as their 'net book value' or 'written down value'.

Acid Test
Also known as the quick ratio; see Quick Ratio.

Acquisition
The process by which a company acquires a controlling interest in the voting shares of another company.

Activity Based Costing (ABC)
The practice that measures the cost and performance of activities, resources and the things that consume them.

Age Analysis
A statement analysing the transactions that make up trade receivable/creditor balance into discreet 'ageing' periods.

Amortisation
An accounting adjustment to take account of the diminution in value of a fixed asset over its economic life. It is often used in conjunction with intangible assets, e.g. goodwill.

Annual Report
A report issued to shareholders and other interested parties which normally includes a chairperson's statement, report of the directors, review of operations, financial statements and associated notes.

Annuity
A series of payments of an equal or constant amount of money at fixed intervals for a specified number of periods.

Appropriation
A term normally used to describe the division of profit generated.

Asset
An item of value. Also the accounting term used to describe the items which a business owns or possesses.

Asset Turnover

Also know as Sales Generation: see Sales Generation.

Auditors' Report

A statutory report on the annual accounts of an organisation resulting from an audit by an independent firm of accountants.

Authorised Share Capital

The total number/value of shares that a company can issue, as set out in its memorandum of association.

Balance Sheet

A statement showing the financial position of a company in terms of its assets and liabilities at a specified point in time.

Bank Borrowings

Includes bank overdraft and bank loans.

Beta

A relative measure of volatility determined by comparing a share's returns to the market's returns. The greater the volatility, the higher the beta, and vice versa.

Brand Accounting

A term associated with carrying brand names as intangible assets in the balance sheet.

Break-Even Analysis or BEA

See Cost-Volume-Profit Analysis or CVP

Break-Even Point

The volume of activity or sales at which total revenue equals total cost.

Budget

A financial and/or quantitative statement, prepared and approved prior to a defined period o time, of the policy to be pursued during that period for the purpose of attaining a given objective.

Budget Centre

A generic title to describe all responsibility centres; see Profit Centre.

Budgetary Control

A system of setting budgets, recording activity and evaluating ongoing performance.

Budgeting

The process of setting budgets

Business Value

The value generated by the free cash flows of a business from an explicit planning period and the continuing period beyond in which all providers of funds have a claim. It is a measure of value before the addition of marketable securities and the deduction of debt.

Called Up Share Capital

That part of issued share capital for which funds have been called up, e.g. a company that has authorised share capital of 1 million but has only issued or called up 80% or 0.8m.

Capital Asset Pricing Model (CAPM)

A technique associated with deriving the cost of a business' equity from the risk free rate, the business' beta, and the market risk premium. The formula for its calculation is:
Cost of equity = risk free rate + (beta(market risk premium))

Capital Employed

The funds used to finance business. Normally measured in 'total assets' or 'net' i.e. total assets less current liabilities.

Capital Expenditure

The purchase of fixed assets.

Capital Investment Appraisal

The evaluation of proposed capital projects that is sometimes referred to as project appraisal.

Capital Structure

The composition of a company's sources of long-term funds, e.g. equity and debt.

Capitalisation

The recognition of an item of cost previously written off against periodic profit as a fixed asset carried in the balance sheet.

Cash Flow

The amount of cash flowing into or out of a business during a prescribed period of time

Cash flow 'Drivers'

Means by which free cash flow estimates can be generated and consist of:

1. Sales growth rate
2. Operating profit margin
3. Cash tax rate
4. Fixed capital investment
5. Working capital investment

Cash Flow Forecast

The expression of the amount of cash expected to flow into or out of a business over a prescribed period of time (e.g. 1 year) analysed by shorter time periods (weekly, monthly, daily).

Cash flow statement

A statement that analyses cash flows historically. It is sometimes encountered showing three types of activity:

Investing activities
Financial activities
Operating activities

Chairperson's Statement

A statement by the chairperson of a company, normally included as part of the annual report, and which contains reference to important events.

Common-Size Analysis

A method of analysis by which data in the income statement and the balance sheet are expressed as a percentage of some key figure, like revenue.

Companies Acts

Acts of parliament that specify legal requirements of companies on a wide range of activities, including accounting.

Company

A legal organisation set up by registration under the Companies Act, or by Act of Parliament or by charter, and having a life independent of its members.

Company Limited by Shares

A company where the members are liable for the company's debts only to the amount they owe in their shares.

Compounding

A technique for determining a future value with knowledge of the present value, the time period and the interest rate.

Consistency

An accounting principle meaning that the treatment of particular items should be the same from period to period.

Consolidated Accounts or Group Accounts

Accounting statements where the accounts of a holding company and all its subsidiaries are amalgamated into one, as though it were a single entity.

Contribution

The difference between the sales revenue and the marginal cost of sales.

Contribution per unit

The difference between the selling price and the marginal cost per unit.

Contribution/Sales Ratio

See Profit/Volume Ratio.

Corporate Report

The annual published financial report of an organisation.

Corporate Value

Where a business holds investments in other businesses that are not captured in the calculation of business value, any such benefits have to be added to determine corporate value.

Cost Allocation

Where an item of cost can be allocated directly to a cost centre.

Cost Apportionment

Where an item of cost cannot.

Cost Centre

A location, person or item(s) of equipment that costs may be ascertained and used for the purpose of cost control.

Cost Driver

The event or forces that are the significant determinants of the cost of business activities.

Cost of Capital

The cost of long-term funds to a company.

Cost of Debt

The cost of loans to a business calculated after tax.

Cost of Equity

The cost to a business of financing its share capital that is typically calculated using a dividend valuation approach or the Capital Asset Pricing Model.

Cost of Sales

The costs that are attributable to the sales made. It is usually before the deduction of selling, distribution and administration costs.

Cost Unit

A normal unit of quantity of a product, service or time in relation to which costs may be ascertained or expressed e.g. per 100, per tonne.

Cost – Volume-Profit (CVP) Analysis

A technique for analysing the relationship between costs, volume and profit, for example to determine the break-even point. (See Break-Even Point).

Creative Accounting

The name given to a number of approaches by which companies can exercise considerable judgement to produce results which put them in the best possible light, whilst staying within the letter of the law.

Creditor Days

The number of days of trade payables 'held' by the business.

Creditors

See Trade Payables. The amounts of money owed and payable to suppliers of goods or services by the business.

Cumulative Preference Shares

Preference shares which are entitled to a deferred dividend if the fixed dividend is not payable. If there is a period of poor profits during which dividends are not paid, the arrears must be paid in future years.

Current Assets

Those assets of a company that are reasonably expected to be realised in cash, or sold, or consumed during the normal operating cycle of the business. They include inventory (inventory), trade receivables (trade receivables), short-term investments, bank and cash balances.

Current Liabilities

Those liabilities which a company may rely upon to finance short-term activities that include trade payables (trade payables), bank overdraft, proposed final dividend, and current taxation.

Current Ratio

A measure of short-term solvency that is calculated by dividing current assets by current liabilities. It gives an indication of a company's ability to pay its way within one year.

Debentures

A source of borrowing for a company, of a long-term nature and usually stating the rate of interest and when repayment is to occur.

Debt

The total amount owed by a company to external providers of funds.

Debtors

See Trade Receivables. Amounts owed to a company by its customers.

Debtors Days

The number of days of trade receivables "held" by the business.

Depreciation

An accounting adjustment to take account of the diminution in value of a fixed asset over its economic life.

Differential Cost

A cost which differs between two ore more alternative courses of action.

Diluted Earnings per Share

Profit after taxation divided by the weighted average of ordinary shares, after allowing for full conversion rights attaching to convertible securities and the allotment of shares under option schemes and warrants, and with a corresponding adjustment to income for interests.

Direct Cost

A cost directly attributable to a product or service.

Directors' Report

A report from the directors of a limited company to its shareholders, included in the corporate annual report.

Discount Rate

The amount by which future cash flows should be discounted to reflect the reducing value of money over time.

Discounted Cash Flow (DCF)

A technique for calculating whether a sum receivable at some time in the future is worthwhile in terms of value today. It involves discounting, or scaling-down, future cash flows.

Dividend

The proportion of the profits of a company distributed to shareholders.

Dividend Cover

This indicates the number of times the dividend is covered by earnings attributable to shareholders.

Dividend Yield

The dividend per share (gross of tax) expressed as a percentage of the market price of a share.

Double-Entry Bookkeeping

A system of bookkeeping whereby every transaction is recorded twice in the books, once as a debit and once as a credit. This system is widely used and underpins the main financial statements produced by an organisation.

Earnings Per Share

Earnings attributable to shareholders divided by the weighted average number of ordinary shares in issue during the period. The calculation and result is shown by way of note in a company's annual report.

Economic Value

The value of an asset which is derived from expressing all of its potential cash flows (over its lifetime) in terms of present worth.

Equity

The sum of issued share capital, capital reserves and revenue reserves which is also known as shareholders' funds, or net worth.

Equity Risk Premium

The excess return above the risk-free rate that investors demand for holding risky securities.

Equity Share Capital

The share capital of a company attributable to shareholders.

Exceptional Items

Costs and revenues that relate to normal business activities but are exceptional only in terms of their value.

Exception Reporting

A system of variance accounting where only those major/significant variances from standard or budget are reported.

Explicit Costs

Anything that is used in the running of a business, i.e. rent, electricity, staff, and is incurred when a monetary transaction is made.

Financial Reporting Council

The body responsible for the setting and enforcement of accounting standards in the UK.

Financial Reporting Standards (FRS)

The name now adopted for UK accounting standards which are required by the Accounting Standards Board, replacing Statement of Standard Accounting Practice.

Financial Risk

The risk that results from a significant dependency upon capital funded by debt and which typically requires to be serviced by non-discretionary interest payments.

Financial Structure

The way a company's total finances have been arranged. The balance between various sources of funding, including short-and long-term finance.

First In First Out (FIFO)

The price paid for the material first taken into inventory. Issues from stores are priced based on the oldest material taken into inventory.

Fixed Assets – (non-current assets)

Those assets which an organisation holds for use within the business and not for resale. They consist of tangible assets, like land and buildings, plant and machinery, vehicles, and fixtures and fittings; and intangible assets like goodwill.

Fixed Costs

A cost that tends not to vary with the level of activity. Fixed costs are often determined by management decisions to invest in plant and equipment; once undertaken these result in period/time related costs and often bear little resemblance to activity.

Flexible Budget (Flexed Budget)

A budget which, by recognising the differences in variable, semi-variable and fixed costs, changes in relation to the level of activity attained.

Floating Charge

A charge against assets as security for a debt. It is a general claim against any available asset of the company.

Free Cash Flow

The cash freely available to the providers of finance.

GAAPs

Generally Accepted Accounting Principles.

Gearing

See Leverage. Expresses the relationship between some measure of interest-bearing capital and some measure of equity capital (or the total capital employed).

Going Concern

An accounting principle meaning that an organisation is assumed to continue in operational existence for the foreseeable future. The value of some assets would e different if the organisation were to cease trading.

Goodwill

The difference between the amount paid for a company as a whole and the net value of the assets and liabilities acquired.

Gross Profit

The basic difference between the money received from sales and the costs of making the product.

Hurdle Rate

A term which describes the rate of return that must be achieved for proposed capital expenditure to be acceptable in economic terms.

Income Statement

See Income statement. A statement showing the difference between receivables and payables and what profit (or loss) has been made over a period of time.

Incremental Budgeting

A means of estimating future fixed overhead costs by adding a predetermined percentage to the previous accounting period's actual costs.

Incremental Fixed Capital Investment (IFCI)

Investment in new assets to enable intended sales growth to occur.

Incremental Working Capital Investment (IWCI)

Investment in additional working capital, such as inventory (inventorys of materials), to enable intended sales growth to occur.

Indirect Cost

Cost incurred other than direct costs, i.e. not charged directly to the product sold. In other words, the costs of production, selling and administration of a business, other than the direct costs of producing its products of services. Often know as overhead.

Institutional Shareholder

A pension fund, insurance company of similar organisation devoted to the professional investment of savings.

Intangible Assets

Assets the value of which does not relate to their physical properties, e.g. goodwill and brands.

Interest Cover

A measure of income gearing (or how comfortably the interest can be paid out of profits).

Interim Reporting

Half yearly unaudited reports required to be produced by quoted public limited companies.

Internal Rate of Return (IRR)

The rate of discount at which the present value of the future cash flows is equal to the initial outlay, i.e. at the IRR the net present value is zero.

Interest Payable
Money payable (but not necessary paid) on interest bearing debt.

Inventory
1. Items held for conversion at a later date into sales, including materials, finished goods, components, bought-out parts and work in progress. Included in current assets.
2. A fixed amount of paid-up capital held by a inventoryholder. Also, in USA, the equivalent of shares.

Inventory Days
The number of days inventory 'held' by the business.

Inventory Turnover
A measure indicating the number of times inventory is 'turned over' on average in a given period (usually one year).

Issued Share Capital
The number and value of shares issued to ordinary shareholders.

Key Ratio
A term sometimes given to the profitability ratio. In the UK this is usually defined as profit before tax plus interest payable expressed as a percentage of net capital employed.

Labour Cost Variance
The difference between the standard cost of labour allowed for the actual output les the actual wages paid.

Labour Efficiency Variance
The difference between the standard hours of labour allowed less the actual hours at the standard price.

Labour Rate Variance
The actual hours at the difference between the standard rate less the actual rate.

Last In First Out (LIFO)
The price paid for the material last taken into inventory. Issues from stores are priced based on the most recent material taken into inventory.

Lease

An asset hired rather than bought, on which rent is paid.

Leverage

See Gearing. Expresses the relationship between some measure of interest-bearing capital and some measure of equity capital or the total capital employed.

Liabilities

The financial obligations owed by a company, these can be to shareholders, other providers of debt, trade payables (trade payables) and other payables (trade payables).

Limiting Factor

Internal and/or external factors which may limit a firm's ability to make infinite profits.

Liquid Assets

The difference between current assets and inventory (inventory).

Liquid Ratio

Liquid assets divided by current liabilities. It attempts to show a company's ability to pay its way in the short term.

Liquidity

The ability of a business to pay its way.

Loan Capital

Finance borrowed, typically at an explicit rate of interest.

Long-Term Liabilities

Liabilities that are not due for repayment within one year.

Machine Hour Rate

An actual or predetermined rate. Calculated by dividing the cost apportioned (to a cost centre) by the actual or forecast machine hours for the period.

Management Accounting

The provision of information required by management in the formulation of policies, planning and controlling business activities and selecting appropriate courses of action from available opportunities.

Marginal Costing

An approach which uses marginal costs as the basis for decision making. Each unit of production is expected to cover marginal costs and make some contribution to fixed costs. CIMA definition: Assigns only variable costs to cost units while fixed costs are written–off as period costs."

Market Value of Equity

The product of the market value of shares and the number of shares issued. Often referred to as market capitalisation.

Master Budget

The end result of the budgeting process expressed in terms of an income statement, balance sheet and cash flow statement.

Matching

An accounting principle which ensures that costs their associated revenues.

Materiality

An accounting convention meaning that the non-standard usage of an accounting practice is permissible if the effects are not material.

Material Cost Variance

The difference between the standard cost of materials allowed for the actual output and the actual cost of materials used.

Material Price Variance

The actual quantity at the standard price less the actual price.

Material Usage Variance

The standard materials allowed less the actual quantity at the standard price.

MB Ratio

The relationship between the market value of equity and the book value of equity (shareholders' funds).

Memorandum of Association

The document that contains the basis of the legal constitution of a company – whether or not its liability is 'limited', its purpose and whether it is public or private.

Minority Interest

The proportion of shares in subsidiary companies which is not held by a holding company. Profit attributable to minority interests and accumulated balances are shown in the consolidated financial statements.

Net Assets

Total assets minus Current Liabilities minus Trade payables: amounts owing after one year.

Net Book Value (NBV)

See Accumulated Depreciation.

Net Capital Employed

The sum of non current (fixed) assets, investments, current assets minus current liabilities.

Net Current Assets

See working capital.

Net Interest Income

Interest receivable less interest payable.

Net Present Value (NPV)

The difference between the discounted value of future net cash inflows and the initial outlay.

Net Realisable Value

The value of an asset which is equivalent to its sales proceeds minus costs of disposal.

Non Current Assets

See Fixed Assets. Those assets which an organisation holds for use within the business and not for resale. They consist of tangible assets, like land and buildings, plant and machinery, vehicles, and fixtures and fittings; and intangible assets like goodwill.

Operating Profit

What remains after costs of sales, administrative and distribution costs have been deducted from sales turnover – i.e. before extraordinary and exceptional items, tax, interest, etc.

Operational Gearing

Investment in fixed assets that, in response to changes in volume, need to be funded by regular inflows of profit/cash to ensure business viability.

Opportunity Cost

The notional cost that arises from being unable to undertake the next best alternative course of action.

Ordinary Shares

Shares which attract the remaining profits after all other claims, and, in liquidation, which attract the remaining assets of a company after trade payables and other charges have been satisfied.

Overdraft

A facility granted by a lending body like a bank whereby credit can be obtained, the interest payable being contingent upon the extent to which the facility is used.

Overhead Cost

See Indirect Cost.

Payback Period

How long it will take to recover the outlay involved in a potential investment opportunity from net cash inflows.

Payments

The payments in cash made by the business.

PE Ratio

One of the most significant indicators of corporate performance which it is widely quoted in the financial press. It is calculated by dividing the market price of a share by the earnings per share (or the total market value by the total profit attributable to shareholders), i.e.

$$\text{PE Ratio} = \frac{\text{Market Price of a Share}}{\text{Earnings Per Share}}$$

PE Relative

A means of comparing a company's PE ratio with the market as a whole:

$$\text{PE relative} = \frac{\text{PE of the company}}{\text{PE of the market}}$$

Peer Group Analysis

An approach involving the analysis of peer group companies which can be used in conjunction with financial information relating to a company to estimate its value.

Period Cost

A cost related to the passage of time rather than the volume of output,e.g. depreciation.

Perpetuity

A special case of an annuity in which cash flows are assumed to be received forever (in perpetuity).

Prepayments

Sums paid out in one year for the benefit of a future period. A current asset.

Present Value Rule

A rule which explains why in a world of certainty accepting all projects with a positive NPV maximises the wealth of shareholders.

Prime Cost

The cost of direct materials, labour and expenses incurred in producing a product.

Principal Budget Factor

The most important limiting factor for a business.

Private Company

A company with at least two members which has the word 'Limited' or Ltd' after its name and is not a public company – i.e. it cannot offer its shares on the open market.

Profit

The difference between the wealth of a business at the start of a period of trading and its greater wealth at the end of that period.

Income statement

See Income Statement. A statement showing the difference between receivables and payables and what profit (or loss) has been made over a period of time.

Profit Centre

An area of responsibility for which the manger has control of revenues and associated costs.

Profit Margin

See Return on Sales.

Profit/Volume Ratio

The ratio of contribution per unit to selling price per unit. Also known as Contribution/Sales Ratio.

Prudence

An accounting convention meaning that provision should be made for all potential costs, whereas profits should not be accounted for until realised.

Public Limited Company (plc)

A limited liability company which has a share capital, has at least two members, is registered under the Companies Acts and has the letters 'plc' after its name (in Wales the letters 'ccc'will be found). It may offer its shares to the open market.

Published Accounts

The statutory accounts that organisations like quoted public limited liability companies are required to produce annually.

Quick Ratio

The ratio of trade receivables (accounts receivable) plus cash t current liabilities. Also know as the acid test.

Quoted Company

A public limited company with a inventory exchange listing and which is able to sell its equity and/or debt openly in the market.

Quoted Investments

Investments in another company which has its shares quoted on a inventory exchange.

Ratio Analysis

The use of ratios to make comparisons between different organisations and/or different periods in time.

Realisation

A convention of accounting which recognises only those profits which have been realised in the accounting period.

Receipts

The receipts in cash received by a business.

Reducing Balance Depreciation

A method of depreciation whereby the periodic amount written off is a percentage of the reduced balance, i.e. (cost less accumulated depreciation).

Relevant Data

Relevant data for decision making is future oriented – that is yet to be incurred.

Relevant Range

The range of output over which an analysis of costs remains valid.

Replacement Fixed Capital Investment (RFCI)

Investment in fixed assets to maintain the current level of activity.

Replacement Value

The value of an asset derived from the cost of replacing it with an identical or similar item.

Reserves

Part of equity capital and consisting of retained profits, surplus values created by the revaluation of assets, and other surplus sums arising from the sale of shares. Typically the largest part of reserves is represented by accumulated profits attributable to ordinary shareholders which have not been distributed by way of dividends but which have been reinvested in the business.

Residual Value

Value generated beyond the planning period. Sometimes known as the terminal or continuing value.

Retained Earnings/Profits

Profits after tax minus dividends paid to shareholders kept in the company after all commitments have been met and shareholders paid a dividend.

Return on Capital Employed

Profit (before or after tax) expressed as a percentage of an appropriate measure of capital employed. A measure of the profitability achieved on capital employed (often measured in terms of total assets less current liabilities in the UK). The ratio is:

$$\frac{\textbf{PBIT}}{\text{Capital employed}}$$

Where PBIT is defined as profits before the deduction of interest payable and tax. Where the capital employed is total assets this is known as Return oN Total Assets (ROTA); where net assets, Return on Net Assets (RONA).

Return on Equity

The percentage rate of return provided to equity investors.

Return on Net Assets

Profits (usually before tax and interest payable) expressed as a percentage of net assets. Net assets are normally considered as total assets less current liabilities.

Return on Sales

Profit (usually before tax and interest payable) expressed as a percentage of sales revenue. The ratio is:

$$\frac{\text{Profit}}{\text{Sales Revenue}}$$

A measure of the profitability of sales which reflects the combination of cost and pricing structures of the business. Also known as Profit Margin.

Revaluation Reserve

A reserve capital created when assets are revalued.

Revenue

See Sales (Turnover). Income derived from the principal activities of a company, net of value added tax (VAT).

Risk-Free Rate

The most secure return that can be achieved.

Rolling Forecast

A forecast, of prescribed duration, which extends automatically as time elapses.

Sales

See Revenue (Turnover). Income derived from the principal activities of a company, net of value added tax (VAT).

Sales Generation

Also know as Asset Turnover or Asset Utilisation. A measure of the efficiency with which the assets of a business generate their output. The ratio is:

$$\frac{\text{Sales}}{\text{Assets (net or total)}}$$

Sensitivity Analysis

A commonly used approach to assessing risk whereby input variables are changed individually to determine their relative effect upon financial results.

Share Capital (Issued)

The product of the total number of shares issued and the nominal value of the shares.

Shareholder's Funds

Another name for equity.

Shareholder Value

A measure of value calculated as follows:

  Business Value
+ Marketable Securities or Investments
= Corporate Value
– Market Value of Debt and Obligations
= Shareholder Value

Shareholder Value Analysis

A valuation approach which considers in broad terms that the value of a business to a shareholder can be determined by discounting its future cash flows using an appropriate cost of capital.

Share Premium

The excess paid for a share, to a company, over its nominal value.

Short-Termism

A term associated with managing for today rather than tomorrow and beyond.

Solvency

Having enough money to meet all pecuniary liabilities.

Standard Cost

A cost prepared prior to a defined period of time; calculated I relation to a prescribed set of working conditions in respect to material quantities and prices, labour hours and rates with an appropriate share of overheads.

Standard Costing

Control technique that reports variances by comparing actual costs to pre-set standards so facilitating action through management by exception.

Standard Price

A predetermined price on the basis of a specification of all the factors affecting that price.

Statement of Standard Accounting Practice (SSAP)

The accountancy bodies' recommendations for good practice in accounting matters in the United Kingdom. Now replaced by Financial Reporting Standards.

Straight Line Depreciation

A method of depreciation whereby an equal amount is written off the value of a fixed asset over its estimated economic life.

Tangible Assets

Assets having a physical identity such as land and buildings, plant and machinery, vehicles etc.

Time Value of Money

A concept which is an integral part of the discounted cash flow technique used in capital investment appraisal. It recognises that cash flows in the later years of an investment opportunity cannot be compared with cash flows in the earlier years.

Total Assets

The sum of non current assets, investments and current assets.

Trade payables

A person or business to whom trade debt is owed and (in the balance sheet) the total of such sums; in USA known as accounts payable.

Trade receivables

An individual or organisation who owes money; in USA known as accounts receivable.

Trade Payables

The amounts of money owed and payable to suppliers of goods or services by the business.

Trade Receivables

See Trade receivables. Amounts owed to a company by its customers.

Weighted Average Cost of Capital (WACC)

The cost of equity before tax and the cost of debt after tax weighted according to the relative proportions of each in the total capital structure.

Trading Profit

Profit from the operations of the business: gross profit less overhead costs.

Turnover

Revenues from the sale of goods or services, usually after deducting any sales or value added taxes and duties, trade discounts and goods returned.

Unit Cost

The cost of one unit of output.

Variable cost

A cost that tends to vary directly with the level of activity.

Variance Accounting
The recording and reporting of actual results compared with standard or budgeted levels of performance.

Work in Progress
Items held that are not in their original state, but which have been partly made ready for sale (manufacturing, construction, etc.). Also used for project accounting where projects run over a period end.

Working Capital
The excess of current assets (inventory, trade receivables and cash) over current liabilities (trade payables, bank overdraft etc.).

Written Down Value (WDV)
See Accumulated Depreciation.

Z Scoring
A scoring technique derived from a statistical technique (multiple discriminant analysis) that is used for predicting companies likely to fail financially.

APPENDIX C
REFERENCES AND SUGGESTED FURTHER READINGS

Chapter 1

Suggested further readings

- Barclay M. J., Smith C. W. and Watts R. L., (1995), The Determinants Of Corporate Leverage And Dividend Policies, *Bank of America Journal of Applied Corporate Finance*, Volume 7 Number 4, Winter, pp. 4-19.
- Brennan, Michael J. (1995) Corporate Finance Over the Past 25 Years, FM: *The Journal of the Financial Management Association*; Summer, Vol. 24 Issue 2, p9-22
- Bussa, Thomas, Knight, Rory. *Risks That Matter: Sudden increases and decreases in shareholder value and the implications.* (Thomas Buss, Global Director, Business Risk Services, Ernst & Young and Dr Rory Knight, Chairman, (2003), Oxford Metrica).
- Chambers, T., (2003), Value reporting: A bigger, more accurate picture than traditional financial reporting, *Ivey Management Services*, July/August *http://64.233.161.104/search?q=cache:fOLq3qj71i8J:www.iveybusinessjournal.com/view_article.asp%3FintArticle_ID%3D434+value+reporting&hl=en&ct=clnk&cd=1*
- Clements A., (1997), An unreliable guide, *The Treasurer*, September, p.25-27.
- DeLoach, J. W., (2000) *Enterprise-Wide Risk Management* , Financial Times-Prentice Hall, London, p. 5 – 19.
- Deloitte Development LLC, (2005) *Disarming the Value Killers – A Risk Management Study.*
- Deloitte Development LLC,(2005), *Assessing the Value of Enterprise Risk Management.*
- Frankfurter, G.M. & McGoun, E.G., (1997), Toward Finance of Meaning: What finance is, and what it could be, *Journal of Investing,* Fall.
- Funston, Rick, (2003)'Creating the Risk Intelligent Organization' (2003), *Internal Auditor,* April 2003.
- Global Association of Risk Professionals, (2003) Operational Risk Survey – 2003,, copyright 2003. Electronic download available here: *http://www.garp.com/surveysandresearch/Response/Feb2004.asp*
- Mills, R., W. (1995) Accounting, Finance and Strategic Issues, *Manager Update*, Autumn 1995 - Volume 7 / 1.
- Opler T. and Titman S., (1994), The Debt-Equity Choice: An Empirical Analysis, *Ohio State University Working Paper*, December.
- Pearson C., (1997), Modern financial theory - its uses and abuses, *The Treasurer*, September, p.24.
- Wright, P. and Keegan, D., (1997) Pursuing Value: The Emerging Art of Reporting on the Future, *PW Papers*, Price Waterhouse LLP.

Chapter 2

Suggested further readings

- Ashkenas, Ronald, N., DeMonac, Lawrence J. and Francis, Suzanne C. (1998) Making the Deal Real: How GE Capital Integrates Acquisitions, *Harvard Business Review*, January-February, pp. 165-178.
- Boquist, John A., Milbourn, Todd T. and Thakor, Anjan V., (1998) How Do You Win the Capital Allocation Game?, *Sloan Management Review*, Winter, pp. 59-71.
- Bowman, Edward H., Singh, Harbeer, Useem, Michael and Bhadury, Raja (1997), When Does Restructuring Work?, Wharton School, University of Pennsylvania, Philadelphia.
- Healy, Paul M., Palepu, Krishna G. and Ruback, Richard S.,(1997), Which Take-overs Are Profitable? Strategic or Financial, *Sloan Management Review*, Summer, pp. 45-57.
- Sharpe, Paul and Keelin, Tom, (1998) How Smithkline Beecham Makes Better resource-Allocation Decisions, *Harvard Business Review*, March-April, pp. 45- 57.

Chapter 3

Suggested further readings

- Black A., Wright P. and Bachman J. E., (1998) *In Search of Shareholder Value: Managing the Drivers of Performance*, Pitman Publishing, p.13.
- Frigo, Mark L., (2003) Strategy and the board of Directors, *Strategic Finance*. Montvale: Jun .Vol.84, Iss. 12; pg. 8
- Mills R.W., (1994), *Finance, Strategy and Strategic Value Analysis: Linking Two Key Business Issues*, Mars Business Associates Ltd., p.49.
- Mills R.W. and Weinstein W.L., (1996) Calculating Shareholder Value in a Turbulent Environment, *Long Range Planning*, Vol.29, No.1, pp.76–83.
- Mills R W. and Print C., (1995) Strategic value analysis, shareholder value and economic value added - what's the difference?, *Management Accounting*, February, p.35-37.
- Rappaport A., (1986), *Creating Shareholder Value: The new standard for business performance*, The Free Press.
- Sheeler, Carl L., (2004) A Misunderstood Aspect of Business Value: The Market Approach, *The CPA Journal*. New York: Oct .Vol.74, Iss. 10; pg. 50, 2 pgs
- Villiger R.and Bogdan, B., (2005), Nature Biotechnology, Volume 23, Number 4, April.

Chapter 4

References

- Aaker, D.A., (1989) Managing assets and skills; the key to a sustainable competitive advantage, California Management Review, Winter.
- Ansoff, H. I., (1984), Implanting Strategic Management, Prentice Hall, New Jersey.
- Copeland, T., Koller, T. and Murrin, T., (1994) *Valuation*, McKinsey & Co.
- Kay, J., (1993), *Foundations of Corporate Success: How Business Strategies add value*, Oxford University Press.
- Mauboussin, M. and Johnson, P., (1997) Competitive advantage period 'CAP': the neglected value driver, *Frontiers of Finance*, Credit Suisse First Boston, op.cit., p.9.
- Miller, M. and Modigliani, F., (1961), Dividend policy, growth and the valuation of shares, *The Journal of Business.*
- Prahalad, C. K. and Hamel, G., (1990) The core competence of the corporation, *Harvard Business Review*, Vol.68, No.3, May/June, pp.79–93.
- Porter, M. E., (1980), *Competitive Strategy: Techniques for Analysing Industries and Competitors*, The Free Press.
- Rummelt, R. P., (1991), How much does industry matter?, *Strategic Management Journal,* Vol., No.3, March, pp.167-186.
- Slywotzky, A.J., (1996), *Value Migration*, Harvard Business School Press.
- Williams, J.R., (1985), A new way to understand business competition, Working Paper, Graduate school of Industrial Administration, Carnegie-Mellon University, May.

Suggested further readings

- Mills, R.W. and Weinstein, W.L., (1996) Calculating shareholder value in a turbulent environment, *Long Range Planning*, Vol.29, No.1, pp.76–83.
- Ogilvy, J., (1996) *Probabilities: Help or Hindrance in Scenario Planning*, GBN Publication on Internet ,June.
- Porter, M.E., (1985), *Competitive Advantage*, The Free Press.
- Rappaport, Alfred (1992) CFOs and Strategists: Forging a Common Framework, *Harvard Business Review*; May/Jun92, Vol. 70 Issue 3, p84-91
- Rappaport, Alfred, 10 Ways to Create Shareholder Value, *Harvard Business Review*; Sep2006, Vol. 84 Issue 9, p66-77.

Chapter 5

References

- Mills, Roger W. and Sawers, A., (1999) (Critique) How Sloan Built cars and value at General Motors, *Financial Director*, June, pp. 28-32.

Suggested further readings

- Bacidore, J., Boquist, J.A., Milbourn, T.T., and Thakor, A.V., (1997) The Search for the Best Financial Performance Measure, *Financial Analysts Journal*, May/June.
- Bennett-Stewart III, G., (1991), *The Quest for Value*, Harper Collins, New York, pp. 289-298.
- Bill Birchard, (1999), Metrics For The Masses: When it comes to EVA, don't take training the rank and file for granted, *CFO Magazine, May*.
- Biddle, G. C, Bowen, R. M. and Wallace, J. S., (1997), 'Does EVA® Beat earnings? Evidence on associations with stock returns and firm values', *Journal of Accounting and Economics*, 24, 301 – 336
- Chen, S. and Dodd, J. L., (1997), Economic Value Added (EVA®); an empirical examination of a new corporate performance measure, *Journal of Managerial Issues*, Fall, Volume 3, Number 3, p.318.
- Davis, H. A., *Cash Flow Performance Measurement: Managing for Value*, (1996), Financial Executives Research Foundation, Inc. Morristown, N.J
- Dodd, J. L. and Johns, J., (1999), EVA® reconsidered, *Business and Economic Review,* Columbia, Apr-Jun.
- Doherty, Neil A., (2005) Risk Management, Risk Capital, and the Cost of Capital., *Journal of Applied Corporate Finance*; Summer, Vol. 17 Issue 3, p119-123.
- Henderson, Glenn V., Jr., (1979) In Defense of the weighted average cost of capital, *Financial Management* (pre-1986). Tampa: Autumn 1979.Vol.8, Iss. 3; pg. 57, 5 pgs
- Johnson, H. T., (1992), *Relevance Regained: From Top Down Control to Bottom Up Empowerment*, The Free Press, New York.
- Kincheloe, Stephen C. (1990) The weighted average cost of capital--the correct discount rate, *Appraisal Journal*; Vol. 58 Issue 1, p88, 8p
- Picken, David H, Mak, Stephen, (2001), Risk analysis in cost planning and its effect on efficiency in capital cost budgeting, *Logistics Information Management*. Bradford.Vol.14, Iss. 5/6; pg. 318, 10 pgs.
- Ross, I., (1999) EVA® in Europe, *The EVAngelist*, January.
- SEC Workshop on 'The Reporting of Intangible Assets', Washington, 11-12 April 1996.

- Shaked, I., Allen, M. and Leroy P., (1997) Creating Value Through EVA® - Myth or Reality, *Journal of Strategy and Business*, Issue 9 , Fourth Quarter.
- Shinder, M. and McDowell, D., (1999) ABC, The Balanced Scorecard and EVA® - Distinguishing the Means from the End, *EVAluation*, Volume 1, Issue 2, April.
- Stern. J., (2000) Why companies' accounts distort economic facts, *The Sunday Times*, April 16, Business Section, p.6.
- Young, S. D., (1999), Some Reflections on Accounting Adjustments and Economic Value Added' *Journal of Financial Statement Analysis*, Vol. 9, Issue 2, Winter, pp.7-19.
- Young, David, (1997) Economic Value Added: A Primer for European Managers, European Management Journal, Vol 15, No 4 August, pp 338-343.

Chapter 6

References

- Banz, R.W., (1981), The relationship between return and market value of common stock; *Journal of Financial Economics*, Vol.9, pp.3–18.
- Chen, N., Roll, R. and Ross, S., 'Economic forces and the stock market,' Journal of Business, Vol.59, 1986.
- Dimson, E., Marsh, P. and Staunton, M., (2000), *Century of Investment Returns*, London Business School/ABN Amro.
- Fama, E. F. and French, K.R., (1992), The cross-section of expected stock returns, *Journal of Finance*, Vol.47, June, 1992
- Keim, D.B., (1982) Size related anomalies and stock return seasonality, *Journal of Portfolio Management.*
- Roll, R., (1982), The turn of the year effect and the return premium of small firms, *Journal of Portfolio Management.*
- Sharpe and Cooper, G.M., (1972), Risk, return class of New York Stock Exchange common Stocks, 1931 1967; *Financial Analysts Journal,* Vol.28, March/April, 1972, pp.46–52.

Chapter 7

References

- Bain, (2000), Survey on Real Options, *The Financial Times*, October 18.
- Ballou, B. and Heitger, D., (2005) A Building-Block Approach for Implementing COSO's Enterprise Risk Management – Integrated Framework, *Management Accounting Quarterly,* Winter, Vol. 6, No.2

- Blume, M. E., (1971), On the assessment of risk, *Journal of Finance*, vol. 26, 1971, pp. 275-288.
- Bussa, T. and Knight, Dr R., (2003) Ernst and Young and Oxford Metrica, *Risks that Matter: Sudden increases and decreases in shareholder value and the implications, www.oxfordmetrica.com/pdf/RisksThatMatter.pdf*
- Credit Suisse First Boston, (1997) *The Cost of Equity: Revising methodologies*, 12 December.
- Culp, C.L. (2002), The revolution in corporate risk management: A decade of innovations in process and products, *Journal of Applied Corporate Finance*, Vol. 14, No. 4, Winter.
- Culp, C.L (2002) *The ART of Risk Management: Alternative Risk Transfer, Capital Structure and the convergence of Insurance and Capital Markets*, New York: Wiley.
- Damodaran, A., (2002) *Investment Valuation: Tools and Techniques for Determining the Value of Any Asset*, Wiley, Second University Edition, p.165.
- Deloitte Development LLC, (2005), Disarming the Value Killers – A Risk Management Study.
- Deloitte Development LLC,(2005), *Assessing the Value of Enterprise Risk Management.*
- Ernst and Young and Oxford Metrica (2003)
- Fernández, P., (2003), 75 common and uncommon errors in company valuation, IESE Business School, Madrid, June 14. *(fernandezpa@iese.edu)*
- Gangemi, M, Brooks, R., and Faff, R., (1999) 'Mean reversion and the forecasting of country betas: a note.', *Global Finance Journal*, Vol. 10 Issue 2, Fall/Winter, p.233.
- Global Association of Risk Professionals, (2003) Operational Risk Survey – 2003,, copyright 2003. Electronic download available here: *http://www.garp.com/surveysandresearch/Response/Feb2004.asp*
- Godfrey, S. and Espinosa, R., (1996) *Journal of Applied Corporate Finance*, Fall.
- Mills, R.W., Weinstein, W.L., Favato, G., (2006), Using scenario thinking to make real options relevant to managers: a case illustration, *Journal of General Management*, Vol. 31, No. 3, pp 49-84.
- Meulbroek, L. (2001), A Better Way to Manage Risk, *Harvard Business Review*, February, Vol. 79, No. 2, pp. 22-23.
- Meulbrook, L.K. (2002) A Senior Manager's Guide to Integrated Risk Management, *Journal of Applied Corporate Finance*, Vol. 14, No. 4, Winter, pp. 56-70.
- The Committee of Sponsoring Organizations (COSO) of the Treadway Commission, (2004) Enterprise Risk Management—Integrated Framework, Executive Summary, Sept.

Suggested further readings

- Baldoni, Robert J., (2004), The journey to successful enterprise-wide risk management, *Directorship*; Vol. 30 Issue 3, p10-15
- Briggs, R. and Edwards, C., (2006) *The Business of Resilience - Corporate security for the 21st century*, ISBN 1 84180 163 1, *www.demos.co.uk*, 2006.
- Booz Allen Hamilton, (2005), Convergence of Enterprise Security Organizations
- Dixit, Avinash K. Pindyck, Robert S, The Options Approach to Capital Investment, *Harvard Business Review*; May/Jun95, Vol. 73 Issue 3, p105-115
- Fortino, M., (2005) Creating A Value-Adding Approach to Enterprise Risk Management, Western Independent Bankers – Director's Conference, San Diego. *http://64.233.161.104/search?q=cache:lTQy-VCbl6EJ:www.wib.org/past_seminars/dir_conf_past/dir_05/presentations/fortino_presentation_dir05.pdf+Deloitte+Creating+A+Value-Adding+Approach+to+Enterprise+Risk+Management&hl=en&ct=clnk&cd=1*
- Luehrman, Timothy A., (1998), Investment Opportunities as Real Options: Getting Started on the Numbers, *Harvard Business Review*; Vol. 76 Issue 4, p51-67.
- McCarthy, Mary Pat and Flynn, Timothy P., (2004) *Risk From the CEO and Board Perspective,* McGraw-Hill, New York, N.Y., pp. 152-153.
- Sullivan, Laura, (2001), Enterprise wide: Building a *Risk Management* program from the ground up, Risk Management. New York, Vol.48, Iss. 12; pg. 24, 5 pgs
- Weinstein, W.L., Blacker, K.B., Mills, Roger W., (2005), Can your Board Really cope with risk?" *IFAC Articles of Merit,* August, pp. 48-52

Chapter 8

References

- Elton, E. J., Gruber, M. J, and Blake, C. R.,(2003), Incentive Fees and Mutual Funds, *Journal of Finance*, 58: 779-804
- Meyer, T. and Mathonet, P-Y., Beyond the J Curve: Managing a Portfolio of Venture Capital and Private Equity Funds, Wiley, 2005.
- KPMG, (2001), *World Class Transactions: Insights into Creating Shareholder Value Through Mergers and Acquisitions. http://www.kpmg.co.uk/pubs/ma_dec05.pdf*
- KPMG, (1999), *Unlocking Shareholder Value: the Keys to Success.*
- KPMG, (1999) *Value Based Management Research Report,* p.4.
- PricewaterhouseCoopers Forecast: *Record cash reserves and a desire for growth will accelerate M&A in 2006*, December 2005. *http://www.pwc.com/extweb/ncpressrelease.nsf/docid/6B314690BEDBDAA3852570D60054A86F*

- Senior Loan Officer Opinion Survey on Bank Lending Practices, US Federal Reserve, October 2005. *http://www.federalreserve.gov/boarddocs/SnLoanSurvey/200510/default.htm*

Suggested further readings

- Agrawal A., J. K. Jaffe and G. N. Mandelker (1992), The Post-Merger Performance of Acquiring Firms: A re-examination of an Anomaly, *Journal of Finance*, Vol. 47, September, p. 1618
- Ashkenas, Ronald N., DeMonaco, Lawrence J. and Francis, Suzanne C., (1998), Making the Deal Real: How GE Capital Integrates Acquisitions, *Harvard Business Review*, January-February, , pp. 165-178.
- Banks, S. and Pape, J-P., (1994) Putting a Price on Success, *Acquisitions Monthly,* February.
- Bernard, V.L. and Thomas, J., (1990) Evidence That Stock Prices Do Not Fully Reflect the Implications of Current Earnings for Future Earnings, *Journal of Accounting and Economics,* Volume 13, pp. 305-340.
- Berry, K., (2005) Hedge funds spur private equity offerings, *Los Angeles Business Journal, June 20, 2005*
- Bowman, Edward H., Singh, Harbeer, Useem, Michael and Bhadury, Raja, (1997), *When Does Restructuring Work?*, Wharton School, University of Pennsylvania, Philadelphia.
- Coopers and Lybrand (1994), *Corporate finance: Survey of critical valuation issues in mergers and acquisitions.*
- Dixit, Avinash., (1989) Entry and Exit Decisions Under Uncertainty, *The Journal of Political Economy*. Chicago, Vol.97, Iss. 3; pg. 620, 19 pgs
- Haleblian, J. and Finkelstein, S., (1999) The influence of organizational acquisition experience on acquisition performance: a behavioral learning perspective, *Administrative Science Quarterly*, March, v44 i1 p29(2).
- Healy, Paul, M., Krishna G. Palepu and Richard S. Ruback, (1997) Which Take-overs Are Profitable? Strategic or Financial, *Sloan Management Review*, Summer, pp. 45-57.
- Healy, Paul M., Palepu, Krishna G. and Ruback, Richard S. (1992), Does Corporate Performance Improve After Mergers, *Journal of Financial Economics*, Volume 31, 1992, pp. 135-176.
- Higson, C. & J. Elliot (1993), Returns to Take-overs- The Evidence, *IFA Working Paper* 173-93, London Business School, Spring.
- James Capel Equity Research, (1995), Pharmaceuticals: In search of Shareholder Value, May.
- James, Mimi Koller, Timothy M, (2000) Valuation in emerging markets, *McKinsey Quarterly;* Special Edition Issue 4, p78-85, 8p

- Jensen, M. C. and Ruback, R. S. (1983) The Market for Corporate Control, *Journal of Financial Economics*, Volume 11, pp. 5-50.
- Kode, G.V.M. Ford, J.C. Sutherland, M.M., (2003),A conceptual model for evaluation of synergies in mergers and acquisitions: A critical review of the literature, *South African Journal of Business Management*; Vol. 34 Issue 1, p27, 12p
- KPMG Management Consulting (1997), *Colouring in the Map, Mergers & Acquisitions in Europe Research Report.*
- Lerner, J. and Schoar, A., *"The Illiquidity Puzzle: Theory and Evidence from Private Equity",* Journal of Financial Economics, 72 (April 2004) 3-40.
- Sabal, Jaime, (2004), The Discount Rate in Emerging Markets: A Guide, *Journal of Applied Corporate Finance*, Vol. 16 Issue 2/3, p155-166
- Timmons, H. Opening Private Equity's Door, at Least a Crack, to Public, New York Times , May 4, 2006, *http://www.nytimes.com/2006/05/04/business/worldbusiness/04place.html*
- Wislon, T., (1997) Evaluating Mergers and Acquisitions, Advanced Strategies for Company Valuation Conference, Euromoney.
- Call for Papers: Special Issue of the Journal of Corporate Finance, Private Equity, LBOs, and Governance, Submission Due Date: January 15, 2006, Special Issue Conference: April 20-22, 2006.
- *deBrauwere*,D., Bank of America Business Capital, 2006 *http://www.bofabusinesscapital.com/resources/capeyes/a01-06-321.html*
- *http://www.dealogic.com/mergers.aspx, http://www.kpmg.co.uk/pubs/ma_dec05.pdf*
- *http://www.pmdzone.com/*
- *http://www.bvca.co.uk/publications/guide/intro.htm*
- *http://www.lpx.ch/english/index.html*
- *http://www.sagientresearch.com/pt/index.cfm*

Chapter 9

References

- Burton WN, Conti D, Chen C et al., (1999), The role of health risk factors and disease on worker productivity, *Journal of Occupational Environmental Medicine*, 41: 863-877.
- CFO Research Services, *www.cforesearch.com*, analysed by Mercer Human Resource Consulting, www.mercerHR.com/CFOstudy
- Eccles, R. G., Herz, R. H., Keegan, E. M. and Phillips, D. M. H.,(2001), The Value Reporting Revolution Moving Beyond the Earnings Game, John Wiley & Sons.

- Ehrbar, A. and Bergesen, M., (2002), A New Approach to Managing Brand and Business Value, *Strategic Investor Relations*, Winter.
- Lev, B. , (2000), *Intangibles: Management, Measurement and Reporting*, Brookings Institute.
- Nicholson, S., Pauly M.V., Polsky, D., Baase, C.M., Billotti, G.M., Ozminkowski, R.J., Berger, M.C., and Sharda, C.E. (2005), *How to Present the Business Case for Healthcare Quality to Employers, Cornell University*, University of Pennsylvania.
- Pauly, Mark V., Sean Nicholson, Judy Xu, Dan Polsky, Patricia Danzon, James F. Murray, and Marc L. Berger, (2002), A New General Model of the Impact of Absenteeism on Employers and Employees, *Health Economics*, 11(3): 221-231.
- Stewart W, Ricci J, Chee E et al. (2003), Lost productive work time costs from health conditions in the United States: results from the American Productivity Audit, *Journal of Occupational Environmental Medicine*, 45:1234-1246.
- van Ark, B., Executive Action #176, January 2006, The Conference Board, 17 January 2006, *http://www.conference-board.org/utilities/pressDetail.cfm?press_ID=2799*
- Wright, P. and Keegan, D., (1997) Pursuing Value: The Emerging Art of Reporting on the Future, *PW Papers*, Price Waterhouse LLP.
- *World Population in 2300, http://www.un.org/esa/population/publications/longrange2/WorldPop2300final.pdf*

Suggested further readings

- Aaker, D.A., Jacobson, R., (1994), The Financial Information Content of Perceived Quality, *Journal of Marketing Research*, Vol. 31, Issue 2, pp 191-202.
- Arthur Andersen & Co, S.C. and The Economist Intelligence Unit, (1992), *The Valuation of Intangible Assets*, Special report, London, January.
- Barwise, P., Higson, C., Likierman, A., and Marsh, P., (1989), *Accounting for Brands*, The London Business School and The Institute of Chartered Accountants in England and Wales, London.
- Blair, M., and S. Wallman, (2001) *Unseen Wealth - Report of the Brookings Intangibles Taskforce*, Brookings Institution , Washington D.C., May.
- Drucker, P., (1998), The Coming of the New Organisation. In *Harvard Business Review on Knowledge Management*, Harvard Business School Press, Boston, 1998.
- Eustace, C.G., (2000), Intellectual Property and the Capital Markets, City University Business School working paper.
- Eustace, C.G. (2001),*The Intangible Economy - Impact and Policy Issues*, Report of the European High-Level Expert Group on the intangible economy. Luxembourg, March (ISBN 92-894-0019-6).

- Goetzel R.Z., S.R. Long, R.J. Ozminkowski, K. Hawkins, S. Wang, and W. Lynch. (2004), Health, Absence, Disability, and Presenteeism Cost Estimates of Certain Physical and Mental Health Conditions Affecting U.S. Employers. *Journal of Occupational and Environmental Medicine*, 46(4): 398-412.
- Greenberg P.E., S.N. Finkelstein, and E.R. Berndt, (1999), Economic Consequences of Illness in the Workplace, *Sloan Management Review* 36(4): 26-38.
- Haigh, D. and Knowles, J., (2004), How to define your brand and determine its value, *Marketing Management*, May/June.
- Kerin, R.A., and Sethuraman, R., (1998), Exploring the Brand Value-Shareholder Value Nexus for Consumer Goods Companies, *Journal of Academy of Marketing Science*, Vol. 26, No 4, 1998, pp 260-273.
- Loeppke, R., P. Hymel, J. Lofland, L. Pizzi, D. Konicki, G. Anstadt, C. Baase, J. Fortuna, and T. Scharf, (2003), Health-Related Workplace Productivity Measurement: General and Migraine Specific Recommendations from the ACOEM Expert Panel, *Journal of Occupational and Environmental Medicine*, 45(4) 349-359.
- McGlynn, Elizabeth A., Timothy McDonald, Laura Champagne, Bruce Bradley, and Wesley, (2003), News Round-up, *Financial Management*, March.
- Matthewman, J., (2003), Intelligence Quotient, *Financial Management*, October.
- Nicholson, S., Pauly M.V., Polsky, D., Baase, C.M., Billotti, G.M., Ozminkowski, R.J., Berger, M.C., and Sharda, C.E. (2005), *How to Present the Business Case for Healthcare Quality to Employers*, Cornell University, University of Pennsylvania.
- Oldroyd, D., (1994) Accounting and Marketing Rationale: The Juxtaposition within Brands, *International Marketing Review*, Vol. 11, No 2, pp 33-46.
- Oldroyd, D., (1998), Formulating an Accounting Standard for brand in the 'Market for Excuses', *The Journal of Brand Management*, Vol. 5, No 4., pp 263-271.
- Print, C.F. (2005), Paper for the 8th International Conference on Corporate Governance and Board Leadership, Henley Management College, October.
- Soete, Luc, (2001) Report on European conference on the 'New Economy', 1-2 March, Brussels.
- The Jenkins Report of the AICPA. (1994), AICPA Special Committee on Financial Reporting, 'Improving Business Reporting - A Customer Focus: Meeting the Information Needs of Investors and Creditors,' Jersey City, NJ.
- Ungar WJ, Coyte PC, (2000), Pharmacy Medication Monitoring Program Advisory Board, Measuring Productivity Loss Days in Asthma Patients, *Health Economics* 9(1): 37-46.
- Walker, (2003), The Business Case for a Corporate Wellness Program: A Case Study of General Motors and the United Auto Workers Union, The Commonwealth Fund: *www.cmwf.org.*

- *World Population in 2300, http://www.un.org/esa/population/publications/longrange2/WorldPop2300final.pdf*

Chapter 10

Suggested further readings

Anon, (2005) Value-based management, A to Z of Management Concepts & Models, p386-388

van Marrewijk,Marcel, (2004) A Value Based Approach to Organization Types: Towards a coherent set of stakeholder-oriented management tools, *Journal of Business Ethics*. Dordrecht, Vol.55, Iss. 2; pg. 147

INDEX

Index

D

E